Charles Marcus Church

Chapters in the Early History of the Church of Wells, A.D. 1136-1333

From Documents in Possession of the Dean and Chapter of Wells

Charles Marcus Church

Chapters in the Early History of the Church of Wells, A.D. 1136-1333
From Documents in Possession of the Dean and Chapter of Wells

ISBN/EAN: 9783337003074

Printed in Europe, USA, Canada, Australia, Japan

Cover: Foto ©Lupo / pixelio.de

More available books at **www.hansebooks.com**

CHAPTERS

IN THE EARLY HISTORY OF THE CHURCH OF WELLS

A.D. 1136-1333

FROM
DOCUMENTS IN POSSESSION OF THE DEAN AND CHAPTER
OF WELLS.

BY THE

REV. C. M. CHURCH, M.A., F.S.A.

Subdean and Canon Residentiary.

London:
ELLIOT STOCK, 62, PATERNOSTER ROW.
Taunton: BARNICOTT & PEARCE.
1894

HEAD OF A CROZIER FOUND AT WELLS.
Vide Appendix P.

WELLS CATHEDRAL.

Lift up your eyes to yonder wond'rous shrine,
Mark with what matchless grace and magic power,
Base, buttress, window, battlement and tower
Are gathered into harmonies divine;—
'Twas so they built of old, for well they knew
God's works to be in tune, and all true art
To be but His voice speaking through the heart
Of man,—His instrument; and so they grew
Ennobled in their work, till every stone
Heaved with the breath of life, reflecting there
No broken fragment of an age by-gone,
But every aspiration, thought, and care,
In lifeless form, thenceforth to live,—and stand,
As mute memorials of their heart and hand.

Godfrey Thring.

THESE PAGES ARE WRITTEN

IN CONSTANT MEMORY

OF

JAMES ARTHUR BENNETT, F.S.A.

Late Secretary of Somerset Archæological Society

BY WHOSE LABOUR OF LOVE

THE WELLS CHAPTER DOCUMENTS WERE ARRANGED

IN 1882-1885.

Desiderio tam cari capitis.

CONTENTS.

		PAGE
INTRODUCTION		ix
CHAPTER I.	BISHOP ROBERT, A.D. 1136-1166	1
CHAPTER II.	BISHOP REGINALD, A.D. 1174-1191	37
CHAPTER III.	SAVARIC, BISHOP OF BATH AND GLASTONBURY, A.D. 1192-1205	88
CHAPTER IV.	BISHOP JOCELIN, A.D. 1206-1242.—	
	PART I	127
	PART II	165
CHAPTER V.	ROGER OF SALISBURY, FIRST BISHOP OF BATH AND WELLS, A.D. 1244-1247	239
CHAPTER VI.	THE CHAPTER OF WELLS, A.D. 1242-1333	258
CHAPTER VII.	INTERIOR ARRANGEMENT OF THE CHURCH OF THE THIRTEENTH CENTURY	322
APPENDICES A—Y		352
INDEX		427

ILLUSTRATIONS.

	PAGE
HEAD OF A CROZIER FOUND AT WELLS	*frontispiece*
THE CATHEDRAL FROM THE S.E.	*vignette*
GROUND PLAN OF THE CHURCH AS IN THE THIRTEENTH CENTURY	1
SEALS OF BISHOPS ROBERT OF LEWES, REGINALD, SAVARIC, AND JOCELIN	36
SEALS OF THE BOROUGH OF WELLS, THIRTEENTH CENTURY	127
SEALS OF BISHOPS ROGER OF SALISBURY AND ROBERT BURNELL	238
SEALS OF BISHOPS JOHN OF DROKENSFORD, RALPH OF SHREWSBURY, DEAN GODLEY, AND DEAN AND CHAPTER OF WELLS	258
TOMB OF BISHOP WILLIAM DE MARCHIA, PLATE 1	288
,, ,, ,, ,, ,, PLATE 2	289
TOMB OF BISHOP DROKENSFORD	312
SEAL OF BISHOP DROKENSFORD	313
PLAN OF EARLY LADY-CHAPEL	425
BUILDING OVER OLD WATERCOURSE IN BURIAL GROUND SOUTH OF THE CATHEDRAL	425

INTRODUCTION.

WHEN, in 1869, Mr. FREEMAN was delivering his lectures on the history of the Cathedral Church of Wells,[1] he looked forward to the time in which the documents in the archives of the Bishop, and of the Dean and Chapter, now "locked up in manuscript," should be printed to illustrate the history which he was teaching others to study.

It has been the aim of the Dean and Chapter for some years past to bring into the light those charters and historical documents with which they are entrusted.

In 1870 the Historical MSS. Commission commenced an enquiry into the original documents in the Registry of the Chapter. They were then described as "a mass of parchments almost wholly without

1. *History of the Cathedral Church of Wells*, by E. A. Freeman. Macmillan, 1870.

arrangement and in varying stages of preservation." About two hundred were then partially examined.[1]

In 1880 the whole collection of eleven hundred documents were cleaned, examined and arranged in thirty-six boxes by Mr. W. DE GRAY BIRCH, and a descriptive catalogue of each charter is now in the Library.

In 1881 the manuscript in the Archbishop's Library, Lambeth Palace, No. 729, containing "Ordinale et Statuta ecclesiæ Cathedralis Wellensis," was obtained by the late Mr. F. H. DICKINSON, and permission was given by the Dean and Chapter to Mr. H. E. REYNOLDS to print the text of the MS., and to make extracts from some of the books in the Dean and Chapter Library for his work on "Wells Cathedral."[2]

Between 1882 and 1885 all the Registers, Rolls, and Indenture Books belonging to the Dean and Chapter were calendared by the late JAMES ARTHUR BENNETT, then secretary of the Somerset Archæological Society, and printed by the Historical MSS. Commission.[3] Without this preliminary labour, voluntarily under-

---

1. Report of Historical MSS. Commission, Appendix, 3, p. 351.
2. *History of the Cathedral Church of Wells*, H. E. Reynolds, folio, 1881.
3. *Report X, Appendix 3, Wells Manuscripts*, 1885. The preface to the Report gives an account of the registers which are there entitled R. i, R. ii, R. iii, and this description is followed in these pages.

Introduction. xi

taken and conscientiously carried out, no consecutive history of the church could have been possible.

These are the original documents which supply elementary materials for the chapter history.

Besides these documents, I have found most valuable help from the *Chronicon Wellense*, of Dr. EDMUND ARCHER,[1] a continuous digest of the Registers and original Charters from the earliest time to the death of bishop Drokensford, A.D. 1329. His book, written in the generation succeeding HENRY WHARTON, corrects and fills up the meagre and often inaccurate epitome of Wells history printed by GODWIN and WHARTON.

We find now from these documents that the authorities quoted by WHARTON under the title of the *Canon of Wells*, and by GODWIN, are very far from being the original sources for the early history of the church of Wells. They are rather the traditions of the fifteenth century as understood and interpreted to us by GODWIN and WHARTON in the seventeenth.

---

1. *Chronicon Wellense*, sive *Annales Ecclesiæ Cathedralis Wellensis*.
Edmund Archer, Fellow of St. John's College, Oxford, Prebendary of Combe 9th, Archdeacon of Taunton, 1712, of Wells, 1726, Canon Residentiary, died 1739.

He was a correspondent of Thomas Hearne, and copies of Wells Charters supplied by him to Hearne occupy 176 pages in Hearne's edition of *Adam of Domerham*, ed. 1727. His hand can be traced on the margin of the Registers throughout.

1. The *Canon of Wells* is the title given in Wharton's *Anglia Sacra*,[1] to a composite document—two anonymous tracts of the fourteenth and fifteenth centuries of six folios embedded in the *Liber Albus* (Register iii),[2] which WHARTON has "woven together" to form a continuous epitome of the earlier episcopates.

(a.) *Historia Minor* contains a short catalogue of the bishops, from Daniel the legendary bishop of Congresbury, down to bishop Harewell's time, 1367-1386.

(b.) *Historia Major* is a longer tract of the same kind, which begins with Edward the Confessor's time, and ends with bishop Bubwith, 1406-1424.

2. FRANCIS GODWIN, canon of Wells, bishop of Llandaff, 1601, and of Hereford, 1617, was son of THOMAS GODWIN, bishop of Bath and Wells, 1584-1590. Though he had exceptional opportunities for examining the charters in the Wells registers, he seems to have been content to follow the same epitome which WHARTON has printed, varying his form of statement in the different editions of his book, viz., the English edition, *The Catalogue*, etc., printed in 1601,

---

1. *Anglia Sacra*, p. 551. London, 1691.
2. R. iii, ff. 296-302.

Introduction. xiii

and the Latin, *De Præsulibus Angliæ Commentarius,* printed in 1615-1616.[1]

By the kind permission of the Council of the Society of Antiquaries, I am enabled to reprint papers from *Archæologia,* now recast and enlarged, viz.: " Reginald," vol. l, 1887 ; " Savaric," vol. li, 1887 ; " Jocelin," vol. li, 1888 ; " Roger," vol. lii, 1890.

I am under special obligations to Bishop HOBHOUSE and to Mr. W. H. ST. JOHN HOPE for assistance and correction on numberless occasions in the continuance of this work.

---

1. Vide Wharton's comment on Godwin, *Anglia Sacra*, p. 588. " Qui plus quam 30 annis Canonicus residentiarius ecclesiæ Wellensis erat, et archiva ejus adhuc integra inspexit. Nuper enim direpta sunt, et impio furore mutilata ac discissa a schismaticis in rebellione Somersetensi anno 1685 motâ. Integris tamen monumentis usus vir eruditus plerosque errores admisit."

ORIGINAL AUTHORITIES.

Manuscript.

1. ORIGINAL CHARTERS in 36 cases,
    Charters, Grants, etc., from A.D. 958.
2. LIBER ALBUS (R. i), in 298 folios.
    Cartulary and Chapter Acts, *circa* A.D. 1300-1393.
3. LIBER RUBER (R. ii), ff. 1-77, parchment; ff. 78-378, paper.
    Cartulary, *circa* A.D. 1215-1513. Chapter Acts, A.D. 1480-1513.
4. LIBER ALBUS II (R. iii), f. 456.
    Charters, etc., *circa* A.D. 1380-1450.
5. COMPUTUS COMMUNARII. 25 Rolls.
    A.D. 1327-1560.
6. FABRIC ROLLS. 9 Rolls.
    A.D. 1390-1565.
7. ESCHEATORY ACCOUNTS. 36 Rolls.
    A.D. 1372-1560.
8. INDENTURE BOOKS.
9. CHARTER OF QUEEN ELIZABETH, 25th November, 1591.

Transcripts and Printed.

10. ORDINALE ET STATUTA. Lambeth MS. 729. Quarto, parchment, in Lambeth Library, transcribed at Wells in 1634 for archbishop Laud.
    Printed in *Wells Cathedral*, H. E. Reynolds, 1881.
11. DEAN COSYN'S BOOK. A manuscript book of 357 pages, small quarto, partly parchment, chiefly paper; transcripts of statutes, etc., 1506.
12. STATUTA ECCLESIÆ CATHEDRALIS WELLENSIS. Folio of 155 pages, parchment, bound in rough calf, in handwriting of seventeenth century, transcripts in same order as No. 10, with more entries.
13. CHRONICON WELLENSE by archdeacon Archer, 1723-1739
    Latin manuscript, quarto, 315 pages. A digest of Wells history and documents to A.D. 1329.
14. CHYLE'S HISTORY, *circa* 1686.
15. WELLS CATHEDRAL, H. E. Reynolds, folio, 1881.
16. REPORT OF HISTORICAL MSS. COMMISSION, Report X, Appendix 3, "Wells MSS," J. A. Bennett, 1885.

WELLS CATHEDRAL CHURCH
Ground Plan as in the Thirteenth Century

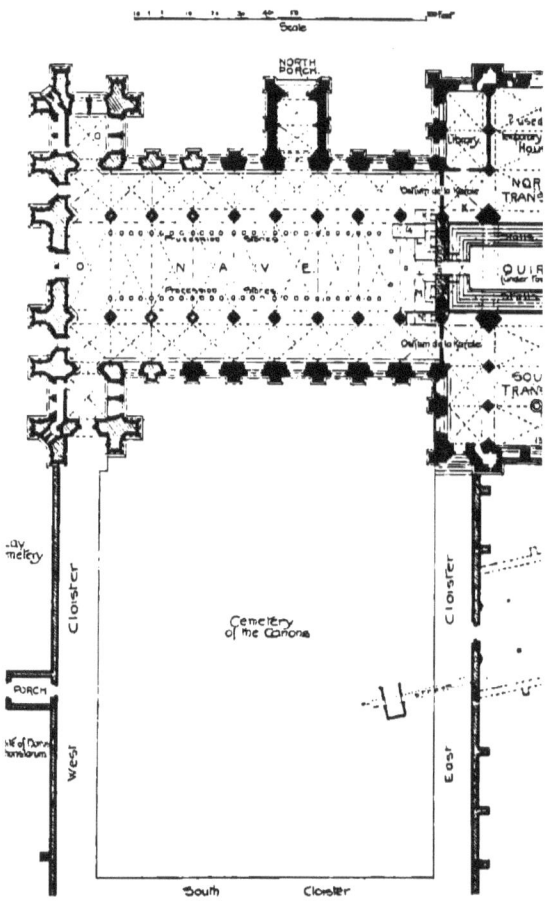

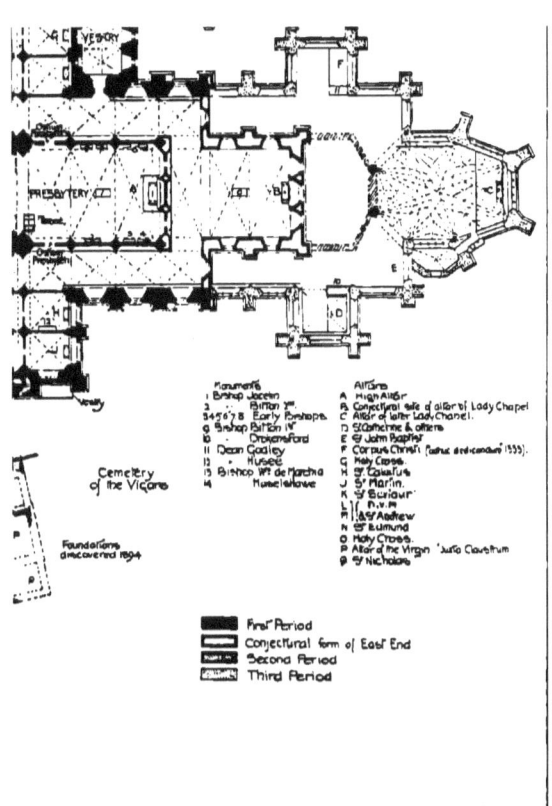

CHAPTERS IN THE EARLY HISTORY OF THE CHURCH OF WELLS.

CHAPTER I.

Bishop Robert, A.D. 1136-1166.

ACCORDING to a "strong and consistent tradition" missionary priests were settled at Wells in the newly conquered Saxon land between the Mendip hills and the moorland, early in the eighth century. <small>Eighth century.</small>

Sherborne had been made the seat of the bishop of these western lands, and Aldhelm was consecrated first bishop in 705. He died in missionary labours in 709, in the little wooden church of Doulting, which stands on the Mendip watershed, looking down through its western valley to the Severn sea. Aldhelm's counsel had led Ine to refound the old religious house at Glastonbury,[1] at the head of the marshes of the Brue. He probably also planted this frontier station at Wells for the vale and fen country of the Axe.

Here rose up the first Saxon church of St. Andrew, by the side of the springs of water which "gush out

---

1. "Ejus monitu Glastoniense monasterium a novo fecit." Will. Malm. *Gesta Pont.*, ii, p. 196, v. 209 (Rolls Series).

like a river" from the limestone rock, and soon became known as "the great fountain of St. Andrew."

<small>Tenth century.</small>

Two hundred years later, when, under Edward son of Alfred, Wessex was recovering from the harrying of the Danes, the West Saxon bishopric was again subdivided, and the church of Wells, then served by a company or "college" of priests, became the spiritual centre of the surrounding country, and the seat of the bishop of Somerset. The priests, living under the rule of the bishop, and dependent upon him for their maintenance, became the "canons of St. Andrew." Perhaps at this time the old church of St. Andrew was made more worthy to be the seat of the bishop. Perhaps it was at this time of deliverance from the Danish terror that another church was founded in the growing town, and dedicated in the name of St. Cuthbert, the patron saint of Alfred. A deep devotion was solemnly inculcated from father to son, for several generations of the house of Alfred, towards St. Cuthbert.[1]

During the tenth century the revival of discipline and learning was going on under the successors of Alfred. Glastonbury was the chief scene of monastic and educational reform under Dunstan and Ethelwold, and the stream of endowment flowed strongly thither.

The Benedictine monks of Glastonbury could look without jealousy from their Tor upon the little church of Wells in the distant shadow of the hills, almost

---

1. Perhaps also we may see a remembrance of these Danish times in the sculptured martyrdom of King Edmund of East Anglia on the capitals of the north porch; it may be a reproduction by later builders of the story they found carved on the early Saxon church. The tragic story of the fall of the East Anglian king, A.D. 871, in Alfred's lifetime, must have been deeply graven on the memories of the sons of Alfred.

encircled by their own possessions, served by a few secular canons under the rule of a bishop who was sometimes chosen from their own house.

But in the eleventh century, under Giso, 1061-1088, the foreign bishop from Lorraine, contemporary with Edward the Confessor and living over the Norman Conquest, contemporary also with the decline of Glastonbury under unthrifty abbots, the possessions of the see grew by royal endowments and episcopal gifts, and the number of the canons increased. Bp. Giso, A.D. 1061-1088.

In the Wells chapter library are copies of charters already published and well known, of local endowments of the see in the time of Giso. There is the original charter dated from Rome, April 25, 1061, given by pope Nicolas II to Giso after his consecration, "confratri et coepiscopo," confirming to him and his successors all that pertained to the see at present, all that he should acquire in future.[1]

There are copies of charters, from king Edward,[2] with grants of Chew and Wedmore, and of Milverton and Mark from the lady Editha, in 1062,[3] and the charter recapitulating all the possessions of the see in 1065.[4] There are the grants in 1066,[5] from William as king, to "St. Andrew the Apostle" of thirty hides

---

[1]. This charter is printed in full fac-simile in Hickes' *Thesaurus*, vol. i, p. 177, "as it does not exist in the *Bullarium Romanum*—it is a very beautiful and valuable example of Italian writing of the time."

[2]. R. i, f. 14. Kemble *Cod. Dipl.*, 834-839.

[3]. R. i, f. 17. *Cod. Dipl.*, 917, 918.

[4]. R. iii, 241. *Cod. Dipl.*, 816. Eyton, *Domesday Studies*, i, 145. "The charter is instructive on matters of topography, and shows, if not any genuine grants, yet still what the church of Wells claimed before the Conquest."

[5]. R. i, f. 14. *Cod. Dipl.*, 976.

at Banwell,[1] and of Winsham "for the use of the canons of Wells,"[2] and of the church of Wedmore by Matilda, William's queen, at Giso's frequent solicitation, in 1075.[3]

In 1086, two years before Giso's death, the great Domesday Survey had been made. A review of the *Terra Gisonis Episcopi* enables us to see the result of Giso's diplomacy, and to estimate the possessions of the see at that time.

The *Terra Gisonis Episcopi* then included more than one twelfth of the shire, it was measured at 280 hides, or about 50,000 acres, and valued at £333 10s., with thirty-seven free tenants and an adult population of 854.[4] It was the second ecclesiastical estate in extent and value, and next after the abbey of Glastonbury, which had a hidage of 442, a population of 1390, and a revenue of £460 8s. 8d.

The bishop had fifty hides as his own demesne at Wells, on which the canons of St. Andrew were his tenants, with fourteen hides assigned for their support; they also held eight-and-a-half hides at Litton, and four hides at Wanstrow. These canons were the staff of

1. R. iii, f. 246. cf. *Somerset Archæological Proceedings*, vol. xxiii, p. 49.
2. R. i, f. 49.
3. R. i, f. 58. The controversy as to Harold's treatment of Giso has been fully discussed by Mr. Freeman. Archer, writing after review of all the charters in the registers, gives his opinion "ex his chartis apertissime constat quam plane et omnino ficta et commentitia ea quæ canonicus noster (the 'canon of Wells') et Godwinus narrant de Haroldo patrimonium Gisonis diripiente, de Gisone, regnante Haroldo, sponte sua exulante, et de cæteris ecclesiæ Wellensis possessionibus ab eodem confiscatis." Archer was writing 1730-1739.
4. Dugdale's *Monasticon*, xiii, f. 288, ed. 1819. Eyton's *Domesday Studies*, ii, pp. 23 and 43; i, p. 142. One half nearly were moor and forest lands.

the church, the ministers of the bishop, his counsellors,—but his tenants at will—under Benthelius the archdeacon, as the bishop's officer, and Isaac the "Provost," the steward. In complete dependence upon the bishop, their position and services in the church were entirely subservient to the character and policy of the bishop of the time.

We have two notable instances of the precarious position and tenure of the canons in the times of Giso and his successor.

Giso, coming from Lorraine where the semi-monastic rule of cathedral life for secular canons had been established, found a small and humble church at Wells (*mediocrem*), a few canons there, (*quatuor aut quinque*), without any conventual house, without refectory or cloister, or the necessary ecclesiastical buildings. He introduced the much stricter discipline of his own country, built cloister, refectory and dormitory for the canons, and obliged them to live together as a celibate brotherhood.[1] A provost, elected out of their own body, had charge over the property and internal management of the brotherhood, "qui bonis eorum exterioribus curam impenderet et interius fratribus."

Giso was one of the bishops who consecrated Lanfranc in 1070. He was at the synod of London in 1075 when it was decreed that the seats of bishops should be transferred from villages to cities, and among others that of Wells to Bath, and he must have forecast the great change and uprooting of his "family" and college at Wells which this would cause.

---

1. *Historiola* "De primordiis Episcopatus Somersetensis," in *Camden Soc. Publications*, p. 22:—"regulariter et religiose cohabitare."

But the move was delayed until after his death. When in 1088 John of Tours the successor in the see obtained from William II the grant of the abbey of Bath[1], the seat of the bishop was transferred to Bath, Wells lost the preeminence which it had held for two hundred years as the *sedes præsulea*, and became as one of the manors of the see, but retaining a collegiate church.

Bp. John of Tours, A.D. 1088-1122.

"Andrew gave place to Peter, the elder brother to the younger."

With this removal of the bishop and the loss of title and dignity to the see, a great change came over the position of the canons of St. Andrew. Bishop John broke up the ecclesiastical establishment which Giso had built up. He destroyed alike the conventual buildings and the canonical discipline, and the canons once more lived in houses in the town, *cum populo communiter.*[2]

Their lands were farmed out to Hildebert his brother, the provost or steward, with a rent-charge upon them of sixty shillings to each canon, ten in number. The provost devised them by will as private property, subject only to rent-charge[3] to John the archdeacon, his son, and he to his brother Reginald, the precentor.

---

1. *Wells Charters*, No. 2. See for text and commentary Freeman's *Norman Conquest*, Note F to vol. i, p. 137.

2. *Historiola*, p. 22. It is not said that he built a house for himself on the ground: this addition only appears in the fifteenth century writer and Godwin.

3. *Historiola* "partem reddituum ecclesiæ Welliæ contra canones distraxit et Hildeberto dapifero suo distribuit redditus ecclesiæ equiparantes xxx libras et ultra."

After the death of bishop John, Godfrey, his successor, tried in vain to recover the lands from John the archdeacon, but the hand of Roger bishop of Salisbury, the chancellor, then prevailed against him with the king, and at his death he left to his successor the church and canons suffering grievously from the exactions which their subjection to the provost had brought upon them.

Bp. Godfrey, A.D. 1123-1135

Robert of Lewes succeeded to the see in 1136. With Robert a new stage in the history begins.

Bp. Robert, A.D. 1136

Like Osmund at Sarum, and Remigius at Lincoln at the close of the eleventh century, so Robert in the twelfth century is the second founder of the cathedral church at Wells. He founded the constitution of the chapter; he was the first builder of the new church; and by granting the first charter of freedom, as over lord, to the burghers of his town, he was the first maker of Wells as a borough.

We can glean comparatively little from contemporary notices of his personal life. He was of a Fleming family, but born in England;[1] a monk of the Cluniac order and of the Cluniac house of St. Pancras, founded by William de Warenne earl of Surrey, in 1091, at Lewes in Sussex. He owed his first appointment as prior of St. Swithin, Winchester, to Henry of Blois, himself a monk of Cluni, the brother of king Stephen, who, as abbot of Glastonbury from 1123 to his death in 1171, and bishop of Winchester from 1129, afterwards papal legate from 1139 to 1143, was the prime minister and most powerful man in the kingdom during the troubled reign of Stephen.

1. *Florentii Wigorniensis Continuatio*, ed. B. Thorpe (English Historical Society), p. 95. "Flandrinensis . . natus in partibus Angliæ." *Historiola*, p. 23, anno 1174.

Robert, after having been employed by abbot Henry at Glastonbury on some temporary commission,[1] was elected in 1136 bishop of Bath, and confirmed in the temporalities of the see, by Stephen, at Westminster, in the Easter feast.

Bp. Robert's appointment. The full text of his appointment to the see is given in a charter, which illustrates the relations of the king towards the church, and the procedure in the appointment of bishops at this time.

King Stephen, *rex Anglorum*, addressing the archbishop and the great men of the realm, makes grant of the temporalities of the see to "Robert bishop of Bath" by canonical election, and confirmation by royal and popular approval, "canonica prius electione precedente, et communi nostro concilio voto et favore prosequente." The king confirms to the bishop all grants which former kings have made to former bishops.[2]

The charter is attested in public audience at Westminster during the Easter solemnities, and subscribed by the three archbishops, of Canterbury, York, and Rouen, and others, "audientibus et collaudantibus omnibus fidelibus meis hic subscriptis;" and Robert was consecrated by his friend and patron Henry of Winchester.[3] This was the first appointment Stephen

---

1. *Historiola*, 23, "miserat uti rebus abbatiæ disponeret."
Another Robert was prior of Glastonbury during Robert's episcopacy in 1159. R. iii, f. 26. And he, or yet another Robert, was also prior of St. Swithin's and abbot of Glastonbury after abbot Henry's death in 1171. Adam of Domerham, ii, p. 305, ed. Hearne, 1727.
The Glastonbury writers do not mention this mission of Robert of Lewes to Glastonbury.

2. R. i, f. 15, "Carta regis Stephani concessa Johanni (*sic*) episcopo Bathon." "*Johanni*" is evidently the copyist's mistake for "*Roberto*." There is no date of the year to the charter, but on the margin a later hand has written 1136.

3. *Florentii Wigorniensis Continuatio*, ii, 95.

had made. He had landed from Boulogne in the December before with little following, and had obtained the support of London and Winchester, where his brother the bishop had induced bishop Roger of Salisbury, the justiciar, to make over to him the royal treasure. Thus strengthened, he returned to London for formal election and coronation. He had been crowned, not without misgivings, by archbishop William on St. Stephen's day, 1135-6, in the presence of the two bishops of Winchester and Salisbury.

A council of clergy was held in April at London, in which they had petitioned Stephen to defend the liberties of the church, and to give effect to her counsels and decrees.[1] Either at his coronation or at this council Stephen had given a short charter in which he confirmed generally the laws and liberties of the kingdom, and promised to respect the canonical election of bishops, and to fill up vacant sees without unnecessary delay. There was therefore good reason that the ancient form of precedent should be carefully set out, and attested in this first charter of the first bishop's appointment in Stephen's reign.

State of the Kingdom, A.D. 1136-1154.

Henry of Blois was not yet papal legate, and there is no mention of papal confirmation of Stephen's appointment.

Though we know little of Robert's personal life, it is evident that the Cluniac monk must have been a man of vigour and sagacity to obtain the recognition of the politic statesman bishop Henry.

His after life showed his power of administration in those difficult times. In the first part of his life as

1. *Gesta Stephani*, p. 17 (Rolls Series). Stubbs' *Constitutional History*, i, pp. 320-322.

bishop his connection with bishop Henry attached him to the side of Stephen, and in his zeal for the king's cause he nearly lost his life in the faction fights between Bath and Bristol in 1138.

His diocese was one scene of that unparalleled lawlessness which contemporary chroniclers have painted so graphically during the reign of Stephen.

In those years 1138-1139 Stephen was at Bath and besieging Bristol.[1] From there he turned aside to blockade the castle of the Lovel family at Castle Cary, which he forced to surrender. He then marched across the Mendip hills against William Fitzjohn of Harpetre. The castle of Harpetre was taken by surprise and burnt. The bishop's own lands suffered from this predatory baron who stretched forth his hands across the Mendips and "unjustly took from bishop Robert the fee of Dinre"[2] (Dinder) which was not restored during his episcopate.[3] Another insurgent, William of Mohun, lord of Dunster, from his inaccessible castle on the shore of the Severn sea (" quod pulchrè et inexpugnatè in pelagi littore locarat ") sallied " out to ravage all that region with fire and sword, and turned a region of peace into discord and rebellion, mourning and woe." " The realm was rent in two ; some lords inclining to the king, some to the empress. Neither of them could exact command or enforce discipline ; both allowed to their supporters every sort of licence for fear of losing them. In every province numbers of castles had sprung up, and there

1. *Gesta Stephani*, p. 41 (Rolls Series), anno 1138, p. 51, 1139.
2. R. i, f. 333.
3. R. i, f. 60, " *Carta de feodo de Dinre* records the restoration by William de Harpetre, the son, to Reginald, successor of Robert, in 1178."

were as many tyrants as there were lords of castles, and they fought among themselves with deadly hatred. They spoiled the fairest regions with fire and rapine, and destroyed almost all the provision of bread. Many bishops ('non tamen omnes sed plurimi') took arms, joined with the barons, fought in battle, divided the spoil, built castles, oppressed the people, and public fame branded especially the bishops of Winchester, Lincoln, and Chester."[1]

In the centre of this endless agitation bishop Robert was quietly working out the new constitution and the new fabric of his church at Wells, which, as a house built upon the rock, was to stand the storms of many generations.

Bp. Robert at Wells. First sketch of the constitution of the chapter.

The charters of Robert's time are few, but each of them has important bearing upon the history of the church of Wells. They are as landmarks and starting points, giving a direction to the course of later government and the progress of events.

Carta de ordinatione prebendarum et institutione communæ.

This first charter belongs to the year 1136, the date of his own consecration. He set himself at once to the recovery of Wells from the state of humiliation under which it had been left by the rule of bishop John of Tours.

The charter is the first draft of the constitution; it is incomplete, but it is virtually the incorporation of the Chapter.[2]

1. *Gesta Stephani*, p. 100, anno 1143.
2. R. i, f. 31. R. ii, f. 41. R. iii, f. 2, 3. cf. *Drokensford's Register*, f. 24. Dugdale's *Mon.*, ii, 293. It has been misquoted by Wharton, A.S., 561.

He says he had acted in council with the archbishops, bishops, and chief persons of the Church. The charter was drawn up in the presence of bishop Henry of Winchester, and afterwards confirmed by the two archbishops, William de Corbeil, of Canterbury, and Thurstan de Bayeux, of York, and by the bishops Roger of Sarum, William of Exeter, and Simon of Worcester.

The date of the charter is fixed conclusively by the signatures of archbishop William, and William Warelwast bishop of Exeter, both of whom died in 1136.[1]

In this first draft of the constitution he was applying to Wells principles worked out by Norman bishops in the English cathedral churches at the end of the previous century, but he was prompted immediately by sympathy with the pressing wants of his church and clergy.

He found the church "suffering intolerably from the oppression of the provostship"—" invenimus ecclesiam indebitis prepositurae oppressionibus supra modum afflictam."

The ministrant body were suffering from the claims of the provost, who doled out to them a bare subsistence from the lands which had been bequeathed to the church for their maintenance. Powerless for united action in the absence or negligence of the bishop, they were as chaplains or curates of the bishop and stipendiaries of the provost.

His aim was to constitute a self governing community, with a spiritual head and officers, who should

---

1. Stubbs *Episcopal Succession*, anno 1136.

have their share in the home government of the church, with freehold endowments separate and distinct from the lands of the bishop, secured alike from misappropriation by the bishop or his officers as of late, and from the grasp of the crown when the temporalities passed to the crown on a vacancy of the see.

Accordingly he instituted a dean, an officer of dignity and authority to preside and rule the canons, invested "with the like dignities and privileges and authority as in other well ordered churches." And lest the office should suffer from the like usurpation (" ne in eadem ecclesia pristina tribulatio locum denuo vendicaret,") the office was endowed with its own lands which secured independence and dignity; "decanum illic ordinavimus, concessis sibi dignitatibus libertatibus et consuetudinibus canonicis ecclesiarum Angliæ bene ordinatarum." *Institution of the deanship.*

The deanship is the only office here instituted and the framework of the constitution is now imperfectly sketched out; but bishop Robert had before him the models of other cathedral churches where the capitular system was at work, and to these Wells was gradually assimilated.

"The Norman bishops," Mr. H. Bradshaw says,[1] "had brought with them into England a form of government for the cathedral churches which they had followed in their own churches of Rouen and Bayeux,[2] whereby the canons obtained a separate and inde-

---

1. *Lincoln Cathedral Statutes*, ed. Bradshaw and Wordsworth, pp. 30, 36.
2. H. Bradshaw, pp. 35, 36. "It is at Bayeux that we find the precise pattern followed by St. Osmund at Salisbury in the ordering of the offices of 'decanus, cantor, cancellarius, thesaurarius, four archdeacons, subdecanus, succentor.'"

pendent position, and the home government of the church became vested in them as a body, the Chapter."

In the previous generation, about the same time at York and Lincoln in 1090, and at Salisbury in 1091, that form of constitution was instituted for the government of these cathedral churches which became the pattern for all secular chapters subsequently erected. About the same time, "shortly before 1150, the bishop of Lincoln, Robert de Chesney, had been persuaded on his accession to the see to bestow upon his chapter the fullest privileges which had been accorded to the chapter of Salisbury by their founder, and this example was followed by other bishops both in England and Scotland." The churches were put under the government of officers appointed by the bishop, with definite offices and duties and separate possessions attached to the offices; and with them was a body of canons, with the dean at the head of all, appointed at first by the bishop, but soon elected by themselves.[1]

Each of the officers had a distinct sphere of duty. The dean was president of the chapter and judge in all causes and matters relating to the chapter; the duty of the precentor, the next in importance "in days when the science of worship was so serious a matter" was to rule the choir, to lead the chanting, to admit and instruct the choir. The chancellor, called also the *archischola* had both educational and legal work—head of the cathedral school, corrector of the ordinal and service books, keeper of the seal, secretary and legal adviser

---

1. The election of the dean by the canons was the rule in bishop Jocelin's time at least, if not before. R. i, f. 57, anno 1216; Cf. R. i, f. 113.

of the chapter. All ornaments and furniture of the church and the ordering of ceremonial was in the hands of the treasurer. Subdean and succentor were assisttants respectively of dean and precentor.

All these offices are found existing very early in the church of Wells, some, in Robert's time,[1] as dean, precentor, treasurer, subdean, and two archdeacons of Bath and Wells, and all, in the next episcopate of bishop Reginald.[2] The description of these offices is contained in the earliest draft of statutes. The *antiqua statuta* which stand at the head of the successive codes of dated statutes, themselves undated, are a declaration of the " ancient customs of the church when first committed to writing."[3] These statutes supplement this first draft of the charter, and show the next stage in the growth of the constitution.

The division of the lands of the bishop, and the endowment of the dean and the canons with separate estates, was the second part in this charter.

<small>Division of the lands into prebends.</small>

The office of the dean was endowed with the manor of Wedmoreland including Mark and Mudgeley, the island block between the marshes of the Axe and the Brue. He was rector of the churches of Wedmore and Wookey,[1] but charged to support four prebends with 100 shillings each a year out of his estate of Wedmore. The manor of Litton also supplied a prebend which was attached to the deanship.

---

1. R. i, f. 46. R. iii, 292 an. 1159.
2. R. i, f. 25, and Reginald's charter to the Town, in appendix E.
3. R. ii, f. 40, 1. Printed in *Wells Cathedral*, Reynolds, from the Lambeth MS. 729. " Statutes were for the most part looked upon as declaratory of the 'ancient customs of the church.' " H. Bradshaw, p. 37.

The manor of Biddisham was set apart to supply a fund for the support of the fabric and furniture of the church of Wells, and it was the titular prebend of St. Andrew ("ad reparandam ecclesiam beati Andreæ et ornamenta emenda"). Only one virgate of its land was reserved to support a vicar choral at Wells.

Dulcot with Chilcot, Wormestor (Wormister), Wanstrow, Bromley or Bromfield in the Quantocks, each formed a prebend.

Out of Winsham five prebends were made.

The manor of Combe St. Nicholas was given for life to Reginald the precentor, in compensation for his cession of the tenure of the estates received through his uncle the archdeacon from the late bishop John, of whom a kindly mention is here made: "memores beneficiorum quæ ab avunculo suo bonæ memoriæ Johanne episcopo ecclesiæ nostræ collata sunt." But after his death, prebends for the support of five canons were to be formed out of the manor.[2] All these manors had formed part of the endowments of the see as held by bishop Giso.

Robert now made grants of two more prebends from later endowments, viz.: Yatton, and Huish in Brent Marsh with the church of Compton.

Two more prebends were made by the grant of king Stephen of the churches of North Curry and Perreton.[3]

---

1. This endowment was afterwards recast; first, when the subdean held the church of Wedmore, and again by bishop Jocelin, when Wookey became the endowment of the subdean and Wedmore church returned to the dean. R. i, f. 58, anno 1210.

2. In Jocelin's time Combe was divided into fifteen prebends, with a provost or steward who farmed the manor and distributed the fixed sum of £5 to each canon.

3. R. i, f. 11, "Perreton," whether it be North or South Pether-

Altogether twenty-four prebends were made in bishop Robert's time out of the lands of the see now transferred, and made the freehold of the canons.

The charter, though entitled *de institutione communæ*, so far treats only of the division of the lands into prebends assigned to individual canons; it says nothing of the common property, the *communa*, as specifically vested in the corporation. But at the same time Robert confirmed to the canons the grants assigned by his predecessors for special purposes, *e.g.*, half a hide of land in North Wootton with which Giso had endowed the chapel of the Blessed Virgin, and and half a hide with which bishop Godfrey had endowed the rectory of St. Cuthbert, in Wells, at the dedication of this church by him (1123-1135), after reconstruction of the old Saxon church. Later documents contain the evidence that during his episcopate bishop Robert made over the church of St. Cuthbert to the canons, as part of their common property.[1] Other special endowments were made expressly to the *communa* of the canons during bishop Robert's time, by grants of lay lands in the diocese, which, though not enumerated now, appear in the confirmation of the possessions of the see in the early part of the next episcopate.[2]

One specific grant is made for the daily sustenance of the canons, of a tenth of the wine, or of the vineyards, of the bishop, and a charge upon the tithes

---

ton, did not remain attached to Wells. Henry of Blois, Richard de Luci, and William Martel dapifer of the king attest the grant in 1141.

1. R. i, f. 111. R. iii, f. 5, Confirmatio bonorum ecclesiæ per Rogerum episcopum, 1246.
2. R. iii, f. 266, anno 1179.

of the bishop to provide the canons with the allowance of bread. The vineyards are not specified; Glastonbury had vineyards at Meare, Pilton, and Pamborough.

<small>Gradual growth of the constitution.</small> This charter, made in the first year of the episcopate, could only represent the purpose of the bishop and the first outline of his plans. The partition of the lands and the endowment of the canons could only be carried out in the course of after years, as the lands came into the bishop's possession after alienation.

Early in bishop Robert's time Reginald the precentor had surrendered his hereditary tenure. But it was long before the bishop came into quiet possession of all the lands which he had held. The right of surrender was disputed by the nephews of Reginald in the king's court, and it was only at the close of Robert's life that their claims to the lands of Winsham, Mudgeley with Mark and a virgate of Biddisham, and Wanstrow, were compromised, at a cost of seventy marcs, and they made public renunciation of all pretensions.[1]

<small>Grant of Huish with Compton.</small> Again, in the charter of 1136 Robert made a grant of Huish in Brent to the canons, but it was not until 1159 that he was able to execute his purpose. Huish was a member of the manor of Banwell, which remained for some time in lay hands, after Banwell had been restored to the see by William at the Conquest.

The recovery of Huish, and the conveyance of it to the church, are made the subject of a deed of great formality.[2]

In a charter addressed to Theobald the archbishop,

---

1. *Historiola*, 26, 27. R. i, f. 36. R. iii, f. 15. Among the witnesses are Richard the dean, which fixes the date after 1160.

2. R. i, f. 26. "Carta ecclesiæ de Hiwys in Brent marisco."

the bishops, and the whole diocese, he names the lay-lords by whom the lands had been held in succession during his episcopate and his purpose obstructed, and now, fearing lest the manor of Huish should be lost to the church ("metuentes ne in jus et rem perpetuam laicorum transferetur") he publicly declares that it is made for ever a prebend in the church of Wells, that thereby "the number of the canons there serving God may be increased, and the praises of God may sound forth more joyously." It is remarkable that a synod of the diocese seems to have been called to attest this deed, which is dated with great precision of year and month, and epact and indiction, in the fifth year of Henry "the younger" and in the twenty-third year of the episcopate, 1159. Peter, prior, and the convent of Bath, Ivo, dean, and "the convent" of Wells, the abbots of Muchelney and Athelney, Robert prior of the monks of Glastonbury, the priors of Montacute, Taunton, and Bruton, archdeacons Robert of Wells and Thomas of Bath, "et multa clericorum turba" attest the deed.

There are some other charters in the registers which supplement the first charter of ordination, and which represent rules probably instituted by Robert. One for instance regulated the succession of the prebends for the year after death, that on the vacancy of a prebend, two parts of the revenues were assigned to the *communa* of the canons, who were bound to maintain the obituary services for the deceased during the year after death, and the third part belonged to the estate of the late canon. Each canon was bound to pay tithes to the parish church near to which his prebend was situated; *Charters supplementary to the institution of prebends.*

he was in no wise to diminish the value of the prebend, but to leave it stocked as he had received it.[1]

<small>Division of the psalter among the prebends.</small>

The daily recitation of the psalter by the members of the chapter, formed part of the consuetudinary introduced by the Norman bishops in the twelfth century elsewhere, and it is ordered in the earliest draft of statutes, the *antiqua statuta*, at Wells. This usage can be traced to very early times in the ordinances of the churches of Lincoln and Salisbury, as of Wells.

" The earliest recorded statute to be found at Lincoln, is one concerning the division of the psalter for daily recitation: it is an ordinance based upon the " ancient institution," *antiqua institutio*, of the church, and drawn up by the dean and chapter, and confirmed by St. Hugh, bishop, 1186-1200."[2]

An order in the *antiqua statuta* of the church of Wells directs that "the whole psalter shall be said daily for the brethren and benefactors of the church of Wells, and two masses each week shall be celebrated for living and dead."[3]

<small>Existence of vicars choral.</small>

Together with the institution of prebends, the existence of the vicars choral seems to be coeval with the earliest establishment of the constitution, though not part of the constitution, but an offshoot from it. It was a natural result from the endowment of the canons with prebendal estates.

We have seen that in the charter of 1136 it was ordered that the prebend of Biddisham should provide

1. R. iii, f. 3; R. i, f. 29.
2. H. Bradshaw in *Lincoln Cathedral Statutes*, p. 37
3. R. ii, f. 42.

a vicar in the church of Wells, for whom a special endowment of land was set apart, *una virgata terræ*.

The custom grew up very soon that every prebendary who undertook to reside in part, and to claim any share in the *communa*, was bound to provide a substitute in his absence, *vicarium suum*, subject to the dean's approval, and under the authority of the dean and chapter. There is no mention of vicars in the *antiqua statuta*, but they were engrafted into the cathedral system before the end of the twelfth century.[1]

Such was the first outline of the capitular constitution of the church of Wells in the twelfth century. From henceforth gradually the canons of the cathedral church became a distinct corporation, with a head in the person of the dean, at first appointed by the bishop, soon afterwards chosen by the canons. All the canons and dignitaries were appointed by the bishop. But whereas hitherto the bishop had been the head of his canons, as an abbot was the head of his monks, now by degrees the chapter became a separate body, with interests and possessions of its own, distinct from those of the bishop—a corporate body, entitled the " Dean and Chapter," to whom was committed the home government of the cathedral church. Each member of the chapter became a separate corporation sole, distinct alike from the bishop and his brother canons, in the possession of a prebend as his freehold.[2]

General result. The canons a corporate body, "dean and chapter."

1. In Savaric's time, Charter No. 16, the abbot of Bec held the church of Old Cleeve as his prebend : he was to be non-resident but to pay four marcs to his vicar in the church of Wells.
2. Freeman, *Cathedral Church*, vol. ii, pp. 49, 65.

22   *Chapters in Wells History.*   [CHAP.

Relations of the chapters of Bath and Wells adjusted.

When the "dean and chapter" of Wells had been constituted, the relations of the two chapters of Bath and Wells required careful readjustment.

Since the transfer of the see to Bath, there had been doubtless a change in the mode of election of the bishop. The canons of Wells had lost the position which they had held from the earliest times, and probably the formal election of bishops Godfrey and Robert had been exercised by the monks of Bath alone.

Either experience, or forecast of strife between the two bodies must have moved Robert soon to make provision for settling the relations of the canons and the monks. We find that the constitutional relation of the two sees was laid down during his episcopate and confirmed by papal confirmation. A charter of Hadrian IV, in 1157, formally recognised Bath as the bishop's seat, sanctioned Robert's title as bishop of Bath, and confirmed him in all the possessions of the see.[1]

Another papal charter by the next pope, Alexander III (1159-81) confirms the title and recites these articles of arrangement made for the harmonious relations of the two chapters.

(*a*). The two churches of Bath and Wells to be equally seats of the bishop.

(*b*). The bishop to be elected by representatives of the two chapters.

(*c*). The prior of Bath to notify the election to the archbishop of Canterbury.

(*d*). The bishop to be enthroned in both churches, and first in the church of Bath.[2]

---

1. R. ii, f. 45, anno 1157; R. iii, f. 268.
2. R. ii, f. 46, an. 1176.

These terms, acted on in the election of Reginald the successor to bishop Robert, received the formal sanction of the Roman court in the year after his election, 1176—at the request of the dean and chapter. But there was no change or addition to the title of the bishop "of Bath" at this time, and not for many years later.[1] No bishop was called "of Bath and Wells" before bishop Roger in 1244.

This sketch of bishop Robert's constitution for his church, may be closed in the words of Henry Bradshaw, which also are a prelude to the future history of the chapter.

"The *capitulum* or chapter had originally been the body of *clerici* most nearly connected with the bishop's see, and forming as such the bishop's immediate council.

"But by the latter part of the eleventh century this body had begun in many ways to develop a substantive existence of its own. The need of an organisation for the management of the mother church of the diocese, whether from the importance of that church, or from the necessarily frequent absence of the bishop, led to the creation of a systematic form of home government; and, in order to create and foster a due sense of responsibility, it became a matter of good policy for the Bishops to confer very great powers and privileges

---

1. Godwin incorrectly says, "Bishop Robert set down the order that the bishop should be called bishop of Bath and Wells," following the fifteenth century writer, the "Canon of Wells." Archer, *Chronicon Well.*, p. 29, corrects him and Wharton, "Canonicus noster et Godwinus, quin et ipse Whartonus, haud satis perspicuè rem narrant. Nullus etenim Episcoporum 'Bathoniensis et Wellensis' nuncupatus est a prima sedis translatione per Joannem Turonensem facta usque ad annum 1244."

upon the body, to which this home government was entrusted."[1]

The fabric of the church. While Robert was building up the framework of the constitution, he was also rebuilding the fabric of the old Saxon church of Wells.

But we must look to the registers of the church of Bath for any contemporary notice, scanty as it is, of this great achievement.

The only evidence which the Wells documents supply is an allusion in one charter,[2] and an incidental record one hundred years later in an inventory of the possessions of the church, of an endowment made by bishop Robert at the dedication of the church which in 1246 was then called the "old church," *in dedicatione veteris ecclesiæ.*[3]

It is a remarkable instance of the fragmentary and incomplete character of these materials of history that such an event as the reconstruction and consecration of the cathedral church should be almost unnoticed in the contemporary records at Wells.

All that we learn from the Bath writer is that Robert was a builder at Bath in completing the church which John of Tours had begun, and that the church also of Wells was built by his design and help, and afterwards dedicated with a solemnity which made it memorable.[4]

He dilates on the dedication of the church in the

1. H. Bradshaw, in *Lincoln Cathedral Statutes*, p. 31.
2. R. i, f. 46.
3. R. iii, f. 4. "Confirmatio bonorum ecclesiæ per Rogerum episcopum," A.D. 1246. Lights for the high altar were to be provided from lands at Dultingcote by the grant of bp. Robert, "in dedicatione veteris ecclesiæ."
4. *Historiola*, p. 24. "Porro non est oblivioni tradendum quod ecclesia Welliæ suo consilio fabricata est et auxilio."

presence of three bishops, Jocelin of Sarum, Simon of Worcester, and Robert of Hereford.

The death of Robert de Bethune, bishop of Hereford, on April 16, 1148, fixes the date of consecration to the early part of that year. As if in fresh recollection of the event, the writer tells how the consecration was marked by the grant from the bishops present, of one hundred days of remission of penance to all who should keep the anniversary of that day by coming to the church.[1]

The later writers, the canon of Wells and Godwin, enlarge somewhat on this meagre account. They speak each in much the same terms of the ruinous condition of the church.

The fifteenth century writer in Wharton, says "dedicavit ecclesiam Wellensem. Multas ruinas destructionem ejus in pluribus locis comminantes, egregie reparavit."[2]

Godwin follows "whereas our church of Wells at this time was exceedingly ruinous, and likely every day to fall to the ground, he pulled down a great part of it and repaired it."[3]

This is all we are told of Robert as a builder of the church of Wells.

There is enough to lead us to look for evidence in the architectural features of the fabric which may correspond with the date of this consecration of some part of it, in 1148. This date, at least, must be the starting

---

1. "Magnum, mirificum, et memorandum collatum est donativum."
2. *Anglia Sacra*, p. 561.
3. Godwin, Lat. ed., 1614; Engl. ed., 1601. Archer quotes and comments on their statements:—"Unde vero ista hauserunt non constat."

point for all enquiries into the architectural history of the present church.

The church which Robert was rebuilding was the Saxon or "Romanesque" church of Wells, in which Dudoc and Giso were buried, each in their places on either side of the high altar.[1] Mr. Freeman would have us conceive of this "the old church of St. Andrew" as built in the old Romanesque "style of England which prevailed before the great improvements of Norman Romanesque were introduced in the eleventh century,—small, and low, and plain, with massive round arches and small round-headed windows, with one or more tall, slender, unbuttressed towers, imitating the bell towers of Italy."[2] It was such a church which Robert was now rebuilding.

In the church of Bath which he is said to have partly rebuilt or finished he must have had before him a more finished example of that "later variety of Romanesque which had been imported into England under Edward the Confessor, from Normandy, and which is called the Norman style," in which John of Tours had been building.

But the associations of Robert were not limited to Normandy, and he was living and building at a time in the twelfth century when the earlier Norman architecture was undergoing a change, and the pointed arch was beginning to take the place of the round massive arches of the buildings of the first part of the century.

---

1. *Historiola*, 21, "Giso sepultus est in ecclesiâ quam rexerat in hemicyclo (a round arch) facto in pariete a parte aquilonali prope altare, sicut Dudoco prædecessor ejus sepultus est a meridie juxta altare."

2. Freeman, *Cathedral Church*, p. 24.

He was connected with the great abbey of Cluni, planted in Burgundy in the tenth century, and now in the height of its fame and prosperity. His own Cluniac monastery of St. Pancras, at Lewes, which had been dedicated at the close of the last century, 1091, by bishops Walkelin of Winchester, Gundulf of Rochester, and Ralph of Chichester, had lately been enlarged and rebuilt, while he was at work on his own churches at Bath, and Wells.

A year or two before the church of Wells was consecrated in 1148, the church of his old home of St. Pancras at Lewes, had been consecrated for a second time, and Robert of Bath was one of the bishops who, with Henry of Winchester, and Ascelin of Rochester, assisted Theobald the archbishop.

Though there could be little or no likeness between the two churches of St. Pancras at Lewes and of Wells, yet there is an interest in noting the remarkable features of the church with which Robert was familiar while he was building at Wells. " The convent of St. Pancras of Lewes, taking the mother church of Cluni as a desirable model, added to the presbytery an eastern transept, with an apse in each arm and a lofty lantern at the crossing, and, beyond this, an apse with five apsidal chapels encircling its aisles."[1]

Robert had also as another pattern, the church of old Sarum, which bishop Roger, " the greatest builder of his day," was building at his death in 1139 ; and the church of the abbey of Malmesbury, in which the pointed arch appears, is ascribed also to bishop Roger.

---

1. *Archæological Journal*, vol. xli. " On the Cluniac priory of St. Pancras, Lewes," by W. H. St. John Hope.

These works of bishop Roger, Mr. Freeman says, "brought to perfection that later form of Norman architecture, lighter and richer than the earlier type which slowly died out before the introduction of the pointed arch and its accompanying details. . . The greater lightness and richness of Roger's work became the fashion in the days of Henry the Second (1141-1189), and when the fashion had once been set lightness and richness went on increasing. . . Now all forms of Romanesque, the architecture of the round arch, were to give way to the fully developed architecture of the pointed arch. . . The germ which we see at Malmesbury grew up by slow and easy steps into the full growth of Lincoln and Salisbury. . . Before the twelfth century had run its course the fully developed pointed architecture had reached its perfection, not at the hands of a Frenchman at St. Denis, but at the hands of the saint whom the imperial Burgundy gave to England, St. Hugh at Lincoln 1186-1200."

If then on these grounds of architectural history, it does not seem so impossible, or improbable, that the pointed arch found its way as an architectural feature into the church which Robert was building at Wells in the middle of the twelfth century, we may hesitate before we accept the assumption that "whatever was the extent of bishop Robert's work, it is certain that not a single bit of detail of his building is to be seen in the present church;" that "whatever was built in the days of Robert has utterly vanished;" and that here "one of the massive piles of that day has utterly gone without leaving any trace of itself."[1]

1. See Freeman, *Norman Conquest*, v. 638-641; *Cathedral Church of Wells*, pp. 67-69.

But if we know little of the construction of the fabric by bishop Robert, we have evidences in his charters that he was active not only in building, but in furnishing his restored church, and in promoting due order and reverence of worship therein. *Bp. Robert in the church*

The one charter in which allusion is made by Robert to his dedication of the church contains a grant of lands at Dulcot and Chilcot, of half a hide and half a virgate to one who had been long engaged in some way in his service, Ralph Martire, "qui per longa tempora nobis servierat." *Grant of lights to the high altar of St. Andrew.*

These lands were charged with the perpetual obligation of providing three lights, one of three pounds weight, and two of two pounds each, for the high altar on the vigil of the festival of St. Andrew.[1]

This grant was confirmed by bishop Roger in 1246.[2]

Another charter has a double interest. In it the bishop appears both as chief pastor and ordinary in his cathedral church, and also as lord of the manor granting a charter of freedom from tolls to his burghers of the town.[3] *Statute to remove markets from the church.*

The preamble recites that whereas the noise and disorder of markets held in the church and the vestibule of the church (*atrio ecclesiæ*), bring dishonour to God, disturbance to the ministering priests, and hin-

---

1. R. i, f. 46; iii, f. 292. Hyginus, the precentor (this may be a mistake by the later copyist for Reginaldus), two archdeacons, Robert of Wells, Thomas of Bath, Robert subdean, William the treasurer. John the provost, Peter prior of Bath, William prior of Bruton, are among the witnesses attesting this grant. Ivo the dean and others, confirm it.

2. R. iii, f. 4.

3. R. iii, f. 245. "Carta Roberti episcopi de nundinis Wellensibus in cimiterio non faciendis; (*cimiterio* is written over *atrio* by a later hand).

drance to worshippers, lest the church should become a den of merchandise, *spelunca negotiationis*, the bishop orders that henceforth, markets on the eves and festivals of the Invention of Holy Cross (May 3), of St. Calixtus (October 14), and of St. Andrew (November 30), shall no longer be held near the church, but in the broad places of the town, *in plateis villæ*.

We realize the scene suggested—the stalls and booths in the square in front, against the doors, and on the steps, within the porches, or in the nave itself of the church; market people standing and chaffering around the doors, coming with baskets and goods into the church, kneeling before shrines and altars. Such was the scene at the west door, and in the nave of the old church, and on the ground outside, where afterwards, when the later hand wrote the title to the charter in the register, "*in cimiterio*," instead of "*in atrio*" was the great cemetery.[1]

As God's minister careful for the reverence due to His house of prayer, he removed the markets from the west front of the church to the square of the town. At the same time, as an act of grace from the lord of the manor, he made a grant to the burghers of his town that the tolls due to his officers at those markets should be remitted for ever, " ut quieti de teloneo in perpetuum permanerent."

This charter, made before 1160, is attested by Ivo the dean, Reginald the precentor, Robert and Thomas archdeacons, Ralph Martire and others. It is one in that series of local municipal charters whereby the

---

1. R. i, f. 64. See the arrangement in 1243, for the cemeteries round the church.

boroughs of England grew up into independent self-government.[1]

The charter fixed the time at which these free markets should be held, and an interesting question arises why these festivals should have been chosen. *Festivals and fairs.*

The festival of St. Andrew was of course kept with special ceremonial as the feast of the patron saint. The other two days may have been chosen as the great markets of spring and autumn. But there may have been other historical reasons why these two festivals were days of special observance in the church of Wells.

Leodgaresburgh, afterwards Montacute in Somerset, had been the scene of the "Invention," the discovery, in the days of Cnut,[2] of a relic of the Holy Cross which had been transported by oxen taking their straight way as by divine monition, like the kine of Bethshemesh, until they came to Waltham in Essex. There in later days earl Harold had raised over the sacred relic the great church of secular canons, rival of St. Peter's Westminster, which was consecrated in the presence of Edward and the great men of the land, among whom bishop Giso was present, on Holy Cross day, 1060.

The cross of Waltham, once the cross of Leodgaresburgh, became the special object of the devotion of Harold's life—the rallying cry of the men who fought around his standard on the fatal day of battle, which was the day of St. Calixtus, October 14.

1. Charters No. 5; cf. R. iii, 245-6.
2. "Regnante Cnuto et Anglis imperante—in loco qui dicitur Mons acutus quem Lutegaresberie compatriotæ appellant." *Tractatus de inventione Sanctæ Crucis*, ed. Stubbs, 1861.

Could it be that an altar of the Holy Cross had been raised in memory of the "Invention of the Holy Cross" of Leodgaresburgh and endowed in the church of St. Andrew in Wells by earl Harold himself, in Giso's time?

Nor again can we forget that it was on the day of St. Calixtus, the third of these days of observance, that Harold fell in battle and William the Norman won the kingdom. The bishop at that time was Giso the foreigner, whose sympathies and hopes would rather be with the conqueror than with Harold. Could Giso have dedicated the altar in the aisle of the south transept in the name of this saint, as a courtly compliment to a powerful patron, or in gratitude for lands recovered and endowments given?

Whatever may have been the reason for the selection of these festivals or for their original institution, we know that there were three altars with these dedications in the church in bishop Robert's time.

The escheator's accounts in the chapter archives contain evidences that the offerings made at these markets (*nundinæ*) were paid, and formed part of the revenues of the church through succeeding ages, until all record of them ceases in the years of general confiscation in the sixteenth century.[1]

Charters by Henry II. Two charters of Henry II in Robert's episcopate mark the recognition by the crown of freehold rights of the bishop and of the dean, as lords in their respective estates; the one a grant to Robert to enclose his parks throughout the county, thereby securing his freedom from the usurpations of the king's officers of

---

1. *Escheatory Rolls, passim* until A.D. 1544. *Hist. MSS. Report,* p. 284.

the forests,[1] and about the same time Ivo, the dean obtained a charter of "free warren" on his lands at Wedmore[2] which gave him like immunity in his manor.

Ivo, the first dean, was succeeded by Richard of Spakeston (Spaxton on the Quantocks) in 1160, and he survived the bishop and the interregnum of eight years which followed Robert's death in 1166.

Richard of Spaxton, second dean, A.D. 1160.

Through these thirty years of national strife and of disputed succession to the throne, Robert was mostly engaged in these works of home administration, but at times he was also taking part in the public affairs of church and state.

In 1141 he was with bishop Henry at Winchester, at the public reception of the empress Matilda, after Stephen had been taken prisoner at the battle of Lincoln; when many of the bishops, headed by Henry of Winchester and Bernard of St. David's, shifted for the time their allegiance from Stephen to the empress.[3]

In 1153 he assisted as witness to the compact made between Stephen and the young duke Henry of Anjou, and he was present at Henry's coronation at Westminster, December 19, 1154.[4] In October of that year he had been one of the consecrators at Westminster of Roger de Pont l'Evêque archdeacon of Canterbury to the archbishopric of York.

In 1162 he was one of the fourteen bishops present at Canterbury at the consecration of Thomas the chancellor to the archbishopric of Canterbury, and

1. R. i, f. 15.
2. R. i, f. 58.
3. Will. Malmb., ii, 188.
4. Matt. Paris.

he witnessed the first stages of the great quarrel between Henry and his archbishop.

In the midst of these public acts, it is pleasant to find him also engaged in a work of pastoral visitation in his diocese. In contrast to the lives of worldly bishops and savage barons with which the chronicles abound in these stormy times, the memory of at least one saintly life has been rescued by contemporaries from total oblivion.

Bp. Robert and St. Ulfric

A memoir of St. Ulfric, a Somerset hermit, one of the English stock, is preserved in the pages of Matthew Paris the monk of St. Albans,[1] and of Gervase of Canterbury.[2] Priest at Compton Martin, his birthplace and home, afterwards hermit in a cell near the church at Haselbury,[3] wearing a shirt of sackcloth, and over it a long coat of chain armour which, in keeping with the character of the times, a friendly knight had given him, Ulfric fought out twenty-seven years of lonely spiritual conflict, the wonder and awe of the neighbourhood for his ascetic life. His fame for visions brought, as is said, at one time Henry I and his queen, at another, the boy Henry of Anjou, to visit him in his cell to hear things to come. Humble of spirit and kindly of speech to those who sought him, echoes of heavenly harmonies were wont to resound behind the closed lattice of his cell. Bishop Robert visited him there, was present with him at his deathbed, and buried him in his cell, from whence his body was moved afterwards to the church of Haselbury,

1. Matt. Paris, *Chron. Major*, ii, 205 (Rolls Series), anno 1154.
2. Gervase, i, 130 (Rolls Series).
3. Haselbury Plucknett, near Crewkerne. The rectory was a prebend in the church of Wells.

where the fame of miracles worked at his tomb in "St. Ulfric's aisle" kept alive his memory.[1]

Bishop Robert died in 1166, August 31, in the thirtieth year of his episcopate, and he was buried before the high altar of the church of Bath.

The first part of his episcopate belonged to the times of anarchy in Stephen's reign, 1136-1154; the last twelve years coincided with the beginning of the constitutional settlement and literary activity of Henry II's reign.

He who sketched out the draft of the constitution of the chapter of his church in 1136, lived to work out its details for thirty years. When he had finished and consecrated the eastern part of the fabric in 1148, he had yet eighteen years more to carry on his buildings westward.

He was one of the active spirits of the twelfth century, who steadily but quietly leavened the world for good amidst the turbulence and wickedness around. He lived in the middle of the twelfth century, at a time in which there was a great preparation for the outburst of intellectual and political life in the thirteenth century.[2] Friend of Henry of Blois, his survivor, "who concentrated about him all that remained of the enlightenment and refinement of English and Norman society," and of archbishop Theobald, "who

1. Matt. Paris, *Chron. Maj.*, ii, 205; Dugdale's *Monasticon*, vi, 218; extract from Leland's *Collectanea*, i, f. 645: "Robertus episcopus Bathon. sepelivit eum in ejus cella. Osbernus parochus de Haselberye transtulit corpus Sti. Wulfrici in aquilonarem partem altaris ecclesiæ.

2. Bishop Stubbs' *Lectures on Medieval and Modern History*, Lect. vi, vii. He draws out an estimate of the debt that the thirteenth century owed to the twelfth.

preserved and handed on the traditions of Bec and of Canterbury, which had gathered round Lanfranc and Anselm," he was contemporary also with the lawyers of the court of Henry, and the younger literary men who formed the school of St. Thomas, the *eruditi Sancti Thomæ*, such as John of Salisbury, Ralph de Diceto afterwards dean of St. Paul's, and Reginald "the Italian," son of bishop Jocelin of Sarum, the intelligent traveller and diplomatist, who after eight years of vacancy in the see was his successor as bishop of Bath.

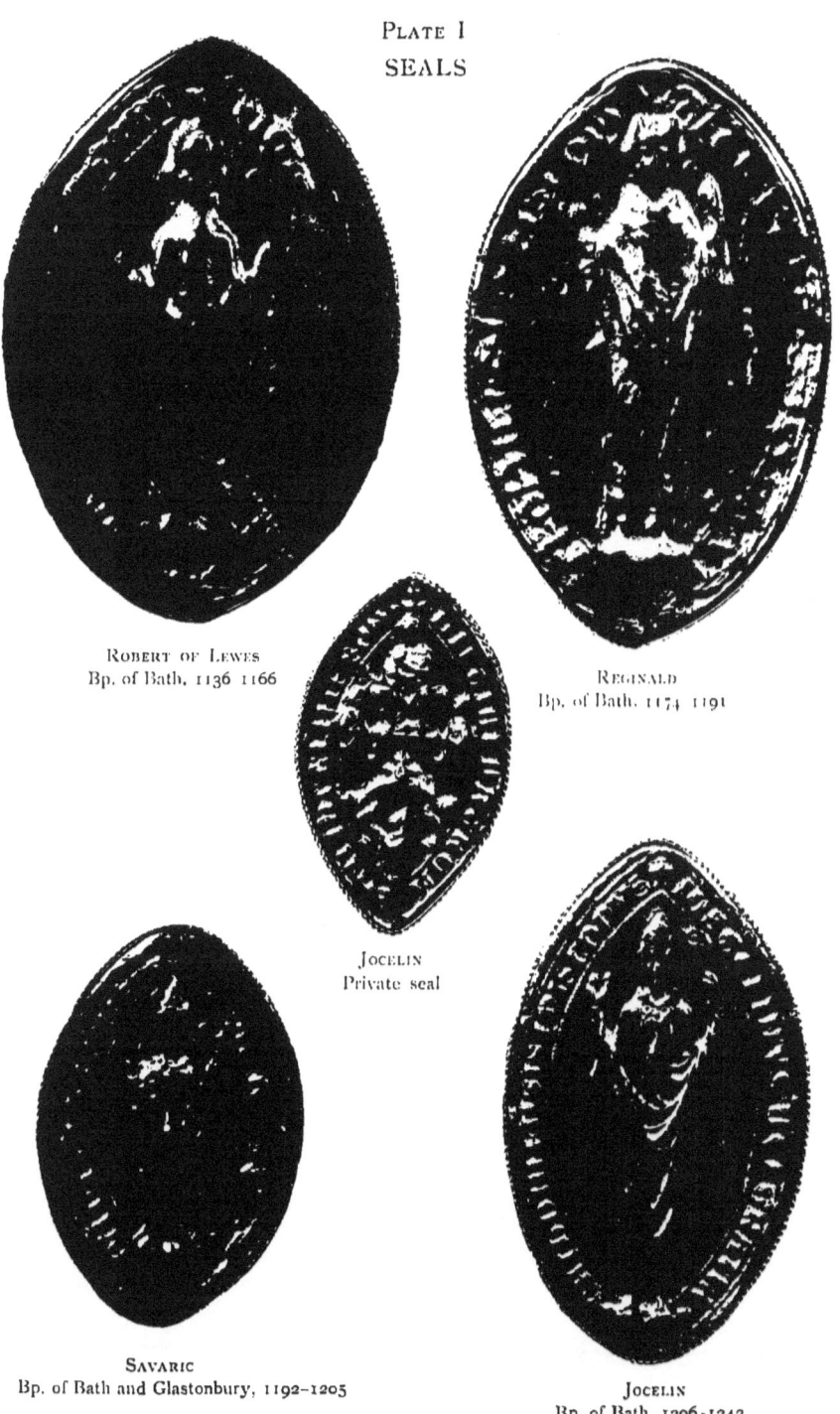

PLATE I
SEALS

ROBERT OF LEWES
Bp. of Bath, 1136-1166

REGINALD
Bp. of Bath, 1174-1191

JOCELIN
Private seal

SAVARIC
Bp. of Bath and Glastonbury, 1192-1205

JOCELIN
Bp. of Bath, 1206-1242
Bp. of Bath and Glastonbury, 1206-1219

CHAPTER II.

Bishop Reginald, A.D. 1174-1191.

I VENTURE to think that bishop Reginald Fitzjocelin deserves a place of higher honour in the history of the diocese, and of the fabric of the church of Wells, than has hitherto been accorded to him.

His memory has been obscured by the traditional fame of bishop Robert as the " author," and of bishop Jocelin as the " finisher," of the church of Wells ; and the importance of his episcopate as a connecting link in the work of these two master-builders has been comparatively overlooked. The only authorities followed for the history of his episcopate have been the work of the *Canon of Wells,* and bishop Godwin. But Wharton, in his notes to the text of his author, comments on the scanty notice of bishop Reginald ;[1] and Archer, our local chronicler, complains of the unworthy treatment bishop Reginald had received from Godwin, also a canon of his own cathedral church.[2]

---

1. " Reginaldi gesta historicus noster brevius quam pro viri dignitate enarravit." Wharton, *Anglia Sacra,* i, 871.

2. " Historicus noster et post eum Godwinus, nimis breviter gesta Reginaldi perstringunt quae pro egregii viri dignitate narrationem magis applicatam de Canonicis istis Wellensibus merita sunt." Archer, *Chronicon Wellense, sive annales Ecclesiae Cathedralis Wellensis,* p. 75.

Bishop Reginald Fitzjocelin de Bohun, and bishop Savaric, his kinsman and successor, were the two last in the succession of foreign bishops who held the see of Somerset from the time of Edward the Confessor. Reginald was of the family of de Bohun, of the Côtentin, the north-west corner of Normandy, where two villages—St. George and St. André de Bohun, near Carentan, in a district of plain and canal like Sedgmoor—still mark the cradle of the family. Richard de Bohun, bishop of Coutances, 1151—1179, was his uncle; his father was Jocelin de Bohun, bishop of Sarum, 1142—1184.

Another member of the family, Engelger de Bohun, is mentioned as one of Henry II's evil counsellors who incited Henry against Becket, when at Argentan he uttered the hasty words which led to the murder of the archbishop.[1]

Into this family married Savaric Fitzchana, son of Ralph, the lord of Beaumont and St. Suzanne, and of Chana his wife, daughter of Geldewin, a Dane, lord of Saumur. He himself was made lord of Midhurst, in Sussex, by Henry I.

His son, Savaric FitzSavaric, inherited the lands of de Bohun; but, dying childless, he was succeeded in his inheritance by his nephew Franco de Bohun, son of Geldewin FitzSavaric and his wife Estrangia. Savaric, bishop of Bath, 1192, in succession to his

---

1. W. FitzStephen, in *Materials for History of Becket*, vol. iii, p. 129, (Rolls Series), " Engelgerus de Bohun, quidam inveteratus dierum malorum," gave the counsel, " Let him be crucified." Cf. *Register of St. Osmund*, i, f. 206 (Rolls Series).

cousin Reginald Fitzjocelin de Bohun, was younger brother of Franco de Bohun.[1]

Reginald Fitzjocelin was born about 1140, before his father, the bishop of Sarum, had been admitted to the priesthood, yet so shortly before, that the question could be raised as an objection to his consecration to the episcopate in after years. Sufficient testimony was at that time brought forward to satisfy and to remove objections. Either as born of Italian blood, or from early residence in Italy, he bore the name of "the Lombard" or "the Italian." The schools of Lombardy, Pavia, Bologna, Padua, whence had come to Normandy Lanfranc and Anselm, were famous. The towns of Lombardy were asserting their independence of the emperor at this time, and Henry's wide-reaching continental policy, and the foreign marriages of his sons, were bringing Englishmen into close relations with Italians and Germans, as well as with French.[2]

Herbert of Bosham, in his life of St. Thomas, names "Reginald the Lumbard" among those attached to the archbishop in his earlier days abroad. Though he laments his defection afterwards, in the time of the archbishop's quarrel with Henry, he describes him at this time as a young man high-spirited, intelligent, prudent beyond his years in council, active and able.[3]

1. Bishop Stubbs in *Gentleman's Magazine*, Nov., 1863, and Preface to *Epp. Cantuarienses*, p. lxxxvi, note, has supplied materials for genealogies of bishops Reginald and Savaric.

2. On Henry's relations with Italy, France, Germany, v. Stubbs' *Pref. to Benedict of Peterborough*, ii, p. xxxi. On Italian affairs of interest in England at this time, v. Stubbs' *Pref. to R. Howden*, ii, p. xcii.

3. Herbert of Bosham names some Lombards among the

From the letter of Peter of Blois archdeacon of Bath, to Reginald when archdeacon of Sarum, we know that he combined a keen love of hawking with attention to business.[1] These qualities would have been likely to have brought the young ecclesiastic into favour with the chancellor in his earlier days.

In 1158 Becket, then chancellor, was sent on an embassy to Paris, with a large suite and much pomp, to arrange the betrothal of Henry's eldest son, then a boy of seven, to Margaret, daughter of Louis VII. The marriage compact was finally completed, not without a quarrel and a reconciliation between the two kings, in 1160.[2] Perhaps Reginald joined Becket about this time, and, as Becket's friend, passed into favour at the French court. In 1164, he received from Louis VII of France a piece of court preferment, succeeding therein the king's brother Philip as abbot of St. Exuperius in Corbeil. The deed of gift, of which the original is extant among the chapter documents of Wells, entitles him "archdeacon of Sarum," and recites that the preferment was due both to his own merits

---

"eruditi" of Becket's followers, together with Reginaldus Lumbardus; Lumbardus of Piacenza, afterwards archbishop of Beneventum, Becket's teacher in canon law; Humbert Crivelli, of Milan, afterwards archbishop of Milan, and pope Urban III in 1185, and others. Herbert thus describes Reginald :—

"Reginaldus natione Anglus, sed sicut educatione et cognomento Lumbardus, pro aetate prudens et industrius, animosus et efficax in agendis, qui extra patriam aliquanto tempore nobiscum fortiter stans, cito doloris nostri fuit principium." *Materials for Life of Becket*, iii, p. 524.

1. Peter of Blois, Ep. 61. He reminds him when archdeacon of Sarum, "curam non avium sed ovium suscepisti," and warns him of the danger, "si non oves avibus antefertis."

2. R. de Diceto, vol. i, p. 302 (Rolls Series), an. 1158. They were betrothed 1160, p. 304.

and also to the solicitations of his friends—"donavimus pro honestate suâ, et pro amicorum suorum prece."[1]

The year of his appointment to the abbey of St. Exuperius was the year of the archbishop's quarrel with the king.

On January 25, 1164, the Council of Clarendon was held, and, after the meeting at Northampton, Becket withdrew from England to Pontigny. Bishop Jocelin of Sarum, father of Reginald, had been the leader and spokesman of the bishops in the vain attempt to mediate between the king and the archbishop, and to conciliate the archbishop after the scene at Northampton. He and Gilbert Ffolliot, bishop of London, became thenceforth the objects of Becket's violent hostility, and he excommunicated the two bishops, together with John of Oxford, dean of Sarum, and others of his opponents, from Vezelay, on Whitsun Day, 1166. In this quarrel Reginald took his father's side, and withdrew from Becket's party.

Peter of Blois about this time intercedes for Reginald with one of Becket's court, and defends him for having left the archbishop in duty to his father, whom the archbishop had denounced. But Reginald had now taken the king's side. His education, ability, foreign experiences, and conciliatory temperament soon made him one of the most acceptable of Henry's diplomatists at the court of Rome, where the quarrel between two violent and headstrong men was mainly fought out.

In 1167 he was at Rome with John of Oxford, dean of Sarum, and Clarembald, abbot of St. Augustine's,

1. Charter No. 7. The text is quoted in Appendix C.

when they obtained from pope Alexander the prohibition to the archbishop against publishing his censures pending the attempt at reconciliation.[1] He was there again in 1169, and accompanied to England the legates Gratian and Vivian, who were sent to effect the reconciliation;[2] and he then incurred Becket's violent abuse for his activity and influence at Rome on the occasion.[3]

In 1170, June 14, Roger, archbishop of York, together with the bishops of London, Sarum, Durham, and Rochester, crowned the young king Henry in Westminster abbey. The anger of the archbishop and primate blazed out afresh at this violation of the prerogative of the see of Canterbury. A formal reconciliation was effected with the king for a time; but at the close of this year the six years' struggle between king and archbishop reached its tragic end when the archbishop was struck down by his murderers, the four knights[4] of the court, in the transept of Canterbury cathedral church, December 29, 1170.

Reaction in favour of the cause of "the martyr" at once set in. Henry, shocked at the outrage and sacrilege, and alarmed at the consequences to his kingdom and to himself, sent at once an embassy to Rome, of men selected as "acceptable to the court of Rome, and well able to plead the king's cause,"[5] of whom

1. W. FitzStephen, in *Materials for Life of Becket*, iii, 99 (Rolls Series).
2. *Ib.* vi, 565 (Rolls Series).
3. *Ib.* vii, 59 (Rolls Series).
4. Three of the four knights held lands in Somerset: Reginald Fitzurse—Richard Breto—William de Traci.
5. Gervase says (i, 233, Rolls Series): "misit nuntios spectabiles et admodum loquaces." R. Howden gives the names, vol. ii, p. 26

Reginald archdeacon of Sarum was one. The letter to the king reports the result of the mission—they had arrived on Palm Sunday, and had been treated with little respect by the cardinals and denied audience by the pope who was at Frascati; the king's name was execrated; Maundy Thursday, the day of public absolution or excommunication by the pope, was approaching; Henry's excommunication and the interdict of the kingdom of England was threatened. With the greatest difficulty[1] they obtained suspension of the interdict, and it had been averted by their pledging themselves that the king would stand to judgment and submit to sentence from the pope. So the interdict was averted; but the excommunication of the murderers and of all concerned was proclaimed. The legates were sent to England or Normandy to receive Henry's submission. The king's purgation and penance at Avranches followed in the next year (May 21, 1172); the canonization of St. Thomas, ordered by the pope, was proclaimed on Ash Wednesday, 1173, and December 29 set apart as the festival of St. Thomas of Canterbury.[2]

According to one of the conditions required from

(Rolls Series); Rotrodus, archbishop of Rouen, who stopped in Normandy; Aegidius bishop of Evreux; Roger bishop of Worcester; Richard de Blosseville, abbot of La Valasse; Reginald archdeacon of Sarum; Richard archdeacon of Lisieux; Richard Barre and Henry Pinchun, clerks. For the letter giving report, R. Howden, vol. ii, p. 25.

1. Gervase adds (*ibid.*): "aliam viam supplicandi, more scilicet Romano sunt aggressi—vix tandem quingentis marcis interpositis admissi sunt."

2. Bull for the canonization of St. Thomas, dated March 13, 1173. R. de Diceto, i, 369.

Henry by the papal legates, Henry now proceeded to fill up the English sees which he had kept vacant during his quarrel with Becket.

Reginald Fitzjocelin was nominated to the see of Bath, which had been vacant more than eight years, since bishop Robert's death in 1166. He was duly elected by the two chapters, the prior and convent of Bath and the dean and canons of Wells[1] in conformity with bishop Robert's provision ; and his election was confirmed at the Council of Westminster, in April, 1173. At the same time the sees of Winchester, Ely, Hereford, Chichester, and Lincoln were filled up ; and Richard, prior of Dover, the late archbishop's chaplain, was nominated to the archbishopric of Canterbury.

But the young king Henry, under the influence of his father-in-law Louis of France, protested against the nomination of bishops in England without his consent, and lodged an appeal against their consecration at Rome. Reginald was selected to accompany the archbishop-elect to Rome to obtain the pope's confirmation. They started in the autumn of 1173. There were tedious delays and diplomacy with the Roman chancellery ; but at last Richard was consecrated archbishop by the pope at Anagni, on Low Sunday, April 7, 1174, and received the pall and his appointment as legate.

The consecration of Reginald and the other bishops-elect was deferred under various pretexts until the return to England.[2]

---

1. The act of pope Alexander, reciting and confirming the joint action of the two chapters, is contained in charter 40. Cf. R. i, f. 94 ; R. iii, f. 266. It is quoted in *Roger*, Appendix A.

2. Howden, ii, 59, *Reginaldi Epist. ad regem*, May 5, 1174. He says, " My own consecration and that of the others are deferred. Our lord the pope has determined to settle nothing until reconciliation between you and your son shall be brought to pass." *Rym. Fœd.* i, 31.

Soon after, they left Rome on their homeward journey—one which has many points of interest for us. The travellers crossed the passes of Mont Cenis, and stopped for a time at St. Jean de Maurienne, in the territory of the count of Savoy.

It was at this wayside station, on the old road between France and Italy, that Reginald, notwithstanding the delays interposed at Rome, was consecrated bishop of Bath.

The chronicles do not tell us the causes which brought about his consecration. We are left to infer them from concurring circumstances, by which this distant Alpine district was being brought into close connection with England, and with our own diocese in particular.

Henry had been negotiating in 1173 a marriage, for political purposes, between his son John and the eldest daughter of Umbert, count of Maurienne. Early death in that year saved her from this fate.

In the terms of the marriage settlement, by which certain places commanding the passes of the mountains would have been secured to Henry, Reginald archdeacon of Sarum had been named as one of the arbitrators on the king's side, in case of any change being made in the terms. Some business arising out of these settlements, and the closing of the arrangements, may have caused Reginald's delay at this time at St. Jean de Maurienne.[1]

[1] R. Howden, ii, 41, 45. Cf. Benedict, who gives the document. By the settlements the passes of Mont Cenis, and four castles commanding them, would have been secured to Henry and put into his hands. In November of the same year Frederick Barbarossa entered Italy through the Mont Cenis passes, burnt Susa, and besieged Alexandria, lately built by the Lombard League. Vide Stubbs's *Pref. to Benedict*, p. xvi, on Henry's projects.

The presence of Reginald in these parts was opportune for another purpose which Henry had in view at this moment.

Henry had undertaken to found three religious houses in England, in partial performance of his penance for the violence of his words against Becket. He had enlarged and reconstructed the religious foundations at Ambresbury and Waltham, and changed the religious orders of the inmates; and he was now planting the first house of the Carthusian order in England. The site which he had given was at Witham, on the borders of the royal forest of Selwood, in the diocese of Bath. Henry was seeking a prior for the new house from the parent house of the order, the Great Chartreuse in the "desert of St. Bruno," near Grenoble.

One of the envoys of the count of Savoy had told him of the fame of brother Hugh of Avalon. "Such a man as would not only ensure success to his new foundation, but would fill the whole church with the beauty of his holiness."[1]

The Great Chartreuse was within easy reach of St. Jean de Maurienne, and letters were sent to the archbishop and to Reginald, to use all endeavours to induce Hugh to come to England, to take charge of the Carthusian colony at Witham.

The bishop-elect of the diocese in which it was planted was the fit person to invite Hugh in Henry's name, and doubtless it was felt that he would speak with more effect if he were the consecrated bishop. So, with this end in view, as we may conjecture, ob-

---

1. Vide *Vita S. Hugonis*, p. 54. (Rolls Series). Cf. Preface, p. xxi.

jections at Rome were overcome, and Reginald's consecration was hastened.

Reginald was required to purge himself by oath of any complicity in the murder of St. Thomas. Testimony sufficient was given to establish the legitimacy of his birth. He was consecrated by archbishop Richard and the archbishop Peter of Tarentaise, in the church of St. John at Maurienne on the vigil of St. John the Baptist, June 23, 1174.[1]

Then, as bishop of Bath, in company with the bishop of Grenoble, he journeyed to the house of the order in the "Eremo" or desert of St. Bruno, enclosed under the pines and crags of the Grand Som and between the torrents of the Guier "Mort," and the Guier "Vif," entering it probably from Grenoble on its south-east side, by Sappey and St. Pierre de Chartreuse.

Hugh of Avalon, with much reluctance, and only by order of his bishop, undertook as his mission the charge of the new priory in England; and it was the first act of Reginald's episcopate to obtain for England and to plant in his own diocese of Somerset, Hugh of Witham, known afterwards to the whole church as St. Hugh of Lincoln.

---

1. "Juga quoque montium transcendens intra valles Morianae, in ecclesia S. Johannis, et in vigilia S. Joannis Baptistae, Batoniensem electum consecravit, archiepiscopo Tarentasiae praesente, manum etiam apponente; accepta prius purgatione Batoniensis electi, quod mortem beati Thomae neque verbo, neque facto, neque scripto procuravit scienter. Alii juraverunt quod, sicut opinabantur, conceptus fuit priusquam Jocelinus pater suus ad gradum sacerdotii promoveretur." R. de Diceto, i, 391. (Rolls Series). Archbishop Peter had been present at the betrothal of prince John with Aalis, daughter of the count of Maurienne. Cf. Walter de Mapes de Nugis Cur. Dist., 2, 3, p. 69. The archbishop was afterwards canonized.

Then the archbishop and bishop Reginald continued their journey to meet Henry in Normandy.[1]

In the first days of August they were at St. Lo in the diocese of his uncle the bishop of Coutances, and in his own country of the Côtentin, and on the fifth of August, 1174, he consecrated the church of St. Thomas at St. Lo, dedicated to the memory of his old master, now the newly-canonized St. Thomas the Martyr.[2]

This church, probably the earliest consecrated to the martyr canonized only the year before, and consecrated by the bishop who had been active against him, son of a bishop whom he had excommunicated, is a monument of the sudden revulsion of feeling which his murder had caused. It is still standing, though long since desecrated; containing architectural signs of the period of its consecration in the flat semi-Norman buttresses on the outside, in the massive round columns of the nave, and the apsidal end with six pointed arches resting on the Norman columns.[3]

---

1. "Archiepiscopus, Batoniensi comitatus episcopo, Burgundiae promontoria, campestria Galliae, Neustriae littora, cum aliqua remoratione transcendit, pertransiit, attigit." R. de Diceto, i, 391. (Rolls Series).

2. The document is preserved in the archives of St. Lo. *Som. Archæological Proceedings*, xix, ii, 94.

3. The nave of the church is about 144 ft. long, by 30 ft. wide, and is divided from aisles 15 ft. wide by six massive Norman columns on each side. Two central columns on each side, larger than the rest, support a tower. Pointed arches rest on the columns.

It is a painful instance of thorough desecration. The nave is boarded over above the arches, and is used as an agricultural hall on market days; the upper part is a theatre, approached by a door at the east end and stairs. Under the later tower arches is the stage of the theatre where had been a representation by a travelling company the night before I was there—on Sunday, June 27, 1886. Two traditions about the church were told to me at St. Lo; one, that it was

On August 8 they met Henry on the shore at Barfleur (*Barbefluctus*), just arrived from England after an eventful month. On July 8 he had landed at Southampton from Normandy. He had gone through his three days' humiliating penance at the tomb of St. Thomas at Canterbury: he had crushed rebellion in the midland of England; and, with the king of Scots his prisoner, he had now landed at Barfleur, within the month.

From thence the archbishop and Reginald crossed to England. The archbishop arrived at Canterbury on September 4, to become a witness of the fire which broke out on the next day September 5, 1174 in his cathedral church, and burnt the choir to ashes. On October 6 Reginald assisted at the consecration at Canterbury of the bishops of Winchester, Ely, Hereford, and Chichester, and there made his profession of obedience to the primate. On November 24 he was enthroned with much solemnity by the primate in person, who was then making a visitation of his province as "legate of the apostolic see," in his own church.

It would be interesting to know whether Bath or Wells—the church of St. Peter, or the church of St. Andrew—was the scene. Ralph de Diceto says the presence of the legate made the event of the enthronisation especially memorable;[1] but he does not name the place of the enthronisation.

built by St. Thomas when in exile—the other, that he was at St. Lo while it was building, and being asked to what saint it should be dedicated, replied, "to the first martyr"; after events led them to take this as a prophecy and direction with regard to himself.

1. R. de Diceto, i, 398 (Rolls Series): "Intronizationem Batoniensis episcopi Dorobernensis archiepiscopus, dum officio fungeretur legationis visitando provinciam, sua praesentia multo sollempniorem effecit, viii° kalendas Decembris, et futuris reddidit memorialem."

Bath had been the chief seat of the bishop, *sedes praesulea*, from whence the title was derived since bishop John's time, eighty years ago. Bishop Robert had done much in reasserting the equality of Wells with Bath, but Bath was still recognised by the pope, Adrian IV, in 1157, as the *sedes praesulea*.[1] The fair conclusion we are forced to draw is, that the legate on this occasion made Bath as the chief seat of the bishop, the scene of the enthronisation in person, though, no doubt, the bishop was enthroned in both his churches, and perhaps by the legate also, in Wells.[1]

In public life.

In the earlier years of his episcopate, bishop Reginald appears as one of Henry's counsellors in the chief national councils of the reign.[2]

---

1. R. iii, f. 268, 289-293. Confirmation of possessions of Bath abbey, by Adrian IV.

2. (*a*) During Henry's reign—from 1174 to 1189.
Bishop Reginald at Westminster, May 18, 1175. Howden, ii, 72.
At Woodstock, July 1. Howden, ii, 78.
At London, March 16, 1177. Howden, ii, 120, 131.
At Toulouse, March, 1178. Howden, ii, 151, 165.
At the Lateran Council, March, 1179. Howden, ii, 171, 189.

(*b*) During Richard's reign, 1189-1191.
Bishop Reginald was present at Richard's coronation at Westminster, Sept. 3, 1189. Howden, iii, 8.
At the Council at Pipewell, Sept. 15, 1189. Howden, iii, 14
At Canterbury, Nov. 26, 1189. R. iii, f. 13.
At the council in Normandy, March 1190. Howden, iii, 32.
He mediated at "the peace of Winchester," April 25, 1191. R. of Devizes, p. 33, § 42.
He mediated at "the peace of Winchester," July 28, 1191. Howden, iii, 135.
He was at the Chancellor Longchamp's trial, Oct., 1191. Howden, iii, 145.
Nominated Primate at Canterbury, Nov. 26, 1191. Howden, iii, 168.
His death took place at Dogmersfield, Dec. 27, 1191.
Gervase, *Opera Hist.*, i, 512 (Rolls Series).

He was present at the Council of Westminster in 1175, at which acts were passed to repress clerical scandals. At the Council of London, in 1177, he was one of the signatories to the award in which Henry adjudicated on the rival claims of the kings of Navarre and Castille. In 1178, he was of a joint commission, appointed at the request of the count of Toulouse by Henry and Louis VII of France to inquire into the heretical teaching of the sect of the Cathari, who were established in formidable numbers in the country round Toulouse and Albi, and became afterwards known under the name of the Albigenses. Bishop Reginald had for his colleagues on this occasion Peter the papal legate, the archbishops of Bourges and Narbonne, the bishop of Poitiers, and the abbot of Clairvaux. They held their court of inquiry at Toulouse, and reported in condemnation of the heretical teaching of the sectaries. In the next year Reginald was one of four English bishops[1] sent as representatives to the Lateran council, summoned by Alexander III, March 1179, at which, among other acts of historical importance, the Albigenses sectaries were condemned and excommunicated. He returned from the council with a deed of confirmation from the pope, his friend Alexander III, dated March 4, 1179, confirming the rights and possessions of the see.[2]

During the next ten years of Henry's reign he does not appear much in public affairs. On the death of his friend archbishop Richard, in 1184, he strongly

1. The other bishops at the Lateran Council were Hugh bishop of Durham; John of Oxford, bishop of Norwich; Robert Ffolliott, bishop of Hereford.
2. This document is quoted later. See Appendix F.

supported the king's nomination of Baldwin bishop of Worcester to the primacy, against the claims of the convent of Christchurch to have the sole appointment, and afterwards he was influential in conciliating the monks to accept Baldwin. In the dispute which followed between the archbishop and his monks he was appointed one of the pope's commissioners in 1187. After Baldwin's death these events led on to his nomination to the vacant primacy in the last year of his life.

Bp. Reginald in his diocese.

During these years of his episcopate, 1174-1191, bishop Reginald was doing good work in his diocese, and they were years of diocesan life and progress.

Church building was going on around him and under his eye at Bath, at Glastonbury, at Witham, and in other religious houses in the diocese, and gifts and endowments were being made to the cathedral church of St. Andrew in Wells. It was his policy to carry on bishop Robert's work and constitution at Wells, to make Wells the headquarters and centre of the diocese, and to give it a fabric and a ministrant body worthy of the dignity of the cathedral church of the diocese. Probably he resided at Wells: there is no evidence that he ever resided at Bath. Yet Bath was not neglected. The hospital of St. John Baptist, by which the sick and poor of the city had the benefit of the hot waters, was founded by him in 1180, and endowed with lands and tenements in Bath and its neighbourhood, and with a tithe of hay from his demesne lands. It was put under the control and management of prior Walter and the convent of Bath, who also gave their endowments.

Bath.

Walter the prior, a man of learning and holy life,

was a contemporary and friend of bishop Reginald,[1] and he was with him in his last hours, when dying at Dogmersfield.

The register of the priory of Bath contains a list of gifts made by the bishop to the convent, of lands and churches, of ornaments and vestments, of a statue of St. Peter, and also, strange to read, of the body of St. Euphemia, virgin and martyr. He also enriched their library with many books.[2]

At Witham, between 1180 and 1186, prior Hugh was at work laying the foundations of his Charterhouse, with a small band of French monks, meanly lodged, and endeavouring to support themselves under severe and ascetic discipline, in the desert of Witham. The chapel of the Fratry, some remains of which in the transitional-Norman style are to be seen still in the parish church, and the necessary buildings for thirteen monks and about the same number of lay brethren, were finished, and the discipline of the house was organised before prior Hugh was called to be bishop of Lincoln in 1186.

Witham.

The house became the home of those who sought a severer discipline amidst the growing laxity of other monastic houses. Walter prior of Bath, and Robert prior of St. Swithun's, were two of those who entered the house late in life.[3] Sometimes it was found too

---

1. "Vir multae scientiae et religionis." A. S. 585.
2. See appendix D.
3. Richard of Devizes, the chronicler of the "Gesta Ricardi," 1189-1192, a monk of St. Swithun's, paid a visit there to his late prior to whom he dedicated his Chronicle, "to see how much nearer to heaven was the Charterhouse at Witham than the Priory of St. Swithun." He bears his witness to the greater severity of discipline there, not without a touch of sceptical sarcasm. "Robertus prior

severe a life for those who had entered it without counting the cost.[1] Walter left it again before his death. It was the home of retreat year by year for St. Hugh when he came from Lincoln to take up again the simple life of a monk in his cell at Witham.

The bishop, who had been the instrument to bring Hugh of Avalon to England, continued to support his work in the diocese. The king's charter was granted at Marlborough. A chapel had stood in the "Eremo," the desert of Witham on the outskirts of Selwood forest, belonging to the priory of Bruton. The king gave to Bruton the rectory of South Petherton in exchange, and exchanges of land in North Curry were made with the Witham owners.

The house was dedicated in honour of the Blessed Virgin and St. John Baptist. The king granted lands which afterwards became the parish of Witham, and lands on Mendip for a cell of the Charterhouse near Cheddar. The house was exempted from all ecclesiastical visitations and imposts; from all claims of sheriffs and officers of the forest. Bishop Reginald on his part "cum consensu capituli Wellensis," granted exemption from tithes and dues to the Charterhouse in the parish of Cheddar.[2]

S. Swithuni Wintoniae, prioratu relicto et professione postposita, apud Witham, dolore (an dicam devotione?) dejecit se in sectam Cartusiae. Walterus prior Bathoniae prius ibidem simili fervore vel furore praesumserat, sed semel extractus nihil minus videtur adhuc quam de reditu cogitare." R. of Devizes, p. 26, § 30. See also the Prologue.

1. *Reg. Prior. Bath.*, ff. 315, 316.

2. Henry's grant is recited in a confirmation to the prior and convent of Witham by Innocent IV, in 1246, in which the boundaries of the land are set out. Vatican Transcripts in the British Museum. Add. MS. 15355, vol. v, ff. 374-381.

Other religious houses were growing up at the time in the diocese.

The abbey of St. Mary at Glastonbury, the great rival ecclesiastical power which had hitherto overshadowed the church of Wells, separated from it by six miles of moorland, was soon about to go through a period of disaster and humiliation. *Glastonbury*

But under bishop Reginald's episcopate there were friendly negotiations and territorial exchanges and mutual concessions.

Henry of Blois, bishop of Winchester, who ruled the abbey for more than forty years, 1125-1171, had lately died. Robert prior of Winchester, succeeded. By an arrangement with abbot Robert, the church of Pilton was ceded to the bishop to form two prebends in the cathedral church, of which the abbot held one, without obligation of residence, but bound to pay three marcs to a vicar. The canon appointed by the bishop to the second prebend received ten marcs from Pilton. The abbot thus became a member of the bishop's chapter, and the Glastonbury writers deplore the advantage obtained over the abbey by this arrangement, whereby the bishop received the acknowledgment of jurisdiction from the abbot, as one of the canons of his cathedral church.[1]

At the same time, to put an end to a long-standing controversy between the abbey and the church of Wells, the bishop granted the abbot a separate territorial jurisdiction, to be held by a special officer (the abbot's archdeacon) over the churches which were in

---

1. R. i, f. 24, lxix, f. 25, lxxv. Cf. Adam of Domerham i, 235; ii, 351.

the twelve hides of Glastonbury.¹ The church of South Brent, which had belonged to Glastonbury, was ceded to the archdeacon of Wells for impropriation, in lieu of his jurisdiction over seven churches of the Glastonbury archdeaconry which the archdeacon of Wells had claimed, and it has ever since remained impropriated to the archdeaconry of Wells, and in its patronage. The church of Huish near Langport was also annexed to the archdeaconry of Wells by bishop Reginald.²

Great building work had been going on at Glastonbury under bishop Henry of Blois—the builder of St. Cross near Winchester, founder of Romsey abbey, and refounder of Taunton priory. Abbot Robert carried on the work until his death in 1178. Then the abbey was held by the king, and put into commission to Peter de Marci, a Cluniac monk, as administrator of the revenues during the vacancy. While the abbey was in the king's hands, on St. Urban's day May 25, 1184, a fire destroyed the whole of the abbey buildings of Henry de Blois, and only a new chamber which had been built by abbot Robert, with its chapel and the great bell-tower, remained.³

Henry, grieved at the loss sustained by the church while the abbey was in his hands, undertook to rebuild

---

1. The abbey had claimed exemption for the churches of the twelve hides from all local jurisdiction secular and spiritual, under a pretended charter of king Ine, but confirmed by sovereigns and archbishops as a real grant.

The exempt jurisdiction was now conceded, and the jurisdiction of the abbot over the churches made equal to a separate and exempt archdeaconry.

2. Reginald's grant; in Adam of Domerham, ii, 345.
3. Adam of Domerham, ii, 333

the church, and committed the work to Ralph Fitz-stephen, the chancellor, to spend all the available resources of the convent on the fabric. A charter was given by Henry, December, 1184, in which he made himself and his heirs responsible for the fitting restoration. The work was of national interest, the revenues of vacant benefices were applied to the work, and a charge was laid upon certain churches in support. Ralph Fitzstephen is described as munificent in his gifts, and the royal treasury supplied what was required. A great store of relics of saints and worthies buried at Glastonbury was now displayed; and the timely discovery or invention about this time of the bones of Arthur and his queen, and the publication of the Arthurian legend, helped to draw a large concourse of pilgrims, and brought much gain of money to the abbey.

So rapidly grew the work, that in the second or third year after the fire, "on St. Barnabas day, 1186,"[1] or 1187, bishop Reginald dedicated the new church of St. Mary on the spot where the old church, the "*vetusta ecclesia*," had stood. At the same time the foundations were laid and the building commenced, of "the great church," *major ecclesia*, 400 feet in length and 80 feet in breadth. But with the death of Henry,

---

1. Adam of Domerham, ii, 335, describes the work, but does not give the year of consecration, "Ecclesiam Sanctae Mariae in loco quo primitus vetusta steterat ex lapidibus quadratis opere speciosissimo consummavit, nichil ornatûs in ea praetermittens." John of Glastonbury (i, 180) names the year thus indefinitely, "quam dedicavit Reginaldus, tunc Bathoniae episcopus, anno Domini millesimo centesimo octogesimo *circiter* sexto die S. Barnabae."

Mr. Parker says, "more probably 1187." *Somerset Archæological Proceedings*, vol. xxvi, 28.

in 1189, the works were stopped—until 1235. "King Richard's mind was more directed to military affairs than to the building which was begun, so the work was stopped because there was no one to pay the workmen."[1] Soon after began the great war with Wells under bishop Savaric and continued under bishop Jocelin until 1219, in which the revenues of the abbey were consumed by litigation at Rome. No building was carried on again until 1235; and the century had passed before the next consecration of the church then only partially built, on the day of St. Thomas the Martyr 1303.[2]

So far we have followed out bishop Reginald's history, as it is connected with the general history of the time, and described in the chronicles of Henry the Second's reign.

Bp. Reginald at Wells.

But we turn to our own local documents, and to the history lurking in the unprinted manuscripts at Wells, to learn more particularly what was going on at Wells during bishop Reginald's episcopate.

Wells was the bishop's seat all through the time until his translation to Canterbury in the last days of his life.

The charters of his time show his care to tread in the footsteps of his predecessor, and to carry on bishop Robert's policy at Wells: *(a)* by confirming and increasing the privileges of the town; *(b)* by adding to the number of the prebends, and increasing the permanent endowment of the stalls; *(c)* by provision for the building of the fabric of the church.

1. Adam of Domerham, ii, 341.
2. John of Glastonbury, i, 255.

The municipal history of Wells is ancient and interesting. Its early charters are of especial value, as showing the relation of the town to the bishop, and the growth of the town around the cathedral church.

Charters to the town of Wells.

Two charters to the city by bishop Reginald stand at the head of these contemporary records, and are of general as well as local interest.

Early in his episcopate, certainly before 1180, as the names of the attesting witnesses show, bishop Reginald gave two charters to the town.[1]

In the first of these he recites the charter of bishop Robert; and, desiring to follow the footsteps of his venerable predecessor, and at the request of the burgesses, he confirms with further grants their privileges then conferred.

Bishop Robert, as we have seen, had granted to the citizens freedom from tolls on three festival times in the year, viz. on the eves and festivals of the Invention of the Holy Cross, St. Calixtus, and St. Andrew.

Bishop Reginald, in his confirmation of this charter, granted three additional days, viz. the morrow of each of these festivals. He also granted to the burgesses one moiety of the profits arising from the hiring of stalls, which belonged to him as lord.

In the second charter, referring again to the example and the charter of his predecessor, he grants that the town of Wells shall be a free borough; that every one dwelling within its limits and possessing a messuage in the name of a burgage should have freedom of dwelling, going, and coming; also of mortgaging, selling, and granting their houses, except to religious

1. See Appendix E.

purposes. He reserves to the bishop the payment of twelve pence a year out of every house in the borough; forbids sale of raw skins, or hides, within the limits of the borough; grants authority to hold a court for settlement of disputes and for civil and criminal trials, except in cases where deadly wounds or injuries for life had been inflicted, without any fee to the bishop's justices. He reserves to the bishop right of appeal, and right to interfere or revise the sentence of the burgesses if they failed to do justice.

These charters, two of a series of municipal charters beginning with bishop Robert, confirmed and amplified by bishop Reginald and afterwards by bishop Savaric the lords of the manor of Wells, and confirmed by king John, 1202, illustrate the peculiar position and character of Wells as the ecclesiastical city growing up around the church, which Mr. Freeman has described so fully in his history of the cathedral church and elsewhere: "Wells stands alone among the cities of England proper as a city, which exists only in and through its cathedral church, whose whole history is that of its cathedral church. Like other cities, it has its municipal history; but its municipal history is simply an appendage to its ecclesiastical history: the franchises of the borough were simply held as grants from the bishop."

They have a further and subsidiary interest as setting out before us the names and designations of the representatives of the ecclesiastical corporation, of the townspeople and their trades, of the owners of land in the neighbourhood, the names of the farms and villages, contemporary with these bishops of the twelfth century.

Bishop Reginald gathers round him the officers and canons of his cathedral church, the landlords and the burgesses and townsfolk, to witness to the charter which, as lord of the manor, he freely bestows upon them. At the same time, as their lord, he reserves to the bishop the right of administering justice and reviewing the sentences of the town magistrates.

Contemporaries.

In the first of these charters given before 1166, occur the names of some of the first officers of the newly constituted chapter, as witnesses to bishop Robert's charter: Ivo the dean; Reginald the precentor, nephew of the late bishop John of Tours; and archdeacons Robert and Thomas.

In bishop Reginald's charter, between 1174-1180, there are the names of the second generation of officers of the cathedral chapter: there is another dean, Richard of Spaxton, 1160-1180; another precentor, Hildebert or Albert, 1174-1185; another archdeacon, Richard of Bath, with title of local jurisdiction; William the treasurer; Robert the sub-dean: there are the canons Ralph of Lechlade, afterwards archdeacon of Bath, and dean 1216-1220; William canon of Haselbury; and Peter of Winchester, afterwards chancellor, 1185.

In both charters of bishop Reginald we meet with the first mention of a name which was to be more known and honoured than any in the history of Wells, Jocelin, then chaplain, the future bishop.

A large number of names, representing the neighbouring landowners and the townsfolk of Wells, sign on this memorable occasion in the early life of the city, when canons and clerks, burgesses and tenants, were called together by the bishop, their lord, to receive this first deed of city incorporation.[1]

We gather from other charters in the Wells registers, and the attestations to documents belonging to bishop Reginald's time, the names of some more of his contemporaries in the diocese and in the chapter.

The names appear, *nomina tantum* for the most part, of the several dignitaries—dean, precentor, chancellor, treasurer, the three archdeacons of Wells, Bath, and Taunton, subdean, succentor. Two deans were living through his episcopate: Richard of Spaxton, from 1160 to 1180; Alexander, from 1180 until the third year of bishop Jocelin, 1209.

Two archdeacons, Thomas of Wells, and Peter of Blois, archdeacon of Bath, appear in the history of the time as taking part in public events beyond the diocese.

Thomas Agnellus, archdeacon of Wells, is identified as the preacher of the funeral sermon on the death of the young king Henry, in 1183, which bishop Stubbs quotes,[2] as showing that the son was looked upon as a champion of the older party against the reforming tendencies of the father.

Peter of Blois archdeacon of Bath, 1175-1190, is the learned rhetorician and theologian and letter writer and literary adventurer, who was known to all the leading men of the day, an active political agent in Henry's court, and at the Roman Curia—of Henry against Becket—of Baldwin against the monks of Canterbury, but changing sides after Baldwin's death.

1. See Appendix E.
2. Pref to R. of Howden, ii, p. lvii.

In his letters,[1] he appears as archdeacon of Bath before Reginald's appointment to the bishopric; he anticipates Reginald's preferment, and warns him of the responsibilities: he defended Reginald for taking the side of his father in the quarrel with Becket. In after years he complained to Reginald as bishop, of his severity in enforcing discipline upon his deputy in the archdeaconry for nonpayment of a debt. His name does not once appear in the Wells charters, but in 1192 he was archdeacon of London,[2] and died about 1200.

William of St. Faith, a witness to bishop Robert's charter before 1166, was precentor in 1187. In that year the precentor of Wells and the archdeacon of Bath were at Rome working on Baldwin's side against the monks of Canterbury, while their bishop was the pope's commissary in England, and supporting the monks against Baldwin.[3]

Grants and endowments to the church

The latter part of the twelfth century, and the strong reign of Henry II, following the lawlessness and anarchy of Stephen's reign, was marked by an outburst of zeal and liberality towards the church and objects of religious veneration.

It was a time of foundation and endowment of monastic houses, and of prebends for secular canons in cathedral churches.

The registers of the chapter of Wells contain many deeds of gifts of land and churches from clergy and laity made to the church of Wells during bishop

1. *Epistolae Petri Blesensis*, i, *Ep.* 62, 58, 149.
2. R. de Diceto, i, Pref. lxxix.
3. *Epist. Cantuar.* cxxxv, p. 107. *Ep.* ccciv.

Reginald's time. These gifts were employed by the bishop in council with his chapter, in augmenting the common fund of the chapter, or in endowing prebends, or in the maintenance of the fabric.

The funds given to the cathedral church were divided into a common fund for the support of the resident officers of the chapter, and for the foundation of prebends.

These deeds of gift were confirmed by bishop and chapter, by king and pope, to secure their permanent validity. Charters of confirmation of the rights and possessions of the see occur frequently at this time, and serve as compendious summaries of the gradual growth of the property of the see during bishop Reginald's episcopate.

They also show incidentally the state of insecurity as to rights of property, and the care taken by the bishop to obtain the highest legal sanction for the rights and possessions of his cathedral church.

Charters of confirmation.

There are seven such charters of confirmation in the chapter registers of the time—

1. By pope Alexander III, in 1176, given at the request *(pro postulationibus)*, of dean Richard and the canons of Wells. (R. ii, f. 46).
2. By pope Alexander III, in 1179, given to bishop Reginald at the Lateran Council. (R. iii, f. 266). (See Appendix F).
3. By king Henry II, in 1185, at Argentan, confirming former royal grants to Bath and to the see. (R. i, f. 15, 16; cf. iii, f. 333).
4. By bishop Reginald, of gifts made to the see in the early part of his episcopate before 1180. (R. i, f. 24; cf. iii, f. 10).

5. By king Richard I, Nov. 26, 1189, confirming royal grants of his predecessors, with special confirmation to bishop Reginald of an agreement with regard to his land at Dynre (Dinder), and grant of the park at Dogmersfield. (R. i, f. 15, 16; cf. iii, 333).

6. By king Richard I, at the same date, in the first year of his reign, confirming to bishop Reginald the possessions of the see acquired during his episcopate. (R. iii, f. 13 in dors).

7. By pope Clement III, in 1190. (R. iii, f. 260).

The two charters most valuable, as illustrating the history of the diocese at this time, are the charters (1) of pope Alexander in 1179, and (2) of king Richard I, in 1189, ten years after, and two years before bishop Reginald's death.

1. The charter of pope Alexander III, brought back by bishop Reginald from Rome after his attendance at the Lateran Council in 1179, is very full in recapitulation of all the possessions and rights of the see, and also of the bishop's jurisdiction and relation to the great religious houses in his diocese. The bishop has the power of removing the prior of Bath for sufficient reasons, after consultation with the chapter, "or other religious men:" no church or oratory may be erected in the diocese without the bishop's sanction: his rights of authority and jurisdiction over religious houses and churches within the diocese are generally but vaguely defined, with reservation of appeal to the pontifical legate or the Roman court: he has authority to compel attendance at his synod of abbots and priors: none

Charter of pope Alexander, A.D. 1179.

are to officiate in the diocese without his permission: if any monks, or other religious men, clerks or laymen, present themselves or are presented to benefices without the bishop's consent, he may remove them.[1]

<small>Charter of Richard I, A.D. 1189.</small>

2. The charter of Richard I in the first year of his reign, on the eve of setting out for the Holy Land, November 26, 1189, presents a summary of the gifts which had been made to the church during bishop Reginald's episcopate of fifteen years, by which sixteen prebends were founded in the cathedral church, and other grants and privileges were bestowed.[2]

Additional privileges of a special character were also granted by the crown at this time: (*a*) the right of keeping hounds, which his predecessors in the see held, but with fuller privileges of hunting through the *whole* of Somerset, roe and fallow deer only excepted. This was a privilege which, in mitigation of the extreme rigour of the forest laws, as enforced by Henry I, must have been a great boon to the bishops and their officers, and which, from his earlier sporting tastes, bishop Reginald would have been fully able to appreciate. Richard conferred also at this time, (*b*) the more important and permanent benefit to the see of rights of mining for lead (*mineram de plumbo*) throughout all the bishop's lands, and probably in connection with this, (*c*) the power to create a borough and hold market in his land at Radclive, *terra sua de Radeclive*, described as also *portus de Radeclive*, in the manor of Compton Episcopi and Axbridge—perhaps a "hithe,"

1. Appendix F.
2. Appendix G.

or wharf, at the head of the tideway on the Axe, for the exportation of the lead ore of Mendip.[1]

But the list in Richard's charter of confirmation does not exhaust the grants made to the church at this time. In the border country of the west of Somerset were the family lands of three of the knights who had struck down Becket in his cathedral church at Canterbury. The Tracy family had given Bovey in Devonshire to the church. Simon Brito, or le Bret, of Samford Bret, now gave the church of St. Decuman on the headland overlooking the western channel for a prebend in the church of St. Andrew in Wells, and Robert Fitzurse, of Willeton in the same beautiful valley under the Quantock hills as Samford Bret, endowed St. Decuman's with twenty acres of land, and gave land to a manse for a chaplain to serve a chapel at Willeton in the parish of St. Decuman.[2]

In the same district, on the borders of Exmoor, William de Romara earl of Lincoln, founder of Cleeve abbey in 1188, gave the church of Old Cleeve[3] to bishop Reginald; and the church of Wynesford[4] on the Upper Exe, a few miles above the Augustinian priory of Barlynch, was given by the lady Alicia de Roges.

These documents show how the constitution and

---

1. *Ratcliffe* in Stuckey's map, on the Axe, which is navigable so far—*Ratley* in Greenwood's map, in Compton; it is *Ripley* in Ordnance map. R. iii, f. 266.

2. St. Decuman, R. i, f. 40, Carta Simonis Brito; R. i, f. 38, Carta Roberti fil. Ursi; R. i, f. 39, Confirmatio Reginaldi Episcopi, teste Alexandro Decano; R. i, f. 38.

3. Cleeve, R. iii, f. 382.

   Wynesford, R. i, f. 59.

property of the church of Wells were built up at this time, under bishop Reginald's rule.

Between the year after his return from the Lateran Council in 1179 and Henry's death in 1189, bishop Reginald does not appear much in public affairs.

These quiet years of his episcopate had formed an important period in the history of the diocese. Henry II, his old master, who had trusted and employed him on important occasions, died at Chinon on the Loire, July 6, 1189.

Life, A.D. 1189-1191.

A time of restless excitement, of foreign adventure and political struggles at home, followed upon Richard's accession. Reginald, as one of the friends and counsellors of Henry, took a leading part in the first events of his son's reign.

He appears to have been drawn away from his diocese into the political and ecclesiastical intrigues of the court.

Whether justly or not, he incurs the suspicion of having aimed at the chancellorship, and of secretly intriguing for the primacy.

On September 3, 1189, he assisted at the coronation of Richard at Westminster. It was a scene of unusual pomp. In the coronation procession to and from the church, and to and from the altar, Hugh bishop of Durham on the right, and Reginald bishop of Bath on the left hand, walked by the side of Richard.[1] Four

---

[1] "Deinde venit Ricardus dux Normanniae, et Hugo Dunelmensis Episcopus a dextris illius ibat, et Reginaldus Batoniensis Episcopus a sinistris illius ibat, et umbraculum sericum portabatur inter illos. Et omnis turba comitum et baronum et militum et aliorum, tam clericorum quam laicorum sequebatur usque in atrium ecclesiae et sic usque in ecclesiam ad altare." *Benedict*, ii, 81.

barons bore over them a silken canopy supported on four tall lances, and the company of earls, barons, knights, clergy and laity followed in long procession. After Richard had made the coronation oaths, he was anointed and crowned by archbishop Baldwin, the archbishops of Dublin, Rouen, and Trèves assisting, and enthroned by the two bishops of Durham and Bath.

After this, Reginald was at the council of Pipewell abbey, on September 15, when the appointments to the chief offices and vacant bishoprics were made by Richard. The see of Ely and the chancellorship were then given to William Longchamp.

Richard, intent upon an immediate start for the Holy Land, was selling the offices of state, and making conveyances of crown lands and castles and towns to the highest bidders. All who could were buying rights and privileges, offices and benefices; "not only to the confirmation of their own, but to the usurpation of their neighbours' rights"—"et caeteri, quicunque volebant, emebant a rege tam sua quam aliena jura."[1]

It is assumed, on a statement of Richard of Devizes, that Reginald made a high bid of £4000 for the chancellorship, which Richard gave to William Longchamp, though he paid for it £1000 less—" Willielmus Eliensis electus, datis tribus millibus libris argenti, sigillum

---

It was a mark of honour to the see, and perhaps also in this case to the man. Brompton, writing at the close of the thirteenth century (f. 1158-9) says, "Atque istud privilegium etiam hodie praesules Dunelmenses et Bathonienses sibi vendicant." Savaric, as bishop of Bath, took this same place at the coronation of John.

1. Vide Howden, vol. iii, 29, for a list of some of the state offices sold by the king at this time.

regis sibi retinuit, licet Reginaldus Italus quartum millerium superobtulerit."[1] Only such men as St. Hugh of Lincoln or as St. Anselm, could pass through kings' courts and papal chancelleries without taint, or suspicion at least, of worldliness and corruption. Whether Reginald was tempted to offer a high price for the chancellorship or not is doubtful. But it is certain that at this time Reginald was employing his money for the benefit of the diocese in buying from the king confirmations of all the possessions and privileges of the see, and the grant of the manor of North Curry, a costly purchase, which he made over to the canons of his cathedral church.

Reginald was a man who mixed in the world, but he does not seem to have been covetous or personally ambitious as compared with his contemporaries, such as Hugh Pudsey of Durham, Hugh Nonant of Coventry, and the chancellor Longchamp. He appears to have been pushed forward into prominent positions, and employed by others as a counsellor and an arbitrator trusted by both sides, rather than a self-seeking intriguer for high places. In 1191 he was twice employed as one of the arbitrators in the quarrel between the chancellor Longchamp and earl John at the pacification of Winchester, April 25; and again, between the chancellor and the rebellious sheriff of Lincoln, Gerard de

---

1. R. of Devizes. *De rebus gestis Ricardi*, p. 9, § 10, ed. Stevenson. Bishop Stubbs and others assume that bishop Reginald is the person here so named; elsewhere, Richard of Devizes calls him by his ordinary title Episcopus Bathoniensis.

At the same time Hugh, bishop of Durham, paid for the office of justiciar 1,000 marcs; for the earldom of Northumberland, 2,000; and 600 for the manor of Sedbergh. The king, "decem millia libras argenti de scriniis ejus diligenter extraxit." R. of Devizes, p. 8, § 9.

Camville, July 28. He was one of those who opposed the chancellor for his high-handed treatment of Geoffrey; but he took no prominent part in his trial and humiliation in October, 1191.

It was probably his unaggressive and conciliatory line of conduct which led to his election to the vacant primacy, rather than any secret intrigues on his part.

A struggle had been going on since 1187 between archbishop Baldwin and his chapter, the prior and monks of the cathedral church at Canterbury.

Reginald at Canterbury.

Reginald had been forward in supporting Baldwin as the king's nominee, and in conciliating the monks to accept him in 1184. But now, when it may reasonably have appeared that the archbishop was using his authority arbitrarily, he did not shrink from opposition to the king, and from taking the unpopular side of the convent. St. Hugh of Lincoln was on the same side afterwards.[1]

The immediate subject of dispute was the foundation by the archbishop out of some of the funds of the cathedral chapter, of a college and church of secular canons at Hackington near Canterbury. The project gave much offence to the monks who thought they saw

---

1. Vide Stubbs, Pref. to the *Epistolae Cantuarienses*, p. liii for the history of this controversy; and letters to and from Hugh bishop of Lincoln in the collection. Also letters of Peter of Blois. Ep. cxxxv, ccclv. Vide *Vita S. Hugonis*, p. 134-5. At this same time two of the chapter of Wells were Baldwin's agents at Rome, Peter of Blois archdeacon of Bath, and William of St. Faith precentor of Wells.

The letters illustrate Peter's character. Ep. cxxxv, his letter on Urban's death; ccclv, his change of sides in disgust at not having been paid his expenses. So he writes about May, 1191, " perdidi operam et impensas—meisque peccatis exigentibus permisit me Dominus occasione illius archiepiscopi damnose deludi . . ." and he offers his services to the convent.

in it, what was probably the intention, a desire to supplant them in their position as metropolitan chapter, and to substitute a body of secular canons (out of their revenue) who would be more amenable to the primate.

They naturally resisted what in their view must have appeared an act of usurpation and arbitrary authority on the part of their abbot, the archbishop.

The king supported the archbishop; the courtiers, for the most part, went with him. The convent appealed to the pope. The pope Urban III in October 1187, took up the cause of the convent, and appointed a commission, consisting of Reginald bishop of Bath, Seffred bishop of Chichester, and the abbots of Feversham and Reading, ordering them to destroy the building.

With the death of Urban III in 1187, proceedings were suspended. Henry died in July 1189. A new reign began in England. The quarrel was arranged for a time, and archbishop Baldwin went on the Crusade with Richard.

Baldwin's death at Acre was known in England in March 1191.

The monks used the opportunity of the vacancy in the see to overthrow the scheme of the late archbishop, and to secure to themselves the election of his successor.

In May 1191, pope Celestine III issued his mandate peremptorily to bishop Reginald and the commissioners, to execute the order for the destruction of the new buildings at Hackington, and on July 21 they were levelled to the ground.

The monks had succeeded in one of their objects.

They were now eager to secure the election of the archbishop. Reginald is charged with secretly intriguing for the primacy; but there is no evidence that he sought the office, or took any steps to obtain it.[1]

It was likely that his support of the convent, his position as pope's commissioner, and his execution of the pope's orders, should have won him the favour of the monks. He certainly had an active but self-interested agent in his cause in Savaric, his kinsman, who had some mysterious influence with the emperor Henry VI, and with the king of France, Philip son of Louis VII, the patron of Reginald in early life. If Savaric was intriguing for Reginald, he certainly was intriguing also for himself, and for the reversion of Reginald's bishopric of Bath.

Under his influence, the emperor wrote in November, 1191, to recommend the convent to take the advice of Savaric "dilectus consanguineus noster," in the choice of their archbishop. At the same time, Philip of France recommended Reginald as the friend of his father, who had given him the abbey of St. Exuperius in 1164, and as strongly supported by Savaric, "our faithful friend."[2]

The king's justiciars had appointed December 3 for a meeting of council to elect. But before the day, the monks, anticipating the meeting, held a chapter on November 27, to assert their claim and to nominate their candidate.

Elected archbishop, Nov. 27, 1191

---

1. Gervase so says, "clam ambiens." Bishop Stubbs, Pref. *Epp. Cant.* lxxxi, thinks "he was quietly laying his plans for the primacy." See also *ibid.* lxxxix.
2. *Epp. Cant.* ccclxxxi, ii.

The prior tried to sound the archbishop of Rouen, the chief justiciar, as to the person who would be accepted by the king. The archbishop, as Gervase hints,[1] intended the monks to choose himself; if so, he must have failed to make himself intelligible, or to have convinced the prior of his merits. "Would the bishop of Bath be admissible?" The archbishop did not say "yes," but the monks interpreted his looks as favourable. "We elect," cried the prior, "the bishop of Bath." The monks re-echoed the nomination, and laying violent hands on Reginald, thrust him, protesting, imploring, struggling, into the archbishop's chair.

The archbishop of Rouen protested in the king's name; the members of the council threatened further proceedings; but the monks supported their right to elect. Reginald re-asserted his unwillingness, but acquiesced in the election, and announced his intention of awaiting the pope's confirmation, with the words: "anxius, invitus, consentio vel gratulabundus cedo."

But all that had been done was made void by Reginald's death within a month of the election.

He was on his way to or from his diocese, when he was seized with paralysis at his manor of Dogmersfield on Christmas Eve.

The prior of Christchurch was sent for. The archbishop, anticipating his death, ordered him to bring the monk's habit, that he might die as a member of the brotherhood. His last words were, "God willeth not that I should be your archbishop. But I desire to be

1. Gervase, *Opera Hist.*, i, 511. (Rolls Series).

a monk, and one with you. Farewell, and pray for me without ceasing, as one of the brotherhood."[1]

He died on St. Stephen's day. The body was taken to Bath, and buried before the high altar on the day of St. Thomas the Martyr, December 29.

Peter of Blois, no longer now archdeacon of Bath, speaks of him as *magni nominis umbra*, and marks—perhaps with malicious humour—the curious coincidence that his days of death and burial were the feasts of the two saints to whom the church was dedicated, which he had been instrumental in destroying. "It was as if St. Stephen had killed him, and St. Thomas had buried him." But Richard of Devizes, to whom bishop Stubbs gives the character of "an ill-natured historian, who never misses an opportunity of speaking ill," is witness to his love for his church of Bath, and the love of the diocese for him,[2] and has condensed in two lines of a homely epitaph, in which he plays upon his name, a high testimony to his character.

Dum Reginaldus erat bene seque suosque regebat—
Nemo plus quaerat—quicquid docuit faciebat.

Reginald rightly named, himself and his flock ruled well;
How ? What he taught he did ; there is no more to tell.

Reginald's life is connected with interesting scenes and important events in the great reign of Henry II. As a statesman, he was one of the foremost in the

---

1. Ep. ccclxxxviii. "Mihi non videtur quod velit Deus quod vester sim archiepiscopus. Vester autem volo et desidero esse monachus. Valete, et gratia vestri incessanter, incessanter, oretis pro me."

2. "Quam multum diligebat, magis ab ea dilectus." R. of Devizes, p. 46, § 58.

second rank of able men whom Henry gathered round himself.[1]

As a bishop, though he was of another type from the ascetic and unworldly St. Hugh, yet he rose far above the selfish and worldly bishops of his time who were the scorn of Henry.

Reginald had no opportunity of showing whether he was capable of ruling the church of England as primate in those troubled times. We may think it was happier for him and for his reputation, that he had not to undergo the trial. But at least Wells has reason to honour him as one of her chief benefactors, not only in ecclesiastical, but in civil history; zealous and liberal, and wise in government, and a worthy successor of bishop Robert.

Bp. Reginald's share in the fabric of the cathedral church of Wells.
It has been generally assumed by later writers, who have followed the Canon of Wells and Godwin as the original authorities on the history of the fabric, that we have no documentary evidence of bishop Reginald's work on the fabric of his own cathedral church.

The Canon of Wells, as quoted in Wharton's *Anglia Sacra*, and bishop Godwin say nothing of any building works between the times of bishop Robert and bishop Jocelin.

Professor Willis,[2] in his lectures on the church of Wells, passes from bishop Robert to bishop Jocelin, as the next prelate who comes architecturally on the scene.

Mr. Freeman says "We may pass more lightly over the time of the two bishops who came between the

---

1. William of Newbury, III, c. xxvi.
2. *Somerset Archæological Proceedings*, vol xii, part I, p. 17.

first great founder, Robert, and the second great founder, Jocelin. Their time is a most important time in the history of the see of Bath and Wells; it is the most important of all times in the late history of the church of Glastonbury; but it provides but little matter bearing on the history of the fabric, or the constitution of the church of Wells. The next bishop, Reginald, founded several new prebends, but I do not find any mention of the fabric in his time."[1]

But we have additional evidences contained in the chapter registers at Wells, which are of earlier authority than the Canon of Wells and Godwin, and which in some measure supply the blank in the history of the fabric. Professor Willis had access to these registers for his lectures on Wells; and he says, that he " drew from these records many particulars of dates and facts hitherto unknown in relation to the progress of the building in the fourteenth and subsequent centuries."

But, unfortunately, his researches did not extend to the earlier records bearing on this first portion of the history of the fabric.

The first document quoted from his own observation is dated 1286. He exhorts members of the chapter, who have the opportunity, to pursue inquiries into the cathedral registers.

While bishop Reginald was receiving and applying benefactions to the church from the clergy and laity of the diocese, he on his own part was making liberal provision by his own acts, both for the augmentation of the common fund of the canons, and also for the maintenance and progress of the fabric of the church.

1. *Cathedral Church of Wells*, p. 70.

Gifts to the communa.

Early in his episcopate he had made over to the canons the "Barton" or home farm, which was the property of the bishop, free of the annual rent of twelve marks which they had hitherto paid for it.

"We have given to God, and to St. Andrew, and to the canons there devotedly serving God, their barton, free from all service, and expressly (*nominatim*) from the rent of twelve marks, which they were wont to pay to us yearly."[1]

He had also given to the common fund of the chapter the tenths of all mill dues on his manor of Wells, "ad communam canonicorum ibidem deo servientium."[2]

These benefactions to the income of the canons, given in perpetuity for himself and his successors, were accompanied with another gift for his own lifetime to the fabric fund of the church.

Fabric fund, from vacant benefices.

In a deed done in chapter very early in his episcopate, in the presence of the dean Richard of Spaxton, William of St. Faith the precentor, Thomas archdeacon of Wells, and "almost all the canons of the church," he made over to the chapter, specially for the uses of the fabric, all the fruits accruing from vacant benefices throughout the diocese, until the work shall be finished.

This grant is conveyed in a charter which is often quoted in the later history. It recites in the preamble the duty incumbent on the rulers of the church, and his own continual solicitude, that God shall not be dis-

---

1. R. i, f. 25, i, f. 59. "Bertona est villa vel praedium frumentarium." The "canon's barn" is now (1885) converted into the cathedral grammar school, by the liberality of canon Thomas Bernard, chancellor 1868.

2. R. i, f. 40. "Carta de decimis molendinorum de Welles," recited and confirmed by Savaric afterwards.

honoured by the squalor of His house. So, with the assent of the archdeacons and in full council with his chapter, he had set himself to discharge this duty incumbent upon him of providing a fund out of the episcopal revenue from the fruits of benefices during the time they were vacant, which should be entirely applied during his lifetime towards the building of the cathedral church, until, by the help of God, the whole work shall be brought to an end.[1]

---

1. Universis Christi fidelibus ad quos praesens carta pervenerit, Reginaldus Dei gratia Bathoniensis episcopus salutem in Domino et Dei benedictionem. Iis quibus est divina dispositione pastoralis officii cura commissa et ecclesiarum solicitudo injuncta, summo opere providendum est, ut domum Dei ea excolant diligentia quod dignitas Domini in domus squalore non possit devenustari. Hoc igitur zelo ducti, de assensu et concilio archidiaconorum nostrae auctoritatis, ad hoc duximus munimen impendendum, ut ad fabricam Wellensis ecclesiae ad cujus regimen sumus domino disponente admissi, fructus et obventiones vacantium ecclesiarum in nostra diocesi existentium quamdiu vacaverint convertantur, et in usus operationis ex toto cedant, donec per Dei miserantis auxilium consumetur.

Factum est hoc in capitulo Wellensi, praesente Ricardo de Spakeston ejusdem ecclesiae decano, Willelmo precentore, T. archidiacono et omnibus fere illius ecclesiae canonicis." R. ii, f. 14.

"The vacant benefice reverted to the diocesan both in spirituals and temporals. He was the guardian of both, bound to provide for the spiritual care of the flock, and also for the revenues chargeable with that care.

"This custom or rather common law was one of the survivals of the earlier condition of the Church, when the endowments of a diocese were a *diocesan* fund, administered by the bishop and synod, and applied to the support of a diocesan corps of clergy.

"These fruits formed a regular part of episcopal revenue administered by a sequestrator-general, until the Act of Henry VIII which, in order to secure payment of his first-fruits from the incoming incumbent, gave to the incumbent the fruits during vacancy—leaving to the bishop only the duty of husbanding those fruits by a sequestrator, and providing therefrom for the spiritual duties."—Note by bishop Hobhouse.

Bishop Jocelin in 1216, after consultation with dean Leonius and

Contemporary grants to the Fabric.

Other grants follow, which have a special interest as unpublished evidence bearing upon the history of the fabric.

Several of contemporary documents bear witness that some building was going on in the church at the time, and that grants were being made for the completion of the work. The dates of these early documents are not expressly given; they can only be ascertained by internal evidence and the names of attesting witnesses.

There are three grants of churches neighbouring to one another in the district of Castle Cary, made probably by members of the same family the Lovels of Cary, either attested by witnesses who were contemporaries with bishop Reginald, or confirmed by Reginald himself.

(*a.*) Robert de Kari, lord of Lovinton, gives to God and St. Andrew the advowson of the church of Lovinton, with one hide of 160 acres of land, and a messuage near the church.[1]

This deed is confirmed by bishop Reginald.[2]

---

the chapter, granted to the *communa* two-thirds of the revenues of vacant benefices, R. i, f. 59.

Bishop Roger in 1246 claimed all the vacant benefices; but the chapter appealed to the grant made to them by bishop Reginald, and the bishop withdrew his claim upon examination of the charters. The chapter then made a free gift to him of the two-thirds (saving to the archdeacon the third part) in consideration of the debts of the bishopric. But they gave this only for the bishop's life, and their act was not to bind future times. R. i, f. 64. So in after times bishop Bytton and bishop Drokensford made the same claim and received the same answer.

1. R. i, f. 38, cxxx; iii, f. 4.
2. R. iii, f. 61.

(*b.*) Nicolas de Barewe,[1] in ruri-decanal chapter at Cary (*in capitulo apud Kari*), "considerata canonicorum Wellensium honesta conversatione et surgentis ecclesie sue laudabili structura," gives up his life interest in the temporalities of this same church of Lovinton for an annual pension of two shillings.[2]

(*c.*) Alured de Ponson grants the neighbouring church of South Barrow, *in fundo meo sitam*, to God and St. Andrew, to the *communa* of Wells, and to Reginald bishop of Bath.[3]

Among the witnesses are Thomas archdeacon of Wells, Robert de Geldeford archdeacon, Alexander subdean of Wells, etc.

These deeds follow one another in the register, as if, in the mind of the clerk who copied them, they had connection of time and place.

The attestations to these charters fix their dates to the time of Reginald.

A special interest attaches to the charter of Nicolas of Barrow for the insight which it gives, though but a glimpse, into the state of the cathedral chapter at this time.

The motives which prompted the grant of the church of Barrow, perhaps of others, was a desire to support in their work the canons who bore a good reputation in the diocese, and to promote the building of the church, which was now rising in beauty. He makes his grant "in consideration of the right con-

---

1. North Barrow, the next parish to Lovinton. R. i, f. 38.—Cf. R. i, f. 61.
2. R. i, f. 38.
3. R. i, ff. 35, 61.

versation of the canons of Wells and the admirable structure of the rising church."

These terms in the preamble of a formal document have some meaning. They give an interest to the bare names of canons which occur as signatories to these documents of the time, they imply that there was attention to duty and devotion in dean Alexander and the archdeacons and canons, Robert of Guildford, Ralph of Lechlade, William of Martock, and doubtless Jocelin the chaplain, which commanded the respect of their brethren of the ruridecanal chapter of Cary.

And also at this time the church of St. Andrew was rising and becoming an object of interest and admiration to the clergy and laity of the diocese, so that when Nicolas of Barrow and Michael of Aldford and Ralph of Yarlington came up to Wells they would contrast their own little village churches with the proportions and architectural beauty of the buildings rising at Wells, and report that their cathedral church was becoming "exceeding magnifical," and a praise in the diocese.

Again there is another charter which tells more definitely of new buildings at Wells, and of the restoration of older work at this time.

Building at Wells, A.D. 1196.

Martin of Carscumbe, presumably Croscombe, near Wells, makes a grant of three silver marcs towards the construction of the new work, " ad constructionem novi operis," of the church of St. Andrew in Wells, and another two marcs to the repairs of the chapel of St. Mary there, " ad emendationem capellæ beatæ Mariæ ejusdem loci."[1]

1. *Carta Martini de Karscumbe.* Noverit universitas vestra quod ego Martinus dedi deo et ecclesiae beati Andreae in Wellia pro salute

The deed is attested by an unknown witness, Baldwin the chaplain. But it is dated with a precision which fixes it to certain years—"in the second year after the coronation of the lord the king at Winchester."

Two years are possible. Winchester was the scene of royal coronation twice during the last part of the twelfth century.

At Whitsuntide 1170, the young Henry, eldest son of Henry II (sometimes called *rex junior*, sometimes "Henricus III")[1] had been crowned at Westminster without his wife Margaret of France, by Roger archbishop of York. That act had brought down upon Henry the wrath of Thomas of Canterbury for the violation of the privileges of his see, and of the king of France for the slight offered to his daughter. He was crowned a second time, with his queen, in St. Swithun's, Winchester, on August 27, 1172.

If we might take our date as the second year from this coronation, and assign 1174 to this charter, it would fall in the first year of Reginald's episcopate, and it would be the earliest evidence of any architec-

---

animae meae et animarum omnium antecessorum meorum, tres marcas argenti ad constructionem novi operis—et duas marcas ad emendationem capellae beatae Mariae ejusdem loci accipiendas de redditu de Maperton quem dominus meus H. de Novo Mercato mihi in solutionem debiti mei assignavit et in carta nostra confirmavit. . .

Ut haec donatio firma permaneat et inconcussa eam sigilli mei appositione roboravi. His testibus: Baldwino capellano, etc. Anno secundo post coronationem domini Regis apud Wintoniae. R. i, f. 41.

Henry Newmarch (de Novo Mercato) was lord of the barony of Cadbury in Somerset, 6 Richard I. Dugdale, *Baron.* p. 435.

1. Richard of Devizes, *De rebus gestis Ricardi I*, p. 5, § 3. "Ricardus filius regis Henrici secundi, frater regis Henrici tertii." "Henry, son of King Henry the Second, is frequently styled Henry the Third in the early chronicles and contemporaneous State Papers. He died in 1183."

tural work succeeding Robert's consecration of the church in 1148. But it is improbable that the young Henry, though crowned and called *rex junior* and *Henricus tertius* in contemporary documents, would have been called *dominus rex* during the lifetime of his father.

There was another coronation at Winchester in twenty-four years. Richard I who had been crowned in state at Westminster on his accession on September 3, 1189, was crowned a second time after his return to England, as it were "to wipe out the stain of his captivity and his foreign homage," on April 17, 1194, at Winchester. The year 1196 would then be the second year after the coronation, the fourth year of Savaric's episcopate.

In either case the document is evidence that new building was going on in the church at Wells in the latter part of the twelfth century, either by Reginald in succession to Robert, or by Savaric in succession to Reginald; and that there was then a chapel of St. Mary which required and was undergoing repair.

We cannot trace any other documentary reference to the "new work" in Savaric's time. But we have some clue to an earlier chapel, which may be the chapel of St. Mary now under repair.

In the great charter of bishop Robert of the date of 1136, there is mention of "the chapel of the Blessed Mary," which bishop Giso endowed with land in Wotton.

"Dimidiam etiam hidam in Wotton cum virgata terrae quam jocundae recordationis Gyso episcopus dedit capellae Beatae Mariae."[1]

1. R. i, f. 31, "De ordinatione prebendarum."

It may be that Giso built this chapel at the time when he was building the cloister and refectory for his canons, on the ground south of the church, where we know a "chapel of St. Mary near the cloister" was standing afterwards, and is mentioned repeatedly in later documents.

This chapel may have been spared when bishop John pulled down the canonical buildings of his predecessor.

We now see that these documents, relating to the years between 1174-1196, bear witness that building was going on at Wells in the latter part of the twelfth century, and in Reginald's episcopate. *Conclusive evidence that Reginald was a builder of the church of Wells.*

There are no fabric rolls of that date, but the charters of gifts and endowments for the sustentation of the fabric and for the completion of work going on, and the acts of confirmation by bishop and chapter contradict the inferences drawn from the language of the Canon of Wells and Godwin, that nothing was done between Robert's and Jocelin's time.

It is antecedently improbable that Reginald should have left the fabric of his own cathedral church to fall into ruins, or to remain neglected during seventeen years of an active episcopate. It was, as we see, a time of activity and progress in the diocese. The bishop was carrying on Robert's work, "following the footsteps of his predecessors, and led by their example."

He was a vigorous man, a Norman, and might be supposed to have had that love of building which distinguished the race. He was high in favour with the kings Henry and Richard and John his brother. He had travelled much, and must have seen or known of new buildings rising abroad and at home—in his uncle's diocese of Coutances: and at Canterbury, where the rebuilding after the fire of 1174 was going on throughout his episcopate : in his own diocese—at Bath, where he was the restorer of two churches, the founder and builder of the hospital—at Witham, where St. Hugh was building his first church, and preparing for his greater architectural work at Lincoln—at Glastonbury, where buildings of national interest were rising between 1184 and 1193, under Norman workmen, and where he was the consecrator of the first completed part, the chapel of St. Mary.

There would have been sufficient to kindle the ambition of an active ruler to keep up and to beautify the church of Wells, one of the seats of his diocese, which his predecessor had begun to rebuild.

We know now from these documents, and from his own words, that the building of the church was the subject of his care and solicitude. We know that he was promoting the building by a large gift to the fabric fund for his lifetime ; that the work was being carried on, and the church was rising and becoming a goodly structure in the land ; and that new works and repairs of old building were being planned or carried out, to which offerings were made, in the first years of his successor's episcopate.

This evidence is to be borne in mind when we look upon architectural features in parts of the church which, as Professor Willis has said, bear a character "unlike any early English building" . . and "belong to an earlier style, characterised as a transitional Norman," "an improved Norman, worked with considerable lightness and richness, but distinguished from the early English by greater massiveness and severity," and of which Britton says, "that had not the 'Canon of Wells' so particularly mentioned the restoration of the Cathedral by Jocelin of Wells, and bishop Godwin so strongly corroborated his testimony, there could be little hesitation in ascribing the work to bishop Robert, and to the reign of Henry II, 1154-1189."

CHAPTER III.

Savaric, Bishop of Bath and Glastonbury,
A.D. 1192-1205.

" SAVARIC is a person whose career if it could be explored would be very interesting." So wrote Dr. Stubbs in 1865.[1] The history of Savaric is yet to be written.

Some knowledge of his episcopate is necessary for the consideration of the question whether any part of the fabric of the church was his work.

His worldly and eccentric career is a strange interlude between the decorous and beneficent episcopates of his predecessors and that of bishop Jocelin his successor. As a citizen of the world he exercised remarkable influence for his personal ends with the chief personages of his time at home and abroad—popes, emperor, and kings. He was one of the diplomatic agents at the court of Henry VI emperor of the Romans, in the European questions raised by the captivity of Richard.

---

1. Vide *Epistolae Cantuarienses, Pref. and Notes*, p. lxxxvii, by Dr. Stubbs. Also *Gentleman's Magazine*, November, 1863, p. 621. These notes supply material for the pedigree of the families of Savaric and Bohun in Appendix I.

Scanty notes of a paper by the late J. R. Green are to be read in the *Somerset Archæological Society's Proceedings* for 1863.

At home, his annexation to the see of Bath of the abbey of Glastonbury by a circuitous and bold intrigue forms one of the ecclesiastical events which throw light on the relations of Church and State at the time just preceding the Great Charter.

He was connected with the families of Savaric of Le Mans, and Bohun of the Norman Côtentin. His elder brother Franco de Bohun held the estates of Savaric Fitz-savaric his uncle, who had married into the Bohun family and was first lord of Midhurst, in Sussex, in the time of Henry I. The two brother bishops, Jocelin de Bohun,[1] bishop of Sarum 1142—1184, and Richard de Bohun, dean of Bayeux and bishop of Coutances 1151—1179, were his uncles, and Reginald Fitz Jocelin, his immediate predecessor as bishop of Bath, was his cousin.

Through his mother, as is supposed a Burgundian,[2] he was a kinsman of the emperor Henry VI. Names of the Bohun family appear in the registers of Reginald's and Savaric's time and among the canons of Wells.[3]

Savaric's first public appearance is ominous of his masterful character and turbulent career.

Early Life, A.D. 1172—1192.

In the patent rolls for Surrey of the year 1172 he is named as heavily fined, £26 3s. 4d. for striving to

---

1. Vide Appendix I. Pedigree of Savaric, and Bohun family.

2. Dr. Stubbs, vide *Pref. Epp. Cantuar.* p. lxxxvii. Howden, 3, 197.

3. Franco de Bohun attests a charter of bishop Reginald to Glastonbury—John de Bohun was canon at Wells in Savaric's time. There is some reason for thinking Alexander the dean 1180—1209 was a Bohun. Roger de Bohun was canon in Savaric's time, and nephew of the dean, vide Appendix I.

wrest a bow from the king's foresters.[1] Notwithstanding, in 1175 he was archdeacon of Canterbury, appointed at Westminster by archbishop Richard.[2] He was treasurer of the church of Sarum in 1180, where his uncle was bishop.[3] He signs as archdeacon of Northampton in a document in the Wells registers of a date later than 1180, attesting a grant of the church of Carenton (Carhampton), in West Somerset, to bishop Reginald.[4]

On this occasion the only other signatory is one "Dalmatius Seneschallus Lugdunensis," an unknown name suggestive of Savaric's Burgundian connection. The confirmation of this grant by bishop Reginald is attested by Savaric and by Alexander dean of Wells and others.

As archdeacon of Northampton he came under the displeasure of king Henry, and his conduct is matter of complaint to the pope. In June 1186 the king's clerks bring letters from Urban to intercede for Savaric, but with orders to sequestrate his archdeaconry for the payment of his debts.[5]

Though in disgrace with Henry he rose quickly into favour with Richard when king, probably through the influence of Reginald. He was one of the crowd of

---

1. "Savaricus clericus debet xxvi libras et iii solidos et iv denarios pro arcu quam voluit auferre ministris Regis in foresta." *Mag. Rot.* 18 Hen. II. *Rot.* 106, Surreia : quoted by Stubbs.

2. Le Neve, *Fasti*, i, p. 38. Ralph de Diceto, i, f. 403. (Rolls Series).

3. Jones, *Fasti of the Church of Sarum.* V. Osmund Reg. i, 268-299, 312.

4. R. i, f. 24.

5. Benedict, i, p. 356. Ralph de Diceto, ii, p. 105. (Rolls Series).

ecclesiastics and courtiers who started with Richard for the Holy Land,[1] and he was with him at Messina in February 1191. There, by some mysterious means, this disgraced archdeacon who could not pay his debts, and was not yet in priest's orders, obtained private letters from Richard ordering the king's justiciar to sanction in the king's name his appointment to any bishopric to which he might be elected.[2]

These letters were sent to his cousin Reginald. Savaric then betook himself to Rome, where he was already very well known, as the centre from whence he could best work out his schemes.[3]

The see of Canterbury was now vacant by the death of archbishop Baldwin at Acre in November 1190. Savaric, in 1191, was using his influence with the emperor Henry and Philip Augustus of France to obtain letters from them to the convent of Canterbury,[4] recommending Reginald for the archbishopric. Reginald, who had other recommendations as a steady supporter of the convent in the quarrel with archbishop Baldwin, was elected Nov. 27, 1191, but he did not survive his election more than a month, and the see was again vacant. Savaric, while interceding for Regi-

---

1. He was "Cruce signatus" when archdeacon of Northampton. *Abbreviatio Placitorum*, p. 38.

2. Richard of Devizes, p. 28. Ed. Stevenson. Richard was at Messina from Sept. 23, 1190, to March 30, 1191.

3. "Ipse vero Romam concessit sicut qui fuerat Romanis notissimus."

4. *Epp. Cantuar.* ccclxxxi, November 1191. The emperor urges the convent to take the advice of Savaric, "our dear cousin and your good friend."

Ep. ccclxxxii. Philip recommends Reginald as his father's friend, "et propter commendationem a Savarico amico et fideli nostro."

nald, had been working to acquire for himself the reversion of the see of Bath. Reginald before his death showed the king's letters to Walter prior of Bath, and obtained from the convent the nomination of Savaric as bishop. The election rested with the two chapters, the canons of Wells, as well as the monks of Bath, but Walter, archbishop of Rouen, the king's justiciar, without waiting for the assent of the Wells chapter, and in spite of their protests, gave forthwith the king's assent to Savaric's election.[1] Savaric at Rome obtained the confirmation of pope Celestine, and after some delay was by his order ordained priest at St. John Lateran on Sept. 19, and consecrated bishop of Bath the next day, Sept. 20, 1192.

Savaric bishop, and abbot of Glastonbury 1193.

Savaric had thus attained the bishopric through his influence with Richard and his friends in high place. He now made his kinsman, the emperor of the Romans Henry VI, the means of coercing Richard to advance still further his interests.

In the winter of 1192 Richard, returning from Palestine, and tempest-tossed in the Adriatic, was wrecked on the low shore between Venice and Aquileia.

After romantic adventures and escapes, which formed the subject of troubadour lays, he was made prisoner near Vienna, in the territory of his enemy the duke of Austria, Dec. 12, and after confinement at Dürrenstein on the Danube, he was delivered up to the emperor

---

1. Richard of Devizes, p. 46. "Walterus prior et suus sine clero (sc. Wellensi) conventus elegerunt sibi in futurum episcopum Savaricum, et licet clerus reniteretur obtinuerunt."
R. i, f. 93. "Canonicis irrequisitis et reclamantibus."

Henry[1] at the price of 60,000 crowns, and about March 23-30 brought to Speyer.

Throughout the whole of 1193, and to Feb. 1194, Richard was a prisoner in the hands of Henry, who was basely making terms at the same time with Richard for his release, and with his enemies his brother John and Philip of France, for his retention.

News of Richard's captivity had reached England in February 1193. A council was summoned by Walter archbishop of Rouen, the justiciar, to meet at Oxford on Feb. 28 to deliberate on measures to be taken to obtain the king's release. Savaric was there named as a fit agent to negotiate with the emperor as being a kinsman of the emperor and then abroad, and a mission was sent from England to confer with the king, and to arrange the terms of release.

During 1193 Savaric was present at interviews which took place between the emperor and the king. At Worms in June 1193, where Savaric and William bishop of Ely were present, terms were finally arranged. The ransom was 100,000 marcs, and 50,000 more were to be paid as perquisite to the duke of Austria. Walter of Rouen, Savaric, and others, were ultimately made hostages for payment of the ransom, bound not to leave Germany without the knowledge of the emperor. But it was not until after a protest from the princes of Germany at Henry's ignoble detention of his captive after promise of release that

---

1. Henry VI Emperor of the Romans 1190—1197, "son and successor of Barbarossa, inherited all his father's harshness with none of his father's generosity." Bryce, *Holy Roman Empire*, p. 205.

Richard was finally released at Mainz on February 2, 1194.[1]

After a captivity of one year six weeks and three days Richard was again in England.

On April 17, 1194, he was crowned a second time at Winchester, "to wipe off the ignominy of his captivity." But the burden of taxation for his ransom lay heavily on the kingdom.

While Savaric was taking part in negotiations for Richard's release he was not unmindful of his own interests. He is said by the Glastonbury writers to have had power with the emperor to make the king's release in some way conditional on his acceptance of clauses suggested to the emperor by Savaric, in which he pressed his own advancement. According to Richard's own statement, as reported by Adam of Domerham, he had extorted from Richard the exchange of Bath city for the abbey of Glastonbury, and the union of the abbey to the see of Bath, so that the jurisdiction and rights of an abbot should be vested in him, with the title of bishop of Bath and Glastonbury.

There was no vacancy in the abbacy at the time, but this immediate difficulty was overcome.

The abbot was Henry, of Sully on the Loire,

---

1. Vide Howden, 3, 194-231, for notices of Richard's captivity under the emperor Henry. The stations and dates of his imprisonment were—
Speyer, March 21-30. 1193.
Treifels in Rhenish Bavaria.
Hagenau in Alsace, April—May.
Worms, May 28—June 30.
Speyer, December and Christmas.
Mainz, February, 1194.

(Henricus de Soliaco), nephew of Henry of Blois, kinsman of Richard, and appointed by him in 1189. Orders were sent to him by Richard to join him at Hagenau, in Alsace, in April, 1193.[1]

He there learnt from Richard himself that he was beholden to cede in exchange the abbey to Savaric, the kinsman of the emperor, that he must resign the abbey, and should be provided for by the vacant see of Worcester. The abbot entered into Savaric's plans and made his arrangements accordingly.

At this same time Savaric was aiming at a higher prize. The archbishopric of Canterbury which he had sought to obtain for Reginald he now sought for himself.

Two letters from Richard following one another from Worms, in May 28 and June 8, represent Richard's ignominious position and Savaric's pretensions.

On May 28 Richard wrote to the convent of Canterbury on behalf of Savaric.

On June 8 he wrote to Eleanor the queen mother to secure the election to Canterbury of Hubert Walter bishop of Salisbury, and to credit no letters in favour of Savaric, or any other candidate. He is forced, he says, during his captivity to write in favour of persons whom he does not wish to be promoted—" pro quibusdam supplicare quos nullatenus promoveri vellemus."[2]

Hubert was appointed soon after in 1193, and Savaric proceeded to mature his plans for Glastonbury. He obtained letters from the king and William

1. Vide Adam of Domerham, ii, 355.
2. Vide *Epp. Cantuar.* 402, 403.

bishop of Ely (Longchamp) to pope Celestine, asking for papal sanction to the union of the bishopric and the abbacy as the only means of putting a stop to the chronic state of discord between bishop and monks. Abbot Henry had returned to Glastonbury about Michaelmas, and, having made his arrangements without revealing the secret treaty, he left the abbey at Advent, and was consecrated at Canterbury bishop of Worcester, December 12, 1193.[1] Then for the first time did the convent learn that their abbot had betrayed them into the hands of their enemies, and that they had passed under the jurisdiction of the bishop of Bath as their abbot.

Adam of Domerham relates that Savaric was then at Bath and sent for Harold, the prior, and announced to his surprise, "I am your abbot."[2]

The action of claiming possession of the abbey in the king's name, and inducting the bishop by his proxy, was carried out by Savaric's agents, selected from the chapter of Wells.[3] On the part of the abbey a solemn protest from prior and convent addressed to

---

1. Vide Adam of Domerham, 356-7. The betrayal of the abbey has condemned the memory of abbot Henry to infamy in the Glastonbury history, notwithstanding that he obtained for the abbot from pope Celestine the privileges of the mitre and ring, and of blessing the vestments. The "Inquisition of the manors of Glastonbury Abbey," *Liber Henrici de Soliaco*,—the terrier of the abbey in 1189,—was made in his time.

2. It is not likely that Savaric, named as a hostage for the payment of the ransom, was in England at this time. He was at Mainz at the time of Richard's release, which took place on Feb. 2, 1194.

3. Ralph of Lechlade, a well-known name in the chapter registers, afterwards (in 1217-20) dean, in bishop Jocelin's time, is named as proctor.

the pope was laid upon the altar of St. Andrew in the church of Wells.

Bath city at the same time was seized in the king's name.

This bold invasion of the independence of the great and most ancient abbey which until the last forty years had held the primacy among the abbeys of England,[1] though effected by a surprise, was not submitted to without a severe struggle. War between Wells and Glastonbury ensued for the next twenty-five years, until 1219—fought out under the two episcopates of Savaric and Jocelin. Richard and John, with the popes Celestine, Innocent III, and Honorius, were engaged in the struggle. *A.D. 1194-1202.* *War with Glastonbury*

The attempt to restrain the excessive power of the religious houses was being made about the same time at Canterbury, under the archbishops Baldwin and Hubert, and at Coventry, under bishop Hugh Nonant. But Savaric's audacity and strength of will carried him through his struggle with more success than either of his brethren, and he transmitted to his successor the title of bishop of Bath and Glastonbury, with a fourth part of the revenue and a large portion of the manors of the abbey.

The Glastonbury writers are naturally vehement in their complaints of the rapacity and cruelty of the invader and oppressor, and the public opinion of churchmen was generally against him. But the example of the archbishops Baldwin and Hubert, and of

---

1. St. Alban's was made the primal abbey under pope Adrian IV (Nicolas Breakspear) who had been a monk of St. Alban's in 1154.

98   *Chapters in Wells History.*   [CHAP

bishop Hugh of Lincoln,[1] and the support which Savaric received from his successor bishop Jocelin and the chapter of Wells, show that there were good men who saw the importance of checking the exorbitant pretensions to independence of the overgrown monasteries in the diocese. Savaric's attempts to bring the other religious houses of his diocese into closer relation to the cathedral church are a sign that he had a policy which was reasonable and consistent, though it is probable that his leading motives in the annexation of Glastonbury were greed and ambition, his acts were violent and tyrannical, and he certainly showed nothing of the spirit of a reformer.

The struggle illustrates the unsettled state of the relations between Church and State at this time, the growth of papal interference, and the inconsistent and selfish policy of the Roman Curia, which soon pro-

---

1. It is instructive to compare how at the same time another and a very different man was fighting a like battle with the king, and with what different weapons he gained his cause.

St. Hugh of Lincoln in 1197 pressed his claim to the right of patronship (*jus patronatus*) based upon ancient precedent, to the vacant abbey of Eynsham, which had been disputed by the king's ministers.

Hugh's friends tried to dissuade him from entering into a hopeless conflict with the king: but he stoutly prosecuted his suit, and by the oath of twenty-four credible witnesses, cleric and lay, gained his cause in the king's court. *Vita S. Hugonis*, iv, 8, p. 188, ed. Dimock.

The custody of the abbey during vacancy was restored to him, the right of confirming the abbot, and full jurisdiction over the convent. At a conference of abbots and other religious of the neighbourhood at Eynsham, the elected of the convent is presented to the bishop, and his benediction is given at Lincoln. At the feast which he gave afterwards it was the subject of rejoicing that like the Good Shepherd he had gathered into one flock sheep that were of another fold, and had united in federal union under one headship church and abbacy.

voked the national assertion of independence of papal interference in the election of bishops and abbots in the Great Charter of 1215.

There are three stages in the history of the struggle during Savaric's life, according to the Glastonbury historian—

> (*a.*) During Richard's time the wolf was kept out of the fold for five years, 1194-1199.
>
> (*b.*) As soon as John succeeded, the wolf sprang into the fold to devour and to lay waste, 1199-1202.
>
> (*c.*) He was checked by the strong arm of the pope, Innocent III, 1202-1205.

Savaric had been inducted under Richard's grant, then abroad and in captivity. But Richard, on his return to England, resenting Savaric's power over him in Germany, repudiated his concession as a fraudulent exchange forced upon him when not a free agent. He received the appeal of the convent, and refused to acknowledge Savaric as abbot, and put the abbey under the charge of William of Ste. Mère l'Eglise, his prothonotary, afterwards bishop of London. This was probably in the autumn of 1194.[1]

Pope and king were at war. Celestine issued his sanction of the union of Bath and Glastonbury in the Lent of 1195, and a second and stronger mandate to the archbishop followed Richard's action in 1196 or

---

1. The dates in Adam of Domerham are confused; but he definitely assigns this act to the first autumn after Henry of Sully's consecration to Worcester, which took place December, 1193. Ste. Mère l'Eglise is a village in the Côtentin near Carentan. William, bishop of London, is more generally called William of St. Mary-church, but cf. Stubbs, *Episcopal Succession*, anno 1199.

1197, ordering him to put Savaric in possession. Archbishop Hubert, who secretly supported the convent, and had delayed execution of the papal letters, now ordered Alexander dean of Wells, and others of the chapter, to read the pope's letters, inhibiting the convent from electing another abbot, and ordering obedience to Savaric.

The king's officers retired. The abbey was put under the authority of Savaric in October, 1197, by archiepiscopal and papal mandate.

Pope Celestine III died January 8, 1198.

Richard answered Celestine's mandate by writing to the new pope, Innocent III, in favour of the convent, by taking the abbey into his own hands as lord, and giving the monks permission to elect their own abbot. William Pica ("conversione novicius sed medicinae professor") was elected abbot, and approved by the king's justiciar November 25, 1198.

Savaric made the next move. From the manor of Mells he issued his excommunication against William as rival abbot, and laid an interdict upon the convent.

The convent stood out for a time. Abbot William ruled from St. Nicholas' day, December 12, 1198, to the Purification, February 2, 1199; but his attempt to enforce discipline amidst the conflict of authority and factions in the house, united all parties against him, and he left Glastonbury to carry the appeal of the monks before the king in Normandy, and before Pope Innocent at Rome. The convent submitted and prayed for remission of the interdict. By the archbishop's authority the abbots of Sherborne and Abbotsbury withdrew the interdict about Easter,

1199; and, a few days after, the abbots of Malmesbury and Evesham, and the precentor of Wells, as the bishop's representative, received the submission of the monks to Savaric's authority. Such was the state of things when Richard's death took place, April 6, 1199.

We see the unsettled state of relations between pope and king in this period of the struggle.

Papal mandates, illegal by the Constitutions of Clarendon, are published and executed by the archbishop.

The king acts in defiance of them—the bishop excommunicates those who act on Richard's authority—the monastery appeals to both king and pope against the bishop. There is a diversity of treatment by the papal court of the two cases of Canterbury and Glastonbury. In the former case, the pope supported the monks against their archbishop. In the case of Glastonbury the pope sends mandates in favour of the bishop against the monks. Richard is so far consistent, after having repudiated his engagement made to Savaric when a prisoner, that in the year 1198 he forbade the execution of papal mandates alike at Canterbury in favour of the monks[1] and at Glastonbury in favour of Savaric.

It is not easy to trace Savaric's movements through his wandering life.[2]

From the time when he left England with Richard for the Holy Land in December 1189 he was probably absent from England until 1197.

<small>Savaric's movements, A.D. 1189—1197.</small>

---

1. Cf. *Epp. Cantuar.*—Richard's Letters, June 14, 15, 1198, *Pref.* p. cxi.
2. Vide Appendix K.

Since 1194 he had held office as chancellor of Burgundy, or "the kingdom of Arles,"[1] under the emperor Henry VI; and he carried on his contest for the abbey through his agents at Rome and by letters to England.

In 1197 he was sent to England by the emperor, then at Messina struck with compunction and in fear of death, to release Richard from submission made to him when in captivity, and to offer restitution in money or lands for the ransom exacted from him.[2]

Savaric might possibly have used this mission as a means of conciliating Richard to support him in his hold of Glastonbury. But while Savaric was on the journey the emperor died, and the opportunity was lost. We then trace Savaric with Richard at Rouen on October 16, 1197, where he attested the concord made between Richard and the archbishop of Rouen after a quarrel about the castle of Roche Andely,[3] and his arrival in England will have coincided with the execution of the papal mandate for his induction into the abbey.

The abbey was now cowed into submission; but Savaric seems to have been restrained from taking possession or from further aggression—perhaps by his late interview with Richard, in Normandy.

1. "Regnum Arelatense," including Provence, Dauphiné, the southern part of Savoy, and the country between the Saône and the Jura. Bryce, *Holy Roman Empire*, p. 448.

2. Howden says, that Richard when in captivity, "consilio matris suae deposuit se de regno Angliae et tradidit illud imperatori Henrico sexto sicut universorum domino." But as he was invested at the same time with the kingdom of Arles by Henry VI, his homage may have been for that fief only. Vide Bryce, p. 187.

3. Howden, 4, 30. Ralph de Diceto, ii, f. 156.

His friend Celestine died soon after, and a very different pope, Innocent III, succeeded. The monks, supported by the king, were carrying their appeal to him.

During 1198 Savaric was in England, probably for part of the time in his diocese, where some undated charters to the church of Wells and confirmation of his predecessor's grants, in the Wells registers, may belong to this year.

In October of this year—1198—Savaric was one of a commission to arrange Richard's quarrel with archbishop Geoffrey of York, and on the archbishop's appeal to Rome the commissioners were ordered to Rome to conduct Richard's case there.[1]

Savaric had also his own business to transact at Rome. He had just excommunicated the abbot elected by the convent of Glastonbury under Richard's authority, and put an interdict upon the abbey for disobeying the pope's mandate. It was now necessary for him to obtain Innocent's confirmation of his act, and to carry on his own case against the agents of the convent in the Roman Curia.

He was there through the winter of 1198-9, when the news of Richard's death on April 6, 1199, brought him back at once to England to take immediate advantage of John's accession, and to try a shorter method, by influence and by bribes, to obtain from him possession of the abbey which Richard had persistently denied him.[2]

A.D. 1199 in England.

---

1. Howden, 4, 66.
2. "Tam prece quam pretio ejus comparans gratiam." Adam of Domerham, 382.

Savaric found John a ready instrument for his purpose. He obtained at once an order to the archbishop for his public installation as abbot at Glastonbury, and Hubert issued a commission to the archbishop of Arragon and the archdeacon of Canterbury to enthrone him.

Savaric was present at John's coronation at Westminster on Ascension Day 1199. According to the ceremonial observed on Richard's coronation, the bishops of Durham and of Bath, walking on the right and left hand of John, conducted him from the throne to the altar to receive the crown, and back again to his throne.

At Glastonbury.

Then Savaric lost no time in asserting himself. On Whitsunday, June 8, Savaric appeared in person at Glastonbury, attended by the dean Alexander, the precentor of Wells William of St. Faith,[3] and other secular clergy and soldiery. The doors of the abbey were found closed, and were forced open: the cloisters of the church were empty and the monks, all but eight, refused to appear. The sacristy was broken open, and the secular clergy in the vestments of the monks formed the procession of installation. The monks were then shut up in the infirmary, and soldiers took post in the cloisters through the day and night. Next day the monks were summoned to the chapter-house, where some were publicly beaten, threats, promises, cajolery were used with others, and at last the signatures of fifty in number were extorted to a deed addressed to the pope, by which they acknowledged Savaric as

---

3. He appears in the *Canterbury Letters* as one of the agents of the archbishop Baldwin at Rome against the convent of Canterbury.

their abbot, and promised obedience. The names of the commissioners and of witnesses present attested the deed, it was sealed with the convent seal, and then the great seal of the abbey was given up to Savaric.

Savaric was now in full possession. The wolf had sprung in upon the fold, and he entered in to devour and to lay waste.

Deputations went from the convent to Rome to lay their case before the pope.

Martin de Summa,[1] powerful in money and in friends at Rome, was their chief champion, going backwards and forwards throughout the struggle at great personal risks on the journey. Savaric's unscrupulous agents waylaid, robbed, and imprisoned the monks.

Eustace Comyn, afterwards prior and a great benefactor to the abbey, and John of Cossington, are names of the most active agents. William Pica was there now until his death, not without suspicion of poison, in the next year.

Savaric was attending on the king in Normandy in the summer of 1199.[2] He was probably again at Rome during the winter, pleading against the Glastonbury deputation, and he left his agents at Wells to carry on the work of crushing the rebellious spirit of the monks and forcing them to withdraw their agents at Rome. A piteous tale was sent from the abbey to the brethren at Rome of Savaric's outrages and

In Normandy.

---

1. His brother was a Milanese, *miles potentissimus.*—Vide *Royal Letters*, Henry III, 2, 512, and he is called " subdiaconus noster " by pope Innocent. Adam of Domerham, 419.

2. He attests documents from July 1 to September 7 at different places in Normandy.

the sufferings of the monks. Innocent was moved to tears by it, as the brethren report in their answer, and promised that he would protect them. A letter from Innocent of later date (August 28, 1202)[1] relates the complaints which reached him at the time and which roused his indignation against Savaric. The gates of the abbey were closed night and day for a year and more, so that no person, no letter, should pass in or out. Refractory monks were punished, one by the loss of his corrody or pension; another was beaten in Savaric's presence, so that he died from his injuries; others were injured for life by hardships endured. The pope complained that his own letters, received by Savaric in Flanders, had been treated as forgeries and disregarded, and his messengers stopped and robbed. On the feast of the conversion of St. Paul, after Savaric's installation, the prior had called to his aid some of the canons from Wells, among whom was Jocelin, afterwards bishop,[2] who, entering in with some lay people, made a violent assault upon five of the leaders of the rebellion, whom they dragged even from the altar, and carried them off in carts to Wells. There they were imprisoned for eight days, suffering hunger and thirst, insults and mockings, and then were dispersed among other religious houses in the country.

Innocent through this time was trying to arrange matters so as to save the credit of the holy see, and do justice between the parties. He was shocked by Savaric's violence and defiance; he was hampered by

---

1. Adam of Domerham, p. 406.
2. The names occur again of William the precentor, Thomas of Dinant subdean, John de Bohun, and Jocelin, afterwards bishop.

Celestine's policy of concession; so he confirmed Celestine's mandate for Savaric's induction, and he annulled William Pica's election; but he inhibited Savaric from acts of excommunication, of vengeance and spoliation, and he appointed a commission to arbitrate and make award between Savaric and the convent.

The commission consisted of Eustace bishop of Ely; Sampson abbot of St. Edmund's; and Godfrey prior of Holy Trinity, Canterbury. They received their mandate in June, 1201; but, either thwarted or bribed by Savaric, they did not proceed to business until, forced by a second mandate from Innocent, they held their sitting at St. Alban's, on September 8, 1202; and made their award, which was confirmed by the pope, September 23, 1202.

This award was the basis of a concordat which lasted for the remainder of Savaric's episcopate.

The ordinance of pope Innocent, based upon the report of the commissioners,[1] is of general historical interest as an example of the Roman jurisdiction overriding the action of the civil court. It also exhibits the internal economy of one of the largest and the most ancient of the abbeys of England. It contains a lengthy recital of the previous stages of the controversy; comments severely on Savaric's attempt to forestall the settlement by an arrangement in the king's court which is now set aside; gives details of local interest touching the income and property of the house, and the number of the monks; and sketches out a

Peace between Savaric and Glastonbury, A.D. 1202-1205.

---

1. The report is printed in Adam of Domerham, pp. 410-425, and a duplicate MS. copy is among the Wells chapter documents.

scheme for a division of the revenues, and the government of the monastery, "after the pattern of other well-constituted cathedral churches in which are colleges of monks." The award was to be final; if the bishop did not accept it within three months the convent should be restored to its former condition, and the monks should be at liberty to elect their own abbot.

It appeared from the testimony of the older monks that the number in the house had ranged from seventy to eighty, besides twenty-three of the body who held hereditary offices: "hereditario jure constitutos."[1] The nett divisible income after providing for these, and for the necessary wants of the house, such as hospitality, the support of the poor, and fabric repairs, was estimated at £800 per annum. Besides this were the altar oblations, which were set apart for the new buildings of the church. The abbey was a barony of the Crown, bound to the service of forty knights.

The concordat.
The scheme of the commissioners on which the papal award in the ordinance was made, estimated the number of the monks at sixty, with a nett divisible income of £800: it provided—

(*a.*) That to the bishop as abbot should belong ten of the manors with the patronage of all the churches on the ten manors, in order to

---

1. Vide *Liber de Soliaco*, notes to p. 10. The offices of porter, master baker, cook, and butcher, were hereditary (some from Dunstan's time), and occasionally descended to females who acted by deputy, *e.g.* the office of pincerna, "butler," who distributed wine to the guests, was held by a daughter of a former pincerna. This office, and some others held *hereditario jure*, were afterwards bought up by the abbey. Vide Adam of Domerham, p. 531.

yield him a fourth part of the revenue[1]—the abbot's house within the precincts of the abbey[2]—and Meare in the Glastonbury xii hides;

(*b.*) The bishop should be answerable for a proportionate share of the knight's service to the Crown—should bear his share of the debts of the convent, and should make restitution or compensation for lands alienated, for patronage unjustly exercised, for injuries to monks ejected or persecuted during the late troubles;[3]

(*c.*) The appointment and deposal of the higher officers; prior, sacrist, chamberlain, cellarer, should belong to the bishop;

(*d.*) The bishop should have canonical jurisdiction over the prior and the convent.

In the internal government it was provided there should be a common purse in charge of four treasurers elected by the convent. The seal of the abbey was to be kept under four keys, of which the prior and two brethren elected by the convent and a fourth appointed by the bishop should be holders. No deeds should be

---

1. The manors of Pucklechurch, Wynescomb, Badbury in Wilts, Essebury (Ashbury in Berks), Buckland, Lyme, Blackford, East Brent, Berges (Berrow), Cranmore.

2. "Ut habeat episcopus domos juxta capellam beatae mariae quae fuerunt abbatum, cum clausura sua per murum qui extenditur a lardario usque ad angulum prædictae capellae; et ut fiat porta ejus versus forum Glastoniense."

3. Martinus de Summa, "our subdeacon," is expressly mentioned as one who had suffered. His services to the convent and their ingratitude to him afterwards are the subject of complaint to Henry III in 1223 from the Podestá and the commune of Milan. *Royal Letters*, Henry III 2, 215.

signed otherwise than in chapter, in presence of the brotherhood.

This ordinance was accepted by both bishop and convent. Hostilities now ceased for the remainder of Savaric's life—both parties seem to have fulfilled their parts of the arrangement. Adam of Domerham has no further complaint to bring against Savaric—"he even showed himself gentle to all—he began to make many gifts, and he promised more." In compensation, he offered, and they accepted, the exchange of the manors of Kingston and Christian Malford for East Brent and Berrow. He voluntarily ceded the manor of Lyme, which had been the hereditary possession of the cook.

Savaric might well be content. He had won in a struggle of nine years. Having obtained the enforced concession of Richard, and pope Celestine's support, he had held to his claim against the open opposition of the king, the secret antagonism of archbishop Hubert, and the weight of adverse public opinion. John he had probably bribed. He had obtained terms from even Innocent III.

Peter of Blois, in writing to him, had represented to him the general opinion that he was striving for an impossibility in seeking to bring under one mitre bishopric and abbey, and that he need not be ashamed to fail in a contest in which no bishop could succeed.

The protests and appeals to Rome from all sides immediately after his death in favour of the abbey witness alike to the displeasure with which his policy was viewed, and to the extraordinary influence and tenacity of purpose by which Savaric had triumphed.

But the pacification of 1202 was obtained at the cost of much diplomacy and much money, in which both Savaric and the convent must have grievously suffered.

The revenues of the see must have been lavished among the lawyers and officials of the Roman chancellery. Savaric's debts were the subjects of epigrams at Rome, and we have evidence that they followed his successor in the see. A letter from the agents of the convent at Rome in the year preceding the award throws some light upon the expenses of the litigation to them—"the convent must pay their debts at Rome before they obtain their award—their agents had made themselves liable for a loan of 900 marcs, due to the money-lenders of Troyes"; the pope himself writes to the convent that their agents had incurred debts to the amount of 750 marcs, which must be paid to the Roman money-lenders before they can be allowed to depart. Martin de Summa and the brethren intimate to the convent that the pope himself will expect to be remunerated for his services to them.[1]

Savaric did not appear at Glastonbury at this time. He preferred the court of John to either of his bishop's seats, or to ruling over recalcitrant monks at Glastonbury. In the summer of 1199 he was with John in Normandy, during July, August, and September; then we lose sight of him. At one time he is in Flanders, where he refuses to receive the pope's letters, or treats them as forgeries.[2] At another time Innocent men-

Savaric's wanderings.

---

[1]. He says, "Summus pontifex pro ecclesiae nostrae impensis beneficiis remunerari voluerit et sub episcopo nihil recipere curaverit." Adam of Domerham, pp. 399, 404. There is another reading, "ab episcopo." These words have an ambiguous meaning.

[2]. Adam of Domerham, p. 406.

tions having seen him and received complaints from him at Rome of losses to the see during his predecessor's time.[1] He was at Rome probably in the winter of 1199.

During the spring and summer of 1200 John was in Normandy and Aquitaine, where, after his divorce, a second marriage was arranged with Isabella of Angoulême, and he returned for coronation at Westminster on October 8, 1200. Savaric was probably there, as he was certainly in England in October, and he was one of John's court at Lincoln on two memorable occasions in November.[2]

At Lincoln, November, A.D. 1200.

On Wednesday, November 22, William the Lion king of Scotland did homage to John, and Savaric was one of the attesting witnesses. On the Friday, the 24th, he assisted at the burial of Hugh bishop of Lincoln. During that autumn Hugh had paid his last visit to the homes of his youth in Burgundy, the family home at Avalon, and the Great Charterhouse from whence he had come so reluctantly to Witham. He had been taken ill on return to England, and died in his house in "the old Temple near London," on November 17.[3] Thence his body was brought down by stages and arrived at Lincoln on the afternoon of Thursday, November 23. There, unexpectedly to themselves, a large and profligate court were called upon to pay the world's last show of homage to the holy and humble of heart. The king of England, the king of Scotland,

At St. Hugh's burial.

---

1. R. 3, f. 262.
2. He can be traced at Gildeford, October 11, Leddibria (Ledbury), November 6, Upton 7, Feckenham 9, Lincoln 21-24, Geytenton 28.
3. *Vita S. Hugonis*, p. 331, "Proprium diversorium quòd secus Londonias apud vetus Templum possidebat."

the archbishops of Canterbury, Dublin, and Ragusa, fourteen bishops, a crowd of abbots, clergy, and barons met the procession outside the city.[1] The body was attended by the king and barons up the steep hill to the church porch: there it was received by the bishops and clergy and borne to its resting-place for the night before the high altar of the church. The next day, Friday, 24, St. Hugh was laid according to his last injunctions before the altar of the newly-finished chapel of St. John the Baptist, in the north transept of the choir.[2]

Reginald of Bath had been instrumental in bringing Hugh of Burgundy from his cell at the Great Charterhouse to Witham, and had helped and honoured Hugh in his work until he was removed to Lincoln. Now Savaric, Reginald's successor, connected also with Burgundy by birth and office, helped to bear St. Hugh the bishop to his grave at Lincoln.

This is the last appearance of Savaric in public life, as far as we can trace.

We must glance at the sequel of the quarrel with Glastonbury after Savaric's death.

The controversy, which had been set at rest for a time in 1202, broke out afresh immediately on Savaric's death in 1205. No sooner had he passed away than memorials were presented to the pope from all sides, praying for the restoration of the abbey to its former status. John was moved to write to Innocent, and to

---

1. *Vita S. Hugonis*, p. 370.
2. *Vita S. Hugonis*, p. 377. "Sepultus est sicut ipse nobis praeceperat secus parietem non procul ab altare Sancti Johannis Baptistae —a boreali ipsius aedis regione."

encourage petitions[1] throughout the kingdom in favour of the abbey, before the see was filled up.

In a short time, general petitions from the barons, from the bishops, abbots, and priors of England, from the churches of Norwich, Worcester, Sarum, from Abbotsbury and Muchelney, even from Bath and Wells, poured in, representing the evils which had ensued from the proceedings of Savaric, the scandal to the Church, the sufferings of the monks, the poor, and the stranger from the lack of means for alms and hospitality ; and praying for the dissolution of the union between the see and the convent.

The monks of Bath compare the harmony and prosperity of the see and of the abbey under Reginald with the discord caused by Savaric's policy, which, carried out without their assent, had generated quarrels, and tended to the impoverishment of the abbey and the sufferings of the poor and the stranger.

The canons of Wells, of whom Jocelin was one, deplore their disappointment with the fruits of Savaric's policy. They had hoped great things would result, but their church and the convent have alike greatly suffered.

The church of Worcester refers to the three persecutions of regulars in their time—at Canterbury, at Coventry, and at Glastonbury. Innocent had upheld the cause of the monks at the two former, they pray Innocent not to desert Glastonbury.

The monks of Muchelney, looking up to Glastonbury as their patron and protector, contrast the former

---

1. For these letters, vide Adam of Domerham, pp. 425, 437. John was at Glastonbury September 3, at Wells September 5, 1205

glory of the house with its present shame, and derision, and poverty. "What was the need that there should be three cathedral seats in so narrow a diocese, with expense and loss of social and religious unity?"

The church of Sarum laments the weakening of discipline and the loss of hospitality to the poor and stranger.

They all pray for the "reformation" of the great and ancient Benedictine house, and its restoration to former independence.

Innocent, unwilling to revoke so soon his own act and the concessions of his predecessor, yet evidently moved by the strength and unanimity of these petitions, could only evade a decision by declining to make any change during the vacancy of the see, and by giving permission to the convent to prosecute their appeal when the bishop was appointed.

In the decretals of Gregory IX, the answer of Innocent to the petition for a dissolution of the union is made the precedent on which a general canon of the Church is based, that "during the vacancy of a see nothing shall be changed."[1]

After a few months, in May 1206, Jocelin of Wells succeeded to the see. He had been one of Savaric's agents in the union, and whatever may have been the opinion of the chapter, he, personally, was unwilling that a policy carried out at such a cost should at once be abandoned without bearing some fruit. The disappointment of the monks vented itself in bitter invectives against Jocelin, as the successor of Savaric

---

1. *Gregorii Decretalia*, lib. iii, tit. ix, c. i. "Ne sede vacante aliquid innovetur."

in greed and guilt no less than in the see, and in complaints and appeals to Rome. War was again renewed, but Jocelin retained his hold on Glastonbury, and Innocent supported him. Innocent died in 1216. It was not until Honorius had succeeded Innocent that the court of Rome could decently reverse its policy. Honorius advised Jocelin to conciliate—terms were proposed by him, and finally arranged in a pacification at Shaftesbury, the octave of St. John the Evangelist 1218. The abbey obtained their freedom to elect their own abbot, and the union was dissolved, but the cession of four of their manors was the price they paid for independence.[1]

Jocelin retained the position of patron, intermediate between the Crown and the abbey, and therewith the patron's right of guarding the temporalities during vacancy, of granting *congé d'élire*, of confirmation of election, and of restoration of the temporalities, as well as the diocesan rights of benediction and of visitation. He was the holder of the fief immediately under the Crown, whereby he became responsible for the knights' service from the abbey to the Crown.

William was elected abbot by the convent on the day of St. Grimbald, 1219, and was presented to the bishop. On the vigil of the translation of St. Benedict, July 11, 1219, Jocelin as patron admitted and confirmed the abbot whom the convent had elected.

On the next day as diocesan he gave him the benediction.

On the morrow of St. Laurence, August 11, the

---

[1]. *Decree of Dissolution of Union*, by Honorius III, May 17, 1218. R. iii, ff. 263-265.

III.]   *Bishop Savaric,* A.D. 1192-1205.   117

bishop came to Glastonbury, and caused the seal of the convent to be put to the deed of concord.

" And so the monastery of Glastonbury, which had been deprived of the dignity of an abbey for twenty-six years, was restored through pope Honorius, although not altogether, yet to the former state of being under the government of its own abbot."[1]

There is no doubt it was a rude and sacrilegious hand which had seized upon the abbey, and succeeded in a bold invasion of the independence and exemption from jurisdiction of the great religious aristocracy, who had lived in security under the protection of royal charters and traditional reputation for sanctity.

But in justice to Savaric we must remember that the Glastonbury historians are scarcely less severe in their strictures afterwards upon Jocelin, the model bishop, for not surrendering the abbey. The aim was good, and some good result was obtained.

It was well to put a check upon the growing wealth and exorbitant pretensions to independence of the abbey, and to bring it into relation with the cathedral church.

Reginald had attempted to bring the abbot into the chapter of his church, and had given the direction which Savaric followed out with some degree of consistent policy towards the other religious houses in the diocese, and Jocelin was unwilling to relax the hold which Savaric obtained until terms were made which secured some degree of subordination on the part of

---

1. So Adam of Domerham, pp. 469-475, and John of Glastonbury, i, 208. But they still complain that the "jus patronatus" remained with the bishop.

the abbey. The *patronatus* of the abbey, which Jocelin at last secured to the bishop, placed the bishop as patron of Glastonbury, instead of the Crown, saved the abbey from the long vacancies which often took place under the Norman and Angevin kings, and gave some authority to the bishop in the appointment, and some right of visitation and jurisdiction. Later bishops reaped the benefit of Savaric's violent invasion.

Three years more remained before his death in 1205.

In this time we may bring together a notice of his relations with the rest of his diocese.

<small>Savaric at Bath; and at Wells.</small>
The register of the priory of Bath contains a scanty record of his gifts to the convent. The churches of Chew, and Weston, and Compton Dando,[1] are impropriated—two copes are given to the church. When the treasuries of all churches were being emptied to pay king Richard's ransom, Savaric had redeemed from pawn their vestments, crosses, and chalices ("ne conflarentur acquietavit)."[2]

The monks of Bath deserved well of him for their hasty zeal in electing him.

The chapter of Wells, notwithstanding their protest and opposition to his election, had stood by him and been his active agents in the struggle with Glastonbury. They received more.

His acts in the latter part of his life seem intended to make return to them; to secure their privileges and rights, and to increase their endowments by a few additional grants.

1. "Comptona Fulconis de Alneto"—Dando in Somerset. Dawnay in Wilts is the family name.
2. Vide *Reg. Prioratus Bathon.* in Lincoln's Inn Library, Appendix L.

The only charters which bear date belong to the years 1201 and 1203. The registers record confirmation of bishop Reginald's grant of the manors of Combe and of North Curry, of the church of Carhampton, and of the tithes of all mills on his manors. Additional grants are made of the churches of Lideard, of Pilton, and of the valuable manor of Wiveliscombe, given in commendation of "the true and laudable service of the canons, and with the desire to increase their insufficient endowments, and to remunerate their labours."[1]

Three more prebends were added, and at the same time important arrangements were made with other religious houses in the diocese—the church of Sutton was made a prebend and attached to the abbacy of Athelney, and Ilminster to that of Muchelney.[2] In the same way the abbot of Bec in Normandy after some controversy with Savaric held the church of Cleeve as his prebend in the church of Wells. These three abbots henceforth held stalls as non-resident canons in the church and chapter of Wells, and each supported a vicar, to whom they paid stipends to perform their duties.[3] A federal union with mutual share of privileges and prayers after death was established

---

1. R. i, f. 59. Cf. iii, f. 371. "Attendentes quam honeste et laudabiliter in ecclesia Wellensi Domino serviatur, communam eorum tenuem nimis et insufficientem invenimus," i, f. 37, i, f. 23.

2. This charter bears a date, "Actum apud Welles in praesentia venerabilis domini et patris Savarici in pleno capitulo ipsius ecclesiae anno 1201 in crastino beati Andreae apostoli."
R. i, f. 42, 49.
R. iii, f. 384. Sutton, R. i, f. 24, R. iii, f. 369.

3. R. iii, f. 381. The abbot of Bec paid 4 marcs yearly. Cf. Diceto, i, 16.

between the cathedral body and these brotherhoods. There is herein the appearance of a general policy of gathering the heads of the monasteries into the council of the bishop, and making the cathedral church the centre of the diocese.

Savaric appears to have been at Wells for the last time in 1203. By an act in chapter, dated the octave of St. Michael 1203, he exempted the prebends from the jurisdiction of the archdeacons.[1]

Another act, following next in the register, seems to indicate that the violent aggression of Savaric on the possessions of Glastonbury had been followed by invasion of the rights of the Wells chapter. Savaric, the invader of Glastonbury, in his turn now inveighs with indignation at the wickedness of some lay people who "at the instigation of the devil" had not feared to invade the possessions of the church of Wells, and he solemnly gives power to the chapter of Wells, in his absence, of excommunicating all such offenders.

The words of this charter anticipate an immediate and continued absence from his see, on account of urgent and distracting affairs requiring his presence in distant lands: "quia nos exigentibus negotiis interdum ad multa distrahimur, et praeter voluntatem nostram in locis remotioribus demoramur . . . . concessimus (ut non expectata praesentia nostra) liberam licentiam excommunicationis in eos sententiam promulgandi."

This charter of 1203 is the last notice in point of time of his presence at Wells. With these words, so characteristic of his erratic life and imperious disposition, he takes his leave of his see, bequeathing to the

[1] R. i, f. 28.

chapter of his cathedral church this power of excommunication as their weapon of defence against their enemies.

So Savaric, the "malleus monachorum," disappears from our sight. We know nothing of his last years, 1204-5, except his death in a foreign land at "Scienes la Vielle"[1] (either Siena or Civita Vecchia) on August 8, 1205, and his burial at Bath.[2]

There is no mention in the registers of any gifts made by Savaric towards the fabric of the church of Wells, or of work done by him.

Considering his long absence from the diocese, the heavy charges upon the revenues of the see in payment of Richard's ransom, and the expenses incurred at Rome by his litigation, it is not likely that Savaric should have been a builder of the church.

One charter there is, quoted in the foregoing chapter, the date of which has been assigned with probability to the year 1196, which contains a gift towards "the new work," and "the reparation of the chapel of the blessed Virgin." At that date, as we have seen, Savaric was abroad acting as chancellor of Burgundy to the emperor Henry. It is very doubtful whether he had been in his diocese since his consecration. If work was then going on, it is probable that the dean and canons were carrying out bishop Reginald's design. But the ransom of Richard, the prodigality of Savaric, and the troubles of his episcopate, would have crippled also the resources of the canons of Wells; and all

1. So Wharton. *A. S.* i, 563. Senes la Vieille = Civita Vecchia, *Glossary to Benedict*, ii, 114. Howd. iii, 40. Senes la Vieille, = Siena. *idem* ii, 229. Howd. iv, 25.
2. Godwin, p. 442, ed. Richardson.

building, both at Glastonbury and at Wells, was most probably suspended while the litigation was going on.

The weighty condemnation of Savaric's government followed quickly upon his death in the memorials to the papal see which have been quoted.

The lighter satire upon his life, by the wits of the Roman chancellery where he was so well known, appears in a gloss to that same canon in the decretals of Gregory IX, by which, as has been said, pope Innocent's decision in the Glastonbury appeal became a ruling precedent in canon law.[1]

Two sayings then current about him at Rome strike at his extravagance and debts, and at his restless and unsettled life.

His debts were so notorious, yet his English credit, it would appear, so good, that "one could make his prayer that he might have shares among the creditors of Savaric, whose name was legion."

One bill of Savaric's foreign debts still remains to us among the documents at Wells—a power of attorney granted by Speronus de Campomoldo, of Placentia, to Rufinus Molinarius to demand 87½ marcs from the bishop of Bath and Glastonbury, for which the late bishop Savaric had given security. This document, dated Monday, March 9, eighth indiction, A.D. 1219, in the "major ecclesia of Placentia," must have been presented to Jocelin soon after he had resigned the abbey.[2]

---

1. Gregory's *Decretals*, iii, tit. ix, c. 1. "De illo episcopo nomine Savarico dixit quidam alius, ' Domine me pone creditorem in legione, id est in societate multorum creditorum quos moriens reliquit episcopus.' "

2. Charter 24.

The other epigram on his wandering life Godwin has published as if it were the epitaph on his tomb at Bath.

> "*Hospes erat mundo per mundum semper eundo
> Sic suprema dies fit sibi prima quies.*"
>
> "*Through the world travelling, all the world's guest,
> His last day of life was his first day of rest.*"[1]

Savaric has hitherto only appeared as the ambitious and worldly prelate grasping at power. There are acts of his later episcopate which represent him in a different light, as seeking to make his peace with the world.

He was the first of the bishops of Wells who gave definite expression to that peculiar form of religious worship which was beginning to occupy such a disproportionate place in the services of the church, the *cultus* of the Blessed Virgin. He instituted a daily mass in the church of Wells in honour of the Blessed Virgin.[2]

He gives the first example of the fashion which became so common in the church of Wells, as everywhere, of making endowments to obtain intercessory prayers from the living for the dead, and so providing by requiem masses, obits, and chantries for a perpetual memorial of the donors.

He instituted a daily mass for his predecessors in the see, the benefactors to the church, and the faithful departed, with a payment of £10 a-year to the chaplain. By another charter[3] he made over to the canons the

---

1. Godwin de praesulibus, Lat. Ed. 1616. "Bathoniae sepultus cum epitaphio." He omits "the epitaph" in the English edition.

I take the opportunity of adding the admirable translation given to me by my friend and colleague chancellor Bernard, whose help, in many ways, I thankfully acknowledge.

2. R. i, f. 46.

3. R. i, f. 23, *in dors.*

church of Pilton, charged with the payment to two priests who were to celebrate daily for his soul and for his predecessors; and on his obit, or anniversary day, one hundred poor were to be fed, and distribution to be made to all who were present on the occasion.

We may read between the lines of this legal document the act of repentance and the would-be acts of expiation and atonement, according to the view of the worn-out man of the world and the popular theology of the time.[1]

In spite of much that must have offended Jocelin in the character and ways of Savaric, he appears to have found some good in him, for which he could in some way support his policy and follow his footsteps in his own episcopate.

One of bishop Jocelin's first acts was to institute, or confirm by a fresh ordinance, that the service of the Blessed Virgin should be daily sung in the church of Wells,[2] and that a requiem should be sung daily for bishop Savaric and all benefactors of the church 'in the chapel of St. Martin, near the font'—that chapel in the eastern aisle of the south transept, near to which still stands the ancient font, the only relic of the Norman or pre-Norman church.

In 1535 the sum of £6 8s. 4d. was still paid, according to bishop Jocelin's ordinance, for a daily mass, "missa de requiem jam vulgariter nuncupata ' Martyn's masse,'" on behalf of the souls of bishop Savaric, his successors, and all benefactors of the church.[3]

1. Vide Appendix M.
2. R. iii, 127, A.D. 1206, three priests, thirteen vicars to celebrate in turn.
3. *Wells MS. Ledger D.* f. 30. St. Martin's chapel has been used for long years as the "Canons' Vestry."

There is yet another charter of great local importance, as one of the series of charters by which the civil liberties of the borough of Wells were gradually enlarged by the concessions of its lords, the bishops of the see.

Savaric, following in the steps of Reginald, confirms to the citizens the earlier charters granting the freedom from tolls on markets held within the borough on certain days, and the right of the borough magistrates of trying causes not specially reserved for the courts of the lord.

One more fair-day was appointed by Savaric, the anniversary of the dedication of the chapel of St. Thomas the Martyr at the entrance to the town on the Glastonbury road, viz., the morrow of the festival of St. John the Baptist. This charter has a peculiar interest topographically, inasmuch as the boundaries of the borough are marked out by lines which are still traceable as nearly conterminous with the limits of the municipal borough of Wells of the present time.[1]

Following upon the charter of bishop Savaric is the first royal charter given to the borough of Wells, obtained through Savaric's favour with king John, who himself was a frequent visitor in Somerset, and to Wells and Glastonbury.[2] It confirms the previous charters of the bishops, and adds another fair-day by

---

[1]. Appendix N. This charter, and that of king John are carefully preserved among the city records in the town hall of Wells, and have been kindly lent to me by the Mayor and Council.

[2]. Vide *King John's Itinerary*. He was at Wells and Glastonbury, 1204, June 15, 17; 1205, Sept. 3, 5; 1207, Sept. 13; 1208, March 3, 4. *Archaeologia*, vol. xxii, pp. 138-9.

royal authority, viz., an eight days' fair on the "Translation of St. Andrew," May 7.[1]

It is pleasant to take leave of Savaric with the recollection that, whatever may have been his failings and shortcomings, his offences and scandals as a bishop, however little he may have added to the fabric of the church, he has taken his place in the civil history of Wells as one of "the first three" who, with Robert and Reginald, gave the start and direction to the growth and progress of the civil liberties of our borough of Wells.

1. Appendix O.

SEALS OF THE BOROUGH OF WELLS
13th century

CHAPTER IV.

Bishop Jocelin, A.D. 1206-1242.

PART I.

REGINALD and Savaric, bishops of Bath at the end of the twelfth century, were succeeded by Jocelin of Wells, 1206-1242.

In Jocelin we have the instance unique in the roll of the bishops of this see of a native, a "son of the soil," rising through all the grades and offices of the church to the bishopric, living at Wells through the greater part of a long and beneficent life, dying there, and buried among his own people. *Early life.*

There can be no doubt from the documents before us that, as Godwin truly says, "he was not only English, but of Wells also—wholly Wells." "Nec Anglus solum, verum Wellensis etiam, totus Wellensis."

The name Troteman found once only, in the annals of the church of Margam,[1] may have been the Saxon name of the family which was afterwards lost in the territorial name of the father Edward de Welles, after he had acquired lands and houses in

---

1. *Annales de Margam*, f. 29 (Rolls Series).

and about Wells.[1] These he left to his sons, who are described in the documents by no other names than "Hugh, son of Edward," "Hugh the heir," "Hugh of Wells," and "Jocelin, his brother." The family rose under bishop Reginald's favour, probably from small beginnings, for Hugh when bishop of Lincoln in after years did not forget in his will "his poor relations at Pilton and about Wells." We may

---

1. The family of bishop Jocelin can be traced in the documents of the time, *e.g.*—Charter 9.

Certificate by bishop Rainaud, that Walter Pistor of Bath had sold land at Lanferley, to Edward de Welles and to Hugh his heir for five marcs of silver.

The original grant made to Walter by the late bishop Robert had been burnt, and the fee is surrendered at the Hundred Court.

Witnesses: Ralph of Lechlade, archdeacon of Bath; Richard, archdeacon of Coutances; Robert of Geldeford; Robert of St. Lo (de Sancto Laudo); Joceline, chaplain; John of St. Lo; Godfrid the Frenchman, and others. Bishop Reginald was keeping up his connection with his uncle's diocese of Coutances.

Charter 10. Inspeximus of grant by Ralph de Wilton of all his land in Wells to Edward de Welles for ten shillings annually, and a present of fifty shillings, and to Wimarc his wife a gold brooch, and sixpence each to two of his sons. Witness to the original grant: Ralph of Lechlade; Alexander, subdean; Robert Fitzpane, sheriff of Sumerset. Witnesses to the Inspeximus: William of Welesley; Alexander, subdean; Jocelin, chaplain; Peter de Winton, Mathias de Winton, and others.

In other documents we find the names of Sarum dignitaries; *e.g.*, R. i, f. 36.

Agreement between bishop Reginald and William son of Richard of Melbury (Mauleberg) about seven acres near the wood of Wokiole, and a meadow of five acres near Poulesham, is witnessed by representatives of the Wells and Salisbury chapters; bishop Joceline of Sarum; Walter, the precentor of Sarum; Thomas, archdeacon of Wells; Baldwin, chancellor of Sarum; Ralph of Lechlade; Robert of Geldeford; Jocelin, chaplain; Stephen of Tor, canon of Wells, and others.

In another document, Charter 13, among the witnesses occur the names of Edward of Wells, Hugh son of Edward, Jocelin his brother, together with Alexander the dean, Thomas the subdean, William of Dinr (Dinder), William of Weleslia.

suppose the two brothers growing up on their father's land at Lancherley, about two miles south-west of Wells, attached to the household of the bishop, showing early abilities which qualified them to become by degrees leading judges, counsellors, statesmen, and bishops of their day, acquiring by office and legal practice, and by favour of king and bishop, riches and honours, grants of land and preferments in church and state.

Hugh, the elder, became archdeacon of Wells under Savaric; was made chancellor of England by king John, and was one of the custodians, for the crown, of the vacant see after Savaric's death, and bishop of Lincoln in 1209.

The register of the priory of Bath shows that Jocelin was early in the service of the convent, and owed his first preferment to the prior, as also doubtless to the influence of his elder brother, then archdeacon.

There are two charters from prior Robert (1198-1223) to Jocelin of Wells, attested by Hugh the archdeacon, the one granting Jocelin one hundred shillings a year until such time as he shall be provided with a benefice, the other granting to Jocelin his clerk, *clerico suo*, the church of Dogmersfield, saving twenty shillings in the name of pension to the said prior and convent.[1]

Jocelin appears in many Wells charters as chaplain to bishop Reginald and canon of Wells. He was also one of the judges in the King's Court before he was made bishop of Bath in 1206.

---

1. *Registrum Prioratus Bathoniæ*, Lincoln's Inn MS., part ii, p. 15. edited by Rev. W. Hunt for Somerset Record Society.

Hugh, heir and possessor of his father's lands about Wells, and receiving grants of manors from king John, which he made over afterwards to his brother Jocelin for the use of the church, divided his great wealth between Wells and his adopted Lincoln. Jocelin gave all he had received to Wells, the place "he loved so well," in which "he had been nourished from his infancy," where, as his fellow-canons attest before his election, "he had lived in all good conscience before them all his life hitherto."

Thus the two brothers, in a spirit of local patriotism and pious devotion which will compare with that of Florentine citizens and builders of Italian towns, became the makers of their native town.

Jocelin bishop by election of the two chapters of Bath and Wells.

The chapter registers give in very full detail the process of his election—a notable instance of free and unanimous election by the two chapters according to the rule followed in Reginald's case, but departed from in the hurried election of Savaric.

The letters of the two chapters bear highest testimony to Jocelin's character and especial fitness.

The Wells canons, in their letter to pope Innocent IV give a piteous account of the state of their church on Savaric's death; "deprived so long of the comfort of a ruler, tossed with storms and exposed to various oppressions and perils, by which both the property and the persons of the canons have greatly suffered," and they pray for the confirmation of the election of Jocelin so singularly fitted by his character and knowledge of affairs for the office of their bishop.

The instruments of his separate election by the two chapters of Bath and Wells are among the chapter manuscripts. They witness to his connection with the church of Wells from his earliest years, and his irreproachable character. "Cum in sinu ecclesiæ Wellensis a primo lacte coaluerit, et sine querela inter eos conversatus esset." We are familiar with his attestation to documents in Reginald's time, and he appears as a contemporary with Alexander the dean between 1180 and 1209.[1]

King John who was in person at Wells and Glastonbury in the month after Savaric's death, was made to know the unanimous choice of Jocelin, and wrote letters to the pope praying for speedy confirmation of the election.

His personal friends among the bishops, and at last all the bishops of the southern province, wrote letters testimonial to the pope praying for Jocelin's consecration.

It took place in the abbey church of St. Mary, Reading, May 12, 1206.

Consecration, A.D. 1206.

One discordant voice, while all men spoke well of him, arose from the monks of Glastonbury. Their hopes of independence must have been raised to the highest pitch by the strong petitions which were laid before John, even from the chapters of Bath and of Wells, as well as from other churches within and without the diocese, praying for the reformation of the abbey and restoration to former state of exemption from the jurisdiction of the bishop, by which even the king had been moved to join in the prayer to the pope

Glastonbury dissentient.

---

1. See the document and signatures in Part ii, under year 1205-6. The instrument of his election by the chapter of Bath with signatures of the monks is preserved among the Wells Charters; Charter Nos. 45, 46.

that these petitions should be favourably received. But they knew Jocelin as an active agent in carrying out Savaric's policy, and they had little hope of obtaining from him freedom from the concordat established in 1202. There is no sign that the monks were ever consulted as a chapter in the nomination of the bishop.

In the bitterness of their disappointment at Jocelin's election they pronounced him a fit successor of Savaric, not only in office, but in greed and guile. For several years political troubles, and the confiscation by the king of the property both of see and convent, were sufficient to put off all settlement of the controversy. There were also strong reasons urging Jocelin to keep hold of Glastonbury for a time at least, such as the desire of compensation to the see for debts incurred by Savaric in the contest with the abbey, which could be refunded out of the abbey revenues, and generally his sense of the need of restraint of the evils growing out of the independence of the abbey.

Jocelin, before Runnymede, had stood by the king, with Peter de Roches, Hubert de Burgh, and Marshall earl of Pembroke; and king John, notwithstanding a letter to the pope in favour of the abbey, throughout supported Jocelin, and in several deeds forbad the dissolution of the union without his sanction.[1] So Jocelin was biding his time, and making his terms, and, probably in anticipation of surrender of the abbey, he obtained in 1215 from king John, as the monks alleged by purchase, the patronship or protectorate *(jus patronatus)*

---

[1]. *Royal Letters, Henry III* (Rolls Series). Ed. Shirley. Pref. xviii.

of the abbey.[1] With this he obtained the rights which had belonged to the crown, of custody of the abbey during vacancy, of granting the *congé d'élire*, and confirming the election of the abbot, and he was enabled to exercise more freely his jurisdiction in the visitation of the monastery.

But when, under the pontificate of Honorius, the papal court took up the cause of the abbey, Jocelin withdrew from Glastonbury, having secured these ends in some measure, and intent on making Wells his home, and the centre of the diocese.

Jocelin's episcopate admits of two main divisions in time—*(a)* from 1206 to 1219—*(b)* from 1220 to 1242.

Jocelin's episcopate.

In the first he laid out his plans and entered on his work, occupied and harassed by the political troubles in the kingdom and by the quarrel with Glastonbury. The local records say comparatively little of these years.

Soon after his consecration he was swept into the current of civil strife. Though a friend and favourite of king John he accepted the suzerainty of the pope as a check to the king's wayward tyranny: he obeyed the pope's order to publish the interdict, and then fled the kingdom in 1208.

He was abroad about five years. We can trace him in the neighbourhood of Bourdeaux in the year 1211.[2] He may also have been in Spain. Eleanor daughter of Henry II, and sister of John, was married to Alfonso, king of Castile, and he may have visited her. The traveller is shown among the archives of the cathedral of Siguenza,[3] a contemporary account of the

1. See Part ii, under 1214.
2. *Ibid.*, 1211.
3. Dr. Edwin Freshfield, F.S.A., has kindly so written to me.

murder of St. Thomas, given to the church by an English bishop Jocelin, about this time.

Joined by his brother Hugh he remained in exile until the bishops were admitted to peace by the king in 1213. He was by the side of the archbishop, Stephen Langton, when the great charter was forced from John in 1215. Then came the civil war and the death of both king John and of pope Innocent in 1216.

Jocelin was at the coronation of the young king Henry III by the legate Gualo at Gloucester, October 28, 1216, and he it was who administered the oath to the king.

With the new pope Honorius III, the controversy with Glastonbury took a new turn. Honorius advised pacification, and finally the union between the see and the convent was dissolved by Honorius, May 17, 1219.[1]

Jocelin, giving up the abbacy and the title of "bishop of Bath and Glastonbury" retained the rights of patron, and possession of four of the manors of the convent.

It is clear that in the first years of his episcopate he had planned and set on foot much of his work at Wells, and that he had matured during exile arrangements for reform of offices in the cathedral church.[2]

Jocelin at Wells, A.D 1220. About 1220 he had settled himself down at Wells for the remainder of his time.

The year 1220 is marked as a memorable year in England in ecclesiastical matters.

---

1. Adam of Domerham, p. 474, thus definitely gives the date: "XVI° Kal. Junii, Indictione. VII. Incarnacionis dominicae anno M°.CC°. nonodecimo, Pontificatus vero Domini Honorii papae. III anno tercio."

2. Part ii, under year 1209.

The register of the church of Salisbury commemorates three events of the year :
- (*a.*) The foundations of the new church of Salisbury were laid April 28th ;
- (*b.*) At Pentecost the young king Henry III was crowned a second time at Westminster ;
- (*c.*) The translation of Saint Thomas of Canterbury, on July 7, was kept as a national festival with extraordinary pomp.

The Wells registers mark the commencement of a new era of computation. The years are dated from the " Translation of St. Thomas."

It was also the year of the canonization of Saint Hugh of Lincoln, on February 17.

Henceforward Jocelin devoted himself to the work of perfecting the cathedral system at Wells. The undisguised jealousy and hostility of the great Benedictine houses at Bath and Glastonbury made it important to build up Wells as the centre of the diocese, to unite more closely the diocese with the cathedral church, and to give greater strength and dignity to the chapter of secular canons.

It is significant that the first act in the register under the year 1220 was the synod of the diocese at Bath, at which the question arose as to the right of precedency of the prior of Bath or the dean of Wells on the right hand of the bishop. It was decided in favour of the prior, but with the expressed proviso that the church of Wells shall not suffer thereby any loss of jurisdiction or authority.

Interest and illustration is thrown upon Jocelin's work by consideration of what was going on at Salisbury at the same time.

There also two brothers, Herbert and Richard Poore, bishops in succession from 1194 to 1228, were working together for the rebuilding of their church, and for the improvement and due ordering of the cathedral body. In 1214 important cathedral statutes were embodied in the document called by them the "nova constitutio," in which, among other things, acts relating to the residence of the canons, the apportionment of the fruits of a prebend on vacancies, the visitation of prebends by the dean, the dress and demeanour of clerks in choir, and the condition of the vicars choral, were passed.[1]

In 1220 the foundations of the new church of Salisbury were laid, and in 1225 the building of the east end was so far advanced that the high altar to the Holy Trinity, and the altars in the east ends of the north and south aisles to St. Peter and St. Stephen, were consecrated, and on the next day, the feast of St. Michael, the bishop entered the new basilica, and therein solemnly celebrated the divine offices.[2] Jocelin was present on this occasion at Salisbury.

Jocelin had inherited the constitution of his church from his predecessors, Reginald and Robert. He had been observing the work, and sharing in councils, and taking part in the duties of the church under bishop Reginald from his youth, and now, as soon as he was free to give himself up to the diocese, he carried out plans of ritual, of building, and of organisation which had doubtless been long maturing and prepared.

1. Osm. Reg. i, 379. (Rolls Series).
2. Osm. Reg. ii, 39.

By one of his first acts, early in 1207, he had instituted and endowed the daily mass to the Blessed Virgin, to be celebrated with increased devotion by three priests and ten vicars. He still further endowed this service at the altar of the Blessed Virgin in 1215, and again in 1239.[1]

Lady mass re-endowed.

His elder brother Hugh was a zealous co-operator in his plans for building and reorganising.

An early draft of the will of Hugh of Wells in the year 1211, when in exile with Jocelin, shows that thoughts and plans for their church and town were at that time in the mind of the two brothers.[2]

Hugh therein devises 300 marcs towards the fabric the church of Wells, and an equal sum to the church of Lincoln; a larger sum (500 marcs) to a hospital to be built at Wells, and other sums to the *communa* of the canons, and to the vicars.

The hospital[3] afterwards built, and dedicated to St. John the Baptist, was intended for the poor and wayfarers, but with special intention at first for the *cruce signati*, those who had taken upon themselves the cross, or had returned from the Crusades. It was in the course of erection in 1221, and then received from

Priory of St. John the Baptist.

---

1. Part ii, under years 1206, 1215, 1239.
2. *Ibid.*, 1211.
3. "A customary appanage to a bishop's headquarters, which Wells hitherto had lacked. I cannot think that the primary and permanent object of the Hospital of St. John was other than that of similar institutions found, I believe, in *every* cathedral city, viz. the discharge of Christian hospitality to the wayfarer who from risk of disease and certainty of filth could not be relieved at the bishop's gate. The reception of *cruce signati* was a temporary yielding to a temporary demand, and lasted only one generation." Note by bishop Hobhouse.

bishop Jocelin its constitution and a grant of cemetery and bells and chapel, which the chapter confirmed.

Park enclosed. In 1207 we may conjecture that he had begun the palace on the south side of the church. We have evidence that the park on that side of the city was in course of formation. In that year Jocelin obtained two charters from king John.

> (*a.*) The first charter, dated from Harpetre, September 16, in the ninth year of the reign, 1207, gave Jocelin licence to impark land at the south side of the town of Wells, and all those woods being and growing on the south side of the town, with all the liberties and privileges belonging to parks, taking thence what timber he wanted for his own use, and to divert the way which runs through the wood in the middle of it.
>
> (*b.*) The other, dated November in the same year, from Marlborough, supplements this licence by granting leave to include two roads in the park: (*a*) one road running across the park under Tor Hill towards Dultingcote, which he diverted to its present line; (*b*) another through Keward towards Coxley. He was to give up land equivalent outside the park for the public road.[1]

These localities mentioned can be clearly identified. The charters give the right of closing roads at the two borders of the park, east and west, and through the midway, and establish the complete privacy of the bishop's demesne.

1. Part ii—under years named.

(c.) About 1221 the park was more widely extended by exchanges of land at Stobery and Beril and Horrington with the lord of the Glastonbury manor of Downhead, Walter de Downhead, for five acres of meadow in the valley on the south, and towards Keward.

The Close Rolls show that at this time Jocelin was receiving charters giving him licence to cut timber and to stock his park with deer from the king's forests of Cheddar and Selwood,[1] and that he was bringing into cultivation land on Mendip, and getting lead and making iron out of the ore which he had permission to dig.[2]

In 1224 (8 Hen. III) he had licence from the king to bring wood from Cheddar forest "to repair his houses at Wokey."[3]

So that to this time the works upon the palace, and the chapel of the palace, and the manor-house, with its chapel at Wookey, ascribed to him by the canon of Wells, may with probability be assigned.

The dignities and offices of the church had been constituted before his time, and here, as at Salisbury, the vicars choral had been in existence as part of the ministrant body of the cathedral church. *Dignities and offices reconstituted*

It is apparent that his aim was to reconstitute all these offices, and to give greater definiteness to duties, and fuller endowments to all who served the church.

The records tell that when in foreign parts, "in partibus transmarinis," in exile between 1208 and 1213,

1. Close Rolls, 5 Hen. III, 15 Hen. III.
2. *Ibid.*, 19 Hen. III.
3. "Decem frusta ad domos suas de Woky reparandas."

he had designed the remodelling of the dignities of dean, precentor, and chancellor.[1]

After his return he made, in 1216, additional and very precise ordinances for the election of the dean.[2]

In 1221 a very full and special ordinance is made with regard to the treasurer's office, containing—

- (*a.*) A change of its endowment from Evercreech rectory to that of Martock.
- (*b.*) A precise description of the duties of that office, so necessary for the newly-arranged ceremonial of the rising fabric.[3]

Later in his time, in 1237, a change was made in the older arrangement between the dean and sub-dean, by which the prebend of the sub-dean was transferred to Wookey, and the dean took the church of Wedmore. At the same time conflicting relations between the offices of the dean and sub-dean formed the subject of new regulations.[4]

Houses for the canons. Houses were provided for the canons resident, by the purchase and gift of individual members of the chapter and others, and the formation of the " Liberty " began.

The positions of these lands and houses so granted are marked out with much precision on the north side of the church, in relation to the existing *area canonicorum* (probably the present cathedral green) and the *magna porta canonicorum,* the entrance to the church, the " Great Porch," on the north side of the church.

1. Part ii. See under years named 1209, 1216, 1221, 1226.
2. *Ibid.* 1216. R. i, f. 133.
3. *Ibid.* 1221.
4. *Ibid.* 1237.

The north side of the church was the quarter where mostly the houses for the dean and dignitaries of the church were placed, and the portions of ground described now gradually extended northwards and adjoined land which bore the name of "Muntoria" and "Muntorey." Here, afterwards, a college of chantry priests was established by bishop Erghum in 1400, and the name became in later times Mont Roy.

These houses, purchased by individuals and given to the church and the bishop for the perpetual residence of canons, were freed by the bishop from all "secular exactions," town dues or borough jurisdiction, and formed the northern quarter of the "Liberty" in the precincts of the cathedral church. The growth of the Liberty[1] is traceable in the records of 1207, 1219, 1228, 1234, 1236.[2]

The existence of schools in Jocelin's time deserves a more particular notice. In 1236 by a deed of some solemnity Thomas Lock, son of Adam Lock, *cementarius* (bishop Jocelin's master builder presumably), with the written consent, by charter, of his mother and his father's executors, makes over lands in "La Mountereye" to the chaplain of the bishop and he to the church of St. Andrew, and to the chancellor, for the use and endowment of schools. The master of the schools is to have a house, and he is to keep the buildings in order, and they are to be inspected once

Schools.

---

1. "Liberty," a privileged area freed from some liabilities; in this case from those of the borough and parish. A lane called "Canons' Walk" ran from opposite the north porch of the church to the North Liberty nearly opposite the "Canons' Barn," and on the west side of the present Vicars' Close.

2. Part ii, under those years.

a year by the chancellor and other canons. The master and scholars are to be present at the anniversary services for Roger the chaplain, and to pray for his soul; and every Wednesday and Friday the scholars are to sing an antiphon in honour of the Blessed Virgin at the school.[1] These schools in the Muntory are named in later records as "scholæ grammaticales," different from the school of the choristers. The "domus choristarum" was on the west of the cloister.

A charter of the date of 1213 may imply the earlier existence of schools under Jocelin's supervision at that time.[2]

Prebends. The number of prebends left by Reginald at thirty-five, and increased under Savaric by the three assigned to the abbots of Bec Muchelney and Athelney, was now under Jocelin raised to fifty or more by the division of the large manor of Combe into fifteen prebends and the addition of Wiveliscombe and others.

Vicars choral. The vicars choral not yet incorporated, but supported for the most part by their several masters among the canons whose places they served, and by a charge laid on the prebends as stall wages, now received regular "quotidians" or grants of daily supplies of bread, which were increased and changed into money-payments in the last years of Jocelin's life.[3]

Vicarages. The formation of perpetual vicarages was carefully enforced by Jocelin, requiring a fixed charge and a division of tithes to be made by those holding the rectories, to whom the churches were impropriated.

1. Charter 30. R. i, f. 33. "Domus in usum scholarum."
2. Part ii, under 1213 and letter of pope Innocent III, to bishop Jocelin, in Charter 20.
3. Part ii. under 1234, 1239, 1241.

It had been throughout an object to him of great solicitude to augment the common fund of the chapter.

In the last years of his life, he made gifts to the chapter of the manors of Cheddar, North Curry, and Winscombe, and the advowsons of Congresbury, Mudford, Lideard, Winscombe, and St. Cuthbert's of Wells. By substituting money for the quotidians of bread to all members of the ministrant body in the church, and increasing the scale of payments, conditional on the fulfilment of allotted periods of residence, he left a permanent legacy to the church and established a claim to the gratitude of succeeding generations.[1]

Grants to the communa.

So far in all this, it is to be observed that Jocelin was not the creator of the constitution or of the order and gradation of the several offices of the church. But he was re-organising, reforming, and expanding the system under which he had grown up, with statesmanlike purpose and wise adaptation to the needs of the time. And he gave such a fresh spirit and life to the church, and so left the impress of his master-hand by the finishing strokes to the work of his predecessors, that his name is connected with the whole ordering and constitution of the church of Wells of the thirteenth century.

The question arises what was the style of the bishop in Jocelin's time?

The title of the see.

Jocelin of Wells has generally been styled by later writers, "bishop of Bath and Wells:"[2] they have

1. Part ii, under year 1242.
2. As an exception v. p. 49 of the *Diocesan History of Bath and Wells*, S.P.C.K. 1885, and the *Genealogist*, July and October, 1885.

followed therein the printed works of Godwin and Wharton.

Godwin, in his catalogue of the bishops, says of Jocelin, that after giving up Glastonbury he resumed the title of bishop of Bath and Wells; "stilum repetiit a duobus antecessoribus (Roberto et Reginaldo) usurpatum; dictus jam posthac, non Glastoniensis (sicut primis consecrationis annis) sed Bathoniensis et Wellensis Episcopus; quo etiam omnes deinceps successores constanter usi sunt."

Wharton repeats the statement, and supports it by alleging the authority of a charter of bishop Robert.[1]

But Archer, in his *Chronicon*, writing about 1726, exposes the mistakes by which Godwin had misled others. He corrects Wharton as to the alleged charter of bishop Robert, by which the relation between the two sees was supposed to be arranged: he shows that the charter, which Wharton has quoted, does not exist, and that there is no evidence of the assumption of the title of Bath *and Wells* earlier than the date of Jocelin's successor in 1244-5. Archer says: "The canon of Wells, and Godwin, and even Wharton himself, are not clear on this subject, for not one of the bishops is styled of '*Bath and Wells*' from the first translation of the see by John of Tours until the year 1244. Then first of all the bishops, Roger, who succeeded Jocelin, took his title from both the churches; but all the others held the title of bishop of Bath alone, with the exception of Savaric, who, after he had procured the union of the

---

1. (V. *Anglia Sacra* i, 563, and note *t*, p. 561, ed. 1691) "exstat compositio in Registro *Drokensford*: quam ante annum 1139 initam esse constat."

abbey of Glastonbury to the see of Bath, called himself 'of Bath and Glastonbury.'"[1]

How is it to be accounted for that Jocelin never took the title of Bath and Wells? One can only suppose that he was unwilling to incur the jealousy of the Bath chapter. He inherited from his predecessor Savaric the title of "Bishop of Bath and Glastonbury," but he did not use it consistently. Sometimes his name appears in deeds and attestations with this double title, sometimes with that of "Bath" alone, but never with the title of "Bath and Wells."

It is manifest that Bath, the *sedes praesulea*, the *mater ecclesia* since 1091—the seat of the ancient abbey —the important city, *civitas Bathoniensis*—was most jealous of the rising ascendancy of Wells, under Robert, Reginald, and Jocelin. Jocelin made Wells to be in reality the chief seat of the bishop, and when forced to drop the title of "Glastonbury," he had expressed to the pope Honorius a desire to have compensation for that loss by being permitted to add "Wells" to his style;[2] yet he never did assume it;

---

[1] "When Wharton says that the record of a convention of 1136 to this effect exists in the Register of bishop Drokensford, the illustrious author falls into an error by confounding with it another charter of bishop Robert not to the point, viz. the charter 'de decanatu,' which is attested by the same witnesses set out by Wharton, one of whom is William archbishop of Canterbury, who died 1136."
Archer, *Chronicon Wellense*, f. 29. "De decanatu" is a later marginal insertion on the charter "de ordinatione prebendarum."

[2] Vide letter of Honorius III to Pandulf the legate. He bids that the register be searched, and if it be found that Wells be the ancient *sedes praesulea* to give permission to Jocelin to assume the title. "Viterbii, iv, Kal. April. pontificatus anno quarto, 1220." Vatican Transcripts, Ep. 679. Pandulf had other things to do.

and in his own documents and seal he calls himself to the last *Jocelinus Episcopus Bathoniensis*.[1]

The prerogative of Bath was formally acknowledged at a diocesan synod held at Bath in 1220, when the right of precedence was in question, and the prior of Bath was adjudged the seat at the right hand of the bishop, rather than the dean of Wells. Bath obtained precedence in form and title; but, notwithstanding, the ascendancy of Wells was being established, to the annoyance of the Bath chapter. The chapter of Bath made a bold attempt to establish their supremacy, to the exclusion of Wells, in the election of Jocelin's successor. Their diplomacy at the Roman Court, which involved them in ruinous expense, obtained a confirmation of their election, and an empty acknowledgment of priority of title, but the enforcement by order of Innocent IV, that the full title of *Bath and Wells* should henceforth be inscribed on the seal of bishop Roger and his successors.[2]

The Fabric in Jocelin's time.

Original documents now enable us to fix certain historical landmarks of time within which the fabric of the church was built, down to the end of bishop Jocelin's life.

The first portion of the church was built and conse-

---

1. See Part ii, anno 1214. Jocelin's seal of dignity bears his effigy, with the marginal legend: ✠ IOSCΛLINVS : DΛI : GRATIA | BAThONIΛNSIS : ΛPISCOPUS. His counterseal has Our Lady and Child sitting on a seat which is supported by St. Andrew and St. Peter; in base under a trefoiled arch is the bishop praying. The legend is: ± : ḣII : TIBI : PATRONI : SINT : IOSCΛLINΛ : BONI. Seals of the bishops. Plate 1.

2. Pope Innocent's Letter, Lyons, May 12, 1245. Vide Letters in Vatican Transcripts in British Museum, Add. MSS. 15353, vol. v, p. 235. Cf. R. i, ff. 93-96.

crated in or before 1148; within the time contemporary with bishop Roger of Salisbury, the builder of Malmesbury, and with Henry of Blois abbot, and builder at Glastonbury, bishop of Winchester, and builder of St. Cross.

Bishop Reginald carried on the work between 1174 and 1191, while William of Sens, and William the Englishman were building at Canterbury, and while the rebuilding of Glastonbury after the fire of 1184 was going on.

Between the years 1206—1242 bishop Jocelin repaired, enlarged, completed, and consecrated the church anew; while, at the same time, the neighbouring church of Salisbury was rising from its new foundation in 1220, and his brother Hugh was at work on the church of Lincoln.

There could have been little building going on at Wells at the beginning of Jocelin's episcopate. The political troubles, the interdict upon the kingdom, and Jocelin's exile from 1208 to 1213, when the revenues of the see were seized by the crown, the struggle with Glastonbury until 1219, were causes sufficient to check any building upon the church. Not until after Jocelin's return from exile in 1213, not until after the final concord had been made with Glastonbury, August 11, 1219, could Jocelin have begun the completion of works left unfinished more than twenty years before, and the repair of older parts which were suffering from longer periods of dilapidation.

When we search for documentary evidence of building during Jocelin's episcopate, we are disappointed at finding so little. One charter belonging to the years

1217—1220, shows that some work was going on at least within those dates.

When Ralph of Lechlade was dean under Jocelin, 1217-1220, Alexander a canon gave for his life the produce of the arable land of the rectorial glebe at Henstridge, half his meadow in Ridgehill and pasture adjacent, and one silver marc from the altarage of Henstridge, to dean Ralph and the chapter of St. Andrew in Wells for the fabric of the church, "ut fabrica celerius ad optatam consummationem mea sedulitate consurgat." He gives this in lieu of the sum assessed upon his prebend by the chapter; and it is to be paid quarterly into the hands of the canons who had charge of the fabric.[1]

We gather from this charter that an assessment had been levied upon the canons for the fabric at this time, that Jocelin had begun to rebuild, and that voluntary offerings over and above the assessment were being made, in this instance at least, to promote and hasten the work.[2]

Beyond this charter we have very little documentary evidence about the fabric in Jocelin's time before the year 1239.

Outside our documents there are other evidences of building operations. The Close Rolls of Henry III[3] contain grants to the fabric in 1220, of sixty large oaks, *grossa robora*, from the forest of Cheddar; in 1224, of one penny a day remitted from the rent of Congresbury manor, "ad operationem ecclesiæ Wellensis"; in 1225,

1. R. i, f. 21; iii, f. 383.
2. The levy of one fifth by Jocelin is referred to as a precedent in 1248. R. i, f. 69.
3. Rot. Lit. Claus. pp. 425, 583, 595.

of five marcs annually for twelve years; in 1226, of thirty oaks "for the fabric of the church of Wells"; and of smaller wood, *frusta*, to repair the bishop's house at Wookey.

We can understand how the work taken up after 1219 would go on and increase under favouring circumstances. After the composition with Glastonbury in 1219 the see was enriched by the ceded manors of the abbey. Bishop Hugh of Lincoln, brother of bishop Jocelin, was making gifts of manors and advowsons to the see, and perhaps other gifts, such as that of Alexander of Henstridge, were enriching the see, which had been poor and impoverished between 1196 and 1219; and Jocelin was enabled to bring to completion his work of twenty years by consecration in 1239, and then to go on to augment the endowments of the church.

There had been so much built and renewed by Reginald and by Jocelin since the consecration by Robert, in 1148, that reconsecration was necessary.

Consecration, A.D. 1239.

The bishop mentions the consecration of the church twice in the introduction and preamble to two charters given to the church about this time. In the year 1239, in a charter confirming to the chapter the manor and church of Winscombe, given "on the morrow of St. Romanus," he thus states the fact of the consecration.

"Omnibus Christi fidelibus ad quos praesens carta pervenerit Jocelinus Dei gratia Bathon. episcopus, salutem in Domino.

"Noveritis nos in dedicatione ecclesiae nostrae Wellensis quam die Sancti Romani mense Novembris anno Incarnationis Dominicae 1239, in honorem Sancti Andreae Apostolorum mitissimi dedicavimus, dedisse et concessisse et hac presenti carta confirmasse pro nobis et successoribus nostris in dotem ejusdem ecclesiae nostrae, et decano et capitulo nostro Wellensi, manerium de Wynescumbe.

"In cujus rei robur et testimonium datum Welliae in crastino Sancti Romani anno Incarnationis Dominicae 1239, et pontificatus nostri anno xxxiv." [1]

In the next charter, three years later, his words record that having done his work as builder of the fabric, he was now bent upon increasing the endowment of the ministrant body.

Increase of endowments

In the last year of his life (1242) he increased the "quotidians," the daily apportionment of the common fund of the canons, and made ampler provision for the maintenance of every member of the cathedral staff:

"Omnibus Christi fidelibus praesens scriptum visuris

---

1. There is a curious variation in the date of the day of consecration. The bishop himself fixes the date as "the day of St. Romanus, in the month of November."

Matthew Paris, iii, 638 (Rolls Series) names the day of St. Romanus as the day of consecration, but fixes the date as August 9,—"quinto idus Augusti die scilicet S. Romani"—*i.e.* the day of St. Romanus, martyr. The day of St. Romanus, confessor and bishop, archbishop of Rouen, in the Sarum Calendar, is October 23. In the Calendar of the Leofric Missal of the latter part of the tenth century November 18 is marked as the day of St. Romanus. "Passio Sancti Romani."

The same day, November 18, is marked in the calendar of the church of Milan as the day of St. Romanus, martyr, of Antioch. There is no mention of St. Romanus in the later Roman Calendar. Did Jocelin consecrate the church on October 23 or November 18? It is an interesting question whether the day of our dedication feast should be October 23, according to the Sarum use, or November 18, following the earlier Ambrosian and Lotharingian Calendars. Godwin assumes that October 23, the day of St. Romanus, bishop and confessor, was the day of consecration—if so, Jocelin, when he wrote "mense Novembris" must have meant the tenth of the kalends of November, an inexact and unusual method of computation.

vel audituris Jocelinus Dei gratia Bathoniensis episcopus salutem in Domino.

"Postquam ad episcopatus officium nos promoveri permisit altissimus, omne studium adhibuimus et adhuc adhibemus, ut cultus divini nominis et decus ecclesiae nobis commissae temporibus nostris cumuletur et amplietur; quicquid ad dispositionem, utilitatem, et ornatum ipsius ecclesiae respiciat semper cogitantes, et ad effectum pro viribus nostris deducere festinantes, ecclesiam Sancti Andreae Wellensis quae periculum ruinae patiebatur prae sua vetustate, cui, Jesu Christo Salvatore nostro permittente presidemus, ipsius auxilium invocantes aedificare caepimus et ampliare; in quâ de sola sua gratia adeo profecimus quod ipsam divinis precibus et sacris unctionibus, cum altaribus, vasibus, vestimentis et reliquiis ad divinum cultum explendum in eadem devote solempniterque consecravimus. Et quia ecclesias aedificantibus non solum de aedificio ipsiusque consecratione cogitandum est verum etiam de ministrantium alimentis, &c." . . . and then he passes on to the subject of the "quotidians": "Acta in capitulo Wellensi sextodecimo Kal. Nov. anno Incarnationis domini nostri Jesu Christi Mill° cc°. xlii. (1242) et pontificatus nostri tricesimo septimo."

This charter is sealed by the bishop and the dean John Saracenus.

The words describe the completion of the work which Jocelin had undertaken by the repair and enlargement of the church which he found unfinished, old and ruinous in parts, and suffering from neglect and dilapidations of time. They occur in the preamble to a charter relating mainly to another subject, the increase of the endowments yet remaining to be done. So the words are general and not precise in their review of what has been done. And when read in connection with bishop Reginald's words and acts, and with the history of the time intervening between Reginald and Jocelin, they ought not to be wrested into the assumption of a claim on the part of Jocelin, that he was the rebuilder of the whole church.

Reconsecration was necessary from the changes and additions which had been made both by Reginald and Jocelin since bishop Robert's consecration, nearly one hundred years before, in 1148; and it was enforced by the orders of the papal legate, according to which several other churches were consecrated about the same time.

The state of dilapidation and partial ruin in which Jocelin says he found the church might well have been the effects of some twenty or thirty years of neglect of an unfinished building, in such times, under the wasteful episcopate of Savaric, the confiscation of king John, the civil war, the intolerable exactions of papal legates, and the local quarrels with the great rival power at Glastonbury going on to 1218-19.

One more document completes the contemporary history of the fabric at the death of Jocelin. It implies that the buildings were completed according to Jocelin's plans at his death.

Jocelin died November 19, 1242.

Arrangement of burial grounds.

No arrangements had hitherto been carried out for the burial ground outside the church; but now, when the building on the west and south sides was completed, the ground was laid out around the newly-consecrated building by a statute of chapter passed on July 9, 1243, during the vacancy of the see, probably in accordance with Jocelin's provision and ordinance.[1]

"1243. Jul. 9 Die Jovis proxime post translationem beati S. [Thomae][2] deliberatum est de sepultura Willelmi de Chiue (Chew) canonici ; statutum est inde ut de caetero canonici residentes sepeliantur in claustro per ordinem secundum dignitatem ordinis et conditionis, ita quod majores minoribus proponantur [nisi forte sepulturas alibi vel in ecclesia vel extra designaverant in vita sua][3] et ut incipiat sepultura eorum ad ostium ecclesiae versus austrum, adeo prope sicut fieri poterit, et ut extendet se usque ad angulum claustri directe et sic deinceps ; cautum est etiam ut nullus laicus vel vicarius sepeliatur inter eos, sed vicarii sepeliantur in caemeterio versus orientem retro capellam beatae Mariae [et alibi in caemeterio] laici vero in caemeterio versus occidentem et incipiat sepultura eorum juxta hulmos ibi plantatos juxta locum illum ubi consuevit esse Hastillaria et sic extendet se versus occidentem—ita quod de caetero nullus laicus sepeliatur ante ostia ecclesiae versus occidentem—majores autem personae de ecclesia sepeliantur in nave ecclesiae si voluerint ipsi, vel amici eorum. Predicta statuta sunt de canonicis nisi in vita sua de corporibus suis aliter ordinaverunt."

This charter gives evidence that the church was considered finished at the time of Jocelin's death, so

1. R. i, f. 64, *in dors.*
2. Partially erased.
3. In a later hand.

that the ground on the west and south could be laid out for burial ground. The door of the newly-constructed west front opened out on the burial ground kept inviolate from markets since bishop Robert's order a century before, and now become the lay burial ground. The south-west portal led out to the cloister girt about with walls, and to the burial ground of the canons. East of the eastern walk of the cloister was a chapel of St. Mary and the burial ground of the vicars.

The church of the time of Jocelin was finished.

It had been the work of the earlier builders to raise the stately porch at the northern side of the church, the great " Porch of the Canons" *magna porta canonicorum*, opposite the houses of the canons which clustered on that side of the church.

It was Jocelin's work to raise the southern doors, rich with Early English tracery leading into the cloisters and the cemetery which was the last resting place of the canons, and leading outward to the palace ground on which he was building.

These contemporary documents supply links in the chain of the history of the fabric which have hitherto been wanting. They place in due relation the several workers in the great fabric. They enable us to correct the traditions of later writers, who ascribed all the work to one great benefactor.

Judgments have been swayed by deference to the supposed authority of the printed statements of the Canon of Wells and Godwin.

It is time that we were set free from subjection to those authorities as decisive on this period of the architectural history of the church.

The Canon of Wells, writing of Jocelin, says: "Ipsamque Ecclesiam vetustatis ruinis enormiter deformatam prostravit, et a pavimentis erexit dedicavitque."

This is the description of a building allowed to fall into shapeless ruin, *enormiter deformatam*, by a century of neglect and decay.

The rebuilding of the whole church is attributed to Jocelin, from pavement to vault, "prostravit et a pavimentis erexit."

Bishop Godwin enlarges upon the text of the Canon, and describes, with more pretention to exactness, Jocelin's work.

In the English edition he says:

"Moreover, in building he bestowed inestimable summes of money. He built a stately chappell in his pallace at Welles and another at Owky, as also many other edifices in the same houses; and lastly, the church of Welles itselfe being now ready to fall to the ground, notwithstanding the great cost bestowed upon it by bishop Robert, he pulled downe the greatest part of it, to witte all the west ende, built it anew from the very foundation, and hallowed or dedicated it October 23, 1239."

He varies and amplifies his statement in the Latin editions of 1614-1616.

Under certain variations in detail the language of these two authorities is decisive, that in their view there was no building going on at Wells in the time between Robert and Jocelin; and that Jocelin pulled down and rebuilt the west end and the greatest part of the church.

These statements representing the later tradition of the fifteenth century are opposed to both documentary and architectural evidence.

They have not been received without weighty protest even by those who have accepted the writers as original authorities from whom there was no appeal.[1]

Britton, writing in 1847, says, " There is, in fact, such simplicity in all the more ancient parts which include the nave and transept, and the walls of the west part of the choir there, that had not the canon of Wells so particularly mentioned the restoration of the cathedral by Jocelin of Wells, and bishop Godwin so strongly corroborated his testimony, there could be little hesitation in ascribing it to bishop Robert, and assigning them to the reign of Henry II." He continues— " The north porch might still more decidedly be referred to the same period, for it possesses so many characteristics of Norman architecture, that there can be no doubt of its having been erected before the Pointed style had obtained its full ascendancy."

Another writer comments on the difficulty of reconciling with the architectural evidence, " the only known authority for the history of the cathedral (viz. the so-called canon of Wells) which, assigning nothing of the existing church to Robert or Reginald, attributes everything to Jocelin. If internal evidence were with history or tradition I would not complain : but it is dead against it."[2]

It is evident that the church bears unmistakable signs of two very different styles of building, in the

---

1. Britton, *Architectural History of Wells*, p. 88.
2. *Wells Cathedral*, Murray, 1861. Note part iii, attributed to Mr. Sharpe.

west front and in the nave and eastern part. The west front is built in the fully-developed Early English style in which Salisbury, Ely, and Lincoln are built. Mr. Freeman expresses the general judgment that Jocelin was the builder of the west front.[1] There is more division of opinion as to the date of the rest of the church.

The church which Jocelin consecrated is generally understood to take in the west front, the nave, north porch, transepts, and the three western arches of the eastern limb. It takes in the three towers up to the point where they rise above the roof of the church.

Mr. Freeman says, "The west front within and without differs widely in its architectural detail from the arcades of the nave and transepts." . . . Again, he says of the style of the nave, " It has a good deal of the earlier Romanesque leaven hanging about it ; its mouldings and the clustering of its pillars are much less free ; the abaci or tops of the capitals are square or octagonal instead of round ; it makes no use of detached shafts, often of marble, which are so abundantly found in the west front."

Professor Willis tells us that the west front is of later date than the nave, and the western part of the nave is later than the eastern part, the choir, and the north porch ; and he enters into detail in his description of differences and breaks in the building. In his lecture at Wells, conducting his audience from east to west in the order of the building, he drew their attention to

---

1. *Cathedral Church of Wells*, pp. 74-76. Prof. Willis in *Somerset Archæological Proceedings*, vol. xii, part i, p. 18. Mr. Irvine started another view, that Reginald was the builder of the west front. *Somerset Archæological Proceedings*, vol. xix, part ii, pp. 13, 14, 23.

breaks and stoppages in the work, and signs of differences of construction, which must occur in a building which, in the vicissitudes of centuries, has experienced repairs by different hands. But a general uniformity, broken by regular diversity, is observable in the nave.

If then the west front is of later date than the nave, and it is the work of Jocelin, finished in 1239, to whom shall we ascribe the rest of the church, which is "unlike any Early English building, and belongs to a style on the whole fifty years earlier?"

With this transitional architecture before us in the north porch and nave, and these documents which speak of buildings going on in the twelfth century, may we not claim that in the nave of Wells we have a remarkable example of transitional architecture intervening between the Norman and the Early English styles?

We may conjecture that the general design of the parts east of the west front belonged to Robert and to Reginald, though the actual work was stopped somewhere in the nave, and the whole has been greatly remodelled in details by successive builders in after years. If, as we are told, all Robert's work has perished, we may at least see in the three western arches of the choir Robert's work recast by Reginald. If there is one point in the nave where it is allowable to conjecture that the great break between Reginald's and Jocelin's work may have taken place, it will be in the part westward of the north porch, where the three last arches of the nave run on to the west front.

Here, Professor Willis remarks, the masonry improves: here the forms of sculptured foliage and human heads are more free and natural, more characteristic of the later workmen: here he considers that we have the work of a later date. *Here* we may conjecture that Reginald's work stopped : *here* was the new work suspended in 1196, when troubles threatened the church under Savaric, when the war with Glastonbury began. *Here* may have been for the next three and twenty years, between 1196-1219, the gaping chasm between the unfinished nave and the older front, which, from its age, was showing signs of decay and was ready to fall, "pro sua vetustate patiebatur periculum ruinæ."

What if Jocelin, after 1219, began to build at the west end, pulling down the old Norman work to the ground, raising up on its ruins the new work in the rich Early English style of the period, rivalling his brother's work at Lincoln? What if he then joined it on to the unfinished nave of Reginald, building up the three western arcades of the nave in the earlier style of his predecessor, and uniting here, in one glorious whole, his own new work with the work of Reginald and of Robert?

It would have been a noble architectural achievement for the last twenty years of a troubled episcopate.

If he did this and no more than this, it would not be difficult to imagine how the tradition would have grown that he was the builder of the whole church. We can understand how after-generations who immediately inherited the benefits of Jocelin's wise legislation and generous benefactions should have cherished the memory of the latest builder, as though he were the one and only builder, of the church of the thirteenth century.

He was of Wells: he, as chaplain and canon and bishop, had grown up, and lived, and died, and was buried, among his own people: his grave and memorial tomb was with them in their church, honoured the more as it was the tomb of the first bishop buried at Wells since the seat of the bishop had been transferred to Bath one hundred and fifty years before. Each generation had before their eyes that part of the church which was Jocelin's undoubted work, gradually rising under the hands of successive builders to the height of its western towers, looking over the burial place of the dead and the homes of the living. Generation after generation saw the deeply recessed niches, the six hundred tabernacles gradually filled with sculptured imagery, telling the whole tale of earth and heaven, of man's fall and resurrection, of the Lord's advent in mercy and in judgment, and of the long roll of saints and worthies of the race of their own land.

It might well be that by the time of bishop Bubwith, when the Canon of Wells wrote, more than a century and a half after Jocelin's death, the tradition had taken root that Jocelin of Wells, who had raised the western front, had been also the architect of the whole church, and that as builder, legislator and benefactor, "there had been none like before him, neither after him had any risen like unto him." "Qui sibi similem anteriorem non habuit, nec huc usque visus est habere sequentem."[1]

But now with these contemporary documents before us, we put in a plea that justice should be done to

---

1. Canon of Wells, in Wharton, A.S. 564.

Robert and to Reginald, who have gone before as builders of the church.

"Vixere fortes ante Agamemnona." Jocelin was last and greatest, but Reginald ought to hold the second place of honour between Robert the "author" and Jocelin the "finisher,"—"the first three" master builders of our holy and beautiful house of St. Andrew in Wells.

Obscure and doubtful are the earlier stages of the architectural history of our church, as of so many of the other great churches which were raised up about this time throughout the land. Few and scanty are the records preserved in contemporary registers. As in the ancient temple at Jerusalem no sound of tool was heard while it was in building—noiselessly the fabric rose into being—so our church has grown up in silence; no portion of the building or sculptures can be assigned with certainty to any one known architect.

We may think we can trace in our local documents the names of one or two of those employed in the work at Wells and elsewhere about this same time. Families of masons (*cementarii*) at Wells, of the names of Lock, father and son, and Noreis,[1] Norreys, and one Deodatus (fit name for some cunning stone worker in the service of the sanctuary) are found in connection with members of the chapter of Wells, and with other workmen of different occupations at both Wells and Glastonbury; John Faber, John the goldsmith, and David the dyer *(tinctor)*, and Simon the colourist *(pictor)*. A member of a family of the name

1. Gaufridus de Noiers was the name of St. Hugh's architect at Lincoln.

of Buneton, established in Glastonbury in 1249, and afterwards in Edward II's time called "de Buneton," "the sculptor," is possessed of lands and houses at Glastonbury, and gives name to a street in Glastonbury called after their own name,[1] Buneton Street. Another name also is now found at Wells, famous throughout England for his architectural works, Elias de Derham — known at Salisbury as canon, *rector ecclesiæ* and architect between 1220 and 1229—known at Canterbury as one of the "incomparable artificers" of the new shrine of St. Thomas in 1220—and at Winchester as master of the works in the King's Hall, 1230-6. He appears at Wells as an early friend of the brothers Hugh and Jocelin, and their companion in exile—he is named co-executor with Jocelin of the first draft of bishop Hugh's will in 1212—in 1236 he is seneschal or steward of Jocelin at Wells, and as such attests the conveyance of houses by the family of the masons Lock, which formed the first church school of Wells. Matthew Paris records his death in 1245.[2] Others of the family, probably from Dyrham near Pucklechurch in Gloucestershire are among the canons.

But, beyond these shadowy names, we know nothing certainly of the actual builders who planned or executed "this immense and glorious work of high intelligence"—who raised the "alta campanilia," to their first stages—who spread the branching roof of the nave—who designed or carved the canopies and niches, tabernacles of life-like statuary, *spirantia signa*,

1. "In vico qui vocatur Boneton in villa Glaston." Appendix R.
2. *Chron. Majora*, iv, 418. (Rolls Series). Part ii, Appendix R.

in that noble gallery of early Christian art displayed on the breadth of the west front, which Flaxman described as "the earliest specimen of such magnificent and varied sculpture united in a series of sacred history that is to be found in western Europe," and which in their decay, after six centuries of existence, still raise the admiration and mysterious wonder of each passing generation.

Jocelin was living in a period of continuous growth and new development: he was unfolding and extending the system which he inherited: he was working on the fabric as he worked on the constitution of the church, repairing, rebuilding what was dilapidated or unfinished in the earlier building, adding largely new and beautiful work. He left the church sufficiently completed for the ritual of his time in fabric and interior arrangement and endowment, as he left the ministrant body of the church enlarged and all but complete in number, more richly endowed, with offices more defined and reorganised, and working with more efficiency.

Within these years of troublous times, during the lawless tyranny of John and the weak misrule of Henry, and the arrogance and intolerable exactions of papal legates, Jocelin was quietly working for the good of the church of God in his own home, as restorer, builder, legislator, reformer.

He has left to his native city a church equal at least in architectural grace and interest to any of the rivals of its day at home or abroad, and surpassing all in the design and execution of the sculptures of its matchless west front.

DRAWN from the wells of some diviner spring,
   Rose—like a fountain leaping in the sun—
   His thoughts high heavenward, ere his work begun,
Great Jocelin,—who made his day-dreams ring
With harmonies before unheard, and wing
   Their flight in voiceless words, and deeds undone
   Till he had shaped his yearning thoughts in stone,
And then, God-guided, taught the dumb to sing:
Apostles, prophets, saints, and martyrs rise,
   Angels, archangels, with their silent song,
Tier above tier before our wondering eyes,
   Who thro' unwearying years their strains prolong:—
And o'er the passing crowd they yet shall raise
Their great " Te Deum " to the end of days.
                                Godfrey Thring.

CHAPTER IV. PART II.

Chronicon of Jocelin, bishop of Bath, 1206-1242, in Archer's "*Chronicon Wellense.*"

Annus Domini.	Cyclus Solis.	Cyclus Lunæ.	Epacta.	Litera Dominicalis	Pascha.	Indictio.
1205	10	9	9	B	Apr. 10	viii
6	11	10	20	A	Ap. 2	ix
7	12	11	1	G	22	x
8	13	12	12	FE	6	xi
9	14	13	23	D	Mar. 29	xii
1210	15	14	4	C	Ap. 18	xiii
11	16	15	15	B	3	xiv
12	17	16	26	AG	Mar. 25	xv
13	18	17	7	F	Ap. 14	i
14	19	18	18	E	Mar. 30	ii
15	20	19	29	D	Ap. 19	iii
16	21	1	11	CB	10	iv
17	22	2	22	A	Mar. 26	v
18	23	3	3	G	Ap. 15	vi
19	24	4	14	F	7	vii
1220	25	5	25	ED	Mar. 29	viii
21	26	6	6	C	Ap. 11	ix
22	27	7	17	B	3	x
23	28	8	28	A	23	xi
24	1	9	9	GF	14	xii
25	2	10	20	E	Mar. 30	xiii
26	3	11	1	D	Ap. 19	xiv
27	4	12	12	C	11	xv
28	5	13	23	BA	Mar. 26	i
29	6	14	4	G	Ap. 15	ii
1230	7	15	15	F	7	iii
31	8	16	26	E	Mar. 23	iv
32	9	17	7	DC	Ap. 11	v
33	10	18	18	B	Apr. 3	vi
34	11	19	29	A	23	vii
35	12	1	11	G	8	viii
36	13	2	22	FE	Mar. 30	ix
37	14	3	3	D	Ap. 19	x
38	15	4	14	C	4	xi
39	16	5	25	B	Mar. 27	xii
1240	17	6	6	AG	Ap. 15	xiii
41	18	7	17	F	Mar. 31	xiv
42	19	8	28	E	Ap. 20	xv

The year begins on March 25th at this time.

A.D. 1205

7 John. See of Canterbury vacant.
8 Innocent III. See of Bath vacant.
Alexander, dean.
Aug. 8 Savaric died.

Archer, f. 90. Custody of the see. Hugh archdeacon of Wells, and William de Wrotham archdeacon of Taunton appointed by the king custodians of the see. W. Prynne, *History of King John*, etc., iii, 9.

January 2. Savaric's debts. Cf. Rot. Lit. Claus. p. 61—The king orders payment of a debt from Savaric of £100 to bishop Peter of Winchester to be paid to the custodians of the see, by the executors of archbishop Hubert's will, he having at his death money in hand belonging to Savaric.

James Savage and Master E. de Derham were the executors.

Dated Clarendon 2 January in the 7th year.

Sept. 10. Confirmation of manor and church of North Curry to the *communa*. King John confirms to the canons the manor and church of North Curry, the lands of Hatche and Wrentich for the *communa*; grants the right of holding a market every Wednesday. R. i, f. 9; R. iii, f. 25 in dors.

"Datum per manus Hugonis de Welles archidiaconi Wellensis apud Bristoll 10mo die Septembris anno regni nostri septimo."

Concordat for election of bishop between chapters of Bath and Wells. The vacancy in the see is made the occasion of formulating a *compositio*, based upon the precedent followed in the election of bishop Reginald between the two electing bodies to regulate future elections :[1]

1. The process in the election of bishop Reginald, and this of

Robert the prior and the convent of Bath, Alexander the dean and the canons of Wells, agree to meet in a convenient place to elect.

The prior shall announce the choice, and in the name of the whole church shall challenge objection *(postulabit*[1]*)*—if the prior be elected the dean shall so act.

The elected to be installed in the church of Bath. Should the priory be vacant at the time dean and canons promise that they will not hinder the installation at Bath.

Prior and dean seal this compact. R. i, f. 56.

Prior, sub-prior, and two monks, appointed proctors for the chapter of Bath, notify by letter to the king their appointment and assent to whatever shall be determined in conjunction with the canons of Wells. Dean Alexander, William of St. Faith, precentor, Thomas, subdean, and Ralph of Lechlade, canons, are appointed proctors of the chapter of Wells. R. i, ff. 54, 55.

The proctors unanimously elect Jocelin of Wells, canon, to be bishop, and by a deed signed and sealed publish the election to the two chapters. R. i, f. 55, in d.; R. i, f. 57.

bishop Jocelin, are recorded in full in the report of the Commissioners appointed in July, 1242, to settle the dispute after bishop Roger's nomination. Vide "Charter No. 40."

1. "Postulabit." Archer quotes Gibson's Codex, vol. i, p. 122, "Postulatio est concors capituli petitio (*i.e.*, nemine contradicente), ut is in prælatum promoveatur sive adsumatur, qui non propter animi vel corporis vitium sed ob alium defectum propter quem non est inhabilis ad prospiciendum ecclesiæ (veluti quia est minor triginta annis aut laicus in minoribus ordinibus aut illegitimus) eligi nequit." It was a "si quis," giving notice of nomination, challenging objections.

Letters of notification of the election are sent by the prior and convent of Bath, and similar letters by the dean and chapter of Wells, to the king, the archbishop of Canterbury (though *sede vacante*) and pope Innocent. R. i, f. 54 ; i, f. 55.

The subscriptions of the prior and monks of Bath,[1] and of the dean and chapter of Wells are appended to their acts.

The letter of the chapter of Bath describes Jocelin: "Clericum ecclesiæ nostræ et canonicum Wellensem, virum industrium, literatum et honestum." R. i, f. 64.

The chapter of Wells lament that "their church has been for so many years deprived of the comfort of a guide and ruler; tossed with storms and exposed to various oppressions and extreme perils. (R. i, f. 28.) For while Savaric has been absent, and too negligent of his charge, things at Wells have gone from bad to worse; the canons have been oppressed and trampled on by wicked men, unrestrained by fear of God or reverence for man ; some have attacked the persons, others the property of the canons. In the hope of applying a remedy to these evils they unanimously, and in conjunction with the chapter of Bath, have elected to their bishop, Jocelin, one of their canons, a deacon, industrious, learned, honest, of great experience in business—whose early life and character are well-known to us, inasmuch as he has grown up among us from his infancy, and has lived among us without reproach."

" Cujus profecto vita, moresque probabiles incognitae

---

1. The letter is printed in full in Introduction, p. 41, to "Account of the Priory of Bath," by Rev. W. Hunt. Somerset Record Society Publications.

nobis esse non poterunt cum in sinu ecclesiæ nostræ a primo lacte coaluerit, et sine querela inter nos hactenus conversatus."

They implore Innocent to assist in remedying this their desperate condition, by granting confirmation of Jocelin's election without delay. R. i, f. 55.

Cf. Inspeximus in 1242, of all the deeds relating to election of Jocelin, in Charters 39, 40, 41.

The names of the canons and clergy of Wells follow the instrument of election.

+ Ego Alexander Wellensis decanus.
+ Ego Willelmus precentor Wellensis.
+ Ego H[ugo] Wellensis archidiaconus.
+ Ego R[icardus] Cancellarius Wellensis.
+ Ego T. Thesaurarius Wellensis.
+ W[alterus de Gray] Cancellarius domini regis.[1]
+ Ego P[etrus] archidiaconus Bathoniensis.
+ Ego W[illelmus] archidiaconus Tantonensis.
+ Ego T[homas] subdecanus Wellensis.
+ Ego A[dam] succentor Wellensis.
+ Ego Abbas Beccensis canonicus Wellensis.
+ Ego Abbas Muchelnensis canonicus Wellensis.
+ Ego R. archidiaconus Wyntoniensis.
+ Ego magister R[adulphus] de Lechelade.
+ Ego Stephanus Ridel.
+ Ego magister Amandus.
+ Ego P. Canutus.
+ Ego Johannes Chauvel.
+ Ego T. de London.

---

1. Walter de Gray, afterwards archbishop of York, is recorded by Beatson as Lord High Chancellor in 1205, between two turns of the office by Hugh de Wells.

+ Ego Reginaldus Buzun.
+ Ego magister W. de Tantonia.
+ Ego R. de Tregoz.
+ Ego magister T. de Heselle.
+ Ego S. de Elmeham.
+ Ego T. de Tornaco.
+ Ego H. de Welles.
+ Ego I. Capellanus.
+ Ego P. de Inglesh.
+ Ego A. Scottus.
+ Ego Hugo de Wylī.
+ Ego Arnisius de Constantiis.
+ Ego Mauricius de Berkele.
+ Ego Johannes de Bohun.
+ Ego Iterus de Wandestr.
+ Ego Phil. de Lucy.
+ Ego R. de Tymbresb.
+ Ego Radulphus Preciosus.
+ Ego R. de Staweia.
+ Ego R. de Camera.
+ Ego W. de Sarum.
+ Ego H. de Wyfelescumba.
+ Ego A. Lugdunensis.
+ Ego H. de Berkele.
+ Ego T. de Cycestria.
+ Ego I. de Kainesham.
+ Ego magister R. de Wyltoñ.
+ Ego T. de Dundeñ.
+ Ego W. de Dinre.
+ Ego I. de Kalna.
+ Ego R. de Bathonia.
+ Ego N. de Welles.

+ Ego H. de Traco.
+ Ego R. de Berch.
+ Ego R. de Sanford.
+ Ego S. de Tornaco.
+ Ego W. de Cerda.

The dean and 55 sign.

In the same year orders on the treasury to the two archdeacons, as custodians of the see, are given by king John for payment to the proctors of the two chapters, "for expenses in coming to us at Windlesore, and in stay in our court at the election of their bishop," and for payments to the same canons, with the addition of Roger de Sandford. Rot. Lit. Claus. p. 52.

Again, in 7 John, January 20, 1205-6, from Bradenestoke, to the same persons (with the exception of Roger de Bohun) "for expenses in coming to us in Dorset and Wiltesir." Rot. Lit. Claus. p. 63. Roger de Bohun, as if forgotten, is the subject of a separate order, on the next day, January 20.

On February 7, from Lexinton, to the proctors for coming to the king at Lexinton. Rot. Lit. Claus. p. 67.

The proctors of the two chapters went to the king, and were with the court, pending the confirmation, from November to February. Rot. Lit. Claus. p. 56.

"Rex. etc. baronibus de Scaccario. Computate cum H. (Hugone) archidiacono Wellensi et W. (Willelmo) de Wrotham archidiacono Tantonensi custodibus episcopatus Bathoniensis de exitibus episcopatus Bathoniensis xx marcas quas liberaverunt priori Bathoniensi, et canonicis Wellensis ecclesiae ad expensas suas veniendo ad nos apud Notingham et apud Windlesore et in mora eorum in curia nostra ad electionem episcopi faciendam ; et xxv solidos liberatos magistro Rogero nepoti decani Wellensis de termino sancti Michaelis ; et xxv solidos liberatos Thomae Turnay de eodem termino et xii solidos vi denarios liberatos Herveo de Tracey de eodem termino de praebendis suis quas habuerunt ante tempora Savarici quondam Bathoniensis episcopi et xiii libras xviii solidos iii denarios et obolum in expensa nostra apud Glaston. per unam noctem et apud Pilton per aliam noctem et xi denarios liberatos H. (Hugoni) archidiacono Wellensi de redditu suo antiquo de Glaston. Teste meipso apud Windlesore quarto die Novembris, 7 Johannis regis." Rot. Lit. Claus. p. 56. Prynne Hist. tom. iii, p. 9.

A.D. 1206.

f. 92.
Letters testimonial of all the bishops, and of the province of Canterbury, uniting in prayer for confirmation of Jocelin's election.

8 John.   1 Jocelin, bishop of Bath.
9 Innocent III.   Alexander, dean.
The bishop of London (William de S. Mere l'Eglise),
     „   Hereford (Egidius de Bruce),
     „   St. Asaph (Reiner),
     „   Llandaff (Henry of Abergavenny),
     „   Bangor (Robert of Shrewsbury),
     „   St. David's (Geoffrey de Henlaw),

To the legate jointly write to the legate, John Ferentinus, cardinal of St. Maria in *Via Lata*, and in vacancy of see of Canterbury, urge that he will give audience to the proctors of Bath and Wells, and ratify the election. R. i, f. 54.

Robert, bishop of Bangor, a friend of Jocelin, writes specially in attestation of Jocelin's great deserts, and prays for confirmation. R. i, f. 55.

King sends letters missive with Jocelin to the legate, and requests his confirmation. R. i, f. 54. *King's missive to the legate, April 23.*
The same bishops write jointly to the pope. Robert of Bangor writes specially. R. i, f. 54.
Another letter is written by the bishop of London and ten other bishops of the province of Canterbury to the legate and to the pope. R. i, f. 56. *Letters to the pope.*

5. Kal. Junii. On Trinity Sunday Jocelin is consecrated bishop of Bath in the chapel of the abbey of St. Mary at Reading. *f. 93. Consecration of Jocelin. May 28, 1206*

The bishop of London consecrates, and nine other bishops assist. (Matt. Paris, *Hist. Angl.*, ii, 107, Rolls Series.) " Jocelinus de Welles in episcopum consecratur Bathoniensem."

In capite jejunii, on the morrow of Ash Wednesday, bishop Jocelin in council with his chapter ordained that the mass of the Blessed Virgin should be celebrated daily before her altar (*ante altare suum*) by thirteen vicars, of whom three were priests ; one to celebrate weekly with ten vicars assisting, until the number of the vicars should be completed by his ordinance. One penny a day to be paid to each vicar attending vespers, matins, and the other hours of the Blessed Virgin and to the priests in addition another half commons, " ut libentius et devotius ministerio suo insistant."[1] *f. 95. Feb. 15, 1206-7. Cf. under 1215.*

In case of illness a substitute to assist ; but absence without due cause to involve loss of daily stipend. R. iii, f. 127.

1. Cf. *Gesta abbat. Sancti Albani*, i, 284. Abbot William de Trumpington, 1214-1235, instituted "quotidiana celebratio missæ S. Mariæ," " videns quod in omnibus nobilibus ecclesiis Angliæ missa de Beata Virgine ad notam solemniter cotidiana decantatur."

174   *Chapters in Wells History.*   [CHAP.

March 3, 1206-7.
King John confirms to bishop Jocelin, the dean and canons, and to the prior and convent of Bath all possessions, liberties, legal rights and privileges granted by his predecessors.

R. iii, f. 2, given at Taydyngton, anno regni 8°. Cf. Inspeximus by Edw. I, 1324, of all charters given to Jocelin. R. iii, f. 392.

There is a note in Archer, pp. 94, 95, explaining "privilegia usitata," and legal terms in charter, by references to Spelman, Somner, and Cowel.

A.D. 1207.

9 John.   1 Stephen, archbishop.
10 Innocent III.   2 Jocelin, bishop.
                           Alexander, dean.

f. 96. Preaching friars come to England.
In these days Innocent sent into England the Preaching Friars; who, suddenly appearing, filled the land with their preaching, and "rumusculos hominum imperitorum aucupati sunt." Cf. Matt. Paris, *Hist. Angl.*, ii, 109 (Rolls Series).

The monks of Canterbury had elected as archbishop, Reginald their subprior; then, by the king's wish, John de Gray bishop of Norwich. The double election was referred to the Roman court by the king and bishops of the province.

Appointment of archbp. Stephen Langton. June 17.
Innocent cancels both elections, and orders the proctors of the convent then at Rome to elect Stephen Langton, cardinal of St. Chrysogonus. Cf. Matt. Paris, *Hist. Angl.*, ii, 104-106, 110-111 (Rolls Series).

"Stephanum de Langetun, cardinalem, quo non erat major in curia, immo nec ei par in moribus et scientia."

The proctors assent, and on Trinity Sunday Stephen is consecrated by the pope at Viterbo.

Anger of John—and violence in consequence. Matt. Paris, *Hist. Angl.*, ii, 112. Letters pass between the king and the pope. Finally, Innocent orders the bishops of London, Ely, and Worcester to warn the king; and, if he is contumacious, to pronounce an "interdict."

Bishop of London confirms the grants of his predecessors of the church of Scandeford (Shalford) to bishop Reginald in 1175, to be a prebend in the church of Wells reserving dues and right of institution. R. iii, f. 388. Cf R. i, f. 48, and f. 24, containing early history of grant of Shalford by Hamo FitzGodfrey. Appendix G. *[July 2.]*

Two royal charters belong to this year.

(1.) "Johannes, Dei gracia, etc.: Sciatis nos concessisse et presenti carta nostra confirmasse venerabili patri nostro domino J. Bath' episcopo, quod possit claudere totum boscum suum de manerio de Well' qui est ex australi parte ville de Well' et facere inde parcum, et quod possit vertere cheminum quod vadit per medium boscum illum, ita quod de cetero nullum cheminum sit per parcum predictum sine voluntate predicti episcopi vel successorum suorum. Quare volumus et firmiter precipimus quod idem episcopus Bathon. et successores sui in perpetuum habeant et teneant parcum illum bene et in pace, libere et quiete et honorifice, cum omnibus libertatibus et liberis consuetudinibus ad liberum parcum pertinentibus. Testibus, W. Comite Sarr', Hugone de Nevill, W. de Cantilup̃, Thoma de Sanford, Thoma Basset, Matthæo *["De parco apud Welles ex parte australi." Charter Roll, ix John, m. 7. Sept. 16.]*

filio Herberti, W. de Monte Acuto, Roberto de Berkel, W. Malet, Willelmo Revel, Ricardo Revel. Datum per manum nostram apud Herpetre xvj die Septembris, anno ix°."

(2.) Licence to inclose the road.

<small>Nov. 16, the bishop's park enclosed. "De via includenda infra parcum de Welles."</small>

Grant of John to bishop Jocelin to enclose "quantum voluit de chemino regali quod pretendit ab orientali parte gardinii sui versus Dultincot sub monte qui appellatur Le Torre; et quod voluit de chemino quod pretendit per Kiward versus Cokesley, et quod dimittat ad cheminum tantumdem de alia terra extra illud clausum—et prohibemus ne quis eum vel successores suos super hoc disturbat vel molestat. Teste me ipso et W. Cantuar. archiep. apud Merleberg xvi die Nov. anno regni nostri ix°." 9 John. Rot. Lit. Pat., p. 77. Ed. Hardy.

<small>Nov. 26, "de quietatione thelonei."</small>

The king grants immunity from market tolls to the king's treasury *(theloneum)* to the chapters of Bath and Wells, and to the bishop and his men—*per totam terram suam.* R. i, f. 9, n. 5; R. iii, f. 2.

"Datum per manus Walteri de Gray Cancellarii apud Merleberg. xxvi Novemb. anno nostri regni ix°."

<small>f. 97. Glastonbury appeals to Rome for dissolution of union.</small>

The convent of Glastonbury renew their appeal to Rome, and pray for dissolution of the union between the see and abbey. The election of bishop Jocelin was especially odious to them, as he had been a zealous supporter of Savaric's policy against the abbey, "tam in reatu, quam in episcopatu, Savarici successor."

Cf. Adam de Domerham, pp. 441-2.

<small>Holecumb.</small>

Henry of Chichester admitted to the church of Holecumb in Devon by Simon of Apulia, bishop of

Exeter, at the petition of the canons of Wells. R. i, f. 20.

Grants of canonical houses. Formation of North Liberty.

(a) Nicolas of Wells gives to the church of St. Andrew and to bishop Jocelin houses and land— "aream cum domibus suis"—before the great gate of the canons—*ante magnam portam canonicorum*—on condition that they shall be for canons, and shall not be alienated by bishop or chapter from the use of the church. Bishop Jocelin confirms the grant, and liberates the houses from all civil dues—" ab omni exactione et seculari servitio sicut antiqua area canonicorum." f. 97. Extension of Liberty, north of the church.

Hugh, archdeacon of Wells, attests. R. i, f. 19.

(b) Walter of Downhead[1] (Dunheved), with assent of wife and heirs, grants to Adam of Litton (Ade de Lectun) his kinsman, a priest, and to his successor one acre of land in the northern part of Wells and near his house at annual payment of 12 pence to Walter and his heirs.

R. i, f. 28. Witness, Thomas nephew of the bishop, Ralph his brother, Alfred of Downhead, Walter of the Muntory (Walter de Muntoria), and others.

(c) Walter of Downhead grants to Malger of Wells, priest vicar, land between his garden and the land of Adam of Litton, extending from the town to a given

---

1. Walter of Downhead appears in many of the documents of the time. He was a layman holding the manor of Downhead on Mendip under the abbey of Glastonbury, also holding a heritable lay fief in Wells, subject to "regale servitium," and, though in Wells, and apparently in the episcopal manor of former times, to no other. Vide Charter 13.

boundary, "a vico usque ad fossatum," and in breadth 5 perches all but 2 feet, on payment of 12 pence.

R. i, f. 28. Witness, dominus Odo, etc.

f. 98.
(d) Malger grants to Ralph Preciosus, canon, all his land and houses between the messuage which had belonged to Adam of Litton and the messuage of Leobert, clerk, with all the building on it, at an annual payment to Walter of Downhead and Walter of Wyke of 18 pence.

R. i, f. 19, in dors. Witnesses, Richard of Aterbery, Adam Magot, etc.

(e) Ralph Preciosus grants to the chapter of Wells his messuage of Leobert and the land which had belonged to Adam of Litton on payment of the said 18 pence, to be let by the chapter to a canon wishing to reside, and to be inalienable, and subject to an annual fine ("ghersuma,"[1]) to be distributed on the anniversary of his death in equal proportions between the canon and vicars present at the service.

R. i, f. 19, in dors. n 43.

Ralph Preciosus confirms more fully the grant—"mansum meum cum edificiis meis quod est inter mansum qui fuerat Leoberti clerici et terram quæ fuerat Adæ de Lectun"—with provision that it shall be assigned to one of the principal canons resident, or desiring to keep perpetual residence.

R. i, f. 19.

Further transactions under year 1228.—At that time the Kardunville family give their land adjoining

---

1. Note by Archer: "Ghersuma, usurpatur pro 'fine,' seu pecunia data in pactionem et rei emptæ vel conductæ compensationem."

to the land of Malger—"quæ vocatur Muntoria"—to Helias the chaplain, and he, to the chapter.

So we gather from these charters of 1207 that there existed at this time a "close," "antiqua area canonicorum," free from all civil dues, "ab omni seculari servitio," and by grants now made additional lands were added at the north of the church.

R. i, f. 27, in dors. Charters 13—35.

The "Muntoria" was the designation of parcels of this land on the northern part of the town now given to the chapter.

Confirmations of grants made to bishop Reginald by Henry de Traci, of grant by Oliver de Traci, 1186, of pension from South Bovi, or Bovy Tracy. R. i, f. 37. Robert de Courtenay, Hugo de la Pumeraye (Pomeroy), etc., witnesses. Cf. R. iii, f. 109. [f. 99. Bovy Tracy.]

Confirmation to bishop Jocelin of grant made to bishop Reginald by George de Stuble of patronage of church of Estun (Easton in Gordano), by Alexander de Rodolio, and William de la Stuble (Stuteville) in 1190. R. iii, f. 370. Witnesses to the original deed—the vice-sheriff, comes of Somerset and Dorset, William de Morevill, Matthew de Clevedon, Richard Fitzarthur, Reginald de Altaville (Hauteville). R. iii, f. 391. Witnesses to the confirmation, William de Ham, precentor of Wells, and others canons. [Easton in Gordano.]

Grant by Robert de Meisy of advowson of church of Bertun (Barton St. David's) and of a moiety of church of Nunney (Nunniz) to form a prebend, if he so willed. R. iii, f. 401. William de Ham, precentor, witness—sixty shillings out of the church of Nunny was afterwards given to the *communa* by bishop

Jocelin—the prebend does not appear. R. iii, f. 4. R. i, f. 112.

Hospital of S. Lawrence Bristol. King John gives donations to the hospital of St. Lawrence at Bristol. Dugdale, *Monast.* ii, p. 438.

Nunnery at Buckland Monachorum. Loretta, countess of Leicester, founded nunnery at Buckland. Dugdale, *Monast.* do.

The convent of Montacute complain to the king of the prior Durandus, and pray for his removal.

21 Dec. Prior of Montacute deprived. Jocelin is ordered to hold an inquisition; finally he is ordered to deprive him.

Rot. Lit. Pat. anno nono, apud Odiham 21 Dec. "Quod ep. Bathon. deprivet Durandum priorem de Monteacuto ob sua male gesta."

A.D 1208.

10 John. 2 Stephen, archbishop.
11 Innocent III. 3 Jocelin, bishop.
  Alexander, dean.

f. 99. Interdict proclaimed March 24. John refusing to acknowledge Stephen as archbishop, the bishops of London, Ely, and Worcester are ordered by pope Innocent to put the kingdom under interdict. The interdict is proclaimed on the vigil of the Annunciation, March 24, "prima die Lunae in Passione Domini, ix Kal Aprilis." [Easter Day fell that year on April 6. 8 Id. April.]

Jocelin in exile. Bishop Jocelin proclaims the interdict in his diocese, and flies the kingdom with other bishops—London, Hereford, Ely, Worcester—to avoid the king's wrath. The king seizes their property.

The interdict. Matt. Paris. Hist. Angl. ii, 116. "Cessaverunt itaque in Anglia omnia ecclesiastica sacramenta, praeter solummodo confessionem et viaticum in ultima necessitate, et baptisma parvulorum;

corpora vero defunctorum de civitatibus deferebantur sepelienda, et in compitis more canum humabantur."

"Sub hoc tempus," Hugh, archdeacon of Wells and chancellor of the kingdom, "Regis Cancellarius." Matt. Paris, *Hist. Angl.* ii, 120. Dugd. Orig. Judic. p. 6.

<small>Hugh of Wells in favour with the king.</small>

Hugh, judge "ad fines levandos," Dugd. p. 42, receives from the king the manors of Axbridge and Cheddar, as a fee at £20 per annum, and the vill of Axbridge. R. i, f. 108.

"Sub hoc tempus," Hugh, as lord of the hundred of Wynterstoke, releases the episcopal manors of Banwell and Compton of all dues to the court of the hundred of Wynterstoke. R. iii, f. 356. Witnesses—Ralph precentor, magister Elias de Derham, Thomas de Thorn, Simon de Cumba, Hugh de Wells, Petrus de Cicestria, Rob. de Mandeville, etc. Cf. R. iii, f. 347, anno 1214.

The vill of Axbridge was afterwards sold by Hugh to Thomas Walensis, and by him to Maurice of Gaunt, who in 1226 was one of the judges on circuit.

R. iii, f. 356. Cf. R. i, f. 108.

A.D. 1209.

11 John.   3 Stephen, archbishop.
12 Innocent III.   4 Jocelin, bishop.
                           Alexander, dean.

A statute, "de ordinatione decanatus et subdecanatus," dated "iii, Nonas Junii, June 3. Pontificatus anno quarto ineunte." R. i, f. 58.

<small>f. 100. Revision of the constitution of the cathedral church by bp. Jocelin "in partibus transmarinis." June 3.</small>

Bishop Jocelin, with the assent of the chapter, makes exchange of prebends between the dean and subdean —Wedmore to become the prebend of the dean; four marcs annually to be paid stall-wages to the priest vicar. Wookey to be the prebend of the subdean, two marcs stall-wages to the vicar.

In the preamble to this charter Jocelin sets forth (a) his especial affection to the church of Wells—"quae nos in gremio suo genitos et uberibus consolationis suae educatos, in eum statum quem licet immerito tenemus, materna semper affectione produxit."

(b) He states that he has already remodelled the offices of precentor, chancellor, treasurer, and succentor, and augmented the endowments, with the view to induce "residence." Cf. ann. 1217. R. i, f. 49; R. ii, f. 14.

f. 100. Hugh bp. of Lincoln, and in exile.

Hugh is appointed to the bishopric of Lincoln; allowed leave of absence to Normandy, to be consecrated by the archbishop of Rouen. He makes profession of obedience to Stephen as archbishop, and is consecrated by him at Melun, 13 Kal. Jan. Dec. 20. M. Paris, *Hist. Angl.* ii, 120.

John seizes all his emoluments at Lincoln.

Walter de Gray is made chancellor.

From 1208 to 1213 bishop Jocelin is in exile in France. Hugh bishop of Lincoln is with him in 1211.

A.D. 1211.

13 John.   5 Stephen, archbishop.
14 Innocent III.   6 Jocelin, bishop.
    Alexander, dean.

Draft of will of bp. Hugh. Nov. 15, 1211 R. iii, f. 284.

Hugh of Wells, bishop of Lincoln, in exile with his brother bishop Jocelin at S. Martin de Garenne, near Bourdeaux, on St. Brice's day, in the third year of his pontificate, appoints bishop Jocelin and Helias de

Derham executors of his will, and makes disposition of his property between the dioceses of Lincoln and Bath, "de bonis quæ mihi restituenda sunt in Anglia." The whole sum named amounts to about 6000 marcs, of which about 2000 (1967), one-third, were to be distributed among his friends, the poor ("pauperibus de consanguinitate mea,") and pious uses; the rest devoted to churches and religious houses in the two dioceses, after payment of dues to the papal see and to the king:

(a) *In the diocese of Lincoln.*
To the fabric of the church of Lincoln 500 marcs.
To the *communa* of the chapter of Lincoln 500
To the vicars 60
To religious houses in Lincoln 300
To lepers' houses 100
To the construction of an hospital 300

(b) *In the diocese of Bath and to bishop Jocelin.*
To the fabric of the church of Wells 300 marcs.
To the *communa* of the chapter "tam ad opus vicariorum quam canonicorum" 300
To build a hospital at Wells 500
To the hospital at Bath 7½
For distribution among the vicars 40

Other sums were left to lepers' houses at Selwood, Ilchester, and Bath; and to religious houses at Barlinch, Buckland, Barrow, and Cannington.

The witnesses to this early draft of bishop Hugh's will represent some of the "familia" of the bishops in exile—master Helias of Derham, master John of York, master Reginald of Chester; master William Roger and Helias, chaplains; Peter of Chichester, afterwards, in 1220, dean of Wells, William of Ham, afterwards precentor, canons of Wells.

A will of another character and with totally different bequests was made later in life by bishop Hugh.[1]

A.D. 1213.

15 John.
16 Innocent III.

7 Stephen, archbishop.
8 Jocelin, bishop.
Leonius, dean.

f. 101.
Public
events.

The quarrel between the king and the pope was reaching its bitter and shameful end in 1213. In 1212 archbishop Stephen, and the bishops of London and Ely went to Rome to complain of John's outrages.

Sentence of deposition was pronounced by the pope. The legate Pandulf was sent to France and England, to offer John terms of submission, or to pronounce deposition and make over to the king of France his dominions. John refuses submission; the archbishop and bishops retire from Rome, publish in France the sentence of deposition of John, and the king of France prepares to invade England.

M. Paris, *Hist. Angl.* ii, 130. Rymer's *Fœdera*, i, 166.

---

1. In this last will, made at Stow Park, June 1, 1233 (Vide *Giraldus Cambrensis*, vol. 7, Appendix G, ed. Dimock, and Pref. xc, xciii), bequests to the diocese of Bath are chiefly *(a)* to the hospital at Wells "profits from wardships and marriages of certain estates held of the see of Lincoln by military tenure, the heirs of which were under age," *(b)* to his poor kinsfolk round Wells and Pilton, *(c)* to a few private individuals, and servants. His brother Jocelin is appointed executor, together with others from the Lincoln diocese. His will is confirmed by anticipation in a charter of Henry III, dated May 27, 1227, and another dated May 15, 1229.

John and the legate Pandulf meet at Dover. Peace is made between John and the pope. John bound himself to obedience to the pope's orders—to restore the bishops in exile; to recompense them for losses since the interdict by the sum of £8000. *May 13, 1213.¹*

The king writes to archbishop Stephen, bishop Jocelin, and the other exiles, that they can return in peace. Rymer's *Fœdera*, i, 170-173. *May 24.*

The interdict is taken off. *June 13.*

Bishop Jocelin is admitted to peace at Winchester before the king on St. Margaret's day. £750 is assigned to him in indemnity for losses. *July 20.² 13 Kal. Aug.*

Nicolas bishop of Tusculum came as legate. *Sep. 29, 1213.*

Conclave at Reading. Protest of the bishops late in exile. 15,000 marcs granted them in compensation for losses. M. Paris, *Hist. Angl.* ii, 145. Rot. Lit. Pat. 15 John. "Hugh de Nevile solvet episcopis (London, Ely, Hereford, Bath, Lincoln) 15,000 marcas pro rege"—apud Reading, December 12. *Dec. 6. Indemnity to exiled bishops.*

Alexander, dean since 1180, dies and is succeeded by Leonius. *Alexander the dean dies*

Thomas de Tornaco (Tournay) precentor.

Chapter ordinances are now made: *Chapter ordinances, upon Jocelin's return to his diocese. f. 101.*

(a) During the *annus post mortem* the fruits of the prebend to belong to the chapter—two parts to be divided among the canons—one part to belong to the representatives of the deceased, for debts, or alms for the soul.

(b) Dignitaries to be responsible for keeping their

---

1 and 2. Archer corrects M. Paris as to dates of both these transactions.

benefices in tenantable repair—"cum tali instauramento quale recepit."

(c) Allowances for improvements made, to be given as alms for the soul of the deceased. R. i, f. 29; R. iii, f. 13.

f. 103.
Sept. 29.
Vacant prebends and benefices.

(d) After consultation with the church of Sarum, with consent of dean and chapter *de communi voluntate*, (1) that fruits of all prebends vacant by death belong to the chapter; (2) Wedmore, when vacant by cession, not by death, to be appropriated to pious uses in the church of Wells, according to joint consent of bishop and canons; if by death of the dean, to follow the custom of other prebends; (3) fruits of all vacant dignities to belong to the bishop; (4) appointment of parochial vicars to be reserved for canon who shall succeed. Vicars choral to be appointed by bishop during vacancy of prebend. R. i, f. 58; R. ii, f. 14.

Confirmation of Savaric's grant of Lideard as prebend to the chapter.

f. 102.
Sept. 30.
Grants and confirmations.

Chapter to appoint a vicar—"cum cura animarum" —to be instituted by bishop. R. i, f. 45.

Wiveliscombe with Fifhide (Fifehead) chapel made a prebend. Vicar to receive three marcs from the prebend. R. i, f. 59; R. iii, f. 371.

Institutions of perpetual vicarages, and assignment of stipends.

Kingsbury vicarage to be the chancellor's presentation after death of present vicar. R. i, f. 46; R. iii, f. 157.

Ashill (Aishulle) advowson granted by Robert de Vallibus, confirmed by Alicia, his mother. R. 1, f. 39; f. 38 in dors. Witness to the grant—John, bishop of Norwich; to the confirmation, Richard, abbot of Muchelney.

Ilton advowson granted by Benedict, abbot of Athelney.

R. i, f. 38 in dors. Witnesses — Richard, abbot of Muchelney; master Helias de Derham; master John of Ileford; master William de Wells; Helyas chaplain; William de Hamme.

Confirmation by Leonius the dean and the chapter of a lease for life of half a virgate of land made by Iterius, prebendary of Wanstrow, to his nephew Ernulf; to return to the prebend after death. R. iii, f. 383.

Arbitration by bishop Jocelin between convent of Goldclive, Monmouth, and Leonius, dean and chapter of Wells, as to church of Staweia (Stowey), assigned to Goldclive. Pension of 40 marcs to be paid. R. i, f. 36 in dors.

Hinton Monachorum about this time founded *de novo* by Ela, countess of Salisbury. Jocelin confirms. Dugd. *Mon.* i, f. 960.

An instance of intimate knowledge of English diocesan affairs and interference by the pope.

Pope Innocent to Jocelin de Welles, bishop of Bath.

March 28 letter of Innocent III to bp. Jocelin.

"A certain M., a poor scholar now in orders, a teacher in schools, had laid violent hands on his scholars while teaching, and had fallen under censure. He has been absolved by the abbot of St. Victor, the duly appointed *penitentiarius* to receive penitents, and has been absolved—admit him again to his functions, and advance him."

Given at the Lateran, 5 Kal. April 1213, Charter 20.

Through 1213, the pope, by his legate, was protecting John—now his vassal since his surrender of

188   *Chapters in Wells History.*   [CHAP.

the crown at Dover, 15 May—against the king of France and the barons. John repents of concessions to the barons, and bribes the new legate, Nicolas of Tusculum. The bishops appeal against the tyranny and pride of the legate. The barons, under archbishop Stephen, unite to compel John to confirm the liberties of Henry I.

John is carrying on the war in France, and deceiving the barons with false promises.[1]

A.D. 1214.

16 John.   8 Stephen, archbishop.
17 Innocent III.   9 Jocelin, bishop of Bath and Glastonbury.
   Leonius, dean.

f. 104.
April 12.
Nicolas, the legate at Glastonbury attests bp. Jocelin's rights at Glastonbury

Nicolas bishop of Tusculum, papal legate, is at Glastonbury and Bath. Bishop Jocelin obtains from him a public sanction to his title of bishop of "Bath and Glastonbury,"[2] probably with a view to the suit in

---

1. Under this year Archer quotes from R. i, f. 29, a group of charters purporting to be letters from the church of Sarum of earlier date addressed to Ivo the dean, and R. the bishop. He discredits the authenticity and the early date of these documents, and considers that they were drawn up with a controversial purpose in the contention between bishop Drokensford and the chapter. "Conscriptae sunt istae literae ad quas Sarisburienses respondent primo die Octobris anno ut conjecturam facio 1319 cum Johannes de Drokensford episcopus visitationem decano et canonicis minitaretur." Cf. R. i, f. 249. But he admits the ordinance as to the "annus post mortem" into the annals of this year.

2. Bishop Jocelin's "style" is variously found in the documents of the time; in attestations to charters he signs sometimes, as "Jocelinus Bathoniensis."

E.g.   Rot. Cart. p. 170, anno 1207.
       Do.   p. 173, ,,   1213.

the Roman court, which was being moved at this time. R. iii, f. 111.

Cf. Rot. Pat. 16 John, 1215, pp. 129-132, contain several royal letters "ne dissolvatur unio," without the king's assent.

"Nicolas, papal legate, to all men. When lately we were at Glastonbury a certain clerk came and prayed us to cause him to be admitted as a monk and a brother. We therefore have admonished Jocelin bishop of Bath and Glastonbury, 'qui in eodem manerio vices gerit abbatis,' to cause this man to be accepted ; he has consented, and the prior and convent have accepted him. We, at the desire of the said bishop, have issued this letter and appended our seal. Given at Bath April 12." <small>Letter of the legate.</small>

King gives a charter "de libera electione prælatorum," to which Jocelin bishop of Bath and Glaston. is witness. (M. Paris, *Hist. Angl.* i, 367—Spelman's *Concilia*, ii, p. 135.) <small>f. 105. June 15.</small>

Nicolas the legate "auctoritate apostolica" relaxed the interdict throughout the kingdom, "in die Apostolorum Petri et Pauli." <small>June 29.</small>

Hugh, bishop of Lincoln, makes grants to bishop Jocelin and the see : <small>Bp. Hugh's grants to Wells. July 11, 12.</small>

<small>At other times with the title "Bathon. et Glaston."
    E.g. Rot. Cart. p. 202, anno 1214.
          ,,   p. 215, ,, 1215.
          ,,   p. 184, ,, 1216.
          ,,   p. 187, ,, 1216.
Before his consecration he was styled "J. Bathon. electo," (Rot. Cart. p. 63, anno 1206, March 3) and he was consecrated as "Episcopus Bathoniensis."

He is styled "Bathon. et Glaston." in the grant of Magna Charta 1215, and in the reissue of the charter 1216.</small>

(a) Half a knight's fee[1] in Draycot and Roborough. R. iii, f. 339 in dors, and f. 349.

(b) Half a knight's fee in Norton, with freedom from attendance at the meetings of the hundred of Cheddar and Wynescomb. R. iii, f. 350.

(c) The advowson of Axbridge. R. iii, f. 343 and f. 349.

(d) Freedom from dues to the hundred of Winterstoke of all bishop Jocelin's lands in the hundreds of Winterstoke and Cheddar.[2] R. iii, f. 347 in dors.

(e) Manor of Cheddar granted to bishop Jocelin and confirmed by the Crown at this time. Cf. R. i, f. 108.

Cessions by the convent of Bath. Chew.

The prior and convent of Bath surrender:

(a) The advowson of Chew, which they held from Savaric, and all rights in the church; they in return receive a pension of 10 marcs from Chew. R. iii, 294 in dors. Thomas, prior of Glastonbury, and the convent, confirm this grant. R. iii, f. 357 in dors.

Stoke Giffard.

(b) The advowson of Stoke Giffard, f. 106. R. iii, f. 350 in dors.

---

1. Note by Archer, quoting Du Fresne: "A knight's fee," as much land of the value of £20 as was held by a knight who was bound to military service of forty days with the king. "Half a knight's fee" equal to land of £10 value, and held by a knight bound to twenty days' service.

2. "Ut omnes homines absoluti essent de sectis hundredorum istorum scil. de servitio quo feudatarii ad frequentanda comitia hundredariorum tenebantur." Archer.

(c) The advowson of Dogmersfield and pension of 20 shillings. R. iii, f. 35. Thomas, prior of Glastonbury (d. 1215) attests and confirms. R. iii, f. 353, v. *Adam of Domerham*, p. 238. Dogmersfield is made a prebend in the church of Wells. R. i, f. 46, 180.

Dogmersfield; which is made a prebend next year.

Weston church is given to the convent of Bath. R. iii, f. 287.

The king, on advice of the papal legate Nicolas, archbishop Stephen, and others of his council, confirms the union between Bath and Glastonbury and the ordinance made in 1202.

R. iii, f. 17. Rot. Pat. 16 Johan., "de unione Bathon. et Glaston. ecclesiarum,"[1] *Adam of Domerham*, p. 239: "datum per manum Ricardi de Marisco, cancellarii nostri, apud novum templum London. vicesimo primo die Novembris, anno regni nostri decimo sexto."

f. 106.
Nov. 21.
Confirmation by the king of the union of Bath and Glaston.

The king grants to Jocelin the *patronatus* of the abbey. The rights appertaining to the *patronatus* are stated—
(a) That the abbot elect receive the temporalities from the hand of the bishop in lieu of the king.[2]
(b) Do feudal homage and service to the bishop "fidelitatem feodalem facturus et servitia feodalia."

f. 107.
Jan. 9, 1214-15.
Grant of *patronatus* of abbey to the bishop.

1. N.B. Erratum in Hardy's index of Pat. Rolls where the charter is entered under the heading "de unione Bath. et Well. eccles."

2. "Temporalia quæ regalia appellarentur si ad nos pertineret patronatus." The bishop stood in the place of the crown. But the bishop had to find the knight's service due from the abbey barony.

(c) The bishop in the vacancy of the abbey to have the custody and ordination of the abbey, "custodiam et ordinationem abbatiæ" and grant permission to elect, "ut dominus et patronus," dated as above, ix^{no} Januarii, anno sexto.

R. iii, ff. 16, 339. *Adam of Domerham*, pp. 240-42. The attestations of the document indicate the leading men of the king's party on the eve of the concession of Magna Charta : Stephen the archbishop, and the bishops of London, Winton, Ely, Hereford, Lincoln are among them.

f. 107.
Jan. 23,
1214-15.
Whitchurch
in Dorset.

Herbert, bishop of Salisbury, admitted William de Wellia to the church of Whitchurch, Dorset, on presentation of Robert de Mandeville. R. iii, f. 455.

Case between Richard parson of Whitchurch and Jordan Malet clerk about the chapel of Charmouth (Cernneure) adjudicated by abbot of Malmesbury and prior of Bradenestoke, papal commissioners, reserving rights of mother church of Whitchurch. R. iii, f. 455.

Cf. Charters bearing upon Whitchurch (Canonicorum). R. iii, ff. 450-457, and under year 1206, in Dorset.

A.D. 1215.

17 John.   9 Stephen, archbishop.
18 Innocent III.   10 Jocelin, bishop of Bath and Glastonbury.
   Leonius, dean.

f. 107.
Magna
Charta
granted,
15 June.

The meeting " in prato Renningmede inter Stanes et Windleshore" at which bishop Jocelin was present, when king John grants and confirms the great charter of liberties and twenty-five barons are appointed to carry out the provisions.

John secretly sends a statement of his grievances against the barons to pope Innocent.

The pope annuls the charter of liberties granted by the king. M. Paris, *Hist. Angl.* ii, 157-162.

Churches of Chew and Welinton are charged with the payment of 10 marcs each a year in endowment of the mass of Blessed V. Mary "quo canonici Wellenses in servitium beatæ Virginis animos suos magis impense intenderent."

Dated at Dogmersfield. Feast of St. Andrew.
Confirmed by the dean and chapter of Wells.
William de Wilton is persona of Chew.
Stephen de Tornaco of Welinton. R. i, f. 43.
See further under year 1239.

November 30.
Endowment of mass of blessed Virgin Mary.

A.D. 1216.

18 John, d. October 18.   10 Stephen, archbishop.
19 Innocent III. d. July 17.   11 Jocelin, bishop of Bath
1 Henry III.   Ralph of Lechlade,
1 Honorius III.   dean.

The vacant benefices belonged to the bishop. Bishop Jocelin, after consultation with dean Leonius and the chapter, now made over two parts to the *communa* of the chapter, and gave one part to the archdeacons of the place, binding the archdeacons to give two parts of their share in same manner to the *communa*. William of Bardeney, archdeacon of Wells, and

f. 106.
July 5.
Ordinance concerning vacant benefices.

William of Wrotham, archdeacon of Taunton, bound themselves by this ordinance and were appointed custodians of vacant benefices. Thomas, archdeacon of Glastonbury, and Hugh of Bath, not being content to follow this order, Jocelin made over to the *communa* the two parts out of their archdeaconries, leaving to them the third part. R. i, f. 59 ; R. iii, f. 12 in dors.

f. 107.
June 14.
Ordinance for election of a dean.
"Sub hoc tempus," Ralph of Lechlade, canon, is elected dean. The process of election and appointment observed in two former precedents in bishop Jocelin's time " and handed down from ancient days," is now confirmed by statute :

(a) The chapter petition the bishop for licence to elect.
(b) The canons elect from among their brethren.
(c) The chapter present the elect to the bishop and pray confirmation.

The charter is given at Bath on feast of Saint Basil in eleventh year of the bishop's pontificate. R. i, f. 113 in dors.

Pope Gregory IX in 1241 confirmed the election of dean John Saracenus, according to this precedent, and the right of the chapter to elect a dean from among the canons, according to the " antiqua et approbata consuetudo." R. i, f. 57.

There is a full statement of this same process of appointment in case of dean Pemple, 1361. R. i, ff. 247-250 ; and of dean Fordham, 1378, in R. i, ff. 267-278.

July 17.
Pope Innocent III died
xvi Kal. Aug. Pope Innocent died. Honorius III elected pope.

IV.]   *Bishop Jocelin,* A.D. 1206-1242.   195

King John died. Henry III a minor succeeds. <small>Oct. 18.
King John
died.</small>

On the Vigil of St. Simon and St. Jude Henry is crowned king at Gloucester by Gualo the legate and Peter bishop of Winchester; bishop Jocelin administers the oath. M. Paris, *Hist. Angl.* ii, 195. Ann. Waverl. p. 286. <small>Oct. 27.
Coronation
of Henry III.</small>

A.D. 1217.

2 Henry III.   11 Stephen, archbishop.
2 Honorius III.   12 Jocelin, bishop of Bath and
                          Glaston.
                     Ralph of Lechlade, dean.

Jocelin appointed one of the judges on circuit in Somerset and Western counties. Dugdale's *Chron. Series,* p. 7. <small>f. 108.
Jocelin
appointed
judge of
circuit.</small>

Institution of Richard of Aterbury as parson to the church of Charlton Makerel, saving to Robert de Meyse the perpetual vicarage on payment of 50 shillings to Richard and his successors. R. iii, f. 192 in dors. <small>Institution
to Charlton
Makerel.</small>

Confirmation by Thomas the precentor and the chapter of ordinance of bishop Jocelin, made " in partibus transmarinis," in exile, with consent of some of the chapter, remodelling and re-distributing Combe prebend and instituting provostship. <small>Division of
Combe
prebend.
Provostship
of Combe
instituted.</small>

Ten prebends to be made out of the prebend of Combe, to receive 10 marcs each, instead of 10 shillings —one appointed by the bishop to be provost—to pay the others, to hold, besides his own 10 marcs, the church of Combe, and whatever remained over from the fruits of Combe. The provost to pay 3 marcs annually to the vicar choral, the other prebendaries of Combe 2 marcs. R. i, f. 49.

For later arrangements, under year 1234, vide R. i, f. 50, and R. i, f. 205 in dors, and Archer in Hearne's *Adam of Domerham*, p. 214.

May 20. Excommunication of partisans of Louis of France.

The archbishop of York, bishop Jocelin, and other prelates pronounce excommunication on the followers of Louis of France. *Chron. de Mailros*, p. 195.

f. 109. Grant to the fabric by canon of Henstridge.

About this time, Ralph being dean, Alexander, canon of Henstridge, desiring to hasten, as far as lay in him, the building of the fabric of the church of Wells, "ut fabrica celerius ad optatam consummationem mea sedulitate consurgat," gives for his life, in lieu of the sum assessed upon his prebend for the fabric, the produce of the arable land of the rectorial glebe at Henstridge, half his meadow in Ridgehill, and one silver marc from the altarage of Henstridge, to dean Ralph and the canons who had charge of the fabric. After his death the land is to revert to the prebend. R. iii, f. 383.

Cf. R. i, f. 69, where a levy of one-fifth on the prebends by bishop Jocelin for the fabric is referred to in 1248; and cf. Osm. Reg. ii, 7, 9 where, in 1219, the canons of Salisbury pledge themselves to contribute to the new fabric of Salisbury according to the value of their prebends for the next seven years, their prebends to be sequestrated in default of payment (ii, 14), and non-resident canons to pay one-fifth to the communa of the residents. Osm. Reg. i, 366.

A.D. 1218-1219.

2-3 Henry III. 12-13 Stephen, archbishop.
2-3 Honorius III. 13-14 Jocelin, bishop of Bath and Glaston.
Ralph, dean.

R. iii, f. 263, and *Adam of Domerham*, pp. 464-474. <small>f. 109. Dissolution of union between Bath and Glastonbury.</small>
Letter of pope Honorius to bishop Jocelin, reciting the process by which the union was now dissolved:

    (a) Letter of commission to Pandulf, bishop of Norwich, and Richard, bishop of Salisbury to arbitrate between bishop and convent.

Dated "Romæ iv, Id. Junii pontificatus nostri anno secundo," 1218. <small>1218. June 4</small>

    (b) Report of papal commissioners of conference at Shaftesbury on octave of Saint John Evangelist, 1218-9. <small>f. 110. 1218-9. Jan. 3</small>

Abbot of Reading substituted for Pandulf in the commission. <small>1219, May 17</small>

    (c) "xvi, Kal. Junii. Indictione vii.[1] Incarnationis dominicæ anno MCC° nono decimo —Pontificatus Domini Honorii Papæ III, anno tertio," 1219.

Pope Honorius dissolves the union between see of Bath and convent of Glastonbury (Jocelino tandem annuente), and confirms term of composition made at Shaftesbury on octave of St. John the Evangelist, 1218-9, by the commissioners:

    (a) The convent shall elect their abbot;
    (b) The bishop shall retain the *patronatus* granted by the king in 1215;

---

1. Indiction vii, corresponds with the year 1219. Nicolas, *Chronology of History*, p. 58.

(c) The manors of Wynescumb, Blackford in Wedmore, Pucklechurch, and Cranmore, to remain with the bishop;

(d) The other manors assigned by the award of 1202 to the bishop to revert to the convent, Meare, Buckland, Keinton, Christ Malford, Badbury, and Ashbury, but the advowsons of these manors to belong to the bishop.

1219-20. March 29. Pope sanctions bishop's change of style.

Bull[1] of Honorius III, warranting the change of style from Bath and Glastonbury to Bath and Wells.

"Honorius, etc. Pandulfo Norwicensi Electo camerario nostro apost. sedis legato.

"Ven. pater noster Bathoniensis episcopus nobis fecit supplicari ut cum hactenus Bathon. et Glaston. epūs fuerit nuncupatus, ne videatur quasi capite diminutus nuncupandi se Bathon. et Wellen. episcopum sibi licentiam concedere dignaremur, præsertim quia sicut asserit, ecclesia Wellensis ab antiquo extitit cathedralis, prout constat ex privilegio sedis apostolicæ apparere, quamvis privilegium istud in registris quæsitum non potuerit inveniri set illud penes se habere idem episcopus asseverat.

"Estimantes itaque dignum antiquis ecclesiis antiquos reddere titulos dignitatum qui nonnunquam novas novis dignitatibus insignimus, discretioni tuæ per apostolica scripta mandamus, quatenus inquisita super hoc et cognita veritate, si rem inveneris ita esse, predicto epo se nominandi Bathoniensem epum et Wellensem auctoritate nostra concedas liberam facultatem.

---

1. This bull, not quoted by Archer, is here inserted to complete the history of the transactions.

"Viterbii, iv Kal. April. pontif. aº ivº" 1219, 1220. (Brit. Museum Add. MSS. 15,536).

Sanction was thus given for Jocelin's assumption of the style "Bath and Wells,"—the *privilegium* was contained in pope Nicholas' grant to bishop Giso in the chapter archives; but either Pandulf did not issue his licence, or Jocelin did not wish to offend Bath, and did not assume the double title, so far as we know.

On the eve of the Translation of Saint Benedict, at Glastonbury, bishop Jocelin, as patron, admits William the abbot elect; and on the feast, as diocesan, he blesses him. *Adam of Domerham*, p. 476.

f. 110.
1219. July 10

Jocelin is again appointed judge of circuit for this year, and sits at Exeter with other judges. A concord is there made with H. de Traci about advowson of South Bovi—the advowson to belong to the bishop. H. de Traci is granted participation in the prayers of the church of Wells. R. iii, f. 109, in dors.

Jocelin judge in circuit. Bovy Tracy.

Grant of land and houses for canons by Hugh archdeacon of Wells (successor of Hugh now bishop of Lincoln), lying between land and houses of Otho, and of Nicolas of Wells.

Canonical houses. Grant of land to chapter.

R. iii, f. 385. Witnesses, Hugh bishop of Lincoln; Ralph, dean; and Peter of Chichester, canon.

Bull for canonization of St. Hugh of Lincoln; the day of his burial to be kept as a festival, viz. November 17. (xv Kal. Dec.) Dated xiii Kal. Martii.

1219-20. Feb. 17. St. Hugh canonized.

The Dominican brothers come into England.

f. 111. Dominicans in England.

Ralph, the dean, dies.

Peter of Chichester, canon, is elected dean. R. i, f. 45.

Peter of Chichester dean.

A.D. 1220.

4 Henry III.   14 Stephen, archbishop.
4 Honorius III.   15 Jocelin, bishop of Bath.
  Peter of Chichester, dean.

f. 111.
April.
Precedence
in synod of
prior of Bath

Jocelin holds a synod at Bath; the question is raised, whether the prior of Bath or the dean of Wells shall sit on right of the bishop.

Precedence is given to the prior of Bath; "without any prejudice to the rights of church of Wells." R. i, f. 45.

July 7.
Translation
of St.
Thomas.

Institution of the festival of the "Translation of St. Thomas of Canterbury." The jubilee is kept on the fiftieth anniversary of his consecration, is a scene of great splendour, and the day is made an era of computation. Vide M. Paris, *Hist. Angl.* ii, 241-2 on the shrine of St. Thomas, of which Elyas of Derham and Walter of Colchester were the artificers.

April 28.

Foundation laid of the new church of Salisbury. Osmund Reg. ii, 14.

Whitsunday

Coronation of the young king at Westminster.

August 7.
Grant of oak
for fabric of
church from
Cheddar by
king.

Grant from the king to bishop Jocelin of oak timber, " 60 grossa robora in boscis nostris de Ceddar " for the fabric of the church of Wells, "ad rogum quendam faciendum ad operationem ecclesiæ suæ de Welles."

Rot. Lit. Claus. m. 6, p. 425, anno 4 Hen. iii, 1220 apud Oxon. vii die August.

Sept. 19.
Christian
Malford.

Dean Peter and chapter at bishop Jocelin's petition receive Ilditius, nephew of John, cardinal of St. Praxidius, vicar of Christian Malford, " ad firmarium," at a rent of 25 marcs.

The charter is dated " 1st year of Translation of St. Thomas."

R. i, f. 98; cf. R. i, f. 71. This transaction is referred to in 1249, and R. iii, f. 338 in 1245.

February 19, 1220-21. Richard, bishop of Salisbury, admits Hugh of Greneford to the church of Whitchurch at presentation of Robert de Mandeville. R. iii, f. 455.

Whitchurch.

A.D. 1221.

5 Henry III.	15 Stephen, archbishop.
5 Honorius III.	16 Jocelin, bishop of Bath.
	Peter of Chichester, dean.

Jocelin, in council with the dean and chapter, makes ordinances for the hospital of St. John at Wells, lately built by the bishop and his brother, bishop Hugh of Lincoln.

f. 111-112. Ordinance about the hospital of St. John at Wells, founded by bps. Jocelin and Hugh Feb. 19, 1220-21.

(a) The hospital to have chapel and bells—a cemetery for the brethren of the house. Those are named especially who had taken vows of going to the Holy Land, or were under the pledge, if called, of fulfilling their vows ("qui signati erant, et sub signo viventes, si ibidem conversati fuissent.")

(b) The rights of dean and chapter to parochial dues reserved.

(c) The master and chaplains to be appointed by the bishop, but to render canonical obedience to the dean and chapter.

R. i, f. 43, p. 168, the chapter ratify. R. ii, f. 16, in dors.[1]

---

1. Cf. R. iii, f. 248 in dors. Bishop Hugh in the draft of his will in 1211 had set apart 500 marcs "ad construendum hospitale apud

202   *Chapters in Wells History.*   [CHAP.

Oratory at Stathe.

The dean and chapter grant licence to the chaplain of the Lady Matilda, widow of Otho of Wandestre (Wanstrow), to serve in the oratory lately built at Stathe, in parish of North Curry—the chaplain to swear obedience to the dean and chapter, that he will not receive offerings due to church of North Curry or chapel of Stoke, nor alms for annuals or tricennials (30 masses on 30 days in succession) nor for any sacred office without express leave of the parish priest of North Curry. The licence granted only during the lifetime of the Lady Matilda, and during her residence at Stathe. No rights to accrue to any other possessor of the lands. The Lady Matilda and Oliver Avenel swear to observe conditions. R. iii, f. 38.

f. 113. Muddesley exchange.

To this time Archer assigns certain undated charters.

1. Alexander of Muddesley exchanges land in Muddesley with Peter the dean.

Boundaries are given. R. i, f. 44.

Exchange of Martock for Evercreech to the treasurer.

2. The church of Martock impropriated to the treasurer instead of Evercreech.

Jurisdiction of the archdeacon and of the abbot of "Saint Michael in periculo mortis" in Martock and of dean and chapter in Evercreech, reserved. R. i, f. 44 in dors.

Cession of land in Wedmore to dean.

3. Robert of Malherbe son of Henry of Muddesley releases to dean Peter his claim to half a virgate of land in Wedmore, in Bemeston hundred. R. i, f. 59.

Welles." At first a hostel for wayfarers—no mention of monastic brethren—and almshouse for poor and needy—those especially in the first instance out of employment by their vow of joining the crusade.

There were ten priests and brethren in 1350.

In 26 Henry VIII the yearly revenues of master and brethren amounted to £40 (Dugdale) or £41 3s. 6d. (Speed).

4. Convention between Peter the dean and the chapter and William de Ralegh canon of Wanstrow. R. iii, f. 399. *Exchange at Wanstrow.*

5. Walter Rofend grants to Walter de Purl canon of Wells half an acre in Cheddar, near the "curia canonicorum," *i.e.*, rectorial grange and manor house. R. iii, f. 408. *Cheddar.*

6. Benedict abbot and convent of Athelney grant to bishop Jocelin advowson of Sutton church. Witness—Richard, abbot of Muchelney. R. iii, 372, in dors. (cf. f. 81, anno 1198). *f. 114. Long Sutton.*

7. Also grant of advowson of Ilton. R. iii, f. 400, in dors.; R. i, f. 38. *Ilton.*

8. William Fitzarthur grants advowson of Weston (in Gordano). *Weston.*

Witnesses—Thomas de Cirencester, sheriff of Somerset and Dorset; John de Paulton; Henry de Campo florido; William, seneschal of the bishop: Baldwyn de Wayford; Thomas de Alta Villa (Hauteville); William de Bonneville. R. i, f. 43; R. iii, f. 356 in dors.

9. Abbey of Lonley presents to bishop Jocelin one of the monks as prior of Stoke Courcy. R. iii, f. 111 in dors. *Stoke Courcy.*

10. Hugh, chaplain of St. Bartholomew's hospital, London, grants to bishop Jocelin advowson of church of St. George de Heanton (Hinton St. George). R. iii, f. 347 in dors. *Hinton St. George.*

11. Bishop Jocelin grants to Thomas de Avenant, Bishopwoode in Lydiard, with feed for pigs and fuel " fualliam ad ignem." R. iii, f. 347 in dors. *Bishops Lydiard.*

12. Walter of Downhead and Walter of Wyke grant to bishop Jocelin five acres within the park in *Enlargement of bishop's park at Wells.*

exchange for lands at Horrington and Berihal. R. iii, f. 353 in dors. At the same time Richard FitzWalter of Henton grants farm and meadow near Wells. R. iii, f. 353 (Cf. with this king John's charters in his 9th year, 1207, "de via includenda" and "de parco apud Welles ex parte australi.")

Charter 29.
A.D. 1221.

Deed of exchange between Walter of Downhead and William of Wyke and bp. Jocelin.

"Omnibus Christi fidelibus ad quos presens carta[1] pervenerit, Walterus de Dunhieved et Walterus de Wyke salutem. Sciatis nos concessisse et in curia sua quieta clamasse in perpetuum de nobis et heredibus nostris, venerabili patri nostro domino Joscelino Bathonensi episcopo et successoribus suis, totam terram et pratum et quicquid habuimus vel habere debuimus

---

1. Note by bishop Hobhouse. Facts to be gathered from this deed of exchange:
  That there was a bishop's park at Wells, or had been of old.
  That it had been inclosed, *e.g.* "infra clausum parci."
  That laymen had been allowed by the carelessness of the bishops of the twelfth century to acquire rights therein and lands, "terra et pratum."
  That bishop Jocelin was engaged in restoring, if not enlarging, the park, by building a wall which he was carrying over the five acres now exchanged, and also in diverting the road to Doulting, substituting "cheminium exterius preparatum," *i.e.* a roadway outside the park wall.
  The bishop valued the five acres etc. very highly, as appears by the amount given in exchange, *i.e.* :—
  1. Two messuages in "villa de Welles," *i.e.* within the borough by East Wells.
  2. Two parcels of land held by their owner on the side of the way to Horrington (Horningedon).
  3. Ten-and-a-half acres of bishop's demesne at Karswell.
  4. Three acres under Stobery (Staberghe).
  5. Seventeen-acres-and-a-half of demesne at Stobery.
  6 Four acres at Beryl (Berihal).

infra clausum parci de Welles, cum quinque acris terre ex australi parte strate qua consuevit iri versus Dultinge, in quibus levatus est murus predicti parci et cheminum exterius preparatum. Hec autem predicta quieta clamavimus pro escambio quod ab eodem episcopo recipimus, videlicet pro duobus mesuagiis in villa de Welles biestwalles—pro uno scilicet mesuagio quod tenuit Cristina Pighele et pro alio quod tenuit Thudricus Pighel, et pro duobus particulis terre quas predicta Cristina tenuit—una ex boreali parte et alia ex australi parte vie qua iter versus Horningedone, et pro decem acris et dimidia apud Karswelle de dominico ipsius episcopi, et pro tribus acris subtus Staberghe quas Adam Grenne tenuit. Et pro decem et septem acris et dimidia apud Staberghe de dominico ipsius episcopi, et pro quatuor acris apud Berihale. Et pro una apud Ailtredehulle et pro septem acris prati de dominico prato suo de Horningedone. Et ad idem pratum claudendum secundo anno de bosco episcopi clausturam in perpetuum recipiemus. Quod ut ratum sit in perpetuum presenti carte sigilla nostra apposuimus. Hiis testibus, Thomae de Cicestria, Ricardo de Meauleberge, Reginaldo de Wudeforde, Willelmo Forestario, Helia filio Ricardi, Willelmo Coco, et multis aliis."

Of the witnesses, the first was a canon of Wells, two were members of the Wells manor court, as tenants of Melsbury and Woodford ; probably the rest were also

7. One acre of Ailtredehull.
8. Seven acres of meadow (bishop's demesne meadow) at Horrington ; and for enclosing the same in the second year (? every other year) fencing stuff (claustura) was to be given from the bishop's wood.

constituents of the court present at the publication of the deed—" cum multis aliis."

Buckland Dynham.
Letter of Stephen de Tornaco to bishop Jocelin, giving value of vicarage of Buckland. The vicar receives the altar oblations, small tithes (except of wool, flax, and lambs), eleven acres of land at Chescroft and Stockland. R. iii, f. 157 in dors.

A.D. 1222.

6 Henry III.   16 Stephen, archbishop.
6 Honorius III.   17 Jocelin, bishop.
                      Peter of Chichester, dean.

f. 115.
June 11.
Archbishop Stephen held provincial synod at Oxford. Matt. Westm. ii, p. 112.

Burnham.
Roger de Clifford recovered by purchase from the abbey of Gloucester right of presentation to Burnham. R. i, f. 194 in dors.

Bp. Jocelin buys land in London.
Reginald FitzReginald, of Cornhill, sheriff of Kent (selling his land to liquidate his father's fine of £2,116), sells to bishop Jocelin lands and messuage opposite church of St. Helena in London, " where now is Gresham College," for which the bishop has paid 200 marcs "in ghersumam." Boundaries are described as extending through Cornhill, Bishopsgate Street, Broad Street. Witnesses—" Petro (de Roches) Winton. episcopo ; Comite Will. marescallo, rectore domini regis et regni ; Hubert. de Burgo justiciario," etc. R. i, f. 17 in dors.

Cf. William Thorn. decem Scriptores, col. 1878.

                    A.D. 1223.
7 Henry III.   17 Stephen, archbishop.
7 Honorius III.   18 Jocelin, bishop.
                            Peter of Chichester, dean.

Gilbert Gule and his wife Christina, daughter of Thomas de Bolonia, grant or restore all the land which had belonged to Thomas in North Curry to the church of Wells, and swear to defend their right. ^{f. 115. June. North Curry.}

Sealed in chapter at Wells " in die octavarum apostolorum Petri et Pauli, anno a translatione beati Thomae Martyris iii°." R. i, f. 12 ; R. iii, f. 38.

William, abbot of Glastonbury dies, and is buried " in capitulo in parte aquilonari." ^{Sept. 16.}

Robert, prior of Bath, is elected abbot of Glastonbury by the convent. Bishop Jocelin confirms and gives the benediction in the church of Bath. *Adam of Domerham*, p. 478. ^{Election of abbot of Glastonbury}

Thomas succeeds Robert as prior of Bath. ^{Prior of Bath.}

William Flandre de Dinre (Dinder) grants to bishop Jocelin the advowson of the church of Dinder. Robert, abbot of Glaston. attests. R. iii, f. 403 in dors. ^{Dinder.}

Letter of Robert, abbot of Glaston. to bishop Jocelin. " The abbey had promised the church of Hamme to R. de Lexington at bishop Jocelin's request, but the pope's mandate orders the abbey to provide for one Benedict, *scriptor papæ*. They are willing, if their appointment of Benedict satisfies their promise to the bishop." R. iii, f. 110 in dorso.

A.D. 1224.

8 Henry III.   18 Stephen, archbishop.
8 Honorius III.   19 Jocelin, bishop.
                     Peter of Chichester, dean.

f. 115.
April 15.
King's grant to the fabric.

The king grants bishop Jocelin one penny a day out of the rents of Congresbury for five years for the fabric of the church of Wells, "ad operationem ecclesiæ Wellensis."

Godfrey de Mandeville gives advowson of church of Whitchurch in Dorset to bishop Jocelin.

Order made by bishop Richard of Salisbury about the tithes of Wodeton chapel, in parish of Whitchurch, confirmed by dean and chapter of Salisbury. R. iii, f. 450.

August 10.

Letters patent of king Henry III acknowledging aid given by prelates of province of Canterbury to the king when besieging Fulk de Breaute in Bedford. Their grant not to be taken as a precedent. Rot. Claus. i, 655. M. Paris, *Chron. Maj.* iii, 88. R. i, f. 17.

A.D. 1225.

9 Henry III.   19 Stephen, archbishop.
9 Honorius III.   20 Jocelin, bishop.
                     Peter, dean.

f. 115.
February 9, 1224-5.
Hinton charter-house.

Confirmation of Magna Charta by Henry III.

Ela countess of Salisbury carries out the will of her husband William Longsword[1] in the foundation and building of the Carthusian house at Hinton, "in parco

---

1. Archer says, "Sub hoc tempus aut annum insequentem." This should be put under the following year, 1226-7. William Longsword died suddenly March 7, 1226-7. Vide Osm. Reg. ii, 48.

de Henton, in loco qui vocatur Locus Dei; in honorem Dei et beatæ Virginis Mariæ et S. Johannis Baptistæ."

Grant of manors of Hinton and Norton, and the advowson of church of St. Philip at Norton.

Bishop Jocelin and Richard bishop of Salisbury attest.

Cf. Osmund Regist. ii, 118. The foundation charter of abbey of Lacock, founded by the same in 1229, "Locus beatæ Mariæ."

The Osmund Register under this year describes contemporary events at Salisbury: [Jocelin at Salisbury.]

September 28. The first service in the choir of the new church. The bishop dedicates three altars; the high altar to the Holy Trinity, the altars of St. Peter and St. Stephen.

September 29. The archbishop preaches to the people outside; afterwards, the bishop "intravit novam basilicam et in ea divina solemniter celebravit." The cardinal Otho, two archbishops, five bishops—among them bishop Jocelin—are present.

September 30. A chapter was held, in which the obligation of the canons to contribute to the fabric was reaffirmed. The rule of residence was relaxed for the next seven years. Osm. Reg. ii, 37-42.

A.D. 1226.

10 Henry III. 20 Stephen, archbp.
Gregory IX, pope, March 18. 21 Jocelin, bishop.
Peter, dean.

Milverton church, given to bishop Jocelin by William Brewer, *coram rege*, in presence of Stephen, archbishop; Peter, bishop of Winton; Hugh, bishop of [f. 116. Milverton church.]

Lincoln; William, bishop of Exeter; Godfrey of Ely. William of Exeter was nephew of William Brewer, counsellor of John and Henry. R. iii, f. 382; Cf. M. Paris, *Hist. Angl.* iii, 253.

Confirmation by archbishop Stephen, May 1226. R. iii, f. 368 in dors.

As a prebend appropriated to archdeaconry of Taunton.

In 1241 Milverton was made a prebend, value twenty marcs, and appropriated to archdeaconry of Taunton with consent of dean and chapter, and given to William of St. Quintin. R. iii, f. 336 in dors.

Axbridge vill bought by bp. Jocelin.

All right in Axbridge town sold to bishop Jocelin by Maurice de Gaunt for one hundred marcs. R. iii, ff. 341, 351 in dors.

Thomas Walensis confirms grant. R. iii, f. 375 in dors.

Maurice notifies the change of ownership to the townspeople. R. iii, f. 356.

Cf. R. i, f. 108. "The crown had in 1209 granted Axbridge to Hugh de Wells, archdeacon of Wells, as a fee at £20 per annum. The same Hugh granted Axbridge to Thomas Walensis, and he to Maurice de Gaunt, one of the king's justices, and he now to bishop Jocelin," answer to "Quo warranto" in 1280. Cf. under November 7, 1227.

f. 116. Martock.

Ralph, abbot, and convent of " Saint Michael de periculo mortis," in Normandy, grant to bishop Jocelin advowson of the church of Martock and pension from thence. R. iii, f. 287; cf. under year 1221.

" Ordinatio domini Jocelini super thesauraria Wellense." R. i, f. 34 in dors.

Re-constitution of office of treasurership.

Reconstruction of the treasurership as to
  (a) Receipts.
  (b) Duties of treasurer.

Memorandum.—As to the fixtures and stock (*instauramentum*) which belonged to the estate of the dean—to be left at death to his successor—24 oxen, etc. <small>Stock to be left on estates of the dean, precentor, and Wanstrow.</small>

Do.—To the precentor's prebend at Pilton, 8 oxen, etc.

Do.—To the prebend of Wanstrow, 8 oxen, etc. R. i, f. 34. Printed in *Adam of Domerham*, pp. 216, 217.

Grant of West Harptre by William Fitz-John de Harpetre. R. iii, f. 355. <small>West Harptre.</small>

King Henry confirms to bishop Jocelin manors and advowsons ceded by the abbey of Glaston at the final concord 1218-9. Reg. iii, f. 99; cf. iii, f. 393. <small>Jan. 22, 1227. Confirmation of Glastonbury manors to bishop.</small>

Confirmation to bishop Jocelin of grant by king Richard to bishop Reginald of keeping dogs for the chase. <small>Feb. 4, 1226-7.</small>

Confirmation of king John's grant of North Curry to the canons. R. iii, f. 407; cf. R. iii, f. 10. <small>Confirmation of North Curry. Feb. 12.</small>

Foundation of Alba Aula (Whitehall), Ilchester, by William Dacus as a hospital for wayfarers "pauperes debiles peregre profiscentes." Charter attested by archbishop Stephen, d. 1228, and Richard Poore of Salisbury, translated to Durham 1228. Cf. Reg. Drokensford, f. 58. <small>Whitehall at Ilchester founded "circa dies istos."</small>

Honorius III died. <small>March 15. Death of pope Honorius.</small>

Gregory IX elected. *Concilia*, tom. xi, col. 242-309. <small>Election of Gregory IX.</small>

Sub hoc tempus Henry Lovesert gives bishop Jocelin four acres in Winscombe, and a meadow to William of Keynsham, parson of church of St. James at Winscombe. R. iii, ff. 99, 100.

A.D. 1227.

9 Henry III. 21 Stephen, archbishop.
2 Gregory IX. 22 Jocelin, bishop.
　　　　　　　　Peter, dean.

f. 117.
May 26.
Glaston
privileges
confirmed
by king.

Renewal by Henry III of charter of privileges granted to Glastonbury abbey by Henry II, May 26, anno Regni 11°. Reg. iii, f. 23, in dors. *Adam of Domerham*, p. 479.

f. 118.
Oct. 6.
Exemption
of chapter
from fines.

Charter of bishop Jocelin to the dean Peter and chapter—that the dean and chapter shall be exempt from all fines "de murdris, etc.," to the king and answerable only to the bishop. Given at Wells, "Octavis S. Michaelis. Anno pontificatus 22°." R. i, f. 59 ; R. iii, f. 10.

Nov. 7.
Axbridge.
Vill given by
bp. Hugh.

Bishop Hugh of Lincoln grants to his brother Jocelin the vill of Axbridge, and all rights therein. A long list of attesting witnesses ; canons of Lincoln, canons of Wells, and laymen.

Given at Tinghurst " per manum Radulfi de Waravill," canon of Lincoln.

November 7, anno Pontif. 18 . R. iii, f. 342.

A.D. 1228.

12 Henry III. 23 Jocelin, bishop.
3 Gregory IX. Peter, dean.

Archbishop Stephen Langton died. Matt. Paris, *Hist. Angl.* ii, 302.

Cheddar and
Axbridge
confirmed.
May 9.

King Henry confirms king John's confirmation of bishop Hugh's grant to Jocelin of Cheddar and Axbridge. In Inspeximus of Edw. I 1324. R. iii, f. 392 ; cf. R. i, f. 108.

Bishop Jocelin, at petition of dean and chapter, grants to Helias, chaplain and canon of the prebend of Compton Huish in Brentmarsh, formerly a member of the manor of Banwell and held with prebend of Compton. Thomas prior of Bath attests. R. i, f. 27, n. 85 ; R. iii, f. 388 in dors.

Huish in Brentmarsh attached to Compton prebend. August 22.

1. Lucia daughter of John of Kardonville gives to Helias chaplain and canon her land in Wells lying between her brother's land and the Muntoria, which had belonged to Walter Malger, " quæ vocatur Muntoria," subject to land rent of 12 pence to Walter of Downhead and his heirs. Lambert, subdean, attests. R. i, f. 87.

f. 119. Grants of canonical houses at Wells by Helias, the chaplain.

2. John her brother, and Mirabel sister, give the land to Helias on the eastern boundary of the estate, and the *columbarium* there—at rent of two pence. Helias gives in one case 2 marcs, in the other 20 shillings, in recognition. Peter, the dean, attests.

3. Helias gives these lands to the chapter for the use of a resident canon, reserving the rent of 12 pence and 1 marc to be distributed at his obit between the canons and vicars celebrating, by the communars (" præpositi ni fallor, de Comba et Winesham.")
Peter, the dean, attests.

Charter 35—Grant of the " Muntoria," " hodie Mount Roy," by Helias the chaplain. R. i, f. 27 ; cf. i, f. 161, 2.

4. Roger Burgeys gives to Richard son of Ivo Cade, land between that of Ralph Preciosus and of the Kardonville family.

5. Richard grants same to William, a vicar, called " the archdeacon," with half acre in Chalve croft ; with

three shops in High Street of Wells ("in magno vico") subject to the payment of—

    (a) 8 pence to John of Palton.
    (b) 3 „ to Ernisius of Downhead.
    (c) 8 „ to the bishop for one shop.
    (d) 8 „ „ for the other two shops.
    And with provision for his obit.

William, "the archdeacon," gives the same to the chapter, with charge—

    (a) Of 11 pence to the lord.
    (b) Of endowment of his obit with the remainder.

6. William Buche (Buck) of Wells gives to the chapter lands which he had bought from Milo, originally part of the Kardonville lands, "apud Muntoriam," charged with 6s. a year, to be distributed at the obit of himself and Alicia his wife among the clergy there present. R. i, f. 162, 163; cf. Archer's Long Book, pp. 100, 129; and compotus of 1391, pp. 281, 282, Wells MSS.

By these grants three more parcels of land adjoining the land of Walter Malger in the "Muntoria," now called "Mount Roy," on the north side of the church are now taken into the "Liberty." (Cf. grants under year 1207.) Two more obits are now founded, of Elias the chaplain, and William Buche.

This house of William, "apud la Montorie," is granted as a canon's house afterwards to William Burnell, subject to charge of six shillings to be paid to the obits of his predecessors, Lucas Membury and Alice Buche. R. i, f. 111. Edward de la Cnole is then dean, 1264.

A.D. 1229.

14 Henry III.   1 Richard, archbishop.
4 Gregory IV.   24 Jocelin, bishop.
                  Peter, dean.

Royal grants to bishop and dean and chapter:—   *f. 120-1. Crown grants, May 5.*

1. Deafforestation of North Curry manor. May 5, anno regni 13°. R. i, f. 10; R. iii, f. 26.
2. Freedom from tolls, "quietancia thelonei," to all tenants except tenants *in capite* of bishop, dean and chapter of Wells, abbot of Glastonbury, prior of Bath. R. iii, f. 14 printed in app. to Hearne's *Adam of Domerham*, p. 247).   *May 15.*
3. Deafforestation of Congresbury manor. R. iii, f. 395.   *May 15.*

Richard Grant, chancellor of Lincoln, is consecrated archbishop at Canterbury, bishop Jocelin assisting, on June 10, Trinity Sunday. M. Paris, *Hist. Angl.* ii, 318.   *June 10. Jocelin at Canterbury.*

Confirmation by king of donations of Ela countess of Salisbury to Carthusians. Ralph of Chichester, chancellor, and bishop Jocelin attest. Reg. Rad., f. 289.

Foundations of Maurice of Gaunt at Bristol.   *Gaunt Hospital at Bristol.*

(1) Almshouse for one hundred poor and chaplain.
(2) A chantry at St. Augustine's, Bristol. He grants to canons of St. Augustine, the manor of Poulet, mills at Weare and at Radewik, and rents of houses in Bristol for the endowment. Local notabilities attest, lay and cleric: Robert de Gurnay,

William FitzJohn of Harpetre, Robert de Berkeley canon of Wells, Jordan Warr, Gilbert de Schipton, Adam de Budeford, William de Hida, Reginald and Gilbert de Sarum. R. iii, f. 280.

Next year. Inspeximus and confirmation by Robert de Gurnay, for himself and heirs, of above charter, on security of bishops of Worcester, Jocelin of Bath, Richard of Chichester, chancellor, Hubert de Burgh, "Comes Cantiæ et Angliæ justiciar," Anselm bishop elect of St. David's, Stephen de Segrave, John Marshall, Hugh fitz Richard, Jordan la Ware, Gilbert de Sifton, John de Campo Florido, Henry de Veir, Elga de Staford, Ralph Russell, Tervic clericus. R. iii, f. 280 in dors.

A.D. 1230.

14 Henry III.   2 Richard, archbishop.
5 Gregory IX.   25 Jocelin, bishop.
                       Peter, dean.

Exchange of land in Pucklechurch between bishop Jocelin and John of Abbetestun (Abson).

A.D. 1231.

15 Henry III.   3 Richard, archbishop.
6 Gregory IX.   26 Jocelin, bishop.
                       Peter, dean.

Nov. 10, f. 122. Harpetre. Robert de Gurnay confirmed grant of church of Harpetre. Gives four acres of land—two of meadow to bishop Jocelin in Chew. R. iii, f. 269 in dors, and iii, f. 368. Cf. under year 1226. R. iii, f. 342, f. 353.

Arbitration by bishop Jocelin between archdeacon of Wells and Helias, prebendary of Compton, about Huish in Brentmarsh, Easter, March 23, R. iii, f. 389, by which it was determined that Huish belongs to Compton, and is exempt from jurisdiction of the archdeacon of Wells. July 25. R. i, f. 27. *(f. 122. Huish in Compton. March 23. July 25.)*

Royal charter confirming liberties of Cheddar to bishop Jocelin. June 11. R. iii, ff. 394-5. *(Cheddar. June 11.)*

Confirmation of former privileges to bishop Jocelin, dean and chapter of Wells, and prior and convent of Bath. R. iii, f. 394; also quoted R. i, ff. 1 and 2.

Royal licence of making a will and disposing of all property, granted to bishop Jocelin and his executors until Michaelmas following death. R. iii, f. 340 in dors; and iii, f. 348; and f. 395. *(Royal grants.)*

Archbishop Richard dies on return from Rome at St. Gemma; buried in the church of the Minorites. M. Paris, *Hist. Angl.*, ii, 336. *(f. 123.)*

Controversy between rector of Whitchurch and convent of Abbotsbury.

Robert de Mandeville, patron of the church, and Robert bishop of Salisbury, confirm Jocelin's ordinances about church of Whitchurch. R. iii, f. 453.

A.D. 1232.

16 Henry III. 27 Jocelin, bishop.
7 Gregory IX. Peter, dean.

Hugh, bishop of Lincoln, gave patronage of Hameldun and pension from St. Peter's, Stanford, to the bishop of Lincoln. R. iii, f. 192. *(f. 123.)*

Bishop Jocelin assigns tithes to the vicar of Pilton. William Bytton, archdeacon of Wells, attests.

	Roger, abbot, and convent of Athelney confirm the grant of lands of Pitney and Wern, made to parish church of Huish by bishop Jocelin. R. i, f. 40; R. iii, f. 365.
November 8	Jocelin grants church of Evercreech to hospital of St. John in Wells; confirmed by prior and convent of Bath. R. iii, f. 159.
1232-3. Morrow of St. Benedict. March 22.	Jocelin decides controversy between Glaston and Martin de Summis, "subdiaconus dom. Papæ," by giving tenths of church of Butleigh and of Domerham Park to Martin, and £100 to be paid in five years for arrears. R. iii, f. 346 in dors., and f. 347.

Cf. Royal letters Henry III, A.D. 1223. The king's protection is asked by the podestà of Milan in the suit between M. de Summis, a Milanese, and Glastonbury.

Martin de Summis, one of a powerful Milanese family, had been the champion of the convent in their war with Savaric, and now the monks refused to fulfil their bonds to him for his losses in their service.

A.D. 1233.

17 Henry III.   28 Jocelin, bishop.
8 Gregory IX.   Peter, dean.

f. 123. March 25. Rights in Stathmore, Saltmore.	Composition between dean and chapter and John of Alre in chapel of St. Gregory de Stoke apud North Curry as to mutual rights in Stathmore and Saltmore. R. i, f. 12, iii, f. 35.
	Confirmed in curia regis in Hilary term. R. i, f. 134. R. iii, f. 36.
August 15. Weston-by-Worle.	Jocelin ordained that the parson of "Weston prope Worle" should pay to the treasurer from the fruits of the benefice one hundred pounds of wax annually, fifty on "the Passion of St. Andrew," fifty on the "Trans-

lation," and that the treasurer should provide two wax candles to be burnt perpetually before the high altar day and night at every celebration of divine offices in the choir. R. i, f. 214. R. iii, ff. 281, 282.

Composition and *finalis concordia* made about lands in Lamelegh by Stoke, and Wrentich and Garstone, and Huntesham, belonging to the canons. R. iii, f. 31. R. i, f. 13; R. iii, f. 30; R. i, f. 13; R. iii, f. 36; R. iii, f. 23 in dors.

A.D. 1234.

18 Henry III 1 Edmund, archbishop.
9 Gregory IX. 29 Jocelin, bishop.
　　　　　　　Peter, dean.

Hugh, bishop of Lincoln, brother of bishop Jocelin, dies, and is buried at Lincoln, February 10. [f. 124. February 7. Bp. Hugh dies.]

M. Paris, *Hist. Angl.* ii, 375. The character there given of him by the monk of St. Albans, "canonicorum sanctimonialium et omnium religiosorum malleus," must be estimated by considerations of the party spirit between the regulars and the secular clergy. The like character is given by M. Paris to Hugh's successor, bishop Grossetête (iii, 528), and by the Glastonbury writers to bishop Jocelin. *Adam of Domerham*, p. 445. [His character by M. Paris.]

iv. Non. April. 4 S. in Lent, *dominica qua cantatur lætare Jerusalem*, Edmund Rich, of Abingdon, canon and treasurer of Salisbury, is consecrated at Canterbury archbishop. Matt. Paris, *Hist. Angl.* ii, 367. [Edmund archbishop April 2.]

Combe præpositura, consisting of Combe (St. Nicholas) manor and church, and churches of Chard and Wellington, now united with *præpositura* of Wynesham, consisting of Wynesham manor and church. R. 1, i 50 and f. 205 in dors. Cf. *Adam of Domerham*, p. 214. [f. 125-6. Dec. 26. Union of provostship of Combe and Wynesham.]

Ordinance of the bishop, the dean and canons consenting to the union on these terms:

The provost of Combe without cure of souls is charged,

(1) With administration of fifteen prebends, retaining one for himself and paying to each ten marcs; each canon to pay two marcs to a vicar (choral) at Wells—

(2) With support of a vicar at Wells at three marcs—

(3) With payment of twenty marcs to the mass of the blessed Virgin at Wells—

(4) And of ten marcs to the "missa de defunctis."

Formation of perpetual vicarages of—

(a) Wellington. Endowed with lesser tithes and altar gifts of Wellington and Buckland, of mills and of hay, except from the bishop's demesne and that of Sir Gerbert at Welinton.

Vicarage-house assigned on north side of church of Wellington, and on east side of church of Buckland.

(b) Chard. Endowed with lesser tithes and altar gifts of churches of Chard and its chapels (the bishop's lands and mills excepted), charged with payment of three marcs to the provost.

Vicarage-house assigned on east side of church, the bishop to present to Chard and Wellington.

(c) Combe. Endowed with lesser tithes of the mother church and of chapel of Watleston to the amount of five marcs; deficiency to be made up out of provost's lands otherwise exempted from payment to vicarage.

Vicarage-house assigned on north side of road to Stanton (White Stanton).

(d) Wynesham. Endowed in like manner to same amount, and with like exceptions.

The provost to present to Combe and Wynesham. The parochial vicars to be responsible to the bishop "in spiritualibus;" to the provost "in temporalibus." The bishop to have jurisdiction over churches of Wellington and Chard. Dean and chapter to have jurisdiction over Combe and Wynesham. *Wynesham vicarage.*

On death or vacancy of the provostship the fruits to belong to his estate until St. John Baptist's day next.

The value of the vicarage is five marcs. R. i, f. 50 and i, f. 205.

The ordinance decrees the amount of stock, *instauramentum*, and the proportions of land in cultivation on the manors to be transmitted in succession.

The manor of Combe consisted of:
 334 acres—107 in corn, 149 "de avena;"
 78 in fallow (de warecto);
 40 oxen of the value of 5s. each;
 200 sheep (oves et multonias) at 12d. each.
At Wynesham :—16 oxen at 3s. 6d.
  132 sheep at 5d.
  53 lambs at 2¼d.
  6 sows, 1 boar, at 4d.

Cf. Hearne's edition of *Adam of Domerham*, p. 214. *North Curry*

About the same time a vicarage is endowed with tithes and offerings at North Curry by the dean and chapter, reserving "garbas cujusque bladi in horto et in agro"—mills and fisheries and hay.

Richard de Tregoz appointed to serve the church

and chapel of Hache in person or by a fit chaplain. R. iii, f. 38, in dors.

Circa dies istos.

ff. 126-7. Canonical houses in Wells bought and given to the church by Roger the chaplain. Cf. under year 1228.

(1) Thomas Lock, son of Adam Lock the mason, *cementarius*, made over to Roger of Chewton, canon and chaplain, for 10 marcs, his houses in Wells, a croft, and half an acre "in campo Wellensi."

Agnes, his mother, confirms her son's gift. R. i, f. 34. R. iii, f. 161.

Lambert, sub-dean, and Richard de Wells, canon, the executors of Adam Lock, approve and seal the grant of Thomas Lock.

The grant of Agnes is attested by Lambert, sub-dean, master Elyas de Derham seneschal of bishop Jocelin, Richard de Wells, William de Bechamstede, canons; master Vincent, Walter de Bridport, Richard de Langport, vicars; Walter, the chamberlain; Lawrence and Ivo Cade, praepositi of Wells; Deodatus and Thomas Noreis, *cementarii*. Vide Charter 23.

Confirmation by Lambert, sub-dean, of a release of Thomas Lock, son of Adam and Agnes Lock. (Cf. earlier document in Charter 30), A.D. 1229, which contains a first grant of Thomas Lock, conveying land in Stobery to Roger of Chewton.

We have here the names of masons under bishop Jocelin—Adam and Thomas Lock, father and son—Deodatus—Thomas Noreis.[1]

(2) William, son of Peter Canutus, made over to Roger the chaplain his houses in Wells for rent of 18 pence.

1. Vide Appendix R.

A.D. 1235.

19 Henry III. 2 Edmund, archbishop.
10 Gregory IX. 30 Jocelin, bishop.
Peter, dean.

(3) January 14. Peter, the dean, and chapter granted to Roger of Chewton the houses which had belonged to Peter Canutus for 18 pence rent, in consideration of Roger having satisfied the claim of Ernisius of Downhead in the king's court. R. i, f. 35. ff. 126-7.

4 January 13. Roger made over to the church, for the use of a canon of Wells, three houses, after his death on the same rent, on the condition that the *communarius* shall distribute 10 shillings to the canons and vicars present at his obit. R. i, f. 35. Charter 32.

January 13. Dean and chapter confirm this. R. i, f. 35. f. 127.

Roger grants other houses, which had belonged to Reginald of Waltham, to Richard of Kentiswood, chancellor, and his successors, for the use of the schools of Wells, on condition: [Grant of houses for schools, "in usum scholarum" and "domus scholarchæ."]

(1) That the chancellor shall confer them on the master of the schools.

(2) He shall pay rent at Easter of 12 pence to John of Palton, ditto to Henry of Waltham, and 7 pence to the chapter.

Another sum to be spent at his obit in distribution:

(a) To three clerks at three altars of the church;
(b) to sacrist; (c) to boys present, and (d) to poor.

(3) The master shall keep the buildings in order.

(4) The master and scholars shall celebrate annually his obit in "aliquo loco competenti."

(5) The boys, who know the psalms to recite the penitential psalms, others the prayers, and all shall pray daily for the soul of Roger and his family before they leave the school, and they shall sing an antiphon of the Blessed Virgin on Wednesday and Friday on coming to school. R. i, f. 33.

Richard de Wells, Walter de Derham, and dominus Jocelin *canonicus Wellensis*, attest.

Cf. Charter 36. Grant by Katherine, widow of Henry de Waltham, to Roger, of her share of lands.

f. 126 in dors.
Warminster prebend.

Arbitration by Richard, bishop of Durham, between bishop Jocelin and Thomas Mauduit about Warminster prebend and advowson.

(1) Advowson to belong to Thomas.

(2) A portion of tithes to value of 30 marcs reserved to the bishop to form a prebend for a canon of Wells. R. iii, f. 110-111.

John Uffington is admitted by bishop Robert to the prebend presented by bishop Jocelin.

Four marcs are assigned to the vicar choral at Wells, and the land to the prebend, according to arbitration. R. iii, ff. 109-110. These charters quoted by Archer are not now found in the Register. Four folios have been cut out in the Register, but the paging, which is of later date, goes on unbroken.

f. 127.
Patronatus of Glastonbury confirmed to the bishop.

Confirmation to bishop Jocelin of the *patronatus* of the abbey of Glastonbury, April 25, "anno regni 19°" given by the hand of Radulf, bishop of Chichester, chancellor, attested by Richard, bishop of Durham, Walter of Kaerleon, Hubert de Burgh com. Cantiæ, Philip de Albiniato, Godfrey de Craucumb, seneschals. R. iii, f. 15.

Wynescomb church dedicated by bishop Jocelin in honour of St. James. August 26, anno pontif. 30°.   *Winscomb church dedicated.*

Endowment by Henry de Lovesert of the church with four acres.   *Endowed. 1236.*

A meadow to the parson of Wynescomb, and an alder bed "alnetum suum." R. iii, f. 100.

            A.D. 1236.
20 Henry III.   3 Edmund, archbishop.
11 Gregory IX.   31 Jocelin, bishop.
                  William de Merton, dean.

Dean Peter of Chichester dies; his executors are bishop Jocelin, Hugh, archdeacon of Taunton, and William of Bitton, sub-dean. R. i, f. 190.   *f. 127. Dean Peter dies.*

William de Merton elected dean.   *William de Merton dean.*

John of Palton renounces his right to two marcs from the houses of Roger the chaplain, according to his will made over to him by the executors of Roger, William the dean, and Richard Kentiswood, chancellor. R. i, f. 33.

Bishop Jocelin consecrates church of Compton Episcopi, and endows the church with ten acres in the moor to be closed; he grants to Helias, chaplain, canon, and parson of Compton to run eight oxen, together with the bishop's oxen, in the pastures of the bishop's manor. R. i, f. 26.   *f. 128. Compton Episcopi. July 13.*

Confirmation by dean and chapter. R. iii, f. 338.

Bishop Jocelin grants to dean William Merton the houses which Peter, late dean, held, lying between houses of Richard the chancellor and Henry of London, canons.   *Deanery houses. Sept. 19.*

Given by the hand of Master William de Maydenstone (Maidstone) in chapter, Sept. 29, 1236. R. i, f. 43.

The canon of Yatton had leased for ten years the rectory of Yatton to the abbot and convent of St. Augustine's, Bristol. William, provost of Combe, becomes sub-tenant of abbot of St. Augustine, Bristol, as firmarius of Yatton for ten years from 1237 for 45 marcs a-year, the dean and chapter become surety for him on the security of his provostship and all his goods.

Octave of St. Martin, 1236. R. i, f. 61.

A.D. 1237.

21 Henry III.   4 Edmund, archbishop.
12 Gregory IX.   32 Jocelin, bishop.
                          William de Merton, dean.

f. 127. Congresbury to the *communa*. May 1.

Bishop Jocelin gave the church of Congresbury to the canons in augmentation of their *communa*, reserving appointment of a vicar.

Vicarage endowed.

The vicarage endowed with lesser tithes, offerings at altar, and a third of the tithe of hay—the "curia personæ" to belong to canons. Another curia to be assigned to the vicar near the church. A third of ten acres of wood belonging to the church to belong to the vicar—the vicar to pay archdeacon's procurations and "cathedralicum," and a third of all other dues. Wells, in festo St. Phil. et St. Jacobi, 1237. R. i f. 43 in dors.

Jurisdiction of dean and sub-dean.

Arrangement made by bishop Jocelin between dean and subdean as to jurisdiction over town and suburbs. Dean, when present, to take cognizance of all causes, in his absence the subdean; in the absence of both the dean's official.

Members of the bishop's *familia* to be tried by the bishop, or his official, the money fines inflicted on them to go to the fabric of the church; in other cases the fine to belong to the dean or subdean, whichever tries the case, after paying fee of the apparitor. R. i, f. 44.

Confirmation by papal legate Otho (cardinal-deacon of St. Nicholas in carcere Tulliano) of Jocelin's ordinance concerning election of dean, 1216. f. 128. Ordinance of election of dean confirmed.

Bishop Jocelin arbitrates between dean and chapter and Alured, lord of South Barrow, about patronage of South Barrow: South Barrow.

(1) The advowson to belong to the dean and chapter, according to gift of grandfather of Alured to bishop Reginald. R. i, f. 35.

(2) Pension to the chapter remitted.

(3) Jurisdiction transferred to archdeacon of Wells.

(4) The dean and chapter present as vicar the nominee of Alured, Thomas of Alitheford (Alford). R. i, f. 35.

Release by William the chaplain and the brethren and sisters of the hospital of St. Bartholomew, London, to bishop Jocelin of rent of ten shillings, which he used to pay to the hospital on his messuage in St. Clement "de Denissemans churche" (St. Clement Danes), on south side of church towards the Thames, paying yearly a pound of pepper. Land in St. Clement Danes.

Attested by Andrew Bukerell, mayor of London, Richard Renger, Roger le duc, Tervic de Colonia, Stephen de la Strande, Richard Fitzedward. R. iii, f. 348 in dors. Charter 36.

A.D. 1238.
22 Henry III. 5 Edmund, archbishop.
13 Gregory IX. 33 Jocelin, bishop.
William of Merton, dean.

Obit of Peter, late dean, in the chapel of St. Calixtus. Peter of Chichester, late dean, had left land in Merlegh of Wookey to endow his obit. R. iii, f. 131 in dors.

William of Maulesbury (Melbury) had renounced all rights in that land. R. iii, f. 190.

Bishop Jocelin desiring to retain those lands in Wookey in the bishop's hands, and also to carry out the dean's bequest, gave to the church in exchange 60 shillings out of the £7 10s. due from the archdeacon of Wells to endow the mass at the altar of St. Calixtus, to be thus distributed:

1 penny to vicar celebrating.
1 farthing to the vicar assisting.
5 shillings for lights.
10 shillings on the anniversary. R. iii, f. 131-2.
March 26, 1238. R. iii, f. 190.

Thomas, prior of Bath, and the convent attest. R. iii, f. 363 in dors. and f. 364.

Whitchurch. Godfrey de Mandeville gave advowson of Whitchurch Canonicorum to bishop Jocelin. R. iii, f. 450.

William Longsword, earl of Salisbury, granted for himself and his heir William de Bratton, to the canonry of Whitchurch or to the dean and chapter of Wells to make a walled park " ad cuniculos servandos," and surrendered his right of way for his cattle " jus chaciæ," *i.e.* " viam per quam aguntur animalia ad pascua." R. iii, f. 375.

A.D. 1239.

23 Henry III.	6 Edmund, archbishop.
13 Gregory IX.	39 Jocelin, bishop.
	William of Merton, dean.

Bishop Jocelin confirms grant by dean Peter (dated 1236) and the chapter to Robert Gyfard, chaplain of St. Cuthbert's, Wells, of all lesser tithes and offerings, reserving greater tithes, and of vineyards, and mills, and tithes due to the White Monks, and tithes of hay, but these last to belong to the vicar in Priddy, Wytenal, and Chilcote. f. 124. April 1. St. Cuthbert's, Wells made a vicarage.

Vicar to pay a pension of twenty marcs to the chapter. R. i, f. 101 in dors.; cf. R. i, f. 104.

May 2. Bishop Jocelin confirms Lydeard to the canons "ad augmentum communæ." R. i, f. 30; R. iii, f. 408. f. 129. Bishop's Lydeard.

September 30. North Curry, "prædium et ecclesia," confirmed again, subject to the provision for a vicar to be appointed by dean and chapter. R. i, f. 30; R. iii, f. 408. North Curry

Dedication of church of Combe, "in honorem sc̄i. Nicolai," by Stephen, bishop of Waterford, on mandate of bishop Jocelin, but in his presence. Church of Combe St. Nicholas. Consecrated August 9. Endowment.

Bishop Jocelin endowed it, giving the provost of Combe patronage of the vicarage of Chard, the mills of Fordyngton, Hornysbowe, and South Chard, but charged with pension of twenty shillings to the bishop from South Chard.

The vicarage of Chard no longer to pay forty shillings to the provost. Cf. Reg. Drokensford, p. 262 n.

230   Chapters in Wells History.   [CHAP.

f. 129.
October 23.
Dedication of church of Wells.

On day of St. Romanus the church of St. Andrew in Wells consecrated " in honorem S. Andreæ apostolorum mitissimi."

Wynescumb manor and church given to the communa. Vicarage formed.

Wynescombe manor and church are given to the *communa*, reserving

(a) Payment of five marcs to the vicar, to be appointed by the dean and chapter.

(b) Dues to the hundred of Banwell.

This grant is made " on the morrow of the dedication of the church of Wells," thus commemorated in the charter.

Charter of bp. Jocelin.

" Omnibus Christi fidelibus ad quos presens scriptum pervenerit. Jocelinus dei gratia Bathon. episcopus salutem in Domino. Noveritis nos in dedicatione ecclesiæ nostræ Wellensis quam die sancti Romani mense Novembris[1] anno incarnationis dominicæ 1239 in honorem sancti Andreæ apostolorum mitissimi dedicavimus, dedisse et concessisse et hac presenti carta confirmasse pro nobis et successoribus nostris in dotem ejusdem ecclesiæ nostræ et decano et capitulo nostro Wellensi . . . manerium de Wynescumbe, etc.

In cujus rei robur et testimonium presenti scripto sigillum nostrum apponi fecimus.

Datum Welliæ in crastino sc̃i Romani anno incarnationis dominicæ 1239 et pontificatus nostri anno xxxiv." R. i, f. 50 in dors.; R. iii, f. 99; printed by Hearne in *Adam of Domerham*, p. 252.

Nov. 12.
Further endowment of servitium B. V. Mariæ.

On the morrow of St. Martin bishop Jocelin confirmed and made further augmentation of the endowment of the service in honour of the Blessed V. Mary,

1. Erratum in transcript in *Adam of Domerham* — " mense Octobri."

instituted 1206, and augmented in 1215 by grant of thirty marcs. Vide under years 1206-1215.

December 29, " die beati Thomae martyris," bishop Jocelin confirmed to the canons, "in augmentationem communæ," the church of Cheddar, formerly held and conceded by the convent of Bradenstoke. R. i, f. 30. Cf. R. i, f. 30, anno 1188. *Cheddar.*

Resignation by rector and vicar of church of Mudford to bishop Jocelin. *Morrow of St. Hilary. A.D. 1239-40. Mudford.*

Grant of church to the *communa*, "sublevaturus paupertatem canonicorum"; patronage to belong to dean and chapter. R. i, f. 30.

Confirmation of grant of tenths to vicar of St. Cuthbert, made in 1236. R. i, f. 101; and f. 104 in dors. *St. Cuthbert's, Wells*

A.D. 1240.

24 Henry III. 7 Edmund, archbishop.
14 Gregory IX. 35 Jocelin, bishop.
       William, dean.

Confirmation of grant of St. Cuthbert, Wells, "in augmentationem communæ." R. i in dors. *June 4. St. Cuthbert, Wells.*

Confirmation by royal charter of privileges to convent of Hinton Monachorum. Dugd. f. 30 *Mon.* 1, p. 960. *Hinton charterhouse.*

Otho, cardinal legate, orders bishop Jocelin to summon to a synod at London all deans, archdeacons, abbots, and priors in his diocese, in person; all chapters, abbesses, and prioresses by proxy, to appear before him on the octave of All Saints, and to urge the parochial clergy to make offerings, and to invite all to give one- *October 7.*

twelfth of their revenue at least to the aid of the pope. R. i, f. 191. M. Paris, *Hist. Angl.* ii, 431.

f. 129.
Nov. 16.
Death of archbishop Edmund.
f. 130.
Xmas. 1240.
Whitchurch vicarage.

Edmund, archbishop, dies; is buried at Pontigny; his heart at Soysi. M. Paris, *Chron. Maj.* iv, 72, 73.

Vicarage of Whitchurch in Dorset instituted and endowed by Robert, bishop of Salisbury.

A division of the greater tithes between churches of Wells and Salisbury. Patronage of vicarage reserved to bishop. R. iii, ff. 341-343.

Stoke St. Gregory vicarage.

Lands and tenements in North Curry given to dean and chapter by Simon Gyan, with condition of providing a chaplain for church of Stoke, with fifty shillings annually. R. iii, f. 207.

A.D. 1241.

25 Henry III.   36 Jocelin, bishop.
15 Gregory IX.   John Saracenus, dean.

f. 131.
John Saracenus, dean.

John Saracenus, dean—son of Peter Saracenus, *civis Romanus*, an agent of the pope in England. Vide Royal Letters, Henry III, 6, 269, 270, in 1212-1225.

John Saracenus is called "subdiaconus et capellanus papae." R. i, f. 75 in dors.

Cf. Rot. Chart. 1215, 9 July, grant to Peter Saracenus, *civis Romanus*, of £20. 1215, 27 July. Grant to John, son of Peter Saracenus, of church of Skenefrith apud Fekeham.

April 3.
Milverton.

Church of Milverton is annexed as one benefice to the archdeaconry of Taunton by bishop Jocelin, with consent of dean and chapter, and two prebends formed out of it. Woky, April 3, 1241. R. iii, f. 336 in dors.

Confirmation by Thomas, prior of Bath. R. iii, f. 337.

On the morrow of St. Augustine's, "Anglorum apostoli," May 27, at a general convocation of the canons, and in presence of bishop Jocelin, statutes are drawn up— May 27. Statutes defining residence and apportioning share of *communa*.

(a) Defining obligatory " residence," to two-thirds of the year for dignitaries; half the year, either continuously or at intervals for ordinary canons, to entitle them to share in the *communa*. Residence is optional, but distribution of *communa* to be according to "residence."

(b) Revision of the Ordinale.

(c) Leave of absence to vicars for bloodletting to be granted by dean, or, in his absence, by the subdean.

(d) Vicars to take place in choir according to the prebends to which they were admitted.

(e) One audit per year fixed to octave of St. Calixtus.

(f) Bell to be rung to summon canons to the chapter. R. ii, f. 17.

Pope Gregory IX dies. f. 132. August 22.

Pope Celestine IV pope for eighteen days. M. Paris, *Chron. Maj.*, iv, 172, and *Hist. Angl.*, ii, 458.

Innocent IV succeeds. *Concil.* tom. xi, col. 310, 590.

Boniface of Savoy elected archbishop of Canterbury by monks of Canterbury. M. Paris, *Hist. Angl.* ii, 448.

Wynescumb appropriated to dean and chapter at resignation of Walter of Cossington. Dean and Vicarage of Wynescumb chapter inducted as perpetual rectors. R. iii, f. 97, 98. Walter to receive the emoluments of the churches of Mudford and Lovington during life.

f. 133.
Chewton appropriated to Jumièges.
Feb. 17.
Chewton vicarage.

Dean and chapter consent to whatever bishop Jocelin shall determine about church of Chewton. R. iii, 192.

Chewton appropriated to abbey of Jumièges in Normandy. R. iii, f. 183 in dors.; f. 184, and ordinance made by bishop, with consent of convent, regulating endowment of vicarage by the convent, with lesser tithes—a house and 5 marks annually to vicar; a pension of 35 marcs to be paid to the chapter; 3 marcs for a light at the service of the B. Virgin; and 3 marcs to the archdeacon.

Norton sub Hamdon.

The convent of Gresteign accept bishop Jocelin's ordinance about Norton sub Hamdon. Church appropriated to the convent and vicarage instituted, forty shillings pension to dean and chapter, half a marc to the archdeacon. R. iii, f. 185, in dors.

f. 134.

Convent of St. Augustine Bristol, present to the vicarage of Paulet, and bind themselves to proposed payment of tithes of vicar and pension of one marc to the Nunnery of Buckland. R. iii, f. 157.

Charter of Richard de Wrotham.

Richard de Wrotham acquits the bishop and his successors and their men from all charges "de espeltamentis canum," *i.e.*, the "lawing" or mutilation of the feet of hunting dogs—"et de pecunia danda pro espeltamentis," or licences for remission. R. i, f. 39 in dors.

About this time, as was stated afterwards in 1248, a levy of one-fifth on all prebends and canonries for seven years was made by bishop Jocelin. R. i, f. 69;

cf. at Salisbury Osm. Reg. ii, 7, 9, 41; the precedent there set in 1219 and 1235.

A.D. 1242.
26 Henry III.   37 Jocelin, bishop.
1 Innocent IV.   John Saracenus, dean.

Bishops of Salisbury, Exeter, and Worcester certify that they have made inspeximus of charters given by king John to bishop Jocelin in 1214, and by king Henry III in 1235. R. iii, ff. 17, 18, 342; ff. 16, 339.

October 17. Bishop Jocelin in chapter with the consent of the dean and canons increases the quotidians to all members of the church of St. Andrew in Wells.

f. 135. Charter of bishop increasing the quotidians. Oct. 17.

In the preamble to the ordinance he makes a statement of the completion of the fabric of the church.

The church having been built up from a state of dilapidation and enlarged and furnished with all things necessary for the divine offices, and consecrated anew, provision is now to be made for the better maintenance of the staff of the cathedral church. Their emoluments are increased and proportioned to their residence.

Bishop Jocelin by his ordinance

(1) Changed the mode of distribution of the daily quotidians of bread from the canon's barn *(panis de grangia)* to money payments.
(2) Increased the scale of daily payments.
(3) Regulated the scale of payments by "residence in Wells."

Chapters in Wells History. [CHAP.

Scale of quotidians according to

Bishop Jocelin's Statute.		Yearly value. £ s. d.	Earlier usage.
To the bishop.	8 pence. 5 pence.	} = 19 15 5	6 pence. 4 white loaves.
To the "quinque personae," dean, precentor, archdeacon of Wells, chancellor, treasurer.	8 pence. 4 pence.	} = 18 5 0	6 pence. 2 white loaves. 2 black loaves.
To all other canons.	4 pence. 2 pence.	} = 9 2 6	3 pence. 1 white loaf. 1 black loaf.
To vicars-choral.	1 penny.	} = 1 10 5	1 loaf every other day, or half-commons.
To all servants of the church, (a) some;	1 penny.	= 1 10 5	1 commons.
(b) others.	1 halfpenny.	= 0 15 2½	Half-commons.

The residue at the end of the year to be distributed equally between the five *personae* and the canons resident in Wells, conditionally upon the former having resided two-thirds of the year either continuously, or at intervals, the latter in the same way for half the year. Cf. Archer's Long Book, p. 19 in dors. R. i, f. 51 ; R. ii, f. 44, 45 ; R. iii, f. 8.

October 29. Wedmore prebends reconstituted— October 29. Reconstitution of Wedmore prebend.
(a) by union of Mark with Wedmore, as one benefice, to belong to the dean.
(b) A fifth prebend formed thereby, united with the prebend of Dogmersfield formed in 1215. This united prebend to follow the same rules as other prebends. R. i, f. 51 ; R. ii, f. 44, R. iii, f. 449 in dors.

Richard of Dynham, rector of Mark, had resigned the church, and the union is now effected by bishop Jocelin, to settle differences between the dean and the rector of Mark.

With consent of bishop Jocelin and archdeacon of Bath, patron and rector, Robert Bretanche, senior, erected a chapel on his *curia* at Trubbewell, with conditions— Chapel at Trubbewell, in parish of Compton Martin.

(1) That the chapel be subject to the mother church.

(2) That the lord and lady and family attend three times a year on the three principal festivals at the chapel of Empnett (Nempnett), a chapel of the parish church at Compton. R. iii, f. 367 in dors.

Grant by dean and chapter of a shop in High Street, "in magno vico," to John, son of Hugh the cook, at 2s. a year. R. iii, f. 188.

Death of bp. Jocelin, Nov. 19.

xiii Kal. Dec.—vigil of St. Edmund, November 19—bishop Jocelin dies, "plenus dierum, vita et moribus commendabilis." M. Paris, *Hist. Angl.* ii, 468. Archer corrects M. Paris as to the date which he had given, iii Kal. Dec.

He is buried at Wells (R. i, f. 74), in the middle of the choir. R. iii, f. 300.

Burial at Wells.

It would appear that notification to the chapter of Bath of the death of the bishop was not given until after the burial, the canons being anxious to secure the burial at Wells. Some of the monks of Bath were present in the church on the day of burial, and some differences seem to have arisen between them and the canons. R. i, f. 74.

Announcement of death to convent of Bath, Nov. 24.

November 24th. Saturday after the feast of St. Edmund. The chapter send William de Bytton, archdeacon of Wells, and Walter de St. Quintin, archdeacon of Taunton, and William de Maydenston (Maidstone), canon, to inform the chapter of Bath, to deliberate on the election of a successor, and to take steps in conjunction with the Bath chapter to obtain permission from the king to proceed to the election. R. i, f. 73.

The chapter of Bath are hereby warned not to attempt to do anything in this matter apart from the chapter of Wells. R. i, f. 74.

PLATE II
SEALS

ROGER OF SARUM
Bp. of Bath and Wells, 1244-1247

ROBERT DE BERKELEY
Sub-dean, 1233

ROBERT BURNELL
Bp. of Bath and Wells, 1275-1292

ROBERT BURNELL
Counter-seal

CHAPTER V.

Roger of Salisbury, First Bishop of Bath and Wells,
A.D. 1244-1247.

THE episcopate of Roger of Salisbury, first bishop who bore the title of Bath and Wells, is short, but memorable in the annals of the church of Wells.

It was the time when the rule of election of the bishop by the joint action of the two chapters of the monks of Bath and the canons of Wells was authoritatively and finally settled, and the style of the bishop, *Episcopus Bathoniensis et Wellensis*, was officially adopted.

There are two documents, original and unpublished, in the manuscript records of the chapter library at Wells, which are the historical landmarks on the subject in the time between the death of Jocelin and that of Roger his successor, 1242-1247:

> *(a.)* The first is dated July 1242. It is an *inspeximus* of all the documents which recorded the election of bishops Reginald and Jocelin to the see of Bath, attested by bishop Jocelin and by William Brewer, bishop of Exeter, and William de Ralegh, bishop of Norwich.

(b.) The second is the "pacification" between the two chapters—the charter by which the rule of the bishop's election, the *norma eligendi*, was settled, under the authority of pope Innocent IV. It was drawn up by bishop Roger, styling himself "bishop of Bath and Wells," confirmed by the seals of the two chapters, and afterwards ratified by the prior and convent of Bath in their chapter-house, August 19, 1246.

I propose to give in this chapter a sketch of the chapter history between the dates of these two documents, as far as it is contained in the registers of the dean and chapter of Wells.

The church of secular canons at Wells had at this time hostile rivals on each side, in the Benedictine houses of Bath and Glastonbury. These convents claimed earlier and more hallowed traditions, and looked with jealousy on the fostering care bestowed on Wells by later bishops, and by Jocelin especially.

Savaric had laid violent hands on Glastonbury: Jocelin had withdrawn his hold, but in so doing had attached to his see four principal manors ceded by the abbey as the price of independence. He had made Wells to be the *sedes præsulea* of the diocese, and the primacy of Bath had become little more than nominal;

A.D. 1242. and shortly before his death he had taken measures with the view of securing to Wells the pre-eminence he had given to it in his lifetime.

He had bequeathed his body to the church of Wells. This choice of Wells as the place of burial consecrated Wells as the first church of the diocese, and made a great breach in the traditionary honour of the church of Bath, which for the last hundred and fifty years had been the burial-place of the bishops of the see of Somerset.

Again, he had, as it were, left testamentary directions as to the election of his successor in the first of these two documents just mentioned, setting out the precedents of election sanctioned by papal authority, and determining the rule of election for the future.

That charter[1] recorded:

- *(a.)* The sanction of pope Alexander III to the election of bishop Reginald, by act of the Wells chapter alone, in 1174.
- *(b.)* The papal confirmation of the rights of the Wells chapter to be the sole electors, but also the decree that a settlement with the chapter of Bath for joint election should be made.
- *(c.)* That settlement, as exhibited in the process of election of bishop Jocelin in 1206.

The canons of Wells appear to have trusted to the strength of these authoritative precedents, and not to have anticipated any independent action on the part of the chapter of Bath on the death of bishop Jocelin.

But the Bath chapter had determined to attempt the recovery of their position by securing the election of a nominee of their own to the see as soon as vacant.

Reverting to the evil tradition of success in the election of Savaric by secret diplomacy, without the knowledge of the Wells chapter, they thought by a

---

1. Vide Appendix S.

like surprise to secure the election on this occasion before the chapter of Wells was prepared to act.

November 19, 1242. Death of Jocelin.

Jocelin died on the vigil of St. Edmund, king and martyr, November 19. That day was marked by a violent storm, which Matthew Paris[1] thinks worthy of record, when the Thames burst its banks, and boats were plying in Westminster Hall. It was a day of letting out the waters of strife between the two chapters of Bath and Wells.

While the canons were laying Jocelin in his grave in the middle of the choir of the church of Wells, the Bath monks, acting with the secrecy and promptitude of a small and united executive, had already sent a deputation to the king, then at Bourdeaux, to obtain for themselves alone the licence to elect

Nov. 22. Conflict with Bath chapter.

On November 22, the Saturday after the feast of St. Edmund, a deputation was sent by the chapter of Wells to Bath: the two archdeacons, William of Bytton archdeacon of Wells, Walter de St. Quintin archdeacon of Taunton, and William of Maidstone canon and proctor, to announce the vacancy, and to arrange for joint action in the coming election. They were received with coldness, and pretexts for delay were made. Finally, they discover that the Bath chapter had already acted independently. They protest, and threaten appeal to Rome.[2]

The public protest of the chapter is put out after their return by the canons resident, on the feast of St. Lucia, December 13.[3]

---

1. *Hist. Angl.*, iii, 467 (Rolls Series); *Chron. Maj.*, iv, 330
2. R. i, f. 73.
3. R. i, f. 75.

Nearly a month, however, had passed before the non-resident members of the chapter, summoned from the different parts of the diocese, are gathered together on December 19, nominally to proceed to the election of a bishop, but warned that they are summoned hastily to take action against the plots of the Bath monks. Again they send a deputation to Bath, to remonstrate and protest; their proctors, Hugh de Romenal the subdean, and Luke de Membury, with four vicars, Richard of Bytton, John of Chard, William of Brugges (Bridgwater), and David, a clerk. The subdean reads the letters of the chapter in the hall before the prior and some of the monks, but to no purpose. They heard, but did not listen; or, listening, did not answer. "Again and again, yea, thrice," the subdean remonstrates and warns against separate and illegal action. The monks were content silently to await the result of their diplomacy, and the canons return again fruitless. Then the chapter in council make their united protest, and take action. They appoint the dean, John Saracenus, and canon Robert de Marisco as proctors, to act for the chapter in petitioning the king for the *congé d'élire*, and for carrying the appeal to Rome. They write letters to influential friends in England, to Walter de Gray, a canon *(fratrem et concanonicum)*, archbishop of York and chancellor, to the bishop of Caerleon, one of the council of the regency, and to Sylvester de Everdon, also a canon, the keeper of the exchequer *(custos scaccarii)*. They commission Philip de Gildeford, a canon, to carry the letters from the chapter to the king, and he is instructed to obtain the help of Peter

<small>Dec. 19. Protest of canons.</small>

<small>Appeal to king and pope.</small>

Chaceporc, Hugh de Vivone, and Godfrey de Ulward, men about the king.[1]

January, 1242-3.

Meantime, members of the Bath deputation were already at Bourdeaux, and the king had granted to them the *congé d'élire* on January 6. As soon as the king's letters arrived in Bath on January 30, the monks send formal notification to the canons that the election of the bishop will take place at Bath on February 6. The canons are invited to be present and to hear the nomination, "though," say the monks, "the canons have no rights there by law or custom, and by this invitation they do not mean to derogate from their own rights, nor to attribute any rights to the canons of Wells in the election." "Oh the intolerable insolence of these shameless monks," is the outburst of our chronicler—"Tanta erat impudentissimorum monachorum effrenata et intolerabilis insolentia."[2]

February, 1242-3.

Notwithstanding, the canons once more with much meekness and forbearance, on the feast of St. Agatha (February 5), the day before the meeting, write letters asserting their equality of rights in the election, their protest against the separate action of Bath, and their appeal to the apostolic see, and "by the advice of some good men, in the hope of preserving the peace of the two churches, they a third time send their proctors, and with them the three archdeacons, to arrange some common action." Again they are treated with cool contempt, and the prior refuses conference. They present themselves at the hour of vespers at the door of the choir, begging that they might address the assem-

---

1. R. i, ff. 73, 74, 75.
2. R. i, f. 75. Archer, f. 139

bled convent. This is refused by those named as prominent among their adversaries, Master Robert of Thetford, Henry of Bath, and Simon the physician. The monks are made to file out from the church into the cloister, the doors of the choir are shut in the faces of the canons, and they are left protesting before the precentor and two servants of the convent. Next morning (February 6) the monks invite the canons to join in the election: they indignantly refuse. Then, in a scene which must have been exciting, the monks proceed to the election: the precentor excommunicates those who would impede the election: the canons protest to the last. The monks nominate as bishop-elect Roger, precentor of the church of Salisbury, and announce that they present him as elect to the king. Forthwith, the Wells proctors proceed to Salisbury to lay their case before the chapter of Salisbury, and to implore the precentor not to accept this illegal nomination. There, after much altercation, the precentor cautiously replies to their question, that he will wait to see if he is canonically elected, and finally he accepts.[1]

So ended the first act: by sharp practice and high-handed effrontery the monks had so far carried the day. The canons might have taken to themselves the promise "the meek spirited shall possess the earth." But they had other resources. The papal see was now vacant, and in anticipation of the papal election the canons gird themselves for the struggle with their adversaries in the Roman chancellery. A chapter is summoned for the first Monday in Lent, February 27, to consult on the state of affairs and the urgent needs

1. R. i, f. 65.

of the church. Letters are written to the dean announcing the citation of the chapter, describing the fraudulent action of the chapter of Bath, urging him to use his best endeavours at Bourdeaux that the king shall not confirm the election of Roger pending their appeal to Rome, and finally to work for their interests in the Roman Curia, of which "he knew the ways better than they did." They send the subdean to consult with William of York, provost of Beverley, a man of wise counsel and a brother and fellow canon, and they write letters to the king himself, imploring him not to confirm the Bath election.[1] The king throughout held himself neutral between the two parties. He had given the *congé d'élire* to Bath in January "saving the rights of the chapter of Wells." About the same time he had written to the chapter of Wells that he had no intention of interfering with the rights of the dean and chapter, and invited their application to him in turn.

March.
In March the dean and Robert de Marisco were at Bourdeaux, and on March 10 the king writes to the chapter of Wells that he has given to them the *congé d'élire* "if it could be without prejudice to the rights of Bath," and he recommends them to make choice of a fitting person useful to the state.[2]

April, 1243.
On April 25 the king's writ had arrived at Wells, and with it a letter, dated March 24, brought by canon John of Dyrham, in which the king promises that he will do nothing to the prejudice of the chapter during the appeal.

It was now the turn of the canons to make boast of

1. R. i, ff. 76, 77.
2. R. i, f. 78.

the king's licence to elect. They notify formally to the chapter of Bath that they had received letters from the king empowering them to elect, and they summon the monks to Wells for Trinity Monday (June 8) as the day of election, but if the time and place is not convenient they will meet their deputation at Ferenton (Farrington Gurney), the usual place of conference, on the vigil of St. Philip and St. James (April 30) to arrange.

Whether this communication was answered at all or not, the Wells deputation went out to Farringdon on the day they had named. It must have been a goodly company who on that spring morning rode up the Bath road and over the long back of the Mendip Hills. We have the names of the dignitaries and their followers. There were the two archdeacons of Wells and Taunton, Hugh the treasurer, the two proctors, their clerks, and their "vallets"; Nicolas the clerk, and Gilbert de Lentenay, vallet of the archdeacon of Wells; Master Robert de St. Quintin and Wileminus, clerks, and Vigeroys, vallet of the archdeacon of Taunton; David the clerk, and Dudeman, clerk and vallet of Henry the treasurer; R. de Guertrie, vallet of the subdean; Thomas, the huntsman (*venator*), of the late bishop Jocelin, and his vallet Henry of Priddy; Robert Marmion, *armiger* of the archdeacon of Wells.[1]

But not one of the Bath chapter was there to meet this goodly array of dignity. Doubtless the canons felt themselves flouted by the monks, but both parties knew well that they were making an empty flourish of the king's writ, and that the battle must be fought in

1. R. i, f. 78 in dors.

the Roman court. The canons, trusting to their diplomacy at Rome, had no intention of acting on the king's *congé d'élire*.

June, 1243. There was a full meeting of canons in chapter on Trinity Monday, June 8, again summoned formally for the purpose of electing a bishop. First, sentence of excommunication was pronounced upon all who should reveal the greater or lesser secrets of the chapter, especially upon any of the chapter who should maliciously impede the election, or should aid the adversaries, the monks of Bath.[1] Then they write a long letter to the king, and another letter to the queen,[2] full of gratitude, but respectfully declining to act on the king's licence and to proceed to election of the bishop, because they had made their appeal to the apostolic see against the unlawful action of the chapter of Bath. In a postscript they commend to the king's favour John Mansel, a canon, as a friend of the chapter, and beg for the king's gracious consideration of their case.[3]

June 29. Innocent IV, pope. On June 24, 1243, cardinal Sinibaldi, a Genoese, was elected pope, and consecrated on June 29, under the title of Innocent IV.[4] As soon as the news arrived

July, 1243. at Wells, the chapter met on July 31, the Feast of St. Peter ad Vincula,[5] to address the pope and to state their case. They notify that they have nominated as their proctors in the Roman chancellery the dean

---

1. R. i, f. 64.
2. The city of Bath was part of the queen's dowry. Rymer, *Fœd.*, i, 420.
3. R. i, f. 78, 9.
4. M. Paris, *Hist. Angl.* ii, 472.
5. R. 1, f. 79.

John Saracenus, and canon John de Offinton. A public notification is made at the same time of their appeal having been lodged at Rome. The proctors are implored to act with the greatest zeal in the cause of the chapter. The chapter empowered the dean to borrow first 100 marcs for expenses in the Roman court; then 100 more; and the sub-dean holds five deeds for a loan of 220 marcs. This is the first instalment of the vast sums borrowed in this litigation, which afterwards amounted to 2600 marcs. Letters are written by the chapter to powerful men at Rome, petitioning for their favour; we know the names of some, and the price of their assistance. Two cardinals are named: John de Colonna, one of the most powerful of the cardinals, whom M. Paris[1] describes as "a vessel of pride and insolence," one of the papal champions against the emperor; another was Otho, the late legate apostolic in England in 1237. We shall find in the items of expenditure the honorarium of a cardinal entered as £50.[2] During the autumn and winter of 1243 the decision of the pope is awaited, and there were frequent communications between the chapter and their proctors at Rome. In September of this year *(circa festum S. Michaelis)*[3] instructions are given very explicitly to the dean of the line he is to take and of the means he is to employ. The precedents contained in bishop Jocelin's charter, viz., the letters of

September, 1243.

---

1. Vide *Matt. Paris, Hist. Angl.* ii, 479: "Vas superbiae et omnis contumeliae qui inter omnes cardinales genere, castris, et possessionibus secularibus erat potentissimus." He died next year, February 9, the Octave of the Purification.
2. R. i, f. 98.
3. R. i, f. 94.

pope Alexander III and the instruments of Jocelin's election, were sent to the proctors. Resting upon these precedents, they say the chapter might have claimed the sole election, but they will be content if equal rights with Bath according to the precedents of Jocelin's election be secured to them. The proctors, accordingly, are to press urgently that the election of Roger shall be set aside, and that all safeguard be taken that in future the election shall be common to both the chapters. Divers suggestions are then made as to the best or most practicable course for securing freedom of election and perfect equality of rights. Arbitration is suggested, but to no one in England, " because of the power of the great men who will intrude themselves into any election." If it should be in France, let it be to the dean or chancellor of Paris; or to a commission appointed by the pope, of whom certain persons are named as acceptable judges, *e.g.* in England, the bishops of Worcester and Norwich; the bishop, dean, and archdeacon of Lincoln; the archdeacon of Sudbury in Norwich, or of Huntingdon in Lincoln diocese. If in France, to the provost of St. Adomar (St. Omer), in the diocese of Tournay (Morinensis), or to the dean and *magister scholarum* in the diocese of Noyon (Novionensis), or to the archdeacon of Rouen.

Four points, *quatuor articuli*, are specified on which they are to obtain the papal decision:

    (a.) What should be the place of prior election?
    (b.) And of installation?
    (c.) What should be the style of the bishop?
    (d.) Which of the two sees should have the priority?

These instructions are accompanied by a characteristic letter to the dean, which reveals the spirit in which they worked, and the importance they attached to the object. He is told to make friends of the mammon of unrighteousness *(facere amicos de mammona iniquitatis)*, and to spend money freely. "We love our honour more than our money," "and all our money is offered" to gain powerful friends in the court, in order that the adversary shall not prevail, and that a decision to the honour of St. Andrew, "who protects and will repay, may be obtained."[1] They give the dean leave to return when he has done all for the cause, and assure him of their gratitude *(grates copiosissimas)*. At the same time they took the opportunity of putting into the hands of their proctors some other minor matters of litigation. They desire the appointment by the Roman court of the judges they have named to adjudicate their quarrel with Glastonbury and Athelney about neighbouring moors, and the ratification of Jocelin's arrangement of the union of the provostship of Combe and Winsham.[2]

The papal arbitrament came in April 1244. In a letter addressed to archbishop Boniface, and to the clergy and people of the diocese, the pope confirmed the election of Roger. In another letter of April 1,[3] addressed to the prior and convent of Bath, the pope set forth generally in the preamble the solicitude of the holy see to cut off or shorten litigation, for the sake of the appellants. In this case, in order to avoid

April, 1244. Arbitrament of the pope.

1. R. i, f. 94.
2. R. i, f. 96.
3. Quoted in Appendix U.

the evil of a protracted vacancy of the see, the election of Roger is confirmed. But to put an end to strife in future elections, it is decreed that from henceforth the dean and chapter of Wells shall have an equal voice and rights in all things appertaining to the election of the bishop.

This award was equitable and reasonable. Roger, the precentor of Salisbury, the nominee of the Bath chapter, was a good choice. He is described by Matthew Paris as a good man, a scholar and a theologian, *vir eleganter moribus et scientiâ theologiæ præditus*. The monk of St. Alban's implies that the pope was influenced in the speedy confirmation of Roger by the wish to provide for a kinsman in the precentorship he vacated, and that Martin the legate had laid hands on the precentor's benefice immediately on his nomination as bishop elect for some nephew of the pope.[1] The Wells registers give no authority for this gossip of the day.

September, 1244.

The temporalities of the see were restored by the king to Roger, as bishop elect, on May 10, 1244, but he was not consecrated until September 11.

On September 11, Roger was consecrated bishop of Bath in the chapel of the convent of St. Mary in Reading, where Jocelin had been consecrated nearly forty years before.[2] The chancellor, treasurer, and archdeacon of Wells, the subdean, and others of the canons were present. The pope's decree of award in the arbitration between the appellants was read. Innocent set aside the protest of the Wells chapter

1. Matt. Paris, *Chr. Maj.*, iii, 285.
2. R. i, f. 80.

against the election of Roger, but reserved his answer to the questions on the four points, *quatuor articulos de formâ et modo eligendi pontificis*, for a future time. The mandate of consecration to William de Ralegh, bishop of Norwich, was then read.

The Wells chapter made their protest by their proctors against the installation of the bishop in the church of Bath rather than that of Wells, and appealed to the pope's decision on the four points of detail *(de quatuor articulis)*.

Four months after, in January 1244-5, the result of the diplomacy of the Wells proctors at Rome appeared in the answer which came from the pope at Lyons on these four controverted points.[1] In a letter dated Lyons, January 3, 1244-5, addressed to the dean and chapter of Wells, the pope ordained:

January, 1244-5.

Further abitrament of the pope.

(a) That the throne of the bishop should be in each of the churches of Bath and Wells;

(b) That the election should take place in each church in turns, first, in Bath, the next time in Wells;

(c) That the installation should take place in the same church in which the election had been held;

(d) That the style of the bishop in charter and on seal henceforward should be " Bishop of Bath and Wells," *Episcopus Bathoniensis et Wellensis;* "et utriusque ecclesiæ episcopus nominetur, Bathoniensis videlicet et Wellensis, et sic in sigillo contineatur ipsius."

---

1. Vide Appendix U. R. iii, f. 108 in dors.

A few months passed, during which Roger had entered peaceably on his office.

But perhaps from fear of offending his supporters at Bath, who had promoted his election at such cost, the bishop had not yet added "Wells" to his episcopal style and seal. The Wells chapter made complaint to the pope that his mandate had not yet been carried out in this particular.

May 14, 1245. Mandate as to title of bishop.

In May following Innocent wrote again from Lyons[1] a letter terse and peremptory addressed to bishop Roger, in which he reminds him of his former mandate, ordering the assumption of the full title of "Bath and Wells." He learns from the dean and chapter of Wells that the mandate in this particular has been disobeyed, and orders that forthwith the title of Wells as well as Bath shall be borne by him, and inscribed on his seal. Very soon after this the bishop must have adopted the double style. Charters and grants made by him occur in the registers dated early in the following year, as early as January 19, 1245-6,[2] in which he bears the double title of Bath and Wells.

Pacification in August, 1246.

Acting still further on the tenor of this mandate, bishop Roger set himself to draw up a scheme of pacification,[3] by which the claims of the two chapters were finally conciliated, and their joint and equal action in each particular case most carefully adjusted. In a charter dated from Stawey in Chew, August 13, 1246, in which he officially assumes the title of "bishop of Bath and Wells," he recites his solicitude

1. Vide Appendix U.
2. R. i, f. 67.
3. Appendix U.

to cut off all further causes of controversy between the two chapters, and their joint engagement to abide by his mediation and award. He then cites the two bulls of pope Innocent IV upon which his award was based, the one dated from the Lateran, March 23, 1244, the other from Lyons, January 3, 1244-5, and proceeds to make order for the joint action of the two bodies on equal terms under all the possible occasions on which they will be called to co-operate in the election of the bishop, from the moment of the vacancy to the last acts in the consecration and installation.

The charter of pacification was formally accepted, signed, and sealed by the prior and convent of Bath on August 19, 1246 ;[1] and on August 26 (Sunday after the beheading of St. John Baptist), Thomas the precentor was sent over to Wells by the convent of Bath with the deed attested and confirmed in their chapter house.

So the long controversy was brought to an end—the *norma eligendi*, the process of election by the two chapters of Bath and Wells, was finally established, and thenceforth it was acted upon on all occasions. It held good without any further attempt on either side to evade or dispute conditions, until the dissolution of the convent of Bath in the sixteenth century. Wells was then left the sole seat of the bishop, the one cathedral church, but the title of the bishop remained unchanged to witness to the ancient primacy and importance of the city of Bath.

"So Roger," says our Wells annalist, "was the first A.D. 1245. of all the bishops who bore the title of 'bishop of Bath

1. Charters 45, 46, 47.

and Wells' (*Rogerus primus omnium Bathoniensis et Wellensis nuncupatus.*") So in 1245 the bishops who had been styled successively bishops "of Somerset" or "of Wells," from the time of Edward son of Alfred to William son of Rufus, then "of Bath," and of "Bath and Glastonbury" under Savaric and Jocelin, now for the first time, and from henceforth invariably, assumed the double title "of Bath and Wells" from their twin cities of waters under the Mendip hills, whence burst out the springs which, at Bath on the north side,

"With hot currents flow, and from beneath
As from a furnace, clouds of steam arise,"

and on the south rise in "the great fountain of St. Andrew,"

"Like crystal clear and cold as winter snow."[1]

Roger died December 21, 1247, and was buried at Bath. The monks carried to his grave the bishop whom they claimed as their own, the last bishop to be buried amongst them.

Both chapters had paid heavily. The monks of Bath had gained a barren victory in the election and consecration of their candidate. But the fruits of victory rested with the chapter of Wells. They had established their right to equality in the election; and the bishop, whose illegal election they had opposed, became their patron to guard their rights from future

---

1. Hom. *Iliad*, xxii, 149.

ἡ μὲν γάρ θ' ὕδατι λιαρῷ ῥέει, ἀμφὶ δὲ καπνὸς
γίγνεται ἐξ αὐτῆς ὡσεὶ πυρὸς αἰθομένοιο·
ἡ δ' ἑτέρη θέρεϊ προρέει εἰκυῖα χαλάζῃ,
ἢ χιόνι ψυχρῇ, ἢ ἐξ ὕδατος κρυστάλλῳ.

invasion. Moreover, they had won over the bishop to admit their independent privileges and separate jurisdictions, and to confirm them in their estates. During the vacancy of the see they had found their strength, and had exercised their independence in the struggle to establish their rights alike against the rival chapter and the bishop. Under bishop Roger there was the first assertion by the chapter of that separate and co-ordinate power of jurisdiction in the government of the church which in no long time brought about collision between bishop and chapter.

Roger's short episcopate of three years was followed by the episcopate of William de Bitton, the archdeacon of Wells, and the leader of the chapter of Wells in the struggle with Bath, nominated by the Wells chapter, elected with all due and legal formalities by the two chapters without any attempt at opposition from Bath, and consecrated at Rome, June 14, 1248.

CHAPTER VI.

The Chapter of Wells, 1242-1333.

THE strife with the Bath chapter during the vacancy in the see after Jocelin's death exhibits the independent action of the dean and chapter in the home government of the church.

The constitution established by Robert had been developed under the succeeding bishops: the chapter had received from those bishops divers privileges and immunities from ordinary jurisdiction: offices had been remodelled and more amply endowed by Jocelin, and the "dean and chapter" had grown into a strong self-governing corporation.

We enter now upon a new period in the history when the growth of the chapter as the governing body in the cathedral church is one of the chief features. All through this time the bishop is in theory the head of the chapter—he appoints the canons to their prebends and offices, and the canons elect the dean. The bishop is himself a canon : chief among the canons he has his seat in choir and chapter among them : he is head of the church in the diocese, and head of the mother church of the diocese where is the seat of the bishop. But in the course of time this power and headship in the government became delegated to so

Plate III
SEALS

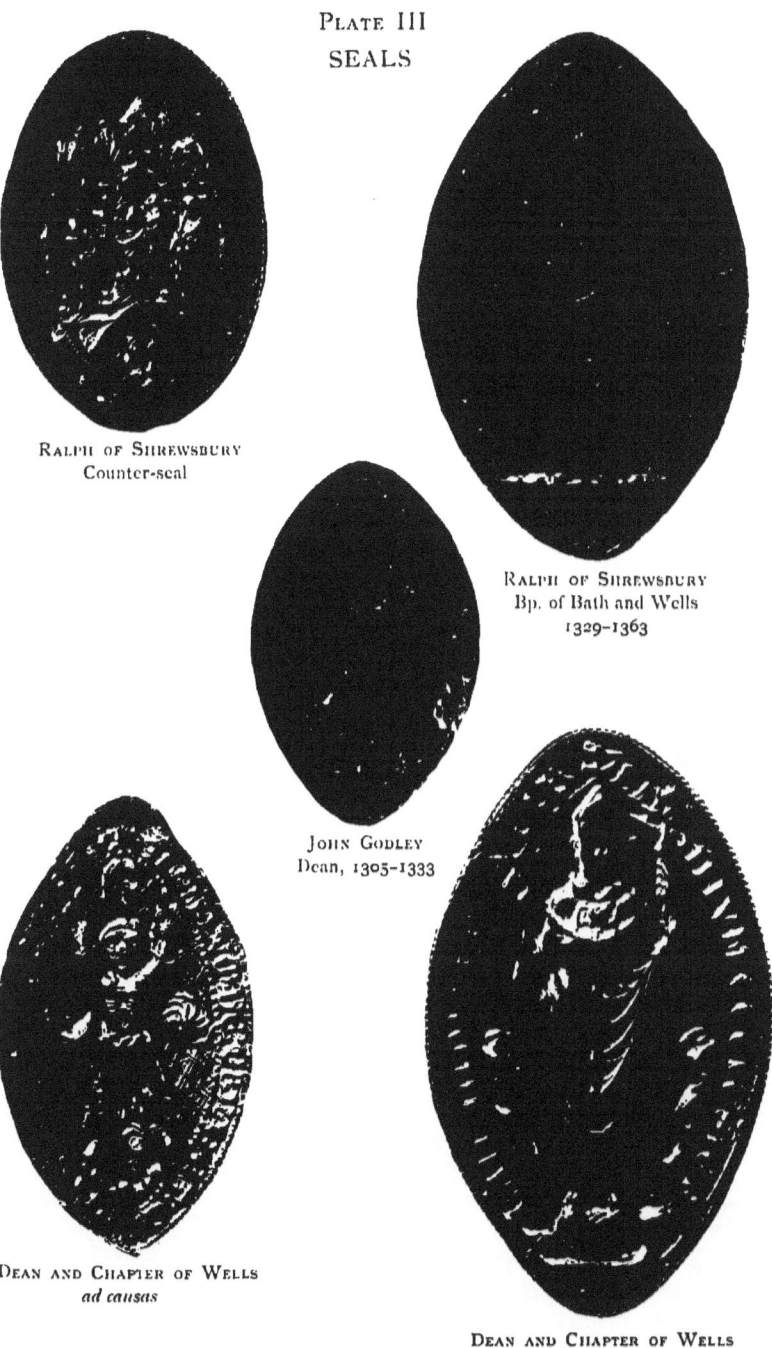

Ralph of Shrewsbury
Counter-seal

Ralph of Shrewsbury
Bp. of Bath and Wells
1329-1363

John Godley
Dean, 1305-1333

Dean and Chapter of Wells
ad causas

Dean and Chapter of Wells

great a degree to the "dean and chapter" by the acts of the bishops, in provision for the internal administration of the cathedral church during their absences and various civil employments, that the bishops lost very much their place and voice in chapter; and the dean and chapter acted as by sole right. Later on in the fourteenth century, when the bishops attempted to recover their position, they were confronted by the acts of their predecessors, and by customs sanctioned by long use, and were forced to modification or withdrawal of their claims. The worldly character of so many of the bishops recommended to the crown for their ability in civil affairs, and their frequent absences from the diocese, led naturally to the concentration of power in the hands of the resident body. On the other hand the deans, elected by the canons from their own body, *de gremio nostro*, often after long experience in the business of the church, naturally took the lead in carrying on internal order and discipline and in promoting the new building of the fabric.

So whereas, hitherto, the chapters in the history of the church of Wells have been marked by names of individual bishops, in the next period the names of the deans, men famous in the congregation, will stand in honourable rivalry with the bishops.

The canons now formed a large and influential body. The distribution of members of the cathedral church through the diocese as holders of prebendal estates, with local responsibilities and duties, bound together the cathedral church and the diocese. Gradually the appropriation of churches to the chapter by the bishops and lay lords had increased the number of canons from twenty-four in Robert's time to thirty-five in that of Reginald and Savaric. Under Jocelin the number was still further increased. After his time the last made prebend of Dinder, created in 1264, completed the number to fifty-three. By degrees, and especially by reason of the increased value of the endowments in Jocelin's time, the dignities and offices in the church tempted the grasping hands of pope, and king, and courtiers. At the time of bishop Jocelin's death, the dean was a nominee of the pope, John Saracenus, appointed in 1241.[1] He was son of a Roman citizen in the pope's body guard who had been the pope's agent in negotiations and embassies,[2] the representative at Wells of the three hundred Italians for whom

---

1. R. i, f. 57. Pope Gregory IX confirms his election, and at the same time the right of the chapter to elect a dean from the canons according to the "antiqua et approbata consuetudo, decanatu vacante."

The process for the appointment of a dean at this time is fully set forth in the Wells Registers, and illustrated by examples in the cases of several succeeding deans until 1547. R. i, f. 57 contains the charter of bishop Jocelin, concerning the appointment, 1216. Cf. R. i, f. 113 in dors.

It sets forth what had been the process in the appointment of two deans during Jocelin's episcopate, and such had been the process handed down from ancient days:

Ut cum decanus ecclesie illius, Domino eum vocante, decesserit, capitulum nobis et successoribus nostris celeriter nuntiare non omiserit, precarique licentiam alium decanum eligendi.

Quæ quidem electio si concessa sit, convocatis fratribus ad diem dictum, invocata Spiritus sancti gratia, talem sibi in decanum eligant personam, qualem ecclesiæ suæ magis viderit fore necessariam et quæ sibi quoad vitam et aliis possit proficere ad exemplum.

Electam personam nobis præsentantes, confirmationem electionis postulantes ut quod nobis est officii circa personam illius sicut decuit, auctore Domino, exequamur.

2. Royal letters, Henry III, in 1217, 1236, 1252.

the pope's legate had desired Henry to find English benefices.

Some of the canons of the day were high in the king's court: Walter de Gray, archbishop of York and chancellor, one of the regency during the king's absence, Sylvester de Everdon, keeper of the exchequer, John Mansel, king's secretary and privy councillor until his dismissal in 1261, Philip de Gildeford, Robert de Marisco, men about the court, all were at this same time non-resident canons.

Of the resident body, the archdeacon of Wells, William of Bytton, was the leader of the chapter, founder of a strong family interest in the chapter, members of which occupied chief places in the church of Wells for at least three generations. The family had come from that same part in the north-west promontory of Normandy, called the Côtentin, in which the Bohuns had their seat. The manor of Bytton, in the Avon valley between Bath and Bristol, had been given by Henry II to Adam of Ammeville near Barfleur, about 1158.[1] It descended from father to son for four generations, and some of the younger members of the family from each generation found home and employment in offices of the church of Wells.

The conflict with Bath called out the energies of the chapter and gave occasion for their assertion of independence of both bishop and pope. Several instances occur. They had appealed in vain to the pope against the unconstitutional act of Bath. Smarting under the adverse decision of the pope, they showed their resentment by rejection of the interference of papal delegates

1. Pipe Rolls, 1158.

in their own chapter affairs. The delegates of the papal commissioners had supported a rival claimant to the archdeaconry of Wells against William of Bytton, and summoned the chapter to appear before them to hear their sentence on a certain day, September 15, 1244. The chapter refused to receive the letter, made formal appeal against the decision of the delegates, and solemnly excommunicated, "accensis candelis et campanis pulsatis," the rival claimant and all of their own body, or of the abbey of Glastonbury who yielded obedience to the delegates.[1]

At this same time, A.D. 1244, August 31, they joined with the chapter of Lincoln in protest to the pope against bishop Grosseteste's invasion of the chapter rights.[2]

Again, in 1247 they showed their jealousy of Roman interference. The chapter refused to allow dean John Saracenus, the Roman nominee, the usual permission to take beneficial leases under the chapter, or to let out the deanery lands, notwithstanding a papal licence, on the express ground that his family had too great influence at the Roman court, "et hoc solummodo propter potentiam suam et suorum quam habent in curia Romana."[3]

Nor were they long in asserting their rival claims against the bishop whom they had received at the papal mandate. They thought him slow in carrying out the order of the Roman court that " Wells " should be added to the style of the episcopate. By immediate

1. R. i, f. 97.
2. R. i, f. 80.
3. R. i, f. 97, "de potentia Saraceni decani."

appeal to pope Innocent they obtained a peremptory order to the bishop, by which the title of "Bath and Wells" was at once assumed in seal and signature in 1245.

They asserted their rights to the sequestrations of all vacant benefices in the diocese on the strength of bishop Reginald's grant of them to the chapter toward the fabric fund, and the bishop was forced to yield. The chapter, satisfied with the acknowledgment of their claims, granted a life interest in them to the bishop in relief of the debts of the see, " debitorum suorum et episcopatus attendentes gravamina, in subsidium et juvamen exonerationis ipsius et episcopatus concesserunt."[1]

At another time they disputed with success the bishop's right to visit any of the prebends of the chapter as exempted by Savaric from episcopal or archidiaconal jurisdiction.[2]

It is a proof of the conciliatory spirit of bishop Roger that the two last years of his episcopate were marked by many acts of favour towards the chapter. He granted to them the custody and proceeds of the deanery when vacant. He supported them in their resistance to the attempt of Glastonbury to recover the ceded manor of Winscombe; and he drew up the Act of Pacification, by which, as arbitrator, he closed the strife between the two chapters, and established their complete equality in the election of the bishop.[3] In his last year he gave his episcopal confirmation of the

1. R. i, f. 64; ii, f. 15; iii, f. 11.
2. R. i, f. 28.
3. Charters 45—47.

possessions of the chapter, which was confirmed also by the prior and convent of Bath.[1]

Such was the successful end of the first trial of strength of the chapter in assertion of their corporate rights, during bishop Roger's time, 1244—1247.

The complete acquiescence of the chapter of Bath in the choice of his successor, William of Bytton, archdeacon of Wells, shows the strength of the Wells chapter. He was elected without opposition by the proctors of the two chapters on February 24, 1248, and consecrated June 14 at Rome, with the double title of the see " Bishop of Bath and Wells."

Bp. William of Bytton, A.D. 1247-1264.

Bishop William's episcopate lasted from 1247 to 1264.

The episcopate of bishop William of Bytton, the first, was chiefly remarkable for his long absences from England, and for his controversies with his chapter at home. He was at Rome at the time of his consecration in June 1248, and probably through the year. In 1253 he and John Mansel, the king's chief counsellor, were sent on an embassy to king Ferdinand of Castile, to negotiate the double marriage of prince Edward to Eleanor his daughter, and of the eldest son of Ferdinand to the English princess Beatrice. He was with the king in Gascony in 1254. Again, he and the bishop of Rochester were the king's secret agents at Rome in 1256-1257, in transacting the king's money negotiations with the pope, to whom Henry, to the great discontent of the nation, had incurred a debt of 140,000 marcs as the price of his acceptance of the fief of Sicily from the pope for his son Edmund.

1. R. iii, f. 4, 5

While at Rome on the king's business he obtained from the pope the confirmation of the possessions and liberties of his see, and also a papal letter to the king, which he bears testimony to the bishop's zeal in the king's cause at Rome, " operosis suis negotiis nuperrime apud sedem apostolicam confectis," and urges the king to restore to the bishop the right of the "patronatus" over the abbey of Glastonbury, which had been granted by king John. But the king, probably under prince Edward's influence, had assumed the chief lordship over the abbey; and the appeal from the pope had little weight at this time of national discontent. The king was forced to dismiss his counsellor John Mansel in 1261, and, with the fall of his friend, the bishop lost all further chance of the king's favour.

While the bishop was occupied with state affairs abroad the chapter was struggling with difficulties in the home government of the church. *Home government.*

The registers give evidence of much activity on the part of the chapter at the time,

(a) In assertion of their independent claims;

(b) In meeting the debts of the church;

(c) In enforcing discipline; and

(d) In ordering and correcting ritual.

They had to hold their own against the bishop's nepotism early in his episcopate, and other occasions of controversy arose:

(a) In 1249 the bishop, in contradiction to his own previous action as a member of the chapter, laid claim to the fruits of vacant benefices. The chapter resisted, on the same grounds with which they had met his predecessor, and no doubt with the same calm confidence in their rights, "cum animi tranquilitate et mansuetudine contra respondebant." The bishop yielded; and then, as before, the chapter, in consideration of the bishop's kindly feeling and the burden of his debts, made a grant to him of the fund for his lifetime, without prejudice to their successors.[1]

Again, in 1250, the bishop collated to the church of Congresbury, though in the patronage of the chapter, his nephew William, archdeacon of Wells. The canons protested, and on the bishop's refusal to revoke his appointment, they cited him to the archbishop's "court of arches," "in ecclesia S. Mariæ in Arcubus." Next year the bishop conceded the claim of the chapter, and revoked his appointment. Then the chapter confirmed his nephew whom he had nominated.[2] These amicable suits were the preludes to more serious controversies in the next century.

A.D. 1244-1248.
The chapter debts.

We have followed the stages in the controversy, whereby the style and title of the bishop of the see were authoritatively determined. But the sketch is incomplete without a short notice of the enormous expense which this litigation must have caused to the two bodies engaged.

It may well be matter of surprise how such litigation could be carried on by small local communities, so great must have been the difficulties of travel, and the expenditure of money involved, in journeys by land and sea to and from Rome, in legal expenses in the Roman courts, and in the purchase of the favour of great men and influential ecclesiastics.

1. R. i, f. 8; ii, f. 15; iii, f. 11.
2. R. i, ff. 100, 101; R. iii, 207.

We have some little insight into the expenditure from the chapter minutes of loans authorised, of debts incurred, and of the resources from whence the money was drawn for repayment.

The first mention of a loan of 420 marcs authorised by the chapter has been noticed in the letters addressed to the dean and proctor at Rome in September 1243.

In the next summer, 1244, the dean probably was on his return home, and the chapter had appointed two fresh proctors, the archdeacon of Taunton Walter de St. Quintin, and Hugh de Romenal the subdean. They go out in October 1244, with authority to make a second loan, equal to £360 of our money,[1] and carrying with them the instructions consequent upon the consecration of Roger.[2] *Oct. 8-10, 1244.*

In April, 1245, the dean returned to Wells, and gave into the hands of the chapter the letters and documents he had taken with him, or had received at Rome from the chapter. Among others he produced the receipt for £50 from cardinal Richard,[3] as "a gift from the chapter," and two sets of letters from merchants at Florence about a loan of 200 marcs which had not been raised, and the letters withdrawn. *April, A.D. 1245.*

Early in October the subdean, who had either come home or had delayed his departure for Rome, was sent to London bearing letters of credit for negotiation of other and larger loans to the amount of 1400 marcs to discharge debts at Rome and in the Roman *October, A.D. 1245.*

---

1. The loan was for £100, and 390 marcs—and that may be multiplied at least by fifteen or twenty, to give an approximate value in modern times.
2. R. i, f. 95.
3. R. i, f. 98.

courts; also to treat about another previous loan of 1200 marcs from merchants of Siena and Florence.¹

Debts met by taxation of prebends. November, A.D. 1245.

So far the chapter seem to have been revelling in unlimited credit. Next month came the time for meeting their liabilities, and they did it manfully. On November 25, 1245, in a chapter in which dean and subdean, treasurer, and other canons who had been employed in these transactions were present, the canons were called to face the payment of a debt of 1775 marcs contracted in the Roman courts, payable in five years from the Feast of the Purification following. They were asked severally if they consented to mortgage their own annual receipts from the chapter estate year by year, until this sum was paid. They unanimously assented, praying only for two conditions, that the surplus, if any, should be divided after payment of debt, and that the incoming dividend of 200 marcs in the next month from the new corn should be divided among the canons.² If the proportionate money value at the two periods is considered, we realise how lavish had been the expenditure in this litigation.

November 11, 1248.

Two years later, or in the first year of the next episcopate, the chapter was again summoned to provide for "the intolerable debts" of the church. An assessment of one-fifth on all prebends for seven years was ordered, the goods of all defaulters to be distrained, and the persons excommunicated.³

Great difficulty was found in enforcing the assessment, and throughout these years suits were going on

1. R. i, f. 98.
2. R. i, f. 97.
3. R. i, f. 69.

against defaulters. Some of the greater and lesser canons had made the payment, but very many, *quam plures*, had not; and distraint, sequestration of prebends, and excommunications were threatened and enforced. The prebendary of St. Decuman owed six pounds for six years to the fabric, and the dean and chapter sold his goods to satisfy their claim.[1]

The abbot of Bec in Normandy was a defaulter; he promised by his proxy to pay for his prebend of Cleeve by a certain day, but the payment was not made, and he was excommunicated.[2]

The abbot of Athelney, also canon of Wells, is cited before the chapter on the charge of having broken his canonical oath by carrying a case against the chapter, on some alleged trespass, before the civil judges; he sent one of his monks as proxy with letters; the chapter refuse to receive his proxy, and summon him in person; he appears in person as abbot, and the case is heard, adjourned, and arranged.[3]

Yet let us look on another fifteen years; the mortgage of the common fund of the chapter, the assessments on prebends, private gifts from local patriotism and devotion, the endowments of particular altars, had come in, to the recovery of the church, and in his last year bishop William, in 1263, could thank God that the church was so nearly relieved from the late burden of debt that he could make over once again the sequestrations of vacant benefices which had been conceded

January 12, 1263-4. Relief from debt.

1. R. i, ff. 69, 70.
2. R. i, ff. 65 and 98.
3. R. i, f. 71.

to him by the chapter for his lifetime, to the fabric fund of the chapter.[1]

Discipline enforced.

(c) The dean and chapter were enforcing discipline and inflicting punishment upon criminous clerks, vicars and canons, by warning, and by deprivation. In the case of some vicars accused of certain great offences, *criminibus enormibus*, they were required to take the pledge of going to the Holy Land, and to be deprived of their commons for three years, and after that time they might be admitted on conditions to be then fixed.[2]

Canon Walter de Purley was suspended for a year for incontinence, and his prebend of eight marcs value was confiscated to the fabric fund. Robert Giffard, another canon, was expelled from church and city for six months and bound to pay sixty shillings to the master of the fabric, *magistro operarum*, and warned of deprivation of his canonry on another offence.[3] As might be expected from the indefinite position held by the vicars at this time, they supplied the more flagrant cases requiring sharp correction and formal dismissal.

It must have added not a little to the difficulties of the chapter that the dean at the first part of this time, John Saracenus, was an alien element in the chapter. While on one hand the canons were called upon to proceed against defaulters in their own body for non-payment of dues, and were enforcing discipline continually on disorderly vicars and upon canons for evil life, they were also obliged to be upon their guard against the intrigues of Roman connections of the dean as well as against the nepotism of the bishop.

1. R. 2, f. 15 in dors; R. 3, f. 11 in dors.
2. R. i, ff. 70, 71; R. i, f. 65.
3. R. i, f. 100.

But in 1253 the dean John Saracenus died, and Giles of Bridport, archdeacon of Berkshire, was elected by the canons. He held the deanery for three years until his appointment to the bishopric of Salisbury in 1256. He has left little record in our registers, except his tenacity in holding his offices in plurality. When elected dean he protested that he did not intend to withdraw from the archdeaconry or any of his other benefices, and appealed to the apostolic see, and when elected to Salisbury he again claimed to hold also the deanery of Wells, and obtained papal letters suspending the election to the deanery as not being vacant. The chapter protested and appointed their proctor and petitioned the pope for right of free election, and then proceeded to the election of the dean.[1]

Giles of Bridport, dean, A.D. 1253-1256.

There must have been some strong men in the chapter at this time thus to hold their own against bishop and Roman agents. Such a man appears in Edward de la Knoll, prebendary of Henstridge, who was now elected by the chapter and confirmed by the bishop as dean, September 1256, in spite of the opposition of the papal officers, and though dean Giles of Bridport was not consecrated bishop until March 11, 1257.

Dean Edward was, like his master bishop Jocelin, by whom he was brought into the chapter, "a son of the soil," from the manor of Knoll in Wookey, where father and grandfather had held land as tenants of the bishops Jocelin and Robert. He lived through three episcopates to September 12, 1284, and by his vigorous administration of nearly thirty years he made the

Edward de la Knoll, dean, A.D. 1256-1284.

1. R. i, ff. 101, 102.

chapter the ruling body and centre of discipline and government. His policy was carried on and developed under his successors in the deanery, Thomas Bytton and Walter Haselshaw. With him began the series of chapter statutes by which the constitution of Robert and Jocelin was modified and adapted to the later times in matters of residence and chapter business, and the Ordinal was from time to time revised and corrected.

Statutes, A.D. 1259.

The statutes of dean Edward in 1259 were promulgated with the will and assent of bishop William, but under the presidency of the dean.

It is important to notice the relative position of the bishop and the dean and chapter, in the home government of the church, as exhibited in these statutes of the thirteenth century.

Henry Bradshaw says, "It is desirable that we should gain a clear notion of what a cathedral statute was taken to be, from the earliest times. It was a provision made to supply the defects of the unwritten custom, discussed and agreed upon by the dean and chapter, and receiving the assent of the bishop, the constitutional head of the whole cathedral body, much as the bills discussed and agreed upon in parliament become law on receiving the royal assent. The statute is made, as a statute, by the dean and chapter; and in those cases when it is thought necessary, the episcopal assent is added, and, this again in the most important cases of all, is ratified by the bishop's seal. But for ordinary purposes of home government, the agreement of the dean and chapter was amply sufficient."[1]

1. Lincoln Cathedral Statutes, p. 38.

In this case where the bishop and the dean were both men of like mind in their devotion to their office, we see this relation in chapter set forth in the official preamble to the statutes. The bishop is present, and gives his episcopal assent and the statutes are made by the dean and chapter in general convocation of the canons.[1]

They begin with a preamble of apology for the necessity of change and innovation on the statutes of bishop Jocelin, then they order a stricter rule of residence than had hitherto prevailed at Wells. Two views of canonical residence had been current. By the "Nova Constitutio" of Salisbury, 1214, it was required that canons should reside continuously for a fourth part of the year, so that a fourth part of the body should always be in residence together with the four chief dignitaries, "quatuor personæ," except when employed in the service of king, archbishop, or bishop. Failure of residence involved the forfeiture of a fifth of the prebend.

Bishop Jocelin in 1240[2] had ordained that the dignitaries who held office, dean, precentor, chancellor, treasurer, should reside continuously for two thirds of the year, but prebendaries not more than half the year, and at any time within the year, "sive continuè sive interpolatim," to entitle them to share in the common fund; for the rest of the year they might reside on the prebend, either serving the cure of souls

---

1. R. i, f. 105. Statutes of 1259, "presente et in capitulo residente viro provido et sagace domino Edwardo decano Wellense, habita deliberatione qua decuit cum capitulo—de voluntate et assensu venerabilis patris domini W. Bathon. et Wellen. episcopi.'
2. R. i, f. 51; ii, f. 17.

in person or appointing the vicar at a fixed payment regulated by the bishop, and no single canon was bound to reside unless he wished. There was then only one audit in the year—on the feast of St. Calixtus, October 14.

But bishop Grossteste at Lincoln in 1239 had tried to enforce the stricter rule of continuous residence for all canons, and had forbidden the tenure of cure of souls by canons.[1]

This stricter rule of residence was now laid upon the canons. Complaints had arisen of inexact computation and unequal distribution. The year was now divided into four terms of thirteen weeks; from Michaelmas to the vigil of St. Sylvester, December 31; from St. Sylvester to the last day of March; from April 1 to June 30; from July 1 to Michaelmas. Four audits were to be held in the year, one in each term, and residence was strictly required within each term, of six weeks and four days for simple canons, of eight weeks for the dean and chief persons, "decano et principalibus personis." Incomplete residence in one term might not be made up in another. A more equal partition of the common fund was ensured; fifty marcs reserved from the revenues of North Curry were to be always in the hands of the communar for division among the residentiaries.[2]

These statutes were passed in chapter March 5, 1259; present, dean Edward; Gilbert de Byham, precentor; John Forte, chancellor; Hugh de Romenal, treasurer; John de Axbridge, subdean; Richard,

---

1. Grossteste Letters, pp. 74-127 (Rolls Series).
2. R. i, f. 105; ii, f. 17; cf. R. i, f. 119; Drok. Reg., f. 26.

succentor; and twelve canons whose names are given.[1]

A second code of statutes was enacted July 9, 1273, under the presidency of dean Edward de la Knoll, in which the Ordinal is again corrected to prevent confusion and irreverence. Four chief quarterly chapter meetings in the year are fixed as audit days, and for the transaction of more important business, at which attendance of canons, or their vicars and proxies, is obligatory, on pain of forfeiture of past quarterly payments. *Statutes, A.D. 1273.*

The vicars choral are now the subject of more direct legislation. A year of probation is appointed for every vicar presented by his master, during which time each shall be under the charge of one of the body appointed by the precentor to be his teacher, *auscultator*, who is to hear and practice the probationer in the musical services, and make report of skill and knowledge and good conduct at the trial, before the whole chapter, at the end of the year.

A preliminary trial of fifteen days shall test the fitness of altogether untried candidates for this admission to probation.[2]

In the election of the bishop in succession to bishop William Bytton great care is shown in observing the formalities which secured the rights of each of the two electing chapters. Prior and convent, dean and chapter *Election of Walter Giffard, bp. A.D. 1264-7.*

1. R. i, f. 105.
2. R. ii, f. 3.
"The *ordinale* or book containing the general rules relating to the *ordo divini servicii*, was the one book absolutely necessary for the right understanding and definite use of the other service books." H. Bradshaw.

send two proctors each to obtain the king's licence. They send two proctors each to Ferenton (Faringdon Gurney) midway between the two towns of Bath and Wells, to fix the day of election. Four proctors from each are deputed to make the election of one of their body, " de ipsis, de gremio seu de collegio ecclesiarum nostrarum."

Finally, on Thursday after the feast of St. Dunstan, Walter Giffard, subdeacon, papal chaplain, and canon of Wells, was chosen bishop, and May 22, 1264, the dean, perhaps in the absence of the prior, made the announcement to the archbishop, and to the king.[1]

Walter Giffard was a statesman-bishop, and his episcopate at Wells was of short duration. Elected in the week after the battle of Lewes (May 14), he was bishop during the year of the "great parliament," and of the battle of Evesham, 1265 ; he was one of the committee of three bishops and three earls chosen by the assembled parliament in 1266, who drew up the "*dictum* of Kenilworth" which gave terms to the baronial party ; and in the next year he passed from the see of Wells to the archbishopric of York. At Henry's death in 1272, he held the Great Seal, and together with Roger Mortimer and Robert Burnell, he was one of the regents until Edward's return from the Holy Land.

William of Bytton the second, A.D. 1267-1274.

His successor was a man of different type, William of Bytton, nephew of the first bishop William, and his successor first in the archdeaconry of Wells and then in the seat of the bishop ; duly elected by the two chapters, he was accepted by the crown in 1267. He had such repute for holiness of life that he was

1. R. i, f. 82

chosen by the archbishop elect Robert of Kilwardly, to be his consecrator as the most saintly of bishops. His episcopate was wholly devoted to his diocese, distinguished only by uneventful acts of home administration, and his memory was kept alive by the local tradition of miracles worked at his tomb. His tomb is with us unto this day.[1]

---

1. Godwin says of the tomb of bishop William the second: "Monumentum ejus situm est inter duas columnas ab australi parte chori ubi marmor videmus pontificis imaginem habens insculptam."

A stone coffin, containing the body of bishop William was discovered during the changes made in the choir under Mr. Salvin in 1848. An eye-witness on that occasion, Mr. J. R. Clayton, then representing Mr. Salvin there, has described the position of the coffin as lying between the second and third columns of the south choir aisle, east of the present screen.

"On the coffin being opened in the presence of dean Jenkyns, it contained a skeleton laid out in perfect order, every bone in its right place; an iron ring, and a small wooden pastoral staff in two fragments; a leaden tablet 10 in. by $3\frac{1}{2}$ with inscription most beautifully rendered in Lombardic characters.

"Hic jacet Willemus de Button secundus Bathoniensis et Wellensis episcopus sepultus XII die Decembris anno domini MCCLXXIIII."

It was noted at the time that "the teeth were absolutely perfect in number, shape, and order, and without a trace of decay and hardly any discolouration."

Godwin in his day reported that "many superstitious people, especially such as were troubled with the tooth ake, were wont (even of late yeeres) to frequent much the place of his buriall."

A monumental slab of dark marble now lies on the floor of the south aisle, not in a line with the coffin, but somewhat east of it, "having a pontifical image graven upon it," the incised figure of a bishop in act of blessing, but with the singular peculiarity that the feet are not engraved.

There is a similar monument with the incised figure of a bishop in Exeter Cathedral, to Thomas (Bytton) bishop of Exeter, nephew of this bishop William. Thomas Bytton was dean of Wells in 1284, soon after his uncle's death, and it is very likely that he laid down this monument to his uncle.

No copy now exists of the seal of bishop William the second, but it is thus described in Drokensford's Register: " Describitur

278   *Chapters in Wells History.*   [CHAP.

The fabric,
A.D. 1248-86.

For some years after 1242 no mention is made in the registers of any work upon the fabric of the church. Only one important event in the fabric history is recorded by Matthew Paris under the year 1248. He says that he heard from the bishop, William of Bytton, consecrated at Rome in June of that year, that an earthquake, felt especially in his diocese four days before Christmas, had thrown down a stone spire *(tholus)* of great weight which the builders were raising on the summit of the church: "tholus lapideus magnæ quantitatis et ponderis qui in summitate ecclesiæ in decorem ponebatur," and that much damage was caused by the fall. He adds that the effects of the shock were felt not so much on the bases as on the capitals of the columns.[1]

Mr. Freeman understands by the word "tholus" the vaulting of the church, and attributes to this earthquake the fall of the vault, and the consequent breaks in the masonry which are to be seen in the eastern

---

sigillum magnum authenticum Will. Bitton in cujus medio erat imago cujusdam pontificis baculum pastoralem tenentis et manum dextram sublevantis in modum benedicentis: a lateribus vero imagines duæ ecclesiæ erant sculptæ cum campanilibus et crucibus suppositis; in circumferentia vero ejusdem literæ continebantur infra scriptæ, *Will. dei gratia Bathon. et Wellen Epûs*. In suprema vero parte sigilli minoris indorsati erant duæ imagines sculptæ, viz. beatorum apostolorum Petri et Andreæ cruces in manibus tenentium, sub quibus imaginibus erat imago cujusdam episcopi genua flectentis et manus sublevantis ad modum orantis. In superscriptione dicti sigilli minoris hæ literæ legebantur: *Crux germanorum, Willelmo sit via morum.*
The brother's Cross! oh! may it be,
William, the rule of life to thee!
One of the "campanilia" in the seal has a spire.
Drok. Reg. f. 152. Ordinatio vicariæ de Wyveliscumbe. Banwell 1262, confirmata 1317.

1. Matt. Paris, *Historia Anglorum*, iii, 42 (Rolls Series).

parts of the nave.¹ If, on the other hand, it was a cap or spire of the central tower which fell upon the vaulting of the transept, at the junction of nave and transept, we may look for differences in the masonry of the transept under the tower and on the columns and capitals of the transept as a mark of this time. But the silence of the chapter registers on such a disaster may suggest that the damage done was less than was reported by the bishop, absent probably at Rome at that time.

With the year 1263, and the restoration of the fabric fund, begins a course of preparation for new buildings. The recovery of the church from the burden of debt was due to the self-sacrificing spirit of the chapter, men of local ties and interests bound up with the city and church in which they lived, men like Edward de la Knoll and the Bytton family, Hugh de Romenal, treasurer, John of Axbridge sub-dean, and others who had pledged themselves to self-taxation of their incomes, and gave liberally of their substance to the church. The Bytton family had become enriched by the church, but some members of it also spent their money liberally upon the church. We can trace John of Bytton, the rich provost of Combe, brother of the bishop, at one time undertaking a loan for the church on his own responsibility, at another making himself answerable for the payment of a pension of 100 marcs to the cardinal Octavian, a patron of the chapter at Rome, giving his money to assist the penury of religious houses in the diocese, building and endowing the

A.D. 1263.

---

1. Freeman, *Cathedral Church of Wells*, 76, 77.

altar of St. Nicholas[1] in the "Cloister Lady Chapel" as the chantry of the family. It was a time when gifts and offerings were flowing into the church for the endowments of altars for memorial services of the departed, some given by the clergy of the church for themselves, or by strangers for their friends, others in return for benefits received during lifetime. It was a time when a change was taking place in the nature of the endowments made by the religious world to the church. Through the last century-and-a-half benefactions to the church had taken the form of endowment by lands and money for the fabric fund or for prebends and offices in the church. Now a greater prominence was being given in the teaching of the Church, to the doctrines of purgatory and indulgences, and to the duty of the living towards the dead, of remembrance before God in prayers and intercessions.

---

1. In 1276 the altar of *St. Nicholas* in the chapel of the Blessed Virgin "near the cloister," constructed by the legacies of John of Bytton, was endowed for mortuary services for himself and his brother bishop William (R. i, f. 22, R. iii, f. 124), and further endowments were made by bishop William the second. (R. i, f. 90, R. iii, f. 188). There seems reason for thinking that this was the burial place of bishop William the first. The endowments of obits made at the altar of St. Nicholas and in the "Cloister Lady Chapel," by the Bytton family, mark this as the mortuary chapel of the family, and the place where the body of the bishop first rested. (R. i, f. 22.) But bishop Drokensford's Register, ff. 123-8 mentions a collation to the annale endowed in memory of bishop William the first, at the altar in "the Lady Chapel behind the high altar" in 1319, and the Canon of Wells and Godwin speak of his tomb as in the middle of the "new Lady Chapel."

Perhaps we may reconcile the earlier and later statements by supposing that when the second and more stately Lady Chapel was raised, the body of the first bishop of the Bytton family, the first bishop buried at Wells since the strife with Bath, was translated to the more honourable place within the church by his great nephew Thomas of Bytton, dean 1284-1292 and afterwards bishop of Exeter.

The foundation of chantries and obits in the church was becoming the fashionable form of religious endowment, by which provision was made by gifts and legacies for the support of priests and chaplains who should offer up memorial and intercessory prayers and masses for the departed.

All such offerings contributed to the richness and adornment of the church, "the offerings for the dead became a source of trade to the living," they supported the ministrant body, they brought worshippers and almsgivers to the church, they fostered the sense of communion between the departed and the generations of the day; and love and enthusiasm for their church, as the common home of the departed and present members of one body, were kindled and perpetuated.

So for forty years the chapter had been recovering from the pressure of debts: they had also been preparing for new buildings. It is in the year 1286 that the registers give the first sign of that building activity which went on for at least the next fifty years. The dean at the time was Thomas of Bytton, one of the third generation of that family in Wells, nephew of the late bishop William, elected by the canons as dean in succession to Edward de la Knoll in 1284. He was second son of Sir Adam de Bytton, and successively precentor, archdeacon, and dean of Wells; in 1292 he was elected bishop of Exeter. There he was builder of the choir and vaulted roof, died September 21, 1307, and was buried near the high altar.[1]

Thomas Bytton dean A.D. 1284.

On the Tuesday after "Quasimodo," April 26, 1286, dean Thomas summoned a full chapter of residents

A.D. 1286.

1. Episcopal Registers, diocese of Exeter, Bytton's. F. C. Hingeston-Randolph, Pref. xxiv.

and non-residents to take into consideration the urgent necessity of finishing the new structure which had been long in progress, and of restoring and keeping up the older fabric, and also at the same time the insufficiency of the means of the chapter for the work, "inspecta ante cetera necessitate urgente quam dicta ecclesia patitur, tam in nova structura jamdiu incepta perficienda, quam antiqua fabrica ipsius reficienda et sustentanda, et ad hec assignatarum insufficientia facultatum."[1]

The canons coming up in great numbers resolved unanimously that each canon should give to the fabric a tenth of his prebend yearly, according to the taxation of Norwich of 1254, for five years, that receivers be appointed by the chapter, and that defaulters should be fined half a marc for failure of payment within fifteen days of the quarter-day, and be further liable to distraint and excommunication.

This resolution of the chapter meeting formed an important precedent which was quoted and acted on in later stages of the work.

The work before the chapter was twofold; to put in repair the old work, and to complete the new structure which had been begun some time before.

We do not know if the repairs required at this time were the repair of the roof or only the normal dilapidations of an old building. The high authority of Professor Willis may be cited that the "new structure" begun, "diu incepta," and as yet incomplete "could be no other than the chapter house."[2]

---

1. R. i, f. 198.
2. *Somerset Archæological Society's Proceedings*, xii, 20.

Hitherto there is no evidence of the existence of a chapter-house, or of any definite place where the dean and chapter were wont to meet in council. They met probably in some part of the church, or in one of the chapels.[1] The important position of the capitular body in the home government of the church, to which they had now attained, demanded that, after the example of other cathedral churches, there should be a worthy council chamber of the dean and chapter where they should daily meet for communion in council, for enactment of discipline, and ordering of ritual.

This chapter act gives the first intimation that this new work had been in progress for some time, and a new start is now taken.

Professor Willis gives the general description of the divisions of the chapter-house as it now exists: "It stands upon a vaulted substructure, by which its floor is considerably raised above the floor of the church. This substructure cannot well be called 'a crypt,' for it is not sunk under ground, the springs of water in the soil forbidding such a building: it is entered from the north aisle of the choir by a doorway and passage. The floor of the chapter-room is reached by a building attached to its western side, which contains a staircase lighted by great windows of early geometrical tracery and leading to the elaborate doorway of the chapter-house. The style of the chapter-room itself is so greatly in advance of the substructure and stairs as to show that a considerable interval of time elapsed

The chapter house.

---

[1]. On one occasion, August 29, 1244, they met in *capella beata Maria*, the southern Lady Chapel probably, to take action against the summons of the papal delegates to meet them in the greater church "in Majore Ecclesia." (R. i, f. 97 in dors.)

between the one and the other." Again, he says, "I conceive that in 1286 the portion of the chapter-house called 'the crypt' was completed."[1] If so, in 1286 there stood on the north side of the church, east of the north transept, a detached octagonal building, on a slightly lower level than the floor of the church, which was the substructure, and the first part of a building as yet incomplete.

Of this "crypt" the thick outer walls, and the mouldings of the wall shafts, the narrow lancet windows with wide splays in each bay, are of somewhat earlier date than the central pillars supporting the vault. The vaulting is remarkable for the way "in which the arches are disposed without the introduction of ribs." Traces of "dog tooth" ornament on two of the capitals betoken an early date in the century. All these are indications that building had been begun awhile, *diu incepta*; had been going on through the time of Edward de la Knoll, through the last forty years, and perhaps, like the undercroft of the palace, even during the later years of bishop Jocelin.

The solidity of this substructure shows that the building was meant to be the basement story of a higher building, and the great size of the central pillar the root of an uprising shaft to stand upon it. At the same time, the massive character of the ironwork of the thirteenth century in the bars and bolts inside and outside of the double doors, the deep sockets in the thickness of the walls on each side of the door and above and below for the drawbars with which the

---

1. Archæological Institute, "Memoirs illustrative of the history and antiquities of Bristol," etc., xxviii.

inside doors were protected, the recess in the thickness of the wall on the south side, are evidences that the building was used as the "treasury" in which all valuables, of money, vessels, documents, were placed. Here it may be was the Sacristy in which the vestments were kept, and also the *thesauraria* of the church.[1] This was the building finished by 1286.

The next stage of building dates from 1286, and from this action of the dean and canons. At this time Robert Burnell was bishop (1275—1292), one of the greatest men in the kingdom as minister of Edward, chancellor, the great lawyer of the time. The year before, 1285, is marked in the constitutional history of England by the promulgation of statutes of great importance, "the culminating point of Edward's legislative activity"[2] the statutes of Westminster, June 28; the statutes of Winchester, October 8. In that year the bishop had obtained a royal licence to raise an embattled wall, *kirnellare*, round the cemetery of the canons and the precincts, *precinctum*, of the houses of the canons at Wells.[3] It is doubtful whether any of this work was carried out by him, if the south wall of the cloister is to be ascribed to Jocelin. The only work ascribed to him by Godwin is the chapel of the palace, and the stately hall which still witnesses in its

Robert Burnell, A.D. 1275-1292.

---

1. R. i, f. 131, in dors. Memorandum. Deeds relating to the churches of Bath and Wells, to North Curry and Wynescumb, St. Cuthbert's, Congresbury, etc., were delivered to Edward the dean to be carried to London at the command of the archbishop on Saturday next before St. Michael, and were brought back by him on St. Crispin and Crispennas day and replaced in the " Treasury "—Oct. 25, 1281.

2. Stubbs, *Constitutional History*, ii, 122.

3. R. ii, f. 18.

ruin to the magnificence of the builder. Burnell was too much engaged in state affairs to be resident long, if at all, at Wells. " He was much employed in Welsh affairs, from which he could ill be spared. So the king was content for a while to let him keep his court of chancery at Bristol," 1284-1285. In May, 1286, he went with the king to Gascony, and was out of England until August, 1289.[1]

But though little resident, the bishop was encouraging and assisting the work which was going on in the church at Wells, by granting indulgences,[2] and by the gift to the chapter, for the fabric fund, of advowsons of churches, Yeovilton, Burnham, Stanton Drew, and Chelwood. He had also taken steps to appropriate the church of Burnham to the chapter, but he died before the appropriation was effected. Bishop Haselshaw afterwards carried out his good intentions. In return, the dean and chapter, in 1306, endowed a chantry for the two bishops at the altars lately constructed at the entrance into the choir, the one in honour of St. Mary, the other of St. Andrew.[3]

---

1. Pat. 14 Ed. III, pt. 1, m. 13. A similar licence with the addition only of the words "et precinctum domorum suorum," is given by Edward III to bishop Ralph, sixty years later in 1341. This royal licence to fortify and embattle the cemetery wall and the precincts was one of several given about the same time to cathedral closes. In the 14th of Edward I, 1286, licences were given to Exeter on January 1; to Wells in April; to Lincoln, Salisbury, and York in May; to St. Paul's in June. Perhaps it was the king's policy to multiply fenced places to give greater security throughout the land.

2. R. iii, f. 389.

3. R. i, f. 164. Chantries of bishops Burnell and Haselshaw founded by dean Godley and chapter of Wells, 5 Kal. Jan., 1306.

A slab of blue lias, 16 feet long, with the matrix of a brass of a bishop, and letters of name mark the site of bishop Haselshaw's

What was the next portion of the work of this time?
A vaulted passage leads from the "crypt" to the
north aisle of the choir, and a doorway in the north
aisle is cut through the older wall of the church.
This was probably the next portion of the work after
1286, followed by the building of the grand stairway
of thirty-two steps leading upwards from the north
door of the transept. This north door was a door of
Jocelin's church, and on the outside the moulding
remains which shows that there was a small vestry
attached to it. It corresponds exactly in position to
the door of the south transept now blocked up by the monument in St. Martin's chapel, which also had a penthouse or vestry on the south side. The ascent of the stairs was lighted by two great windows of early and very beautiful geometrical tracery, and flanked by tiers of stone seats rising with the stairs, which curved round to the portal and double-arched vestibule of the chamber. This we may suppose was the work of Burnell's time, and of dean Thomas and of the canons from 1286 to 1292. Whoever was designer and architect of this noble ascent up to the chapter-house, which is the distinguishing characteristic of the chapter-house of Wells above all its contemporaries, it is a work worthy of the princely builder of the palace hall. The large windows which light the west side of the stairs, and in which the rich brown glass gives screen from the western evening sun which strikes full into the hall, are likenesses, on a grander scale, in form and tracery

The ascent to the chapter-house, A.D. 1286-92.

burial place at the southern entrance of bishop Bubwith's chantry. This also fixes the site of one of the altars, *ad ingressum chori*, and so of the choir screen of the time.
Cf. R. i, f. 52. Dean Husee's obit was ordained there in 1307.

to the windows in the little village church of Acton Burnell, which was built by the bishop at the family manor and castle in Shropshire.

On October 22, 1292, bishop Robert Burnell died at Berwick, while with the king in his Scotch wars. His body was brought to his church at Wells, and buried, but no stone or inscription now marks the burial-place of one of the greatest statesmen, though not a very saintly bishop, of the see. Godwin says, "he lieth buried in the middle of the body of his church under a marble stone somewhat below the pulpit," "paulo infra suggestum."[1] He means the stone pulpit in the nave, built by bishop Knight in 1516. Carter's plan (1798) shows a large slab containing the matrix of a brass in the south of the nave between the third and fourth pillars west of the tower. That has disappeared.

Another and a third stage in the building was going on under bishop William de Marchia 1293-1302, when Walter Burnell 1292-1295, and Walter de Haselshaw 1295-1303, were deans. Haselshaw succeeded to the bishopric, and died 1308.

William de Marchia, A.D. 1293-1302.

William de Marchia, canon of Wells, had been one of the king's agents at Rome in 1284 to obtain from pope Martin IV concession of the tenths from the clergy for five years, for the support of a crusade which Edward undertook to join.

In 1289 he sat with the chancellor Burnell on a commission to hear the complaints brought against the judges during the king's absence in Gascony.

In 1290 he was made treasurer of the kingdom.

1. *De Præsulibus*, 426, ed. 1743.

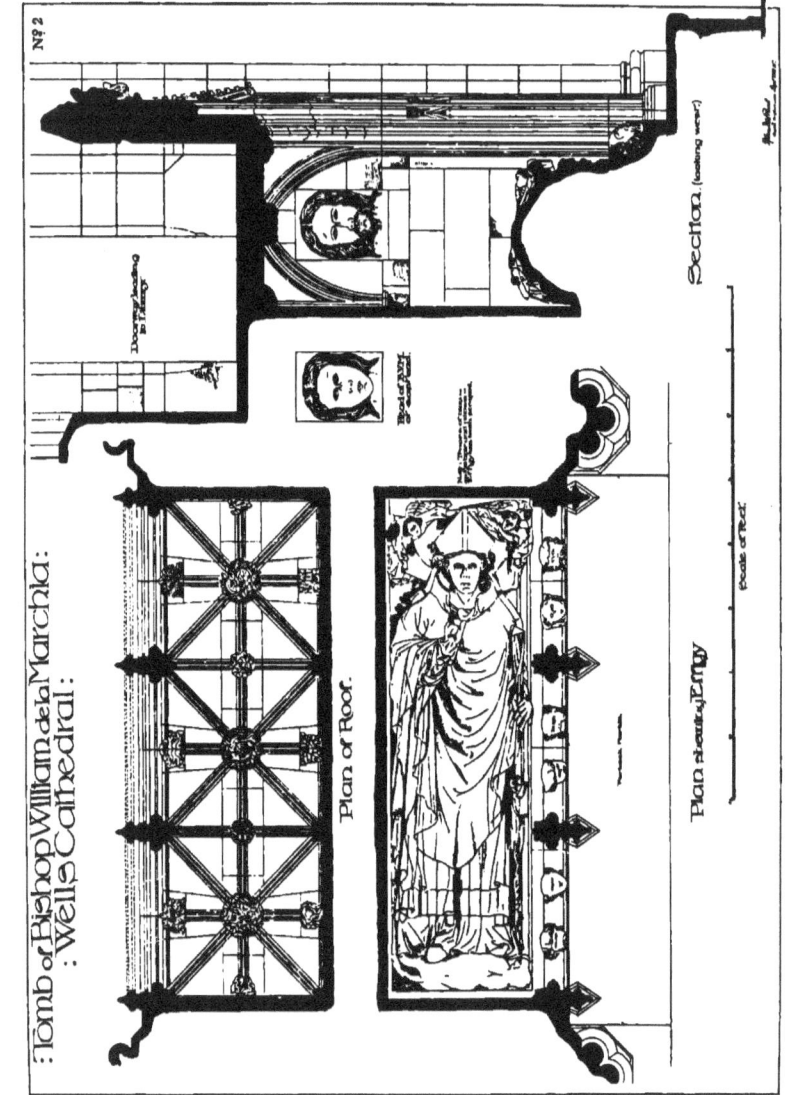

A copy of the deed of submission of the Scottish chiefs to Edward as overlord—in the Wells archives—is attested by him as treasurer in 1291.[1]

He was rewarded with the bishopric in succession to the chancellor, for his services to Edward in financial difficulties.

Tradition has assigned to the time of bishop William the building of the chapter-house. Godwin says " In this man's time the chapter-house was built by the contributions of well-disposed persons." We are familiar with the local habit of ascribing to one man, or period, as to bishop Jocelin and his time, the progressive work of several generations. But in this case so little is recorded of the bishop during his episcopacy, in comparison with his predecessor and his successors, that it has been difficult to account for the tradition, and still more for the extraordinary respect paid to his memory by the dean and chapter, and for their strenuous efforts to obtain his canonization.[2]

One original charter in the chapter archives may suggest a reason for this posthumous gratitude and for the tradition which ascribed to his time preeminently, the building of the chapter-house.

---

1. *Fœdera*, ii, 274, ed. 1727. This deed was sent to Wells to be enrolled in the chapter archives, July 9, 1291. R. iii, f. 22.

2. It is doubtful if his registers could be recovered. Reg. Drokensford, f. 34. "*The bishop to dean.*" "Being much embarassed for want of our predecessors' registers, we bid you cite Robert provost of Wells, and Henry archdeacon of Taunton, the last bishops' executors to render up such as are needful for administration. Give like monition to Antony Bradney executor of bishop William (*i.e.* de Marchia) and his co-executor. If negligent, cite them before us at Chard, second week in Lent." Pucklechurch, February 8, 1310.

The pope Martin IV had granted to Edward a tenth of all clerical incomes for five years in 1284, in aid of a promised crusade. The crusade was deferred, and in 1291 Nicolas IV renewed the grant to Edward.[1] The two chapters of Bath and Wells were the sub-collectors for the diocese under Oliver Sutton, bishop of Lincoln, and John de Pontoise, of Winchester, executors for the kingdom. A deposit of £1,000 was lying in the hands of the chapter, held *in subsidium terræ sanctæ*, while the crusade was deferred. By a deed[2] dated Dogmersfield, January 20, 1295-6, bishop

---

1. *Fœdera*, ii, 274, 499, 517, ed. 1727.
2. Charter, 138. The original document incorrectly endorsed in a later handwriting " Bp. Willm. receives £1,000 for the Holy Land Warrs," and having a fragment of a bishop's seal, is here transcribed. It runs thus :

" Universis videntibus hanc scripturam Willelmus permissione divina Bathoniensis et Wellensis Episcopus salutem in domino sempiternam. Noveritis quod cum nos, Episcopus supradictus, Thomas Prior et conventus Bathoniensis, W. Decanus et capitulum Wellense, recognoverimus per nostrum scriptum obligatorium nostro et cujuslibet nostrum ac ecclesiarum nostrarum nomine, nos recepisse [dep]ositum et habere a reverendo patre O[livero Sutton] dei gratia Lincolniensi Episcopo executore, una cum venerabili patre domino J[ohanne de Pontissera] eadem gratia Wintoniensi Episcopo legitime impedito, super decimis domino E[dwardo] dei gratia Regi Anglie illustri in subsidium terræ sanctæ concessis in regno Anglie a sede apostolica deputato, mille libras bonorum et legalium sterlingorum in pecunia numerata de pecunia decimæ antedictæ restituendum predictum depositum prefato domino Lincolniensi Episcopo vel collegæ suo, aut alteri eorundem succedenti vel succedentibus in officio execucionis predicto, infra unum mensem postquam nos aut aliquis nostrum conjunctim seu divisim per dictum patrem aut collegam suum vel aliquem alium seu alios quem vel quos tangit officium execucionis predictum fuerimus requisiti, prout in scripto hujusmodi obligatorio plenius continentur. Quia tamen depositum mille librarum supradictum ad nostras solum modo manus pervenit, et in nostris ac nostri Episcopatus negotiis feliciter expediendis per nos totaliter est conversum, indempnitatibus prioris et decani predictorum ac capitulorum ipsorum rovidere volentes, dictum de-

William gave to the executors a bond for repayment of this sum of £1,000 whenever it should be required. It appears to have been already borrowed by the bishop and the two chapters conjointly, with promise of repayment on demand within one month. Now the bishop makes himself solely responsible for repayment, and pledges (no doubt with consent of his chapter) the diocesan revenues and his personal property as security for repayment to the collector.

Inasmuch as the money had come into his hands only, and had been spent on diocesan objects "in nostris et nostri episcopatus negotiis feliciter expediendis totaliter est conversum," he promises to hold the two chapters free from all liability "et ipsos indempnes undique quoad hujusmodi depositum conservare."

There is no other evidence to show how this £1,000 was spent, or that it was ever repaid, or called for by the executors. The chapter kept this bond as their security under any circumstances.

At his death the bishop devised a tenth of this sum, 100 marcs (£66 13s. 4d.) to the chapter to be held by them in deposit for the crusade "ad subsidium terræ sanctæ" and "usque ad generale passagium ad terram sanctam proxime faciendum," but with ultimate reversion to his brother, and then to

---

positum predicto patri Lincolnie Episcopo vel collegæ suo predicto aut sibi succedentibus, ut premittitur, vel succedenti reddere seu restituere, quando oportuerit, promittimus bona fide, et ipsos indempnes undique quoad hujusmodi depositum conservare. Et ad hoc fideliter faciendum obligamus nos executores et successores nostros, ac omnia bona nostra presencia et futura ecclesiastica et mundana ubicumque inventa. In cujus rei testimonium sigillum nostrum presentibus est appensum. Datum apud Dogmerfeld xiiij^a kalend Februarii anno domini millesimo ducentesimo nonagesimo quarto."

his nephew Robert Urry, if the crusade were abandoned.

This deposit in after years became a subject of much trouble to the chapter, as hungry suitors wooed them for it, first the bishop, then the king, to whom they granted it for two years. Then the papal nuncio adjudged it to the brother and after his death to the nephew. The chapter, having yielded to the king's demand, were unable to surrender it.[1] These transactions throw some light on bishop William's motives.

We do not know sufficiently the nature of the transaction, but it is probable that the treasurer-bishop, who knew the king and the danger there was lest the sum of £1,000 lying in the hands of the chapter might be swept into the king's coffers, took this method of securing it for the service of the church in his diocese at his own personal risk, and if such a sum, or part of it, was spent by him on the chapter-house it would

---

1. R. i, ff. 119, 132. Receipt by the dean and chapter, Sept. 7, 1311, to the executors of bishop William.

R. i, f. 119; Reg. Drokensford, f. 37. The bishop borrows it until Easter. London, Sept. 13, 1311.

R. i, f. 119. Letter (in French) to Thomas de Berkele, one of the executors from the dean and chapter, "the money is sent to London ' al hostel le deen de Seynt Poul ; ' they pray him to defend them from damage."

R. i, f. 202. The king wishes to borrow it. R. i, f. 159. The D. and C. write to the bishop and lend it to the king for two years, 1312.

R. i, f. 208. Order from official of papal nuncio that the money is to be paid to the brother, 1313.

Probably it was never recovered from the Crown, for it turns up again in the next generation: R. i, f. 205, 208. The papal nuncio in 1340 orders it to be paid to the nephew, according to former injunction made in 1313.

R. i, f. 209. Dean and chapter now plead that the time for reversion has not come, 1340.

reasonably account for the gratitude of the chapter and for his posthumous fame as a benefactor to the church.[1]

There must have been some special reasons, and some high qualifications which won for him after his death very strong testimonials from his contemporaries, and influenced many great persons to join in seeking his canonization, according to the fashion of the time. Money was collected in the diocese for his translation and honourable burial, and the stately tomb in the south transept is a remarkable monument of contemporary gratitude. The letters written by the dean and chapter twenty years after his death bear high testimony to the virtues of his life, as "the good shepherd," and to the effulgence of miracles at his tomb; and the highest personages in the kingdom were moved to use their influence at Rome in support of the prayer of the chapter.[2]

It is pleasant at least to read a contemporary eulogy from those who had lived with him, as a set-off against the detraction which followed his memory from others. The same terms are used in all the letters from the chapter describing him as the man of holy life and the exemplary bishop, "vitæ sanctæ, conversationis

---

1. In 1282 Edward had seized the treasure at the Temple for the Welsh war. Stubbs, *Const. Hist.*, ii, 119.

2. 1324, June 2. R. i, f. 172. Laurence de la Waar, the king's ambassador, is urged to take up the suit for the canonization, against the machinations of John de Britton, the adversary.

1324, June 2. R. i, f. 171. Letters to John de Grandison and to Robert Baldock, the chancellor.

1324, June 4. R. i, f. 172. A précis of letters to influential persons. Bishop Drokensford writes to Rome.

1325, December 4. R. i, f. 174. The king, queen, archbishop Walter, and eight bishops petition the pope for his canonization.

honestæ, bonus pastor in ministerio sacerdotali, pauperibus et miserabilibus personis compatiens, elemosinarius largissimus."

But yet all their efforts were in vain. The "machinations of the adversaries" at Rome were too strong. Matthew of Westminster and Polydore Virgil are quoted by Godwin as representing the grounds of opposition: "they complaine grievously of him (bishop William) as the author of a hainous sacrilege in causing the king to spoile all the churches and monasteries of England of such plate and mony as lay hoarded up in them, for the paiment of his souldiers." Godwin, gives his own opinion that the bishop was made a scapegoat to bear the offence of the king's arbitrary acts in obtaining money. "Edward was a prince that neither wanted wit to devise nor courage to execute such an exploit, and to lay the fault upon another at last, which, how undeservedly soever, might barre him out of the Pope's calender."[1]

Evidences are not wanting that there were "other well-disposed persons" who were contributing at this time to the fabric and the chapter-house. William of Wellington, one of the canons, gave about this time forty marcs "to the needs of the church and to the fabric of the chapter-house." The dean and chapter in 1300, "desiring to return spiritual things for temporal," endowed, with £10 a year charged on the manor of North Curry, an obit for this benefactor at "the altar of Holy Cross, under the bell-tower on the north side of the church."[2]

1. Godwin's *de Præsulibus*, p. 375, ed. 1743.
2. R. iii, f. 284.

Henry Husee, canon, precentor, and afterwards dean in 1302-1305, gave to the chapter £200 on condition that they endowed his obit with £10 annually. His obit was afterwards celebrated at one of the two altars at the entrance of the choir, and his monument was raised by his executors in the chapel of St. Calixtus.¹

Dean Walter de Haselshaw gave £10 a year to the chapter during the lifetime of Walter de Charleton, one of the canons, for which an acquittance was given to the executors of the dean in 1317.²

But whatever may have been the share of bishop William de Marchia and others in obtaining funds for the building of the chapter house in life, and after death, the credit of carrying to completion the last stage of building belongs to dean John Godley (Johannes de Godelee), the greatest builder of the church since Jocelin. Prebendary in 1301, during the last years of bishop William's life and during the episcopate of Walter Haselshaw, he was elected to succeed dean Husee in 1305, and he held office for twenty-seven years until February 1332-3. During his earlier life he must have watched the first stages of the building, the growth of the great ascent, and of the noble portal, and the gradual rise of the outer walls and buttresses of the great octagonal building on the north of the church. At first we may suppose a temporary roof covered in the stone floor raised upon the vault of the substructure. On this floor can yet be traced the diagrams, perhaps of Godley's architect, which may

Dean Godley A.D. 1305-1333.

1. R. iii, ff. 103-109.
2. R. i, f. 140.

have supplied the working drawings for the masons in the interior arrangement of windows and vaulted roof which rose above it in dean Godley's time.[1]

Familiar with the designs of the first builders, he and his master-mason, William Joy, worked them out and brought the whole to its present perfected beauty in the first fifteen years of his government.

<small>Bp. John of Drokensford A.D. 1309-1329.</small>

John of Drokensford (Droxford in Hants) was bishop for the greater part of dean Godley's time, succeeding bishop Walter in 1309, and dying three years and a-half before the dean in 1329.

His register is the first in the series of episcopal registers at Wells; lately edited for the Somerset Record Society, it gives the materials for a fuller knowledge of the bishop's life and times than has hitherto been published.[2]

He was "one of the lawyer-statesman class of bishops." He had held several lay offices under the crown, and was rewarded by an abundance of ecclesiastical benefices. At the time of his election he held office about the king's person as keeper of the wardrobe, he was canon of Wells and of four other cathedral churches, and he held prebends in five collegiate churches, and other benefices in different parts of the kingdom.

"Wells was not used by him as headquarters, save that the dean and chapter furnished him skilled com-

---

1. Mr. Irving writes: "That wonderful collection of working drawings now remaining on the floor of the first chapter-house. There is not such a collection elsewhere in England, and I earnestly hope that such an unique collection may be illustrated by the Society of Antiquaries."

2. *Somerset Record Society*, vol. i, Drokensford's Register, 1887, it is edited by bishop Hobhouse.

missaries for his varied commissions, and Bath was no centre of diocesan action."[1] It is no wonder that as he moved about from one to another of his manors and of his sixteen official houses, he should have left to the dean and chapter the home government of the church, or that with little time to study the annals of his church he should have come into collision with his chapter when he assumed rights of episcopal jurisdiction which had been ceded by previous bishops to their officers in the chapter.

It is to dean Godley that we owe the preservation of early chapter documents and the formation of the first of the chapter registers, the *Liber Albus* (R. i), in the chapter archives. He had known the full value of these early charters in establishing the dean's position in the great controversy with the bishop; and in the last year of his life he ordered that they should be carefully copied, examined by the chancellor and others of the chapter in presence of a notary, "sub manu publica," and enregistered, lest these floating and perishing leaves, which are the treasures of the church, and contain the primary elements of its history, should perish through neglect or age.

A.D. 1332, Liber Albus, Register i ordered by dean Godley.

"Item quod quædam chartæ nostræ, quæ sunt velut thesaurus ecclesiæ, in parte sint debilitatæ, quædam vero quasi vetustate consumptæ, volumus quod per disertos viros concanonicos nostros, præsente ecclesiæ cancellario qui curam et custodiam habet eorundem, circa festum Sancti Michaelis examinentur, et in uno registro de verbo ad verbum conscribantur, et quam citius commode fieri poterit sub manu publica, auctori-

---

1. Preface to the Register by bishop Hobhouse, p. xviii.

tate judicis competentis ad perpetuam rei memoriam publicentur, saltem illæ de quarum consumptione magis timetur."[1]

The registers of bishop and of chapter can now be read together to illustrate and confirm one another. The notices of the building become more frequent though they are few and fragmentary considering the importance of the works in progress. Yet we can trace from these short and scanty chapter acts what an amazing activity was manifested by the chapter in raising those parts of the fabric which distinguish the present church from the church of Jocelin and of the thirteenth century. Within the twenty-seven years of dean Godley's rule,

<small>Work going on under dean Godley.</small>
(a) The central tower was raised and roofed in;
(b) The chapter-house was finished;
(c) The Lady-chapel was built;
(d) The choir was being refitted with new stalls and being prolonged eastward;
(e) The parapet round the whole of the earlier church was renewed.

The chapter records contain the notices, from time to time, which enable us to affix certain dates to most of these buildings during their progress to completion.

---

1. R. ii, f. 24. "The early part of this Register i, or *Liber Albus*, was written" (Mr. Riley says in Report 1 of Historical Manuscripts Commission), "in the reign of Edward I or possibly Edward II." The date is fixed more precisely by this order of dean Godley. Mr. J. A. Bennett says in his preface to the "Calendar of Wells Manuscripts," (Appendix 3 to vol. 10 of Report to Historical Manuscripts Commission): "this volume was probably once bound in black and called the 'Liber Niger,' to which there are references in the chapter acts. The earliest entry is of the time of Edward the Confessor, the last belongs to the year 1393."

During the first decade (1305-1315) no mention of the fabric occurs.

But with the year 1315 commences a series of short notices from time to time which indicate the progress of the works then going on.

In 1315 a commission was sent through the diocese, under the official of the bishop and the official of the dean, to levy money for the work on the tower, "campanile," of the cathedral church. The bishop had assigned to that object the fees received for non-residence and other sources.[1]

Central Tower, A.D. 1315-1319.

In 1318, May 8, an important chapter meeting was held, of which the minutes are given with unusual detail.[2] One of the foremost questions discussed was how to deal with defaulters who had not paid the "decima quinquennalis," agreed upon at a late chapter meeting towards the "new campanile." They were to be proceeded against by censures and sequestrations.

Chapter Meeting, 1318.

It was announced that large sums were coming in for the new campanile from different sources:

Sources of income.

(a) From the tenths of assessments on the prebends of the canons, the *decima quinquennalis;*

(b) From the offerings made at the tomb of bishop William *(de oblationibus Sancti Willelmi)* who was already canonized by popular voice without waiting for the decree from Rome.

(c) From the collections made throughout the diocese by the "fraternity of St. Andrew," a brotherhood formed at this time to raise funds for the

1. Reg. Drokensford, f. 81. "Commissio ad levandam pecuniam concessam fabricæ campanilis Wells." Banwell, July, 1315.
2. R. i, f. 143. Archer sums up the purpose of this chapter meeting, "ad constructionem novi campanilis finiendam."

cathedral fabric. They collected the sums which were given as the "cathedraticum," or by bequest, to the fabric fund. They published the bishop's "indulgences" and letters to stimulate parochial collections, and they carried the year's collection to Wells for an audit now appointed by the chapter, or "paid it to a lessee who had agreed to give a fixed sum to the chapter."[1] Two canons are to audit the accounts of each collector.

In 1318-1319 the central tower was being built. In 1321 it was raised up high enough to be roofed in.

In August 1321 the chapter borrowed £40 (= £800) for building purposes, "quadraginta libras in fabrica ecclesiæ reparanda impendendas,"[2] and on December 23 in that year they acknowledged the grant of one penny in the pound from the benefices of the clergy of the deanery of Taunton for the covering in of the tower, " in subsidium coopertura novi campanilis ecclesiæ Wellensis." They undertake that this voluntary gift shall not be made a precedent for a demand in other times.[3]

So in 1322 we have reason to suppose that the central tower was approaching completion.

Chapter-house, A.D. 1319.

In these same years, while the tower was being built up, the chapter-house was finished. In 1319 the

---

1. See preface to bishop Drokensford's Register by bishop Hobhouse, p. xxv. He compares the "Brotherhood of St. Chad" at Lichfield. The upper parts of the western towers of Tours cathedral church were built by the "Brotherhood of St. Gatien," in the fifteenth century.

2. R. i, f. 155. Bond of the dean and chapter to Richard, "dicto Richeman de Well." for £40 borrowed "per manus R. de Baker custodis fabricæ ecclesiæ Wellensis ad usum ejusdem ecclesiæ." 20 kal. Sept., 1321.

3. R. i, f. 157. December 23, 1321.

chapter meetings were held in the new "domus capitularis ;" perhaps for the first time on the occasion of the contest with bishop Drokensford as to his right of holding there his ordinary visitation of the cathedral church. Hitherto throughout the registers the meetings and acts of the dean and chapter have been described as "in capitulo," but no place of meeting has been definitely named. The word 'capitulum' is used both for the place of meeting of the chapter and for the body itself. For the first time now, at the opening of this controversy, dean Godley summoned the chapter to meet in the "Chapter-house" on the Wednesday after the translation of St. Thomas, July 1319, "in domo capitulari ecclesiæ Wellensis."

"Reverendus vir dominus Joannes de Godelee decanus . . . omnes canonicos per pulsationem magnæ campanæ juxta modum et consuetudinem ejusdem ecclesiæ fecit evocari, quod comparerent in domo capitulari ecclesiæ Wellensis die Mercurii proximi post festum translationis beati [Thom. *erased*] martiris anno domini MCCC^{mo} nono decimo." R. ii, f. 31.

Now and from henceforth, generally, but not universally, the place of meeting is thus named in important chapter acts ; "actum est in domo capitulari."

The chapter had now achieved the completion of their "Domus Capitularis," their council chamber ; the place of business and legislation of the capitular body in its several grades of governors and governed as a great landed corporation in the shire, and the place of discipline and of regulation of ritual of a great religious and educational institution.

The building was for the most part the creation of

the capitular body, and its rise in beauty and dignity was a sign and record of the rise and culmination to power and to independent jurisdiction of the chapter, which now had grown up from small beginnings to a co-ordinate position with the bishop in the home government of the cathedral church, and an independence in the management of its own internal affairs.

In the outer walls and interior arrangement of this noble octagonal chamber, with its fifty-one canopied stalls, in the engaged shafts and rich mouldings and tracery of its eight noble windows, in the tall central pillar branching out, palm-like, to support the vaulting and the roof above, in the characteristic mouldings and distinctive ornaments, such as the ballflower in the window mouldings, we have one of the best examples of the " decorated " order of architecture, at the beginning of the fourteenth century, the years of the second Edward, 1307-1327.

It may as truly be said of the chapter-house of Wells as of its rival at York which lacks the unique stately grandeur of the ascent of winding stair, and the grace of branching central shaft:

> " Ut rosa flos florum,
> Sic est domus ista domorum."
>
> O rose of flowers fairest!
> O house of beauty rarest!

The master builder, William Joy. It is pleasant to be able to record the name of the master builder who was working with dean Godley in the prosecution of these great works. In a chapter act at this time, but of which the actual date is illegible, a life pension of forty shillings is granted by the dean and chapter to William Joy, master of the fabric, "magistro fabricæ," for his faithful services to the church, "pro bono et laudabili suo obsequio nobis et ecclesiæ nostræ," and his services are retained, as hitherto, to superintend the fabric and repair defects.[1] Again in 1329, a further pension of 36s. 8d. is assigned, with the same condition of retaining his services, "quolibet anno et quotiens opus fuerit, inspicere defectus reparandos in ecclesia nostra, et consilium et auxilium impendere."[2]

We cannot fail to remark the coincidence of the conflicts about jurisdiction between bishop and "dean and chapter" with the first mention of the entrance into the new chapter-house.

Conflict between bishop and dean and chapter, A.D. 1319-1321.

The bishop may have wished to mark his formal entrance into the new building by an assertion of episcopal visitation, and a challenge of the alleged immunities of dean and chapter from his ordinary jurisdiction. It may be that he, a great state officer whose duties occupied him much outside his diocese, had yet to learn from the history of his church that the autonomy of the chapter was the growth of long years of custom, and the result of privileges and grants bestowed by his predecessors in the see. But when the charters of Reginald, Savaric, and Jocelin were exhibited to him, he was forced to acknowledge that his rights by common law had been narrowed by custom and special charters, so that the prebendal churches and parishes were exempt from the visitation of the bishop and his archdeacons. It had come to this that the bishop could not visit a prebendal parish

1. R. i, f. 179.
2. R. i, f. 181.

nor summon an offending prebendary, but he must admonish the dean to enquire and to answer corporately before him in chapter-house and to take proceedings accordingly.

The chapter retained throughout all these proceedings their respect for the bishop and acquitted him of personal motives; they so fully considered that he had been instigated to action by his official principal, that after the settlement of the quarrel they petitioned the bishop to remove his official from office, " pro honore sua et pro pace et tranquillitate," as the cause of all the differences that had arisen between them; " a quo tota dissensionis materia inter nos et vos sumpsit originem."[1]

Before the question of jurisdiction had been settled another subject of litigation was moved by the bishop's official. He claimed the two-thirds of the sequestrations of vacant benefices, which had been granted by charters of Reginald and Jocelin to the dean and chapter as a fabric fund. The dean and chapter again protested.[2] But the rights of the dean and chapter were so clearly established by these charters, and they had been so successfully vindicated against former bishops, according to proofs now put forward, that in this case the bishop could not support his officials; he withdrew his right of ordinary visitation, and conceded all the claims of the dean and chapter.[3] The

---

1. R. i, f. 157. William of Edyngton, clerk, was the obnoxious official. He was appointed 2 kal. Oct., 1318. Reg. Drok. f. 196.

2. R. i, ff. 154, 155

3. Reg. Drokensford, f. 175. "Memorandum: the bishop yields to the dean and chapter on points at issue:

(a) Their claim to fruits of vacant benefices.

controversy had lasted two years and more, from July 1319 to August 1321.

It is curious to find as a sequel to this controversy, in the very charter which accompanies the bishop's concession, the practical acknowledgment by the bishop that the chapter was also the guardian of the treasure of the church. He borrows for some special occasion from the treasurer of the church his necessary episcopal apparel, and gives a bond for safe return at a given date, or the value at his death.

On December 15, of this year 1321, he gives a bond to the dean and chapter for two mitres, to be returned at Michaelmas 1323, if required; also a crosier, a gold and sapphire ring, sandals, and gloves; and the value estimated is to be paid by his executors at death.[1]

(*b*) Their wonted jurisdiction over city and prebendal parishes.

(*c*) The wonted jurisdiction of the three archdeacons. On each point with reserve.

Given at the Temple, London, 9 kal. August, 1321." The text of the controversy is published in *Wells Cathedral*, H. E. Reynolds, Appendix H, p. 133, transcribed from R. ii, f. 31, where it fills eight folios; see also R. i, ff. 151, 156. It is curious that the mistake "Johannes Bathon. et Glaston. Episcopus" instead of "Jocelinus" runs through the copy in the registers.

1. R. i, f. 164. The two mitres are valued at £23 6s. 8d., one £10 the other £13 6s. 8d.; the "baculum pastorale" at £6 13s. 4d.; the gloves "cum nodis aureis" and the sandals valued at £2 10s. were all to be restored, "vel eorum estimationem in morte. Blakeford 18 kal. Jan., 1321." To carry on the story a little further, see R. i, f. 182, under date Oct. 23, 1329. Ralph of Shrewsbury had been elected bishop. He writes to the dean and chapter that his predecessor had sold a mitre to a burgess of London and if the chapter desire he will obtain it if possible, to remain *in perpetuum* in the church. They assent, and then they supply by the treasurer the bishop's apparel for his consecration, viz.: One mitre, value 100s.; a crosier, value 10 marcs; a silver censer, value 4 marcs; two silver candlesticks, 12 marcs, all to be restored on St. Michael's day after his consecration. More careful than before, they require receipt and

These were some of the valuables kept in the strong room of the cathedral church, "the treasury" under the chapter-house, together with the muniments of the chapter and the documents of the bishop, of which the chapter were the guardians for the bishop.[1]

During the years that followed, work was silently going on, of which we see the results in 1326-1327. The dean and chapter were collecting money for another "new work," and were making great efforts to obtain the canonization of bishop William de Marchia, as St. William, the local saint.[2]

New work A.D. 1325-1327.

In June 1324, the letters were being written to Rome, to influential persons there by the dean and chapter, and they were using all their influence at the English court to obtain the highest support. At the end of 1325, December 4, the queen Isabella wrote to the pope, and the archbishop and bishops, some of whom were leading members of her faction,[3] united in a petition to the pope for bishop William's canonization "on account of

---

security with oath on the Gospels from the bishop's factor for return on Oct. 23. Bishop Ralph afterwards gives personal receipt and bond for return. Dogmersfield Nov. 13, 1329.

Cf. Inventory of the *tresor* of Carlisle cathedral church in 1325-1332, in *Proceedings of the Society of Antiquaries*, 2nd S. xii, 129.

1. Reg. Drokensford, ff. 161-166. Cf. R. i, f. 131, documents deposited there in 1281.
2. R. i, ff. 171, 172.
3. R. i, ff. 172, 174. Stubbs, *Const. Hist.* ii, p. 370, writing of 1323-6 says: "The weakness of Edward and the policy of the popes, who sometimes played into his hands, sometimes defied him with impunity, had promoted to the episcopate men of every shade of political opinion and every grade of morality. Three of these, John Drokensford, bishop of Bath, Henry Burghersh of Lincoln, and Adam Orlton of Hereford, had been implicated in the late rebellion." These three were among the petitioners, Dec. 4, 1325.

his many virtues and the many miracles which are wrought at his tomb."

But the years 1324 and 1325 were troublous times, and it is evident that much disquietude was felt by the chapter in undertaking these great enterprises and incurring such expenses.

In January, 1325, a summons was addressed to the chancellor, Thomas of Retford, for a chapter meeting to consult on their policy, the state of their finances and the reformation of the church, "super reformatione status ecclesiæ," which had formed the subject of previous conferences, "tractatus." A general convocation of residents and non-residents was called to take counsel in these perilous times, " ad deliberandum de convulso ecclesiæ Wellensis statu atque de rebus fere perditis ad pristinam dignitatem constituendis."[1] The preamble of the summons contains complaints of the oppressions under which the church has been "trodden down;" "modernis oppressionibus conculcata et deformata tot et tantis gravaminibus."

Alarm of the Chapter.

It has been assumed[2] that these strong but vague words of alarm have special reference to that disastrous subsidence of the lately raised central tower, which led to the introduction of inverted arches between the piers of the tower as a means of support. But the recurrence of similar language in chapter acts of following years, and at the same time the con-

1. R. i, f. 169. Datum in domo capitulari Wellen. 13 kal. Feb., 1324-5.

2. As by Professor Willis: "On this evidence he is reported to have said that the piers of the central tower were found to be dreadfully crushed, so as to produce the utmost anxiety for the safety of the building."—Paper read before Royal Institute of British Architects, April 8, 1861.

tinuance of new works of construction, seem to show that no such grave cause of interruption occurred at least during dean Godley's lifetime.

Political troubles of these years of civil war, pecuniary difficulties under the heavy taxation of the clergy, and, local quarrels and disturbances, were cause enough to account for the strong language which the resident canons used in summoning their brethren to give their counsel and support in the costly enterprise before them, which was no less than the reconstruction, *reformatio*, of the eastern part of the church.

Later in this year 1325, on November 10, there is a chapter memorandum that the bishop had given one half of the proceeds of his visitation to the "new work" of the church, and a collector, R. de Wamberg, is appointed.[1]

There is a confirmation of this chapter act in the bishop's register, under date January 30, 1325-1326.

"The bishop then sent a circular to all rectors to stir their people jointly and severally in aid of the 'new work' going on at Wells Cathedral; the collection for this object is to take precedence of all other collections. An indulgence of forty days is promised, and it is ordered that a roll of the benefactors shall be sent in, who shall share in all benefit of the spiritual acts of the cathedral body."[2]

New stalls. The stalls in choir of Jocelin's time, were decaying,

---

1. R. i, f. 173.
2. Reg. Drokensford, f. 242. Indulgentia pro novo opere Cathedralis ecclesiæ Wellensis. Chew, 2 kal. Feb. 1325-26.

old-fashioned, and of bad style, "ruinosi et deformes."
In the new zeal for the beauty of the church they were
thought unworthy, and new stalls were to be provided.
All dignitaries are now ordered to construct their own
stalls: "in vigilia Sancti Martini, 1325, ordinatum fuit
eodem die quod canonici qui sunt in dignitate et officio,
sumptibus privatis faciant stallos suos et ad hoc per
decanum compellentur." It was ordered, moreover,
that each dignitary should spend thirty shillings " in
stallo suo faciendo," and that a tax shall be levied half
yearly up to that amount on each dignitary by a
collector then appointed.[1]

This renewal of the stalls of the choir was part of the "new work" in 1326. But the stalls could not have been meant for the old choir, which was still cramped under the tower arches. The choir and presbytery were to be extended eastward, and to undergo a great "reformation." It was doubtless the anticipation of this great and formidable work which had caused the chapter such anxiety and misgivings in the January before; while the church was in a state of almost "demolition," and while the eastern end was being pulled down in order to build up the new north and south walls of the presbytery, the appearance of things might well justify alarm about the distracted condition and ruinous state of the church. *Prolongation of the choir itself.*

The renewal of their stalls was comparatively a light burden to put upon the canons while such great works were being designed and carried out by the energy of the dean and the resident body.

For, in the same year 1326, another and a fourth

1. R. i, f. 173.

"new work," as part of the great design, must have been well nigh brought to perfection.

<small>Eastern Lady-Chapel A.D. 1326.</small>
The beautiful eastern Lady-chapel, a detached polygonal building, was rising up outside the eastern wall of the church, separated by some distance from it.

There is no mention of it in the register until incidentally we thus learn that it is built, "noviter constructa." On June 4, 1326, the bishop gave canon Michael of Easton a parcel of ground in his garden near to the canon's house, measuring fifty feet from the wall of the newly constructed Lady-chapel, "a muro capellæ beatæ Virginis noviter constructæ," and twenty-eight feet south towards St. Andrew's Well from the old wall of the bishop's garden. A medlar tree in the midst of the garden was reserved for the bishop, and a path of eight feet wide, as if to give him access to it.[1]

So in 1326-27, the central tower, chapter-house, and Lady-chapel were finished, the stalls of the choir were being renewed, and the reconstruction of the eastern limb of the church was going on.

<small>Civil war, A.D. 1326-7.</small>
In that year, 1326, the queen Isabella and Mortimer were in rebellion against Edward II. These western parts of England were the scene of Edward's flight, imprisonment, and murder. In October 1326, the rebel party were at Bristol and the regency was proclaimed. Bishop Drokensford was one of the queen's partisans. Adam Orlton, bishop of Hereford, formerly

---

1. R. i, f. 175.
Cf. Reg. Drokensford, f. 252. "Bishop to canon Mich. de Eston. Grant of garden adjoining his house by the east end of new Lady Chapel and St. Andrew's Well. The medlar to be kept for the bishop with access by path eight feet wide.—1326."

canon of Wells, was the guiding spirit of the queen's party in the deposition of Edward in the parliament of January 1327, and the adviser of Edward's death. Edward was murdered at Berkeley on September 21, 1327.

This year the chapter very nearly lost their dean. Dean Godley was elected bishop of Exeter, but his election was set aside by the pope in favour of John de Grandison, archdeacon of Nottingham, who was promoted to the see of Exeter by papal provision, August 28, 1327.

Yet the work at Wells was ceaseless. There was work to be done in uniting the presbytery and choir of the old church to its new Lady-chapel; the presbytery and choir were to be prolonged eastward, the walls of the present eastern presbytery to be built, the delicate triple arches to support the eastern wall with its unrivalled Jesse window and its gallery of niches and statues under its clerestory, and then the arcading of the processional path behind the high altar which was to unite the Lady-chapel and its transepts with the sanctuary. All this new work was yet to be done, and it was certainly begun in the later years of dean Godley's life. In the years 1326 and 1327 the clergy of the diocese were contributing to this "new work" of the church, "in subsidio novæ fabricæ ecclesiæ Wellensis," and at the same time towards the translation and honourable entombment of William de Marchia, whom the chapter were trying to enthrone as the local miracle-working saint of those latter days.[1]

---

[1]. Reg. Drok. f. 251, May, 1326. R. i, f. 165, Dec. 26, 1326. The clergy of the Axbridge deanery, and (Reg. Drok. f. 267, Sept. 2,

312   *Chapters in Wells History.*   [CHAP.

Death of bp. John, May 9, 1329.

But now the two chief actors in this eventful period were passing away. They were preparing for their end by endowing chantries and ordaining services of commemoration, and of intercession for their souls after death.

Bishop Drokensford had obtained license of mortmain from the king to the amount of £10 per annum, and lands at Okehampton in Wiveliscombe, which were conveyed to the chapter as endowment of his chantry. He united dean Godley with himself in his ordinance for the endowment of a chantry at the altar nearest to his grave. This ordinance was dated 1328-9, March 17,[1] and he died on 9th of May following at Dogmersfield.[2]

His burial place.

He was buried at the entrance of St. Katherine's chapel, the "capella beatarum Katerinæ, Mariæ Magdalenæ, et Margaretæ,"[3] on the north side of the altar, where the tomb shorn of its canopy now stands.

1327), the clergy of the diocese, "omnes et singuli," give one tenth from their benefices for the canonization of William de Marchia and the *novum opus* of the cathedral. The collectors were raising money for these objects in 1328. Reg. Drok. f. 30.

1. Reg. Drokensford f. 306. "Ordinatio Cantariæ." The chantry in the cathedral church at the altar nearest to his grave was still further endowed with houses in Wells. There was to be a daily celebration there for the soul of the bishop and dean Godley. The dean and chapter nominated the chaplain, with lapse to the bishop after one month. Chalice and vestments were given by the bishop to be in the chaplain's charge. Dogmersfield, March 17, 1328-9.

Charter 226 contains further endowments in 1330; Charter 230 in 1332; R. i, f. 184, in 1338.

2. Archer quotes R. i, f. 177, but this folio has been torn out of the register since his time.

3. R. i, f. 181. The dean and chapter appoint two chaplains to celebrate for the souls of Robert Cormailles and the bishop in the chapel of St. Katherine, 1329.

R. i, f. 193. St. Katherine's Chapel is named as the place "ubi sepelitur," 1333.

The Tomb of Bishop Drokensford.
Wells Cathedral Church.

VI.]   *The Chapter of Wells*, A.D. 1242-1333.   313

The process of election by the two chapters took place at once, and Ralph of Shrewsbury canon of

> The canon of Wells says, 'sepelitur ante altare S. Johannis Baptiste,' which is the altar east of his tomb—but more distant.
>
> This notice in the writer of the 15th century has given rise to the later mistake as to the burial place of the bishop, which was by the side of St. Catherine's altar, in front of the altar of St. John Baptist.
>
> The pattern of the tomb is peculiar. The panels of the sides are all blank, saving the canopied heads, which are through-cut from side to side. The heads are ogeed with crockets and finials above, and cusps below. The slabs of Purbeck marble under the recumbent figure (which was highly coloured) are too thin to admit of inscription on the bevel.
>
> A canopy rose overhead from pedestals at the four corners, but the bases of these pedestals alone remain. In each pair of spandrils over the side panels are emblazoned a pair of shields, the same pair again and again. One of these shields is identified as a Drokensford coat by the seal still appendant to a charter of Philip de Drokensford, the bishop's nephew, conveying land in Wiveliscombe for the endowment of his uncle's chantry, 1332, 6th Edward III. Charter, 230.
>
> See Jewers's "Heraldry of Wells Cathedral," 1892, p. 86, where the arms on the seal are described as "four swans' heads, couped and addorsed, in chief a label of three points (*i.e.* the eldest son's difference)."

> The condition of the tomb in the year 1758 is thus recorded: "In a chapell beyond the quire is a curious tomb for bishop John Drokensford. It was neatly arched and painted and gilded, and his effigy lying thereon; which arching was taken down in 1758, when the high altar was being decayed and seemed in danger of falling."— Note from a MS. note-book, formerly belonging to the Rev. Mr. Bowen, one of the priest vicars, in MS. note to Britton's "Wells Cathedral" in the Serel collection of papers in Taunton Museum.
>
> See in Appendix W a further quotation as to the "high altar" in 1758.

S s

Wells, chancellor of the University of Oxford, was elected on June 2nd.

Dean Godley's obits.
Dean Godley had preceded the bishop in office by four years. He survived him for more than three years and a half.

In the year 1330-1, February 21, the chapter, under the presidency of the dean's friend Thomas de Retford the chancellor, marked their sense of the dean's merits as "a defender of the liberties of the church" by ordaining during his lifetime his mortuary services. It is ordained that two priests shall celebrate masses for his soul at two altars, one at the altar of the Blessed Virgin in the "cloister Lady-chapel," *juxta claustrum*, the other at the new altar of Corpus Christi not yet dedicated, "ad altare in honorem corporis et sanguinis Christi constructum, et adhuc dedicandum." Prayers are to be said for the good estate of the dean, his brother Hamelin de Godelee and his friend John de Bruton canons, and for their souls, and the souls of their families and also of the royal family, after death.

A long array of county noblemen attest the deed, which thus takes the form of a public testimonial.[1]

Dean Godley's death, Feb. 9, 1333.
The chapter announced his death within two years after, on February 9, 1332-3, "the Friday after the feast of St. Agatha."[2]

There is evidence that the dean was active to the last in his zeal for the church. In his last year, 1332, he obtained leave of absence from the new bishop Ralph of Shrewsbury, and the answer of the bishop in

---

1. R. i, f. 179. Details of the services to be held at each altar on different days follow.—Wells, February 21, 1330-1.
2. R. i, f. 191.

conveying the licence bears striking testimony to his appreciation of the greatness of the work which had been done, and of the dean's indefatigable zeal in carrying on what yet remained to be done. The bishop thus sets forth the grounds on which leave of absence was sought and granted: "quum ecclesia nostra reparatione seu verius nova constructione indigeat, ac tu domine decane non solum ecclesiam nostram sumptibus tuis propriis reparare et pro majore parte de novo construere, sed et ipsam defensare laudabiliter inceperis, nec possis hujusmodi incepta perficere nisi ad loca forinseca se transferes et remota;" and then he heartily gives him God speed in his mission for the church: "Go where you will in your good purposes for the restoration of our buildings," "Concedimus tibi ut vadas quocunque volueris, quamdiu circa fabricam ecclesiæ intenderis."[1]

In the last weeks of dean Godley's life the young king Edward III and his queen kept their court at Wells, from Christmas to Epiphany 1332-3. The fame of the new chapter-house and Lady-chapel, and the rising presbytery, might well have attracted them.

Visit of Edward III to Wells.

The chronicles of the reign tell of a sumptuous outlay on the occasion: "ubi fiebant multa mirabilia sumptuosa,"[2] but the presence of the court must have made a heavy charge upon the resources of the bishop and chapter, with large and unfinished work upon their hands.

The next year, February 12, 1333-34, when the king

1. Excerpta a Registro Radulphi anno 1332, Harleian MS. 6964, p. 62.
2. "Chronicles of Edward," i, 356 (Rolls Series).

demanded a subsidy for the marriage of his sister the princess Eleanor, the chapter of Wells prayed to be excused, pleading the ruinous and dilapidated state of their church which would swallow up their common fund for more than three years.[1]

Dean Godley's monument. It is remarkable that no monument is known to exist in the church to this greatest builder since the time of Jocelin. It has been reasonably conjectured that the monument, a facsimile of bishop Drokensford's monument, which stands at the entrance to the north transept of the Lady-chapel,[2] corresponding in position to the Drokensford monument on the southern side, may be the contemporary memorial of dean Godley. It would be an appropriate resting-place for the dean, side by side with the bishop, at the entrance of the Lady-chapel which the two had been instrumental in building. At any rate, the Lady-chapel itself is one fair memorial of dean Godley's work. Here and in the chapter-house it may be said of him, "Si quæris monumentum, circumspice."

Review of dean Godley's work. Charters belonging to the years after Godley's death may be selected as a sequel to this sketch of the work on which he had been employed, and they show the yet unfinished state of the church at his death.

---

1. R. i, f. 192. At the same time bishop Ralph sent £40 "in maritagio Alienoræ sororis regis, et excusat se non plus posse dare ob quam plurima sua debita et æs alienum." Excerpta a Reg. Radulphi, f. 64, Harleian MS. 6964, p. 62.

2. It bears a recumbent figure of a priest and a defaced inscription. A vague tradition has supplied the name of dean Forrest (d. 1446) but against evidence: "by his will he directed that the place of his burial should be 'coram summo ostio infra ecclesiam.'" Letter from Rev. F. W. Weaver.

Six months after dean Godley's death, July 15, 1333, the chapter gave formal release to his executors for all sums which had passed through the dean's hands in his several enterprises during office, " pecunias ad dictum opus seu fabricam dicte ecclesiæ receptas."

They were thus enumerated :

> 1. The demolition of the church which had preceded new work begun, "ratione demolitionis ecclesiæ Wellensis et operis seu fabricæ ejusdem ecclesiæ per eum defunctum qualitercunque dum vixit, inchoatæ ; "
>
> 2. Completion of the new works on the fabric and on the stalls of the choir ;
>
> 3. The canonisation of William de Marchia.

They reserved a claim upon the executors for the return of some of the muniments of the church still in their hands.[1]

This deed forms an honourable testimony to the integrity of the late dean as trustee of the large sums which had passed through his hands in these great undertakings, and to the exactness of his accounts now wound up within a few months of his death.

The immediate successor of dean Godley was Richard de Bury, but he soon passed to the bishop's

---

1. Charters 240. The executors named are Hamelin de Godelee, Ricardus de Chudderleigh, Johannes de Chudderleigh, Rogerus de Acton.

The bishop at the same time gave a release in the same terms. Reg. Radulphi f. 84. The chapter document is endorsed : "Duplicata et ideo ista remanebit in scrinio thesaurariæ," and in a later hand, " Release to dean Godelee's executors. Canonisatio dñi Willi de Marchia."

seat at Durham,[1] where he left an honoured name as founder of the great library.

Wybert de Littleton, elected dean in place of Richard de Bury, had died before installation.[2]

Review of the work, in A.D. 1337. Walter de London succeeded August 30, 1335. At a chapter meeting in 1337, he reviews the dangers to the church of Wells, on one hand from external assaults, "concussionibus et oppressionibus plus solito," and on the other from the unfinished state of the works upon the church, "fabrica ejusdem ecclesiæ pro magna parte restauranda." Then he cites the precedents in dean Godley's time, for calling upon the whole body of the chapter to unite in common action to support a common burden, and to provide a remedy for common evils.

The result of those appeals had been that the resident canons, who had borne the burden and heat of the day *(pondus diei et æstus)*, had spent more than £1,000 in the defence and restoration of the church, "mille libras et amplius sterlingorum circa defensionem et restaurationem ecclesiæ impenderant." But there still remained a debt upon the church of £200; and he complains that the non-resident canons, many of whom held the richer prebends, had contributed nothing, "ab omni contributione et subsidio pro defensione et restauratione facienda penitus abstinuerunt." He now called upon them to bear their part, and to be forward in beautifying the house of God, "ad honorem Dei et celeriorem exornationem ecclesiæ." Then it was ordered in chapter that the debt of £200 should

1. R. i, f. 193.
2. R. i, ff. 194-197.

be raised by the taxation of the prebends of all non-resident canons.[1]

Again, in the next year, May 28, 1338,[2] the dean sends out another summons to the chapter in strong terms of distress, first on account of attacks on the liberties of the church growing in violence, " ausibus sacrilegis plus quam solito multiplicatis," and also on account of the dangerous state of the fabric. There had been frequent conferences in chapter on these subjects, but now again the whole body is summoned at the desire of the bishop, "presente et id fieri postulante," in order that one and all should unite in support of the church, and that the fabric now shattered and deformed, " enormiter confracta et deformata," may be finished and thoroughly restored, "expleri et efficaciter expediri."

Causes of distress, in A.D. 1338.

There was enough to justify this alarm of assault from without, in the public affairs of the times, and also there was growing up a local spirit of revolt against the privileges and claims of the bishop on the part of the burghers of Wells, which broke out a few years later, 1343-4, in a riot at Wells, leading to a lawsuit which was finally decided in favour of the bishop.[3] There must also have been much cause of anxiety in the unfinished state of the fabric. The duty lay upon the bishop and chapter of carrying on the design of

1. R. i, f. 200. 1337, March 31.
2. R. i, f. 201.
3. R. i, ff. 241—246, 17 Edw. III. Nov. 8, 20, 1344. Resistance to the levy of tolls at the fairs by the bishop's officers and riot. The king sends commissioners to enquire; they gave three thousand pounds damages to the bishop, and the charter of the city was annulled.

dean Godley in the prolongation eastward of choir and presbytery. When the eastern wall was broken down, and new walls and vaulting were being raised, the eastern part of the church would have appeared fractured and unsightly.

Or, perhaps, now in addition, there were also the warning signs in the cracks visible at this day in the interior arcading of the central tower, telling of settlements and threatening approaching downfall. But no fuller or more special reference to the construction of the great arches of support under the central tower as yet appears in any of the chapter documents of this time.

Here we must close the story of the fabric. The transcript and publication of the register of bishop Ralph of Shrewsbury[1] will throw light upon the next very important period in its history.

Such was the state of the church of Wells at the close of dean Godley's life and at the opening of bishop Ralph's episcopate. So much had been done; central tower, chapter-house, and Lady-chapel, were finished. The parapet round the church, raised upon the semi-Norman corbel table, bears witness by its ball flower in the string course that it is work of this same time. Stall work for the new choir was waiting for the completion of the decorated sanctuary. A wonderful and beautiful series of works had been carried on, the outgrowth of twenty-five years of architectural genius, and enthusiasm, and labour, the memorial of dean Godley. Much more remained to be done to

---

1. This will form the volume to be printed by the Somerset Record Society for 1895.

complete the grand design, and more remains to be told of the progress of the fabric during the vigorous episcopate of Ralph of Shrewsbury.

Yet something has been brought to light from these chapter documents to show who were the builders of the church of Wells, and how the work was done, in the century since Jocelin of earlier fame. Dean Godley and his master builder William Joy, names hitherto little known among us, stand side by side with bishop Jocelin and his builders, Adam and Thomas Lock, Thomas Norris, and perhaps Elias of Dyrham, as the builders of the next period of architectural beauty. They, like Jocelin, were the finishers of works prepared for them by the piety, the gifts, the patriotism, and the labours of the men who had preceded them. They too, like Jocelin, have been the authors of new creations of art which have made the church of Wells a "thing of beauty and a joy for ever."

These were the men who
>   "fashioned for the sense,
> These lofty pillars, spread that branching roof
> Self-poised, and scooped into ten thousand cells,
> Where light and shade repose, where music dwells
> Lingering—and wandering on as loth to die;
> Like thoughts whose very sweetness yieldeth proof
> That they were born for immortality."

CHAPTER VII.

The interior arrangement of the Church of the Thirteenth Century.

THE growth of the fabric has been traced in outline, in former chapters, from bishop Robert's time as far as the beginning of the episcopate of bishop Ralph of Shrewsbury.

From the same documents which have supplied materials for the history, we can perhaps discover the plan and interior arrangement of the church within that time.

Mr. Freeman's words have given us hitherto a general description of the area and divisions of the church. The nave stood perfect from western door to choir screen; the choir, including the stalls of the canons and the throne of the bishop, was under the central tower, stretching possibly a bay eastward, or a bay westward. "The central lantern, not yet driven to lean on ungainly props, with the rich arcades of its upper stages still open to view, rose in the simple majesty of its four mighty arches as the noblest of canopies over the choir below."[1]

---
1. Freeman, *Cathedral Church of Wells*, p. 99.

The eastern limb of the cross contained the presbytery, the void space left to give dignity to the high altar which stood at the square east end of the church rich with the best detail of the thirteenth century. The aisles extending further eastward enclosed a procession path behind the high altar, and between it and a small Lady-chapel at the extreme east end.

This description leaves undefined the line of separation between nave and choir, and the exact position of the choir screen.

Later and more detailed study of the building has led Mr. W. H. St. John Hope to fix with scientific judgment upon this line of separation as running between the columns of the first bay westward from the piers of the central tower, and to draw out the accompanying plan of the choir and presbytery of the church of the thirteenth century.

Position of the choir screen.

The evidence of the masonry and that of the documents both combine to confirm that judgment. Marks on the columns of the first bay and insertions of later stones on the walls of north and south aisles show that a wall stood there, stretching across in that line from aisle to aisle, rising to the height of the capitals of the columns. In the central space between these columns was the choir screen, which bore upon it the roodloft and *pulpitum*, surmounted by the great Cross which looked down the nave. In the centre of the screen was the choir door, and on either side screens either of stone or wood were continued across the north and south aisles, with a door in each giving entrance into the transepts.

At the entrance of the choir, on either side of the

choir door, "ad ingressum chori," stood two altars, one in honour of the Blessed Virgin and the other of St. Andrew, which had been lately constructed in 1306.[1] Before these altars at that time, by order of the chapter, the obits were celebrated of bishops Burnell and Haselshaw, endowed by the chapter with £10 a year, a charge upon the revenues of North Curry, in return for benefactions by those bishops. The grave-stone of bishop Walter Haselshaw, who was buried in 1308, a blue lias slab sixteen feet long,[2] bearing the effigy of a bishop in the matrix of a brass and some letters of his name, lies on the north side of the place where, on this supposition, was the choir door, and before the site of the altar on the north side of the choir door. Here then was the screen which separated choir from nave.

Statutes of dean Haselshaw's time in 1298[3] show that there was reason for separating off for greater privacy the eastern parts of the church, where the ministers of the church were continually on duty in the daily offices, and were guardians of the sanctuary and of the treasury of the church. The nave was a place of public resort, of traffic, and often of tumult. Complaints of the noise and disorder there occur in the statutes of 1298, which forbid games, spectacles, and buying and selling in the nave of the

---

[1]. R. i, f. 52 ; R. iii, ff. 101, 277 ; R. i, f. 164.

[2]. Godwin, *De Præsul.* 427, describes his burial place. "He lies buried under a huge marble in the body of the church towards the north, almost over against the pulpit," *i.e.*, the stone pulpit in the nave. It is also at the southern entrance of bishop Bubwith's chantry, and the step rests partly upon it.

[3]. R. i, f. 215-219, contain the text of these statutes.

church, and enforce on the sacristan greater strictness in keeping order.[1]

The following statute in 1297 regulates the times and occasions for opening and closing the doors of the church and of the choir, with a view to ensure quiet for the church services.

De hostiis aperiendis.

In eodem die ordinatum fuit per decanum et capitulum quod magnum hostium ecclesie sub campanile versus claustrum tam de die quam de nocte sit clausum, nisi quando pro processione vel alia causa necessaria debeat aperiri.

Item quod duo hostia de la Karole ex utraque parte chori sint clausa de nocte; ita tamen quod hostium versus librarium sit apertum a prima pulsatione matutinarum donec post tertiam pulsationem hostium chori aperiatur. Ita quod idem hostium semper sit clausum de die, propter conculcationem librorum ecclesiæ quæ fit per extraneos, et per exclusionem laicorum ne audiant secreta capituli, nisi de precepto alicujus canonici illud contigerit aperiri.

Item quod post *gloria Patri* primi psalmi, hostium chori claudatur et serratur per sacristam dum matutine dicuntur, nisi ex rationabili causa illud oporteat aperiri, et quod hostium versus capellam beate Virginis in claustro, propter cameram necessariam, aperiatur dum matutine dicuntur qualibet nocte.[2]

---

1. "Mercaturas exerceri intra navem ecclesiæ prohibemus omnino, decernentes sacristam si hoc fieri presumpserit graviter puniendum —custodiat etiam ecclesiam melius solito a tumultu.

2. R. i, f. 126, anno 1297, Feb. 18.

Doors of choir screen.

This chapter memorandum is an important landmark in determining the position of certain parts of the church at this time.

It directs that—

(a) The great door of the church, *magnum hostium ecclesie*, under the south-western tower was always to be closed, except on special occasions, as for processions.

(b) The two side doors of the choir screen, the doors *de la Karole*[1] in the aisles, were always to be shut by night. One door is described as near the library "versus librarium," where the books were then kept, and this door was to be kept shut also by day, to prevent intrusion from the nave, and rough usage of the books by the public, "propter conculcationem librorum ecclesiæ quæ fit per extraneos."[2] It was also near the place of meeting of the chapter, and the door was to be closed lest strangers should overhear the chapter conferences, "per exclusionem laicorum ne audeant secreta capituli."

The reasons thus given for closing this door also indicate that the library and the chapter room of that time, the *capitulum*, were near to one another, and were near to one of the side choir doors. That door must have been in the north aisle, nearest the chief door of entrance into the church by the north porch. That door in the screen, *de la Karole*, was only to be opened in preparation for matins, and until the choir

---

1. "Karole," Carol, bears the meaning of a place enclosed with partitions or screens, "Ea voce significari videtur id omne quod aliquid circumseditur et vallatur." *Ducange*, ii, 188, ed. 1883.

2. A list of books lent to Salisbury and returned in 1291, is given in R. i, f. 116.

door proper was opened, viz., between the first and the third bells. The choir door was then opened, and kept open until after the first psalm, and was then closed until the end of matins, that there might not be any going in or out during the service. The other, or south door of the screen, *de la Karole*, was generally closed, but the south transept door which led into the cloister was kept open during matins, to give access from the choir to the *camera necessaria* which was there.

The close neighbourhood of the library and the chapter room at this time is shown by another clause in the statutes of 1298, which orders that the commemoration of the dead forming part of the "missa in capitulo" might be said, either in the library or in the chapter room.[1]

Library and capitulum.

We are led to infer that the *librarium* and the *capitulum* in 1298 were near the north door of the choir, and in the north transept; that the west aisle of the north transept, (now enclosed by a screen of later work, within which are the vestries of the Vicars choral,) was the site of the library, and that the north transept served as the meeting place of the chapter, the *capitulum*, until the great Chapter House, the *domus capitularis*, was built.

The evidence is complete which determines the position of the choir screen, of the choir door, of the altars on each side of the entrance of the choir, and of the screen across the aisles, each with their doors, admitting into the transepts. The choir and the

---

1. "In festis autem novem lectionum statuimus quod dicantur *Placebo* et *Dirige* in capitulo, vel in librario, ab illis qui ad missam capituli sunt ascripti."

eastern part of the church were effectually separated from the nave when the choir door and the side doors were closed.

<small>Choir.
Chorus Cantorum.</small>

Within the screen under the central tower were the stalls of the canons and the seats of the singers, and the throne of the bishop at the eastern end.

<small>" Ordinatio clericorum in choro."</small>

The Dean and the Precentor occupied the two return stalls at the entrance of the choir, the Dean on the south : the two Archdeacons of Wells and Bath respectively held the south and north stalls at the east, and the Chancellor of the church and the Treasurer were next to them. On the right of the Dean were the stalls of the Archdeacon of Taunton "if he be a canon," of the Abbot of Bec, always a non-resident, and of the Subdean. On the left of the Precentor were the Abbot of Muchelney, the Succentor, and the Provost of Combe.

Between these stalls were ranged on north and south sides the senior canons or their vicars, the master of the schools, the priest-vicars, and by special distinction some of the deacon-vicars. In the second form were the junior canons, then the deacons and others in minor orders.

On the lowest form were the boys—first the upper boys who were on the foundation, *pueri canonici*, then the others.[1]

<small>Presbytery.</small>

In the two bays east of the choir was the Presbytery. A door on each side opened into the north and south aisles, the *ostia presbyterii*. The tomb of bishop Jocelin was in the middle space of the floor : the burial place of bishop William the second of Bytton, who died 1274, and his monument, lay between the second and third

---

1. Printed in Reynolds' *Wells Cathedral, Ordinale et Statuta,* p. 1.

pillars on the south side, and in a line with the tomb of bishop Jocelin.[1]

On the stone bench on either side lay the effigies of the bishops of the old Saxon church, Dudoc and Giso, who had been buried on each side of the high altar, and four others whose bones had been removed by Robert or by Jocelin, and their effigies sculptured in Jocelin's time, in honourable commemoration.[2]

Within the third bay stood the high altar of St. Andrew, with the Crucifix over it. Eight lights, to burn in the framework of the Crucifix above the high altar, were to be supplied perpetually by the churches of Wellington and Chew.[3] Lands at Dulcot and Chilcot had been granted by bishop Robert on the covenant that three lights should burn for ever before the high altar,[4] and according to bishop Reginald's ordinance, one large wax light *(mortarium)* was to be supplied by

<small>High altar.</small>

---

1. Vide p. 277.

2. When the presbytery of the thirteenth century church became the choir of the fourteenth, in the time of bishop Ralph, the stalls occupied part of the stone bench, and these monuments were moved nearer the outer edge of the bench.

"Enclosed within the stonework, on which were the sculptured effigies of the early bishops, were boxes containing bones, and leaden tablets with the names of each bishop thereon inscribed. These monuments were opened in 1848, and were moved from the stone bench, where they then lay behind the thirteenth century stalls, to their present positions. There was the obvious evidence that the boxes were of later, probably much later date, than that of the original interment."—Letter from J. R. Clayton, Esq., who was present on the occasion.

3. Two marcs were paid to the treasurer "per manus archidiaconi" to supply "octo cereos in scabellis crucifixi desuper altare sancti Andreæ." R. iii, f. 5.

4. R. i, f. 46; R. iii, f. 292.

the priory of Bruton from the churches of Banwell and Westbury.[1]

Square or apsidal end.
The question has been raised, and will always be unsolved until the old foundations can be discovered, whether the end of the church was apsidal or square.

Professor Willis considered that the end in Jocelin's time was square, with a chapel to the Blessed Virgin behind the high altar. On the other hand those who saw some of the foundations laid bare in 1848 give their testimony that there had been an apse at one time.[2]

The apse would be the form bishop Robert would be more likely to have followed from his Cluniac associations: Jocelin may have changed the apse to a square, and this change in the east end of the church in itself would have involved the necessity of reconsecration.

Two chapels of the Blessed Virgin.
The extension of the north and south aisles of the early church beyond the line of the sanctuary gives reason for supposing that there was an eastern Lady-chapel behind the high altar.

We might assume, as a matter of course, that there was this eastern Lady-chapel coeval with bishop Jocelin's work; but the evidence of the registers is not decisive as to its existence before the latter part of the thirteenth century.

---

1. R. iii, f. 288.

2. "On the removal of the pavement of the choir, in 1848, there were certain excavations in various parts for the insertion of the scaffold supports. The result of this was the revelation of deeply laid stonework which I remember Mr. Salvin declaring to be the foundation of the early apse."—Letter from J. R. Clayton, Esq.

There is mention by bishop Robert in 1136 of the chapel of St. Mary which had been endowed by Giso. Savaric and Jocelin endowed the daily mass at the altar of the blessed Virgin; but the position of the altar or of the chapel is not once named throughout Jocelin's time; whereas in the middle of the thirteenth century, from 1250 onwards, there is frequent mention of the chapel of the blessed Mary, of which the site is definitely described as "set in the south side of the church near the cloister." That chapel is continually mentioned as the scene of obituary services, and especially of the Bytton family.[1] The first definite mention of the eastern chapel "behind the high altar" occurs in 1279. In that year both chapels are named.[2] In the ordinance for the execution of the will of bishop William of Bytton the second, the priest is ordered to celebrate at "the altar in St. Mary's chapel by the cloister," and also two tapers are to burn "in St. Mary's chapel behind the high altar."

Lady-chapel juxta claustrum.

Lady-chapel behind the high altar.

Again in a charter of the year 1298 there occurs an entry of offerings made at the image of St. Mary in the chapel behind the high altar.[3]

It is certain, therefore, that at the end of the century there were two chapels of the Blessed Virgin, one "behind the high altar," and also the chapel "on the south side of the church, near the cloister." There

1. R. i, f. 175; R. iii, f. 175.
2. R. i, f. 4; R. i, f. 120; R. i, f. 128.
3. R. i, f. 128. From the will of one Lucia Laundrey, wife of Nicolas le prest buried in St. Cuthbert's cemetery:

Item lego imagini beatæ Mariæ in capella retro magnum altare in ecclesia beatæ Andreæ Wellensi, unum keverchef de serico, pretio quinque solidos.

is no evidence to determine how far the chapel behind the high altar extended. The documents are silent until in the year 1326 we have evidence of the existence of the Lady-chapel then newly constructed by dean Godley, at the extreme east end, and detached from the church; but the earlier chapel on the south side, *juxta claustrum*, continued to exist until it was pulled down by bishop Stillington and the larger chapel, still called the Lady-chapel, was built by him over its foundations in the latter part of the fifteenth century.

Sacristy and Treasury.

One very important part in the church was the vestry or sacristy where all the sacred things, the *trésor* of the church, were kept.

In the north aisle of the choir a door leads through the vestibule into the undercroft of the present chapter house. This lower building belongs to a date between 1263 and 1284. In the former of these years the chapter, relieved from debt, began the preparation for further building. In 1284 the chapter ordered that the work long begun, "diu incepta," should be carried forward. This was followed by the gradual erection of the Chapter house. The "crypt," or "undercroft," with its two divisions of vestibule and interior chamber was the treasury, and also the sacristy, of the church. The interior octagonal chamber, secured by strong iron staunchions to its narrow deeply-splayed windows, was the treasury, the *thesauraria ecclesiæ*, in which the most valued possessions of the church were deposited, both those belonging to the bishop, his registers, vestments, mitres and jewels, and also the money, sacred vessels, crosses, and vestments of the chapter.[1] It was guarded by its double and heavily-barred doors, which had their bolts and locks both inside and outside, and the sacristan was bound by his office to sleep therein. The outer vestibule with deep recesses was the ordinary vestry of the clergy.

Upon this building, devoted from long time to these two-fold uses, was raised by gradual advances, between 1284 and 1319, the " Domus Capitularis," the chapter-house, the home and place of meeting of the *capitulum*, for which they had long waited, without any settled meeting place. Now, in this lofty and beautiful building of two stories, they had their treasury and sacristy below, their audience chamber above, and there every morning, after the prayers of the third hour and the morning mass, the chapter of the whole body was held for the daily lection and commemoration of brethren departed, for maintaining discipline, hearing complaints, passing judgment, inflicting punishment; for ordering the services of the day and of the week—for sitting in council and drawing up statutes.

" Domus Capitularis."

When the chapter-house, the new " domus capitularis," was entered, in 1319, the arrangements of the stalls in chapter was different from that ordered in choir, inasmuch as the dean and chapter then formed a council gathered round the bishop. This arrangement bore witness to that original idea that the bishop was head of the chapter as his council, always present among them and presiding, which time and circum-

" Ordinatio clericorum in capitulo."

---

[1]. R. i, ff. 131, 181, P. 305. In 1306, R. i, f. 132, deeds and money are ordered to be kept in an iron safe, "in fargurio viridi." " Fargua=fabrica ferraria." *Ducange* iii, 414, 415, ed. 1884.

stances had at Wells considerably modified. The chapter-house was designed for a chapter of fifty canons and the bishop. There were seven stalls in each facet of the octagon under each of the seven windows, forty-nine in all; and one on either side of the double doors of entrance under the eighth window, making fifty-one stalls, including the stall of the bishop.

The stall of the bishop was in the centre of the eastern group of seven under the eastern window, and opposite to the doors. Around him in council sat the officers of the chapter and the officers of the bishop, the hierarchy of the diocese, all, except the dean who was the elected of the canons, appointed by the bishop.

On the right of the Bishop sat the Dean, the Archdeacon of Wells, the Chancellor, the Archdeacon of Taunton, if he were a canon, "si fuerit canonicus,"[1] the Abbot of Bec, and the Subdean.

On the left of the Bishop were the Precentor, the Treasurer, the Archdeacon of Bath,[2] "if he were a canon," the Abbots of Muchelney and Athelney, and the Succentor.

The other canons were in their respective stalls, and the vicars in order as priests, deacons, and subdeacons, on the lower bench.

The boys stood on the floor, on each side of the *pulpitum* or desk, which stood east of the central pillar.

1. Cf. "Choir Stalls at Lincoln," *Archæological Journal*, vol. xxxviii, p. 52.

2. The archdeacons of Bath and Taunton, unless they held prebends, seem to have been outside the cathedral body, as the archdeacon at Lincoln.

This sketch of the interior order and arrangement of the church of the thirteenth century may receive some illustration if we follow the course of the processions in the "Ordinale" of the church of Wells. There is good reason for assuming that the ritual therein prescribed belongs to dean Haselshaw's time, after successive revisions during the thirteenth century.[1]

"It is worthy of remark that the ordering of litanies and processions as detailed in the printed and MS. manuals and processionals of the fifteenth and sixteenth centuries, is verbally identical with that prescribed by the consuetudinaries of Osmund, Wells, and Exeter in the thirteenth or beginning of the fourteenth century."[2]

The order of processions.

Processions of choir and clergy through the church and precincts, the singing of litanies and hymns,

---

1. Neither "Ordinal" nor "Consuetudinary" now exist in the registers of the dean and chapter except in two transcripts. One is a manuscript book of 357 pages, small quarto, partly parchment, chiefly paper, entitled "Dean Cosyn's MSS." It contains very full transcripts, in various handwriting, of the statutes and acts of the chapter. It bears on page 158 the writing "Liber Wilelmi Cosyn Decani Wellen. Ecclesiæ Cathedralis — scriptus et collatus labore et sumptibus suis, anno domini 1506." [1506 is added in margin by a later hand.] All the pages following are in the handwriting of that time and on parchment. The handwriting of the former part is of earlier dates.

The other is a folio of 155 pages of parchment, bound in rough calf, and lettered at the back "Statuta ecclesiæ Cathedralis Wellensis." It is in one and the same handwriting, of the sixteenth century.

It is probable that from this later transcript the copy was made of the "Ordinale et Statuta" now in the Lambeth Library (no. 729), which was drawn up and sent to Lambeth, in obedience to archbishop Laud's monition, by dean Warburton and the chapter, in 1634. It is printed in Reynolds's *Wells Cathedral*.

2. J. D. Chambers' *Divine Worship in England in XIII, XIV and XIX Centuries*, p. 182. 1877.

with readings of scripture and prayer at fixed stations in the circuit of the procession, were most effective methods of instruction, and of impressing upon the minds and feelings of the people the reality and meaning of the sacred things appropriate to each season and particular festival.

The clergy going out from presbytery and choir, into the nave among the people, brought with them, in ways which could be understood and felt by all, expressive signs and illustrations of the subjects for thought and objects of reverence and devotion at each particular season, and urged their people to join with them in prayers and intercession, and in giving thanks.

Procession on Sunday. Every Sunday before the great service of the day, the procession went out of the choir by the north door of the presbytery eastward, the priest sprinkling all the altars, then down the south aisle of choir to the south transept and into the cloister, where the priest entering the cemetery of the canons said the prayers for the dead, and rejoined the procession in the chapel of St. Mary, where was *the first station*.

Thence they returned into the church and to the great Cross in the nave over the choir screen, before which was *the second station*. There followed the " bidding prayer," which at Wells was always given out from the *pulpitum* towards the people. Thence they returned into the choir. The stations where the canons were to stand, on each side of the nave to west door, were marked on the pavement by processional stones.[1]

This manner and order of this procession for the

---

1. These are shown in Carter's plan of 1798.

first Sunday in Advent was observed on all ordinary Sundays throughout the year.[1]

Certain changes and additions were made on particular days and festivals.

On Palm Sunday, after the blessing of the branches and flowers, the line of procession was as before round choir and cloister, and thence through the house of the choristers on the west of the cloister, and out into the cemetery of the laity, " per domum choristarum exeat in cimiterio."[2]

On Palm Sunday.

They went round the cemetery to its extremity westward ; there was the *first station*, and there the Gospel was read by the deacon.

The *second station* was before one of the western side doors of the church, where the precentor began the antiphon, and the boys sang the festal hymn, " Glory, laud, and honour to Thee, Redeemer, King."

---

1. *De ordine processionis dominicæ primæ in Adventu et in aliis dominicis per annum.*

. . . exeat processio per ostium presbyterii septentrionale et eat circa presbyterium—sacerdos in eundo singula altaria asperget. Deinde transeunte processione per ostium cimiterii sacerdos cum suis ministris intret cimiterium canonicorum, aspergendo illud, et oret pro defunctis, deinde redeat ad processionem in capella beatæ Virginis ubi fiat statio. Inde redeant ante crucem in navi ecclesiæ et ibi secundam faciant stationem . . . deinde precibus consuetis dictis chorum intrent et sacerdos ad gradum chori dicat versiculum et orationem.

2. "*In dominica Palmarum sunt quædam specialia annexa.*

" . . . in primis eant per ostium boreale chori circuens chorum et claustrum, et exeant in cimiterio magno per domum choristarum, circuens cimiterium usque ad locum primæ stationis, et ibi legatur Evangelium ab ipso diacono induto ad processionem. . . . deinde eat processio ad locum secundæ stationis, precentore incipiente antiphonam—fit autem secunda statio ante ostium ubi pueri cantant ' Gloria, laus ' ; peracta autem statione eat processio ad ostium occidentale, et ibi intret . . . et fiat statio ante crucem. . . ."

X x

The *third station* was before the other side door, where the priest sang the "Verse" before the people. Then through the central west door they re-entered the church and made their *fourth station* before the Cross, and thence passed into the choir singing the antiphon.[1]

On Ascension Day. On Ascension Day, a procession with banners, the first that of Leo, "the lion of the tribe of Judah," that of Draco the conquered serpent, the last,—passed through choir down the nave to the west door, round the precincts of the church on its northern, eastern, and southern sides, "circumeundo extrinsecus totam ecclesiam," into the cloister by its south-eastern door,[2] and re-entered the church by the west door.

On Rogation Days. On Rogation days, and on days of solemn intercession, the procession, singing "the great litany," passed through the town to the church, or a chapel where a mass was sung, and then returned to the church through the western door, finishing the litany in the choir.

"Eat processio ad ecclesiam in urbe vel in suburbio, et ibi missa cantata, processionaliter redeat ad ecclesiam per idem ostium quo egressi sunt."

On Corpus Christi. On the festival of Corpus Christi[3] four priests, bearing aloft a shrine, "feretrum in quo sit Corpus Dominicum," on four staves, under a silken canopy, passed down choir and nave and through west door, and then made

---

1. "This procession was precisely the same at Sarum, Wells, Exeter, Canterbury, and, as it would seem, at Rouen in the eleventh and twelfth centuries." Chambers, p. 191.

2. Viz.: the door at right angles with the bishop's door at the southern end of the cloister.

3. Chambers, p. 195, "not mentioned in the consuetudinaries, except those of Wells and Exeter."

the circuit of treasury, cloister and cemetery, "circuens thesaurarium, claustrum, et cimiterium"; and returned by the same western door.

Through Lent, on Wednesdays and Fridays until Maundy Thursday, before the commencement of mass, a procession was wont to be made, without any cross, through the north door of the presbytery to the chapel of St. Mary behind the choir, "ad capellam beatæ Mariæ retro chorum"; the responsory having been sung, all present kneel, *se prosternunt*, while the priest sings the *Kyrie eleison* and the 51st Psalm, and standing, says the collect, *orationem*; after the litany has been sung as far as to the intercession "sancta Maria ora pro nobis," they pass round to the west door of choir, and entering there finish the litany.

In Lent.

We pass now from the fabric of the church in the thirteenth century to take note of the different component members of the body then occupying choir and chapter house.

There is a document belonging to the time of dean Haselshaw, in which the number and titles of the prebends then existing are formally drawn out.

The prebends A.D. 1298.

The daily recitation of the whole psalter by the members of the chapter, each member taking his appointed number of psalms, probably formed part of the "consuetudinary" introduced by the Norman bishops, who moulded the constitution of the English cathedral churches in the twelfth century.

Recitation of the Psalter by prebendaries.

The usage can be traced to very early times in the ordinances of the churches of Wells, Lincoln, Salisbury, and St. Paul's, London, though the actual division of the Psalter among the several prebends is of later dates.

The earliest draft of the statutes of the church of Wells contains the order that "the whole psalter shall be said daily for the brethren and benefactors of the church of Wells, and two masses each week shall be celebrated for living and dead."

"Præterea singulis diebus dicetur totum psalterium pro fratribus et benefactoribus Wellensis ecclesiæ, et singulis hebdomadis celebrentur duo missæ pro salute vivorum et defunctorum."[1]

Table of Psalms divided among the prebends in A.D. 1298.

There seems to be good reason for attributing to dean Haselshaw's time the following distribution of the psalms among the prebends.

Though the usage dated from very early times, and from the *antiqua statuta*, yet the actual division of the psalter must have varied with the varying number of prebends through the times of bishops Reginald, Savaric, and Jocelin. It was not until after the imprebendation of Dinder, the last-made prebend, in 1263, that this final division could have been drawn up. Under dean Haselshaw there was a general revision of the "consuetudinary" with a view to enforce stricter discipline and greater reverence.[2] The duty of the canons to recite the psalms assigned to their prebends is enjoined in the heading affixed to the table of prebends and psalms: "Singulis diebus dicat dominus Episcopus hos psalmos cum confratribus et prebendis totum psalterium quolibet die ut patet inferius."[3]

1. R. ii, f. 42.
2. R. i, f. 215; R. ii, ff. 19, 23. "Statuta edita tempore Walteri de Haselshaw," printed in *Wells Cathedral*, H. E. Reynolds, 1881.
3. The table is found in the Cosyn MS. on page 68, and on page 81 in the other copy.—See on p. 335.

Church of the Thirteenth Century.

The following is the list of prebends and their psalms:—

Prebend	Psalm	Prebend	Psalm
THE BISHOP	Ps. i	CUMBA III.	Ps. xxxix
	Ps. ii		Ps. xl
	Ps. iii		Ps. xli
WEDMORE I	Ps. iv	CUMBA IV	Ps. xlii
	Ps. v		Ps. xliii
	Ps. vi		Ps. xliv
	Ps. vii	BOKLONDE	Ps. xlv
CLYVA	Ps. viii		Ps. xlvi
	Ps. ix		Ps. xlvii
	Ps. x		Ps. xlviii
S. DECUMANUS	Ps. xi	MYLVERTON I	Ps. xlix
	Ps. xii		Ps. l
	Ps. xiii		Ps. li
	Ps. xiv		Ps. lii
CUMBA I	Ps. xv	HENGESTRYNGE	Ps. liii
	Ps. xvi		Ps. liv
	Ps. xvii		Ps. lv
CUMBA XII.	Ps. xviii		Ps. lvi
CUMTONA	Ps. xix	TYMBERSCOMBE	Ps. lvii
	Ps. xx		Ps. lviii
	Ps. xxi		Ps. lix
IATTONA	Ps. xxii	AYSHULLE	Ps. lx
	Ps. xxiii		Ps. lxi
	Ps. xxiv		Ps. lxii
HASELBERGA	Ps. xxv		Ps. lxiii
	Ps. xxvi	CUMBA V	Ps. lxiv
	Ps. xxvii		Ps. lxv
	Ps. xxviii		Ps. lxvi
WANDESTRE	Ps. xxix	ESTONA	Ps. lxvii
	Ps. xxx		Ps. lxviii
	Ps. xxxi	ILTONA	Ps. lxix
SCANDERFORDE	Ps xxxii		Ps. lxx
	Ps. xxxiii	CUMBA XIII	Ps. lxxi
	Ps. xxxiv		Ps. lxxii
WEDMORE II.	Ps. xxxv	DUNDEN	Ps. lxxiii
	Ps. xxxvi		Ps. lxxiv
CUMBA II	Ps. xxxvii	CUMBA XIV	Ps. lxxv
	Ps. xxxviii		Ps. lxxvi

CUMBA XIV	Ps. lxxvii	BERTON	Ps. cxi
CUMBA VI	Ps. lxxviii		Ps. cxii
DULTICOTE	Ps. lxxix		Ps. cxiii
	Ps. lxxx		Ps. cxiv
TAUNTON	Ps. lxxxi		Ps. cxv
	Ps. lxxxii	CUMBA VIII	Ps. cxvi
BRENT	Ps. lxxxiii		Ps. cxvii
	Ps. lxxxiv		Ps. cxviii
	Ps. lxxxv	WEDMORE IV	Ps. cxix
WYVELESCUMBA	Ps. lxxxvi		vv. 1-64
	Ps. lxxxvii	CUDDEWORTHE	Ps. cxix
	Ps. lxxxviii		vv. 65-112
ILMYNISTRA	Ps. lxxxix	CUMBA IX	Ps. cxix
SUTTONA	Ps. xc		vv. 113-160
	Ps. xci	CUMBA X	Ps. cxix
	Ps. xcii		vv. 161-176
	Ps. xciii		Ps. cxx-cxxiv
HOLECUMBA	Ps. xciv	WYTCHYRCHE	Ps. cxxv
	Ps. xcv		Ps. cxxvi-cxxxi
	Ps. xcvi	HARPETRE	Ps. cxxxii
WEREMINSTER	Ps. xcvii		Ps. cxxxiii-cxxxvi
	Ps. xcviii	CUMBA XI	Ps. cxxxvii
	Ps. xcix		Ps. cxxxviii
CUMBA VII	Ps. c		Ps. cxxxix
	Ps. ci	WEDMORE V	Ps. cxl
	Ps. cii		Ps. cxli
CORY	Ps. ciii		Ps. cxlii
WORMESTERR	Ps. civ		Ps. cxliii
WITLAKYNGTON	Ps. cv	DYNRE	Ps. cxliv
CUMBA XV	Ps. cvi		Ps. cxlv
MYLVERTON II	Ps. cvii		Ps. cxlvi
WEDMORE III	Ps. cviii	LUTTON	Ps. cxlvii
	Ps. cix		Ps. cxlviii
	Ps. cx		

The numbering of the Psalms is the same as in our Prayer Book.
The Psalms 149 and 150 are not assigned.

We see that the number of the portions into which the psalter was divided was fifty-four. There is another prebend mentioned, that of Biddisham (Bydsam), to which no psalms were assigned.

Number of prebends.

The assignment of the first portion of the psalter to the bishop witnesses to the early and close connection between the bishop as president and the chapter as his council. With this exception, the psalms are assigned to prebends, not to offices or dignities, except where prebends were attached to offices. The number of prebends at this time was fifty-four, but the dean held the prebend of Wedmore annexed to his office, and probably Biddisham: the prebend of Huish and Brent was annexed to the archdeaconry of Wells,[1] and that of Milverton to the archdeaconry of Taunton.[2]

Accordingly the number of prebendal stalls in choir and chapter house was fifty, and the bishop's stall in chapter house made the fifty-first.

All the prebends were nominally in the appointment of the bishop, but both pope and king took frequent opportunities of filling up the stalls with their own nominees and laymen. The registers about the beginning of the fourteenth century contain such instances.

Papal nominations to prebends.

In 1313 it was necessary to enforce the rule of bishop Jocelin's time that the four principal *personæ* in the church should be priests, because the chancellor at that time was not in full orders.[3]

In 1317 John de Orleton held his canonry "by

---

1. R. i, f. 41, by Savaric, before 1206.
2. R. iii, f. 136, by Jocelin in 1241.
3. R. i, f. 119. Reg. Drokensford, f. 26.

favour of the apostolic see," which his uncle, Adam bishop of Hereford, counsellor of queen Isabella, had obtained at the time of his appointment to the see.[1] In that same year three more canons were papal nominees.

In 1320 the chapter protest against the bishop's order to collate one appointed by the pope, "juxta formam gratiæ per summum pontificem factæ." In the same year they refuse quotidians to another, John de Ros, who was also domestic clerk to one of the cardinals and absent at Rome, whom they had appointed at the mandate of Clement V.[2]

Vicars choral. The Vicars choral occupy a prominent place throughout all these times. No organic part of the cathedral body, they grew up from the very first as assistant ministers to the canons when absent or becoming aged or voiceless. They quickly became a numerous body—appointed by individual canons, with the approval of the dean and chapter, but dependent on the will of their masters : at first for the most part ill-paid, homeless, single, and without discipline, their condition called for frequent correction and regulation ; but bishop Jocelin recognised them as part of the cathedral body, assigning them daily quotidians of one penny from the common fund, and they were often men of good position and associated with canons in cathedral offices and duties.

By the statutes of 1273 they were required to have a year of probation after nomination : a teacher, *auscultator*, was assigned to each, by whose testimony

---

1. R. i, ff. 136, 138. Reg. Drokensford, 30, 33, 50.
2. R. i, f. 140.

the probationer's knowledge of psalter and antiphonary and hymnary and of his skill and voice were to be approved,[1] and if he had testimony of good conduct from the other clergy of the church, he should be "perpetuated,"—"si bene morigeratus expertus fuerit, perpetuetur."

The statutes of 1298 are more precise in requirements from the vicars.

These statutes give an insight into the internal working of the cathedral system at the close of the thirteenth century, and deserve some fuller notice.

<small>Statutes of dean Haselshaw, A.D. 1298.</small>

The end of the century was a time for laying down with greater care the duties attaching to offices in the church, for tightening the bands of discipline, and for raising the tone of the whole community to greater reverence and sense of duty. A general convocation of all the canons, "omnium et singulorum confratrum," was summoned to meet on the morrow of St. Andrew, 1298, to discuss and ordain matters affecting the wellbeing of the cathedral church, the chapter, and all who ministered in the church. The bishop, William de Marchia, was not present, nor is any reference made to him as taking part in the proceedings. The statutes which were the result of the three months' deliberations, were publicly promulgated before canons and vicars on the morrow of the day of St. Matthias, February 25, 1298-9.[2]

The preamble is a *concio ad clerum* in which is set forth the claim of the Church to a high standard of devotion and duty in all her members, that they may

---

1. R. ii, f. 3.
2. Haselshaw's statutes. R. i, f. 215, 219; R. ii, f. 219.

instruct the laity, alike by word and good example. It is the work of the clergy to be fervent in prayer and in reading of the scriptures—"in orationibus devotis, et in sacrarum scripturarum lectione." As the church is the house of prayer, habits of reverence, punctuality, and attendance to duty are enjoined upon all her members.

Rules for Vicars.

The vicars choral are more specially addressed as holding a middle position, many of them priests and deacons, others in minor orders and mixing with the world; the danger therefore is great lest ("quod absit") they become negligent of duty and fall away. Precise rules are laid down for the attendance of all with reverence, and punctuality and to the end of the service, at Matins, Prime, high Mass, the Mass of the Blessed Virgin, Vespers and Compline; and six at least on each side are to be present at the canonical hours of 9, 12, and 3; also fines and punishments are prescribed for absence, unless hindered by reasonable causes. Excuses must be stated and allowed at the next day's meeting in chapter before the whole body.

Attendance at Services.

The practice of vicars and *annellarii*[1] coming to the obituary services only when there is a distribution of money is strongly reprobated. They are to be fined at the week's end for as much as they have received.

No Vicar to lodge alone.

The injunctions of previous statutes, especially in 1243 and lately in 1295, that no vicar shall lodge alone, but either with his "master," or with another vicar, which seem to have been disregarded, are now enforced by immediate suspension from choir and with-

---

1. *Annellarii* and *altaristæ* were those who served the altars at obituary and anniversary services.

drawal of commons from some offenders, and the same punishment is threatened on all who shall disobey. The great difficulty of enforcing discipline upon vicars who lodged in unlicensed lodgings was now pressing upon the chapter the consideration of establishing a college house where all might live together. Twenty years after this, in 1318, the scheme had so far advanced that a house was marked out, and the matter was left to dean Godley to draw up terms and to make arrangements.[1] Nothing more was done at that time, but it is to be noted that the dean and chapter were the first to set on foot the scheme which was successfully carried out by bishop Ralph, in the establishment of the "College of Vicars Choral."

The earlier statutes for the admission and probation of vicars are confirmed, with the additional statute that a vicar showing defect of voice or skill shall be removed from office by the dean and chapter, who shall have the appointment for that turn, "absque omni offensa et indignatione præsentatis." Canons are to be punctual in their payments to their vicars, and responsible for the good behaviour of those in their household. As if in preparation for the entrance into the new capitular house, the attendance of all vicars is required at the daily chapter meeting after prime, which is the occasion for the commemoration of the departed, for the reading of the lectures by the reader appointed, for hearing and correcting of faults, and on Saturdays for the ordering of the weekly services by the precentor.

Removal of Vicars by dean and chapter.

---

[1]. R. i, f. 143. "The last convocation determined that a house should be provided for the vicars, the dean to arrange about expenses."

In the meantime it is allowed that on certain occasions the commemoration of the departed may be said either in the ordinary place of meeting of the chapter, or in the library, " in capitulo vel in librario."[1]

The duty of the canons to recite the psalms belonging to their prebends is now enforced by a distribution of the psalter between the bishop and fifty-three prebends; and the same duty is required from the *altaristæ* as an act of intercession for the bishop, the chapter, and other benefactors of the church, and the *tabellarius* is to mark the observance of the duty.

Revision of the ordinal.

A committee of discreet men is to be appointed, "deputentur aliqui discreti," to revise the Ordinal and the Martyrology: another committee of vicars to correct the Antiphonary and Gradual, so that all confusion in the services and material of discord may be removed. Visitors are to be appointed to make a yearly inspection of the canonical houses, and to make valuation of dilapidations; and finally an estimate is drawn up of the separate value of each prebend, according to which the taxation of stall wages due to the vicars is to be regulated, and the proportions due on vacancies, respectively, to the estate of the deceased and to the *communa* of the canons should hereafter be assessed. A taxation of a tenth of all incomes of canons for five years, "decima quinquennalis," is ordered.

Lights before the Cross in nave.

The duty is specially enforced on the treasurer of providing two lights on each side of the Cross in the nave on different festivals, at vespers, matins, and high mass, of sufficient size to give light there, and of

---

1. See pp. 326-7.

supplying incense pure and good, *sicut antiquitus solet*, for the altar purposes.

The mention in these ordinances of clerics, and of boys who had their place in the choir and chapter-house, suggests that a certain amount of educational work was going on in connection with the cathedral church. There were the boys of the choir on the foundation, "pueri canonici," for whom the "domus choristarum" on the west of the cloister was provided. Besides this choir school there were also " scholæ grammaticales," for the younger vicars and youths, and for the purpose of a higher or more varied education, which were endowed with land, certain houses, and a croft, and half an acre in the " Muntoria," which Roger the chaplain of bishop Jocelin conveyed to the chancellor of the church and to his successors, in 1235, to be by them assigned to the master of the schools for the time being, for the perpetual use of the schools and scholars.[1] The "magister scholarum" had his place in choir, as vicar of the prebend of Biddisham.[2] An early charter contains a letter from pope Innocent III, addressed to bishop Jocelin in 1213, directing him to receive into favour a poor scholar who had as a teacher laid violent hands on his schoolfellows and clerks, and had been suspended but absolved, which suggests the existence of schools in Jocelin's time, and Wells as the scene where this had occurred.[3]

Schools.

---

1. R. i, f. 33. "Domus in usum scholarum magistri." R. i, ff. 34, 35. Cf. Charters 30, 36, anno 1235.

2. "Bydsam prebenda sancti Andreæ cujus vicarius est magister scholarum."

3. Charter 20. See p. 187. Another mention is made of these schools in a fragment of a letter from a student at Oxford to his brother, a vicar at Wells, in the fifteenth century. Charter 639.

We have before us now the church of the thirteenth century, as we are able to gather from notices in chapter records the area of the building, and the chapelries and altars within and around the church.

This was the scene where, in Carlyle's well-known words, "painful living men worked out their life wrestle, looked at by earth, by heaven, and hell. Bells tolled to prayers, and men of many humours, various thoughts, chanted vespers, matins, and round the little islet of their life rolled for ever, as round ours still rolls, though we are blind and deaf, the illimitable ocean, tinging all things with its eternal hues and reflexes, making strange prophetic music."[1]

It is easy to criticise and condemn the modes of religious worship of the times that are not our own. It is easy to cite cases of offences and scandals in the lives of men in different orders belonging to the cathedral church, as it is always easy to show how most men live below the ideal of the profession to which they belong.

It is more profitable to mark, in conclusion, the high ideal which representative men in the church of Wells had before their own minds, and made it their duty to enforce upon the community placed under their government at the close of the thirteenth century.

We have seen what Robert and Jocelin planned and fashioned as founders and builders and legislators. The statutes of dean Haselshaw are a landmark marking the highest tide in the ebb and flow of the history during the succeeding century, and they moulded the order and government of the church

[1] Carlyle's *Past and Present.*

during the first years of the fourteenth century, while the fabric was growing in form and beauty.

Here, at Wells, in times of the growth of civil institutions, and of national progress, one high purpose through the ages ran of raising up a building of the highest architectural beauty, as a centre of devotional life, of education, and discipline; a school of music and of art.

It has been the aim in these chapters to draw out a local chronicle from homely materials, and to show how the zeal and efforts of the men of the soil, the landowners, and the clergy of the cathedral church, the clergy and laity in their parishes, the townsmen and artisans, have had their part in working out this purpose and in handing down to us in the church of Wells "this glorious work of fine intelligence."

APPENDIX A.

REGISTER i, FOLIO 31.

De ordinatione prebendarum et institutione commune.

UNIVERSIS sancte matris ecclesie filiis Robertus Bathoniensis ecclesie minister humilis, salutem in domino.

Nostri nos admonet sollicitudo propositi de ecclesiarum nostrarum utilitate per omnia cogitare, ne si qua in eis de neglectu jactura proveniat in supremo debeamus examine culpabiles inveniri. Proinde postquam divine pietatis miseratio nos non nostris meritis, sed dono sue gratie cathedram nos fecit episcopalem conscendere, cure nobis fuit ab ecclesiis sollicitudini nostre commissis propulsare malitiam, omnemque ab eis zeli vel contentionis fomitem radicitus exstirpare.

Quum ecclesiam Wellensem indebitis prepositure oppressionibus supra modum afflictam invenimus et gravatam, ejus compatientes insidiis et calamitatibus condolentes, communicato consilio archiepiscoporum episcoporum aliarumque religiosarum Anglie personarum, exigentibus quoque ejusdem ecclesie canonicis, decanum illic ordinavimus, concessis sibi dignitatibus libertatibus et consuetudinibus canonicis ecclesiarum Anglie bene ordinatarum.

Et ne in eadem ecclesia pristina tribulatio locum denuo vendicaret, possessiones et predia que ad eam fidelium sunt donatione devoluta in prebendis taliter distribuantur.

De Wedmorlanda sex prebendas et decanatum fecimus, ut una videlicet prebenda sit ecclesia de Wedmore cum appenditiis suis, quam ad decanatum omni volumus tempore pertinere. Secunda vero prebenda sit terra de Bidesham, una duntaxat virgata excepta, quam prebendam ad reparandam ecclesiam beati Andree et ornamenta emenda specialiter assignavimus, ut ipsa nihilominus prebenda vicarium debeat invenire.

Reliquam terram de Wedmor cum Mudesleye et Marche et ceteris pertinentiis suis et virgatam terræ in Bidesham superius exceptam, decanum perpetuo tenere statuimus, redditurum exinde quatuor canonicis annuatim viginti libras, singulis centum solidos, et quicquid superesse contigerit suis usibus, cum ecclesia de Woky decanatus nomine noverit attributum.

Luthunam unam prebendam esse volumus decanatui in perpetuum assignatam, Witechurche unam prebendam, Dultingchot et Chellecote unam, Wormestorre et Wandestreu unam, in Wynesham quinque, ut una sit ecclesia ejusdem fundi. Ipsa vero villa tres prebende, quam teneat unus canonicorum redditurus exinde annuatim duas prebendas singulas centum solidorum, residuo sibi in prebendam retento. Quinta autem prebenda sit Bromleya. Cumbam vero tanquam unam prebendam Reginaldo precentori tota vita sua tenere concessimus, memores beneficiorum que ab avunculo suo bone memorie Johanne episcopo ecclesie nostre collata sunt. Post decessum enim Reginaldi tres prebendas et cantariam de villa ipsa faciendas decrevimus ad arbitrium episcopi et decani et totius capituli, ecclesia ejusdem ville quintam nihil-

z z

ominus constituente prebendam. Præterea pro remedio anime nostre, necnon et decessorum vel successorum nostrorum, dedimus beato Andree in Wellis ecclesiam de Yatton in prebendam.

Hiwys quoque in Brentemarisce et ecclesiam de Cumpton quas eidem sancto Andree integre et quiete in perpetuum dedimus patrimonium possidendas, in unam fecimus convenire prebendam.

Dimidiam etiam hydam in Wotton cum virgata terre quam jocunde recordationis Gyso episcopus dedit capelle Sancte Marie, necnon et dimidiam hydam quam pie memorie Godfridus episcopus ecclesie sancti Cuthberti contulisse noscitur in sua dedicatione, decimam quoque vini nostri memorate ecclesie sancti Andree concedimus. Et hac nostre auctoritatis pagina confirmamus amplius, ut nocturne canonicorum vigilie aliquod solatium sortiantur, de chyrsettis et decimis ad sepedictam sancti ecclesiam Andree pertinentibus panem fieri constituimus, canonicorum qui matutinis interfuerint usibus profuturum.

Prescriptam ergo prebendarum distinctionem seu etiam donationem ut rata in posterum et illibata permaneat, sigilli nostri impressione signatis ad posterorum notitiam literis fecimus commendari, rogantes ut omnes qui in episcopatu nobis successuri sunt, quod a nobis pie prorsus et salubri provisione statutum est, ratum habeant, et inconvulsum perpetuo studeant servare, quatenus a bonorum omnium retributore uberes exinde mercedes debeant expectare.

Acta sunt hec in presentia Henrici Winton episcopi, et postea subscriptis testibus confirmata, Willelmo Cantuar. et Thurstano Eborac. Archiepiscopis, Rogero Sarum. Willelmo Exon. Simone et aliis.

APPENDIX B.

CONTEMPORARIES OF BISHOP REGINALD.

(a.) A.D. 1174-1191.

Kings:
  Henry II 1154, 1189.
  Henry III junior, 1170-1183.
  Richard, 1189.

Popes:
  Alexander III 1159-1181.
  Lucius III to Nov. 25, 1185.
  Urban III to 1187.
  Gregory VIII Oct. 20 to Dec. 17, 1187.
  Clement III 1187 to 1191.
  Celestine III 1191 to 1198.

Archbishops of Canterbury:
  Richard, 1174-1184.
  Baldwin, 1190.
  Reginald, Nov. 27 to Dec. 26, 1191.

Deans of Wells:
  Richard of Spakeston. (Bishop Reginald, Charter ii).
  Alexander. (R. i, f. 23, *et passim*; f. 60; f. 61).

Precentors:
  Reginald. (R. i, 36, 1164).
  Albert, or Ilbert. (Bishop Reginald, Ch. ii).
  William of S. Faith. (R. ii, f. 14).

Chancellors:
  Robert. (R. i, f. 25).
  Peter de Winton, 1185.

Treasurer:
  William. (Bp. Reginald, Ch. ii).

Archdeacons:
  Wells: Thomas. (R. i, f. 25; f. 36).
     Robert de Geldeford, 1185. (R. i, f. 38; iii, f. 357).
     Ralph de Lechlade. (Charter 9).
     Richard. (R. i, f. 25, and i, f. 48).
     Godfrid. (R. i, f. 24).
  Bath: Richard of Poitiers. (R. i, f. 48).
     Peter of Blois. (*Ep. Cant.*)

Subdeans:
  Robert. (Bp. Reginald, Ch. i).
  Alexander. (Charter 10).
  Thomas. (Charter 13).

Succentors:
  Galfrid. (R. i, f. 36, 1164).
  Adam. (R. i, f. 61).

Priors of Bath:
  Hugh.
  Walter. (R. i, f. 27).
  Gilbert.

CONTEMPORARIES OF

BISHOP SAVARIC.	BISHOP JOCELIN OF WELLS.
A.D. 1192-1205.	A.D. 1206-1242.
Kings: Richard I 1189-1199. John, 1199-1216.	*Kings:* John, 1199-1216. Henry III 1216-1272.
Popes: Clement III 1187-1191. Celestine III 1191-1198. Innocent III 1198-1216.	*Popes:* Innocent III 1198-1216. Honorius, 1216-1227. Gregory, 1227-1241. Innocent IV 1243-1254.
Archbishop: Hubert, 1193-1205.	*Archbishops:* Stephen, 1207-1228. Edmund, 1234-1240.
Dean: Alexander. (R. i, f. 23).	*Deans:* Alexander (R. i, f. 57), 1209. Leonius, 1213. Ralph de Lechlade(R.i,f.57),1216-1220. Peter of Chichester (R. i, f. 27, *in d.* 1220, 59), 1236. William de Merton (R. i, f. 43), 1236. John Saracenus (R. i, f. 57), 1237-1250.
Precentor: William. (R. i, f. 23; f. 57).	*Precentors:* William de Hamme. (R. i, f. 61 ; f. 57). Thomas de Tornaco, 1213. (R.iii,f. 383).
	Chancellors: Richard de Kenelword, 1235. (R.i,f.33). Thomas of Retford. (R. i, f. 34 ; f. 46). 1213. (R. iii, f. 383).
Archdeacons: Wells : Robert de Geldeford. Hugh de Welles. Bath : Robert de Geldeford. Ralph de Lechlade. Taunton : William de Wrotham. (Pat. 6 John).	*Treasurers:* Peter. (R. i, f. 61). Richard. *Archdeacons:* Hugh de Welles. Ralph de Lechlade. William de Wrotham, 1215. Hugh de Wilton. William de Bardeney, 1221. (R. i, f. 44).
Subdeans: William. (Le Neve). Thomas. (R. i, f. 23, *in d.* f. 57).	*Subdeans:* Thomas. (R. i, f. 57). Lambert. (R. i, f. 27, *in d.*).
Priors of Bath: Walter. Robert. (R. 1, f. 49).	*Priors of Bath:* Robert. (R. i, f. 54). Thomas.

APPENDIX C.

Appointment by Louis VII king of the French, of Reginald, archdeacon of Salisbury, to be abbot of St. Exuperius, Corbeil. Dated Melun, 1164.

CHARTER 7.

IN nomine sancte et individue Trinitatis, Amen.

Ego Ludovicus dei gratia Francorum rex. Nobis honor est, et ecclesiis nostris commodum, quotiens earum curam discretis et honestis committimus viris. Notum itaque fecimus universis tam presentibus quam futuris quod abbatiam sancti Exuperii[1] de Corbolio, Reginaldo archidiacono Salesberiensi, pro honestate sua, et pro amicorum suorum prece donavimus, habendam et tenendam, sicut frater meus Philippus et ceteri ante eum abbatiam tenuerunt et hoc fecimus salvo jure nostro et canonicorum salva etiam ecclesie dignitate ; quod ut ratum sit in posterum scribi [nostra auctorit]ate communire precepimus. Actum Miledu[num incarn]ati M°. C° lxiiij. astantibus in palatio [quorum infra scri]pta sunt nomina et signa.

  S' comitis Theobaldi dapiferi nostri.
  S' Mattei camerarii.
  S' Guidonis buticlarii.[2]
  S' Constabulario nullo ;
Datum per manum Hugonis cancellarii.

---

1. St. Exuperius, "a military saint, one of the companions of St. Maurice."

2. V. Ducange—*Buticlarius.* idem quod pincerna—
  buta = lagena, cupa; butta = dolium, vas vinarium ; buticula, dim. = bouteille—buticularius Franciae — unus e quatuor majoribus palatii officialibus qui literas et diplomata regia subscribebant.

The document is on a small piece of parchment much worn and torn. The letters within brackets are wanting, and are supplied conjecturally.

APPENDIX D.

Gifts of bishop Reginald to the church of Bath.

Vide *Registrum Prioratus Bathon.*, p. 315.

[R]EGINALDUS episcopus hujus loci omnes terras nostras a predecessoribus suis ad opus fabrice ecclesie nostre diucius detentas devote restituit, et que a predecessoribus suis nobis restitute erant affectuosius ab ipso nobis, confirmate sunt. Ecclesiam de Aystona, Ffulconis de Alneto, in usus proprios nobis confirmavit. Ecclesias de Brugges et de Kary et de Radestoke nichilominus in usus proprios nobis confirmavit. Ecclesiam etiam de manerio nostro de Fforda in usus proprios nobis confirmavit et proventus ad fabricam ecclesie nostre assignavit. Oblacionem vero pentecostalem a predecessoribus suis nobis concessam, ecclesie nostre veluti matrici ecclesie Somersetie devotissime confirmavit. Hospitale sancti Johannis in Bathonia ecclesie nostre contulit, et de ipso sicuti de propria elemosinaria nostra nobis disponere concessit. Corpus beate Eufemie virginis et martiris[1] ecclesie nostre contulit, et plures reliquias sanctorum cum capsulis eburneis. Albam quoque preciosam auro textam, amictum quoque, et mitram sancti Petri Tarentasiensis[2] ecclesie nostre adquisivit. Cereum vero ardere ante corpus dominicum et sanctorum reliquias constituit, et quadraginta solidos ad ejus perpetuitatem de ecclesia de Banewelle, per manus canonicorum de Briwtone

---

1. Cf. Stanley, *Memorials of Canterbury*, App. F. p. 280.
2. Tarentasiensis is the reading which Mr. Hunt has supplied. Peter, archbishop of Tarentaise, was Reginald's consecrator, p. 47.

assignavit. Bibliotecam eciam ecclesie nostre, pluribus libris ditavit. Plura etiam ornamenta Ecclesie nostre contulit, scilicet duas capas preciosas et v meliora et majora pallia. Ecclesiam vero nostram cartis regum de libertatibus, et privilegiis summorum pontificum de dignitatibus sufficienter ditavit. Cujus anniversaria dies in albis celebretur, et C pauperes reficiantur, et mensa fratrum copiosius procuretur.

The register of Bath Priory is a manuscript in the library of the Society of Lincoln's Inn, who kindly allowed this transcript to be made in 1885.

APPENDIX E.

1174—1180.

I. *Bishop Reginald's charter to the town of Wells, confirming bishop Robert's charter forbidding markets in the church and its precincts, and giving free markets to Wells.*

MS. IN THE TOWN HALL OF WELLS.

Carta Domini Reginaldi Episcopi Bathoniensis.

UNIVERSIS Christi fidelibus ad quos presens carta pervenerit Rainaldus divina miseratione Bathon. episcopus salutem ab auctore salutis.

Ad universitatis vestre notitiam volumus devenire nos cartam Roberti bone memorie Bathon. episcopi predecessoris nostri inspexisse, et eam in presenti pagina de verbo ad verbum annotasse.

[1] Robertus Dei gratia episcopus Bathoniensis uni-

1. Cf. R. iii, ff. 245, 246.

versis fidelibus tam clericis tam laicis tam Francis quam Anglis, salutem et Dei benedictionem.

Postquam divina vocante clementia pontificatus apicem dignitatis conscendimus summa ad hoc animi intentione desudavimus, ut ecclesiæ beati Andree in Wellis regimini nostro commissæ venerationem debitam impenderemus, et ab aliis impendi faceremus ; et si que in ea prave essent consuetudines eas a liminibus ejus pulsaremus, et honorem ejus et utilitatem quantum in nobis erat amplificaremus.

Nonnullorum autem constat experientie quod tumultus nundinarum que in eadem ecclesia et in atrio ejus hactenus esse consueverunt ad dedecus et incommodum ejusdem ecclesie accidit, cum in ea ministrantibus quam maxime sit importunus, quia et eorum devotionem impedit et orationum quietem perturbat. Verum ne contra vocem divinam domum orationis speluncam patiamur esse negotiationis, statuimus et firmiter precipimus ut quicunque illic in tribus festivitatibus, videlicet in Inventione S. Crucis et in festivitate S. Calixti, et in celebritate beati Andree, negotiaturi convenerint, in plateis ville illius negotiationes suas securi et ab omni prava consuetudine et in quietudine libere exerceant, et nullatenus ecclesiam vel atrium ecclesie violare presumant.

Concedimus etiam consilio clericorum nostrorum et constituimus, ut omnes in predictis festivitatibus et earum vigiliis quieti de teloneo in perpetuum permaneant. Quod quidem in posterum ratum esse volentes presenti scripto commendamus et sigilli nostri impressione roboramus. Testes: Ivo decanus Wellensis: Reginaldus precentor: Robertus et Thomas archidiaconi : Edwardus : magister Eustachius : Willelmus de sancta fide : Radulfus Martre : Willelmus de Atebera : Petrus de Chiu : Walter Pistor : et alii multi clerici et laici.

Nos igitur venerabilis predicti decessoris nostri vestigiis inherentes, ob reverentiam beati Andree Apostoli et ad petitionem burgensium nostrorum Wellensium, omnes consuetudines et libertates negotiatoribus illic in tribus festivitatibus et earum vigiliis venientibus ab eo concessas ratas habentes et in posterum illibatas volumus permanere, adjicientes ut eisdem libertatibus et consuetudinibus in crastino etiam omnium predictarum gaudeant festivitatum, nobis quidem et successoribus nostris de consensu predictorum burgensium conductus omnium seldarum medietas in prescriptis nundinis debet in perpetuum remanere.

Que omnia ut rata et intacta in posterum perseverentur presentis scripti testimonio et sigilli nostri appositione duximus confirmandum.

Hiis testibus : magistro Willelmo thesaurario Well' : Roberto subdecano Well' : magistro Rad. de Lichel : Jocelino capellano : Willelmo de Meleburn : Johanne de Cumb. : Thoma de Dinant. : Gaufrido clerico : magistro Rogero medico : Michaele clerico : Hugone clerico : Henrico de Armentiis : Willelmo de Erleg : Philippo de Wika : Ricardo de Ken : Walerando de Wellesley : Willelmo de Maulerb' : Reginaldo de Wodeford : Eadward de Wellis : Godefr. de Cnoll : Jocelino de Welles : Willelmo de Sept : Henrico bedello. Hugone fabro. Willelmo forestar. Rad. Cade. Huberto filio coci. Alfredo mercatore. Raino.

Ruffe. Gaufr. Ruffo. Rad. Cusin. Willelmo coco et aliis multis.

Endorsed : Carta dñi Regiñ Ep' Bathoñ
   de tribus nundinis concessis . . .

The silk cord and a fragment of green wax on which is the outline of a bishop's robe and a few letters are attached to the earlier of the two charters.

The seal of the other was in fair preservation in 1886; on it is the figure of a bishop in the act of blessing with right hand—a pastoral staff in the left. The legend on it

✠ REGINALDVS DEI GRATIA BATHONIENSIS
   EPISCOPVS.

II. *Bishop Reginald's charter to the town of Wells.*

MS. IN THE TOWN HALL, WELLS.

Carta domini Reginaldi episcopi Bathon.[1]

UNIVERSIS Christi fidelibus ad quos presens carta pervenerit Reginaldus Dei gratia Bathoniensis episcopus salutem in domino.

Patrum et predecessorum nostrorum inherentes vestigiis et eorum auctenticis ducti et docti exemplis, quod ipsi sua statuerunt industria nos roborandum duximus auctoritate nobis a deo indulta.

Concedimus ergo juxta tenorem carte predecessoris nostri pie memorie Roberti episcopi villam Wellie burgum esse in perpetuum et eisdem finibus quibus in eadem carta diffinitum est et prescriptum.

---

1. Copies made from the charters by kind permission of the Town Clerk.

Appendix E.

Volumus etiam et concedimus ut quilibet intra easdem metas messagium aliquid in presentiam possidens vel in posterum possessurus nomine burgagii liberam habeat commorandi, recedendi, et revertendi, simulque domos suas impignerandi, vendendi, necnon et donandi, nisi domibus religiosis, licentiam, secundum propriam sue dispositionis voluntatem, redituum nostrorum integro jure retento, id est de singulis massagiis duodecim denariis annuis.

Volumus preterea si lis aliqua forte dampnosa intra ambitum massagii alicui eorum [evenerit] liberam habeant potestatem ut administrationes concordes fiant, justicia nostra nullam exigente inde consuetudinem vel emendationem donec burgenses in justitia defecerint, nisi mortale vulnus vel dampnum corpori perpetuum inflictum fuerit vel etiam nisi aliquis litigantium justicie nostre querimoniam faciat, salva in omnibus justicia regni et dignitate.

Inhibemus etiam ne aliquis in eadem villa pelles crudas vel coria cruda emere presumat nisi fuerit in luna et lagha burgensium Wellarum.

Huic nostre concessionis et confirmationis testes sunt :

    Ricardus Well. decanus.
    Ilbert precentor Well.
    Henricus Exon. et Ricardus Bath. archidiaconi.
    Robertus subdecanus.
    Johannes de Cumba.
    magister Eustachius.
    Godfridus de Hercredeb.
    Willelmus et Jocelinus capellani.
    Ernisius clericus filius Theobaldi.

Petrus de Winton.
Thomas de Dinan Wellensis canonicus.
Willelmus canonicus de Haselburg.
Adam de Suttone.
Willelmus de Spinenall.
magister Radulphus de Lechelade.
Gaufridus de sancto Giorgio.
Robertus filius Hamo.
Galfridus Giffard.
Godfridus de Dinre.
Walerannus.
Walcelen de Well.
Gaufridus francus.

The seal and counterseal of the bishop are appended.

APPENDIX F.

Confirmation of the possessions of the church of Bath to bishop Reginald, by pope Alexander III. IV Cal. Mart. 1179.

REG. iii, FOL. 266, in dorso.

In hac privilegii confirmatione panis, medo, et capreoli sive porci, quæ presentantur in crastino paschæ de Glaston.

CONFIRMATIO Alexandri venerabili fratri Rainardo Bathoniensis episcopo ejusque successoribus canonice substituendis in perpetuum ; si omnibus fratribus et coepiscopis nostris cogamur ex ministerio susceptæ amministrationis adesse et apostolicum ipsis patrocinium exhibere, tibi tanto fortius tenemur suffragium apostolicæ defensionis impendere et consideratione tue commissam tibi ecclesiam in sua justitia confovere quanto circa nos et Romanam ecclesiam puriorem devotionem genere comprobaris, eamque nobis certioribus indiciis visus es reddere manifestam.

Qua propter venerabilis in Christo frater episcope, tuis justis postulationibus clementer annuimus et Bathoniensem ecclesiam cui Deo auctore preesse dinosceris sub beati Petri et nostra protectione suscepimus et presentis scripti privilegio communimus, statuentes ut quascunque possessiones quecunque bona eadem ecclesia in presentiarum juste et canonice possidet aut in futurum concessione pontificum, largitione regum, vel principum oblatione fidelium seu aliis justis modis prestante domino poterit adipisci firma tibi tuisque successoribus et illibata permaneant.

In quibus hæc propriis duximus exprimenda vocabulis.

Totam civitatem Bathonie cum omnibus consuetudinibus extra et infra ut liberius habet rex et civitatem aliquam in tota Anglia, cum moneta, cum teloneo, tam in campis quam in silvis, tam in foro quam in pratis et aliis terris, insuper nundinas in festivitatibus S$^{ti.}$ Petri et hidagium quod exigebatur de viginti hidis ad eandem civitatem pertinentibus, et omnia placita et leges et justitias et omnes consuetudines omnino et adjutoria et si qua sunt alia quæ Rex Willelmus vel frater ejus Rex Henricus in eadem civitate plenius et liberius habuerunt, quæ ipsi Johanni episcopo predecessori tuo et successoribus ejus in perpetuum concesserunt et cartis suis confirmaverunt, præterea confirmamus, quod manerium de Calveston [Kelston] sit in hundredo Bathonie et in justicia tua, sicut prefatus Rex Henricus concessit et confirmavit, parcum etiam et warennam, bertonam, Hantonam, Fordam, Clavertonam, Lincumban, cum molendinis et aliis appendiciis earum in terris aquis pratis pascuis in bosco et plano cum omnibus consuetudinibus et libertatibus earum eidem civitati adjacentibus et omnia alia ad eandem civitatem pertinentia.

Ecclesiam de Wellis cum universis prebendis suis, et ipsum manerium cum Wochi et Westberiæ cum parco suo cum feodis militum et ffranchelanorum et terris rusticorum ad idem manerium pertinentia cum boscis et planis pratis et pascuis molendinis et vineis aquis et omnibus aliis appendiciis suis.

Ecclesiam de Chyu et ipsum manerium cum omnibus pertinentiis et libertatibus suis.

Villam de Yatton cum omnibus pertinentiis et libertatibus suis.

Villam de Banewel et Villam de Cumton cum portu de Radeclive et parte villæ quam habes in Axebrugg ad Banewel pertinente cum omnibus pertinentiis et libertatibus suis.

Ecclesiam de Ceddre et duas hidas in eadem villæ.

Ecclesiam de Evercrez et ipsum manerium cum omnibus pertinentiis et libertatibus suis.

Terram de Merk que est in Wedmor, quam prefatus Henricus rex predecessori tuo concessit et confirmavit.

Ecclesiam de Kingsbere et ipsum manerium cum hundredo et omnibus pertinentiis et libertatibus suis.

Et ecclesiam de Cerde et ipsum manerium.

Et ecclesiam de Hiwis et ipsum manerium cum omnibus pertinentiis et libertatibus suis in terris pratis pascuis bosco et pasturis.

Ecclesiam de Walenton et ipsum manerium cum Bokelande et ceteris pertinentiis et libertatibus suis.

Ecclesiam et villam de Lidiard cum hundredo et ceteris pertinentiis et libertatibus.

Ecclesiam et villam de Wivelescumb cum hundredo cum omnibus pertinentiis et libertatibus suis et Fifidam similiter.

Ecclesiam de Dorkemefeld et ipsum manerium cum socha sacha et tol et theam et infangenethrop cum omnibus aliis pertinentiis et libertatibus suis in bosco plano pratis et pascuis que memoratus Rex Henricus predecessor tuo et ecclesie Bathoniensi reddidit concessit et carta sua confirmavit ejus successor Henricus rex secundus similiter eandem tibi concessit et reddidit cum domibus Winthorne et carta propria confirmavit sicut jus tuum et ecclesiæ tuæ tenendum in libera et perpetua elemosyna; feodum etiam de Dinra quod idem rex tibi reddidit et ecclesiæ tuæ et carta sua confirmavit, quod Henricus de Tille cum ecclesia de Dorkemefeld et ipso manerio in curia memorati regis tibi et ecclesie tue quiete clamavit.

Apud Gatinton terram de salinis et ipsas salinas et omnes pertinentes in nova foresta et duas hidas in Cherleton. Præterea duos panes certæ quantitatis et duos barilos medonis certæ mensure et duos capreolos vel duos porcos que annuatim in secunda feria pasche tibi redduntur et ecclesiæ Wellensi a monasterio Glastoniensi a tempore beati Dunstani ex ipsius institutione.

Preterea de benignitate apostolica tibi duximus indulgendam ut liceat tibi priorem ecclesiæ tuæ pro manifesta causa depositione digna, cum consilio capituli vel aliorum religiosorum virorum, a prioratu sine contradictione qualibet amovere.

Ad hec apostolica auctoritate statuimus ut a monasteriis monachorum vel monialium et in ecclesiis regularibus que in tuo episcopatu consistunt, eam decreti de cetero habeas potestatem quam predecessores tui et tu ipse usque ad hoc tempora in eis noscimini rationabiliter habuisse. Prohibemus insuper ut infra episcopatum tuum sine assensu et auctoritate tua vel successorum tuorum, salvis autenticis scriptis apostolicæ sedis, nullus de novo ecclesiam vel oratorium construendi habeat facultatem.

Si quando vero abbates vel priores aut alii ad tuam jurisdictionem spectantes qui religiosis locis tui episcopatus precesse noscuntur tibi in his rebelles et inobedientes extiterunt in quibus obedientiam et reverentiam exhibere tenentur, fas tibi sit in eos canonice sententiam promulgare, advocatis autem conventualibus seu parochialibus ecclesiis tue jurisdictionis qui non habent in ipsis ecclesiis quicquid aliud præter jus patronatus easdem ecclesias ordinandi, vel in eis quidquam temeritate propria statuendi sine auctoritate et concurrentia tua omnem intercludimus facultatem metropolitano quoque tuo, sine speciali mandato Romani pontificis in eisdem ecclesiis te inconsulto, nisi causam super his ad eum per appellationem deferri contingeret aut apostolicæ legationis obtentu quicquam statuere liceat, vel rite sive manifesta et rationabili causa sententiam promulgare—præsenti etiam scripto tibi duximus indulgendum ut si quando abbates priores vel aliæ personæ que ad tua synoda venire tenentur et precipue que tibi professionem fecerunt ad synoda vocati non venerunt, in eas de auctoritate nostra nisi canonicam excusationem probaverint, animadversionem tibi liceat canonicam exercere.

Illas autem qui super justitiis tuis quas aliquando tibi nolunt exsolvere vel pro alia causa a te duxerunt appellandum appellatione remota liceat tibi compellere, et infra certum et convenientem terminum quem eis praefixeris appellationem interpositam exequantur vel ad mandatum tuum justa rigorem juris super his pro quibus appellatum est, tibi satisfactionem exhibeant competentem.

Religiosos vero vel alios ecclesiasticos viros ad tuam ordinationem spectantes si qui te presente sive tua vel te absente sive archidiaconi tui licencia, ordines ab episcopis receperunt alienis infra episcopatum tuum, in ordinibus taliter receptis sive tuo vel successorum tuorum assensu ministrare penitus prohibemus. Si qui autem monachi canonici aut alii religiosi viri clerici vel laici in ecclesias tui episcopatus ad presentationem eorum spectantes earum personis decedentibus intrudere seipsos vel alios sine tua auctoritate presumpserint, taliter intrusos dummodo excessus eorum sit publicus et notorius ab eisdem ecclesiis fas tibi sit removere et in ipsas si ad mandatum tuum cedere forte noluerint ecclesiasticam sententiam promulgare, præterea benedictiones et professiones abbatum tui episcopatus nec non etiam institutiones et ordinationes ecclesiarum omnes quae in tuo episcopatu consistunt.

Another page follows with the usual warning and saving clauses.

Then follow the signatures of pope Alexander and the cardinals.

Eighteen cardinals sign.

Datum Laterano, per manum Alberti sancte Romane ecclesie presbiteri cardinalis et cancellarii.

IV Cal. Martis Indictione XI, incarnationis dominicæ anno millesimo centesimo lxxviiij° pontificatus vero domini Alexandri pape tertii anno vicesimo. (1159-1179).

APPENDIX G.

Carta Regis Ricardi de prebendis et terris de novo adquisitis.

REG. iii, FOL. 13.

RICHARD by the Grace of God king of England, etc.

Know that we have granted and by this present charter have confirmed to God and the church of Saint Andrew in Wells, and to Reinaud Bishop of Bath and his successors for ever, all donations of churches and other benefices made to him and the aforesaid church as the charters of the givers do testify, viz.:

1. *By gift of Robert abbot of Glastonbury and the convent there, the church of Pylton and the church of South Brent.*

By a composition between the two ecclesiastical magnates, the bishop and the abbot, whose territories and jurisdictions marched together, two prebends were made by the gift of Pilton, of which the abbot held one, and became a member of the bishop's chapter. By the cession of South Brent, archidiaconal jurisdiction was given to the abbot over seven of the churches of the Twelve Hides of Glastonbury, and was exercised by a special officer, the abbot's archdeacon, exempt from the bishop's jurisdiction.

Pilton is no longer a prebend. The abbot afterwards gave up the prebend. Pilton became a peculiar in the jurisdiction of the precentor of Wells.

2. *By gift of Richard de Camvilla, the church of Hengestrigg, in perpetuam praebendam.*

Henstridge, near Wincanton, on the Dorset border, was the gift of Richard Camville, Henry's envoy to Sicily to conduct Joanna his daughter to be the wife of William king of Sicily, in 1176. He was present at Richard's coronation, 1189, commanded the English fleet which took Richard on the crusade, was justiciar of Cyprus, and died at Acre 1191. Gerard, son of Richard, was sheriff of Lincolnshire, and one of the chief opponents of Longchamp the chancellor during the regency in Richard's absence. He confirms the grant of his father, and archbishop Richard (1174-1184) attests it. Charlton Camvill, now Charlton Horethorne, in Somerset, granted to bishop Robert by Richard de Camville (*Ad. de Domerham*, i, 298), and Clifton Camville, in Staffordshire, bear witness to the family estates in both counties. Henstridge is a prebend at the present time.

3. *By gift of Oliver de Dynham, the church of Bokelande, in perpetuam praebendam.*

Buckland Dinham, near Frome, and Corton Dinham, near Sherborne, probably received names from Dinan, in Brittany, the original seat of a family which had lands also in Devon and Cornwall. Hugh de Dinan held under William de Tracy, also under William de Braosa of the honour of Barnstaple (Berdestaple) in Devon. Buckland Dinham is a prebend at the present time.

4. *By gift of William Fitzjohn of Harpetre, the church of Estharpetre.*

William of Harpetre, one of the family of Lovel of Cary, had before this made restitution to the bishop of his fee of Dynre (Dinder), which his father had taken from bishop Robert. He now added this gift of the church of East Harptre, *in perpetuam praebendam.* East Harptre is a prebend at the present time.

5. *By gift of William Fitzwilliam, the church of Haselbergh, in perpetuam praebendam.*

Haselbury, near Crewkerne, was the scene of hermit Ulfric's life and miracles; his cell there was visited by bishop Robert in 1154.[1] Haselbury is a prebend at the present time.

6. *By gift of Hamon of Blakeford, the church of Scanderford, in perpetuam praebendam.*

Blackford in Wedmore, or near Wincanton: Scanderford in Essex, now Shalford, is a prebend at the present time.

All these gifts are confirmed by an earlier deed of bishop Reginald,[2] and were given during dean Spakeston's time, between 1174-1180.

1. Matt. Paris, ii, 203. *Som. Arch. Proc.* vol. xix, part i, 28.
2. Bishop Reginald's *Confirmatio*, R. i, f. 24; R. iii, f. 10.

7. *By gift of Gerberte de Perci and Matilda Arundel, the church of Compton and the church of Bromfeld.*

Gerbert or Gilbert de Perci gave the church of Childcompton, on the Mendip, "quantum ad dominum fundi pertinet," *in perpetuam praebendam*. Matilda de Arundel, his wife, gave the church of Broomfield, on the Quantock range, "in perpetuam eleemosinam." Childcompton was alienated to Bradenstoke. No longer a prebend.

8. *By gift of Alan de Fornellis, the church of Cudeworth with Cnoll chapel, in perpetuam praebendam.*

Alan de Fornellis (Furneaux), one of Henry's justiciars in 1179, lord of Kilveton, Somerset, held lands in Devon at the time, under the bishop and under Robert, the king's son. One of the same name was sheriff of Cornwall in Richard's reign. Cudworth is a prebend at the present time.

9. *By gift of James of Montsorel, the church of Whytelakyngton, in praebendam.*

The castle of Montsereau, in Anjou, besieged by Henry of Normandy, afterwards Henry II, in 1151, or the great fortress in the earldom of Leicester (Mount Sorel), we may suppose to have been the seat of the family, who now owned Whitelackington, which was Roger Arundel's demesne in 1084. Whitelackington is a prebend at the present time.

Three gifts from Devonshire landowners follow.

10. *By gift of Jocelin de Treminet, the church of Aulescomb, in praebendam.*

Awlescombe, on the south side of the Blackdown

hills, near Honiton, "in agro Devoniensi et diocesi Exon." No longer a prebend.

11. *By gift of Oliver de Traci, the church of Bovey, in praebendam.*

Oliver de Tracy from Traci, near Bayeux in Normandy—a large landholder in Devon, represented the family of William de Tracy, one of the murderers of St. Thomas. William de Tracy held the honour of Tracy, in Devon, consisting of twenty knights' fees, at the same time.

12. *By gift of Radulf son of Bernard, the church of Holcombe and Lameia, in praebendam.*

Holcombe Rogus in Devon, probably. Lameia does not appear elsewhere. There is a Holcombe in Somerset. Holcombe gives name to a prebend at the present time.

13. . . . . . , *the church of Ceddre.*

The name of the giver of the church of Cheddar is omitted here. About this time the prior and convent of Bradenstoke, in Wiltshire, gave all their rights in the church of Cheddar to Alexander, dean and canon of Wells—witnessed by Walter, prior of Bath; and bishop Reginald gave to the convent of Bradenstoke, with the assent of Alexander the dean, and the canons, the church of Childcompton, the dean reserving the jurisdiction over it as once a prebendal church (Dugdale, *Monasticon*, ii, f. 209). R. i, f. 27. In 1240 bishop Jocelin confirmed Cheddar to the chapter. R. i, f. 30.

14. *By gift of the sisters Alicia, Christina, and Sara, the church of Tymberscombe, in praebendam.*

Another sister, Cecilia, is mentioned in the bishop's confirmation act: the husbands are named as consenting parties. One, John de Columpstock, was a Devonshire landowner. Timberscombe is a prebend at the present time.

15. *By gift of Robert de Bolevill, the church of Lideford, in praebendam.*

One Richard de Bonneville (Bonneville on the Toncques, in Normandy) was holding land at this time in Devon. Robert de Boleville, or Bonneville, made the grant in bishop Robert's time. A suit arose with his brother John, which was arranged in 1187 and impropriation made. West Lydford is no longer a prebend.

16. *By gift of Radulf Wac, the church of Doveliz.*

Dowlishwake, in South Petherton hundred, is not mentioned elsewhere in the register.

One Baldwin Wac (Wake) was present at Richard's coronation, and afterwards one of Richard's hostages in Germany. Dowlishwake, near Ilminster, is the church which preserves the name of the family. Howden, iii, 14, and 233.

17. *By gift of Simon Bozun, the church of Karenton.*

In the register of the priory of Bath, the prior and convent grant the vicarage of Karenton to Walter the clerk. Simon Buzun is witness.

Simon Bozun, knight, one of a family of landowners also in Devon, granted Karenton (Carhampton): he retained the appointment for his life to the prebend. It then reverted to the bishop. Carhampton, near Dunster, in West Somerset, or perhaps Carentan, in the Côtentin, Normandy, was the original seat of the family. The Bohun family came from near Carentan, where is S. André de Bohun and S. George de Bohun.

18. *By gift of Stephen son of David, a moiety of the church of Waleton.*

19. *By gift of Matilda de Chandos, the church of Stoweia, in perpetuam eleemosinam.*

Maude de Chandos was heiress of Robert de Chandos, who died 1120, the founder of Goldclive, with Isabella, his wife, daughter of Alured de Hispania, Domesday lord of Nether Stowey. Maude married Philip de Colombiers in 1166, who held eleven knights' fees in Devon and Somerset.

20. *By gift of Alured de Punson, the church of Berewe.*

Alured de Ponsot, or Ponsard, or Punson, lord of South Barrow. One of a group of grants made by Robert of Cary, lord of Lovington, and Nicholas of North Barrow—members of the family of Lovel of Castle Cary.

21. *By gift of Radulf Fitz-William, the church of Werminstere, in praebendam.*

Grant of Warminster, in Wilts, the church of St. Dionysius, by Ralph, son of William (Malet ?).

22. *By gift of Galfrid Talbot, half a virgate of land at Norham, with all the meadow which he had there, in perpetuam eleemosinam.*

Norham, in North Curry hundred.

23. *By our gift, the manor of North Cory with the church and all its appurtenances.*

The church or manor of North Curry, Wrantage, and West Hatch, were grants of crown lands after purchase by the bishop from king Richard, when he was raising money for the needs of the Crusade by sale of lands and offices (R. i, f. 9). They were bought by the bishop from the crown, and made over by him as a benefaction to augment the common funds of the canons, and formed the largest manorial possession of the chapter. The manor of North Curry included the hundred, and was a great lordship.

At the same time, on the same occasion, and doubtless on the same conditions of heavy payments, bishop Reginald obtained from king Richard charters confirmatory of all the grants and privileges made to the see by his predecessors from William II's time.

APPENDIX H.

Monasticon of Somerset in the times of bishops Reginald and Jocelin.

(I am indebted to the Right Rev. Bishop Hobhouse for this table).

Name and Order.	Founder.	Date.
Benedictine.		
Glastonbury.	Unknown.	
Bath.	King Osric.	676.
Muchelney.	King Athelstan.	939.
Athelney.	King Alfred.	888.
Dunster. (Cell to Bath)	William Mohun I.	1080.
Augustinian Canons.		
Bruton.	William Mohun II.	1143.
Taunton.	W. Giffard and H. de Blois, bps. of Winchester.	temp. Stephen and Hen. II.
Keynsham.	Earl of Gloucester.	1167.
Stavordale.	The Barons Lovel of Cary.	12th cent.
Barlinch.	The Say family.	1175.
Woodspring.	The Courteney family.	1210.
Cistercian.		
Cleeve.	De Romará, earl of Lincoln.	1188.
Carthusian.		
Witham.	King Henry II.	1174.
Hinton.	Ela Longespée, countess of Salisbury.	1222.
Cluniac.		
Montacute.	Earl of Mortaigne.	1068.
Alien.		
Stoke Courcy.	De Courcy family.	temp. Hen. II.
A cell to the Benedictine abbey of Lonley, Normandy.		
Nunneries.		
Mynchin Barrow.	Gournay family.	before 1212.
Mynchin Buckland.	W. de Erlegh.	1166 and 1199.
Cannington.	De Courcy family.	c. 1140.
White Hall, Ilchester.	William Denys.	c. 1216.

APPENDIX I.

FAMILY OF BISHOPS REGINALD AND SAVARIC.

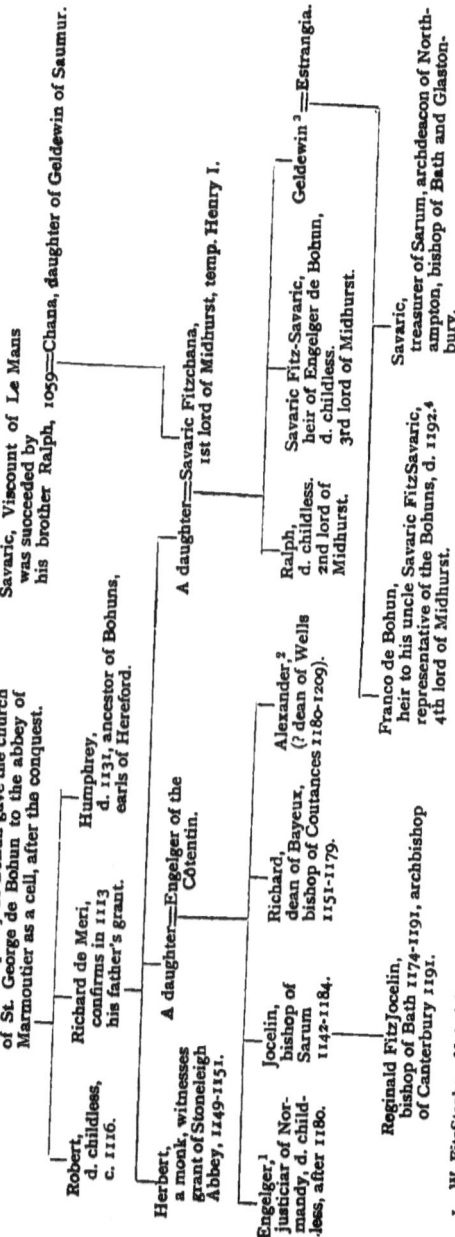

1. W. FitzStephen, *Materials for Life of Becket*, iii, p. 129, calls Engelger "patruus Jocelini Episcopi." Bishop Stubbs suggests there may be a mistake for "Reginaldi." Engelger held lands in S. Marculf in 1180. Vide *Rotuli Scac. Norman.* Lechaud D'Anisy, Caen, 1840.
2. An Alexander was dean during Reginald's and Savaric's time, 1180-1209. Roger de Bohun, "nephew of the dean," is mentioned as canon of Wells, anno 1205. *Pat. Rolls*, 35 Edw. III contains insperimus of 1 Ric. I and Henry III in which mention is made of (*a*) "Savaricus filius Engelgeri de Bohun." (*b*) "Savaricus filius Chana et Radulfus filius ejus, et Savaricus filius Savarici." (*c*) "Geldewinus filius Savarici." Cf. also Madox, *Hist of Exchequer*, i, 561, 6th Henry II "Geldewinus filius Savarici."
3. It is conjectured by bishop Stubbs that there was a Burgundian connection with the emperor Henry through Estrangia, mother of bishop Savaric.
4. Annal. Waverley, ii, 248.

APPENDIX K.

Sequence of events in Savaric's life, and in the annexation of the abbey of Glastonbury to the see of Bath.

Adam of Domerham, pp. 357-425.

1192.	SAVARIC at Rome, consecrated bishop September 20.
1193.	Savaric at Hagenau in Alsace obtains from king Richard consent to the exchange of Bath city for Glastonbury abbey, and union of the churches of Bath and Glastonbury under him as bishop of Bath and Glastonbury.
April.	Obtains letters from Richard, archbishop Hubert, and bishop William of Ely, to pope Celestine, petitioning for papal sanction.
June.	Savaric with Richard at Worms in June is named as one of the hostages for payment of his ransom.
Decemb. 12.	Abbot Henry vacates Glastonbury; is consecrated bishop of Worcester at Canterbury.
Decemb. 8.	Savaric at Bath sends for prior Harold, tells him that he is their abbot.
	Ralph de Lechlade in the name of Savaric takes possession of the abbey by royal warrant.
	The monks lodge a protest and notice of appeal to the pope on the altar of St. Andrew, Wells.
Feb. 2, 1194.	Richard is released at Mainz.
April 27.	Richard is crowned at Winchester.
	Savaric is chancellor of Burgundy to the emperor Henry VI.
Easter-tide.	Prior Harold appeals to the king at Winchester. He is put off by bishop of Ely, who bids the monks await the pope's decision.

The monks send another deputation to Richard in Normandy: are favourably received. Richard revokes his grant obtained when he was in durance, dispossesses Savaric, and places the abbey in the hands of his prothonotary, William of St. Marychurch. *"1st autumn after abbot Henry's consecration." Feast of St. Bartholomew, August 24.*

"In quadragesima sequenti, secundo videlicet anno post promotionem Henrici in episcopum," Savaric at Tours receives pope Celestine's sanction to the union of Bath and Glastonbury and assumes title. *Lent, 1195.*

Savaric obtains from the pope (1) A second mandate. (2) Letters of inhibition addressed to the convent. (3) Mandate of execution to archbishop Hubert, issued by pope Celestine, dated in three documents, May, June, "pontificatus anno sexto, MCXCVI, anno indictionis xiv" (pp. 364-6-7). *1196.*

The papal letters are publicly read in the convent by Savaric's agents from the chapter of Wells. And "completis jam tribus annis et parum amplius post promotionem Henrici in Episcopum," Savaric is inducted a second time. *1197.*

"Die sequenti," the convent send a deputation to the archbishop to protest. He rebukes them for their supineness in not having followed up their appeal to Rome. "Vos vultis somniando negotia vestra perficere, sed Savaricus episcopus non dormit"—"he, by his authority, had hitherto kept Savaric from possession." *Feb. 5 or 6.*

Savaric is sent to England by the emperor Henry to make restitution to Richard. The emperor dies while Savaric is on the journey.

Savaric is with Richard at Rouen. *October 16.*

Archbishop Hubert, forced to act upon the papal mandate, orders obedience to the proctors of Savaric, who with the dean of Wells and others of the chapter *Novemb. 18. modicum post Octavas S. Martini Nov. 18.*

	of Wells take possession in Savaric's name, and the king's officers withdraw. "Acta sunt hæc anno quarto post promotionem Henrici in Episcopum Wigorniensem" p. 370.
1198.	Pope Celestine dies January 8, 1198. Innocent III succeeds.
August 29, in festo decollationis S. Johannis.	Savaric in England during part of the year. Monks sent to complain to Richard in Normandy bring back royal letters to the king's justiciars ordering them to take possession of the convent in the king's name, which is so done.
Sept. 8.	Dean of Wells and prior of Bruton protest in Savaric's name before the convent.
Sept. 29. October.	William Pica returning from Rome directs the convent to send a deputation to meet him in Normandy, to approach the king. Savaric is appointed one of Richard's envoys to arrange matters with Geoffrey archbishop of York.
November.	The monks bring back letters from Richard dated Roche d'Andeli, October 29, giving licence to elect their own abbot, and letters to the pope Innocent III and to the cardinals urging dissolution of the union.
Circa Octavas S. Martini. Nov. 25.	The convent send a deputation to London with the king's letters, and "in scaccario regis" elect William Pica abbot, November 25. Savaric from the manor of Mells excommunicates William Pica and his supporters, and puts the convent under interdict. He is sent to Rome on Richard's affairs.
December 6.	William Pica rules as abbot from December 6, 1198, to the Purification, February 2, 1199.

Savaric's agents from Wells lay violent hands in the church of Glastonbury upon the leaders of the opposition and carry them off to prison in Wells. 1199. January 25. Conversion of St. Paul.

William Pica goes to Rome.

Savaric and the abbot plead against one another before Innocent, at Rome.

The dean of Wells and prior of Bruton proclaim the archbishop's interdict and excommunication of the abbot and convent for disobedience to the pope's letters of inhibition. Thursday before Easter.

The convent submit and pray for absolution. Easter.

The abbots of Sherborne and Abbotsbury in the archbishop's name absolve the convent. 1st Sunday after Easter.

The abbots of Malmesbury and Evesham receive the confession and profession of the convent and administer correction.

    Richard's death. A.D. 1199.

    Savaric returns to England. April 6.

    John's coronation at Westminster. Savaric assists. May 27. Ascension-Day.

    Savaric obtains the king's mandate for installation.

Savaric is installed in person at Glastonbury by commissioners appointed by archbishop Hubert. He takes possession of the abbey, and forces all the members of the convent to act in obedience to him as abbot. June 8. Whitsunday

    Savaric is with John in Normandy. July, August, September.

    Savaric probably at Rome in winter. Winter.

Innocent is adjudicating on the Glastonbury quarrel—removes Savaric's sentence of excommunication of William Pica—inhibits Savaric from further acts of violence—annuls William Pica's election—confirms the union of the see and abbey—appoints a commission to A.D. 1200. June 23. Aug. 22.

	arbitrate and to make award between Savaric and the convent.
Sept. 3.	William Pica dies at Rome.
October 8.	John's marriage with Isabella of Angoulême—second coronation at Westminster.
	John is at Lincoln.
November. " 23rd. " 25th.	Savaric present with the court at Lincoln, at the homage of William the Lion, and at the burial of St. Hugh.
A.D. 1201.	Innocent orders the convent to obey Savaric as their bishop "et specialiter tanquam proprio pastore."[1]
April 21. xii kal. Maii.	Savaric at Wells, grants charter to the city, which John confirms and enlarges by royal charter.
A.D. 1202. June 9.	Innocent sends a second mandate to the commissioners to hold their court.
August 29.	Another letter from Innocent to the commissioners reporting gravamina of convent against Savaric and urging investigation of charges.
Septemb. 24. viii kal. Oct.	Report of the commissioners and award of the pope. "Prima ordinatio ecclesiae Glastoniensis facta auctoritate domini Innocentii III."
A.D. 1203. Octave of St. Michael.	Savaric at Wells—makes grants to the chapter—in anticipation of his absence gives authority to the chapter to excommunicate all invaders of the rights of the chapter.
Aug. 8, 1205.	Dies at Senes la Vielle—either Siena, or Civita Vecchia.

---

1. *i.e.*, as their diocesan and ordinary—also as their abbot.

APPENDIX L.

Gifts of bishop Savaric to the church of Bath.

Registrum Prioratus Bathon. (p. 315).

SAVARICUS episcopus hujus loci, omnes terras nostras a praedecessoribus suis nobis restitutas, omnes etiam ecclesias nobis in usus proprios ad eisdem concessas, affectuose confirmavit et etiam a summo pontifice confirmari procuravit. Praeterea ecclesiam de Chyw ad jus patronatus sui spectantem nobis in usus proprios contulit et confirmavit, ecclesiam etiam de Westoñ injuste a quibusdam alienatam nobis reddidit et in usus proprios nobis confirmavit et a summo pontifice utramque ecclesiam de Chyw videlicet et de Westoñ in usus nobis proprios confirmari procuravit, ecclesiam nihilominus de Comptona Fulconis de Alneto nobis in usus proprios confirmavit—duas capas decenter ornatas nobis contulit. Cum autem in redemptione regis Ricardi omnes thesauri exhaurirentur ecclesiarum, de ratione propria vestes, cruces, et calices nostros ne conflarentur acquietavit. Cujus anniversaria dies in albis celebretur et C pauperes reficiantur et mensa fratrum copiosius procuretur.

APPENDIX M.

Institution of the Mass of the Blessed Virgin.

REG. i, FOL. 46; iii, FOL. 136 in dors.

SAVARICUS Dei gratia Bathon. et Glaston. episcopus.
Omnibus fidelibus per episcopatum suum constitutis salutem et benedictionem. Quum in multis offendimus

omnes, et sine peccato praesens vita non agitur, necessaria habemus sanctorum suffragia ut quum nostris excessibus incessanter affligimur, eorum apud Deum intercessionibus sublevemur.

Inter omnes autem sanctos memoria dei genetricis eo jocundius agitur quo pro fidelibus sedula creditur interventrix existere, et apud Deum majorem noscitur gratiam obtinere.

Desiderantes itaque inter hujus mundi tam varia pericula ipsius patrociniis communiri, communicato capituli Wellensis consilio provida deliberatione statuimus, ut in ecclesia ipsa continua ejusdem dei genetricis virginis habeatur memoria, et in ejus veneratione missa diebus singulis solemniter celebretur.

Alteram praeterea missam pro praedecessoribus nostris episcopis, fratribus quoque et benefactoribus ipsius ecclesiae, cunctisque fidelibus defunctis, in eadem ecclesia providimus diebus omnibus specialiter celebrandam, ut sacramentis salutaribus expiati superis sedibus celerius inserantur.

APPENDIX N.

Charter of bishop Savaric to the town of Wells (c. 1201) in the Town Hall of Wells.

OMNIBUS Christi fidelibus ad quos praesens carta pervenerit.

Savaricus Dei gratia Bathoniae et Glastoniae Episcopus salutem in domino. Quum in praeterito cognovimus praedecessores nostros a multis retro temporibus in augmentum honoris, dignitatis, et reddituum suorum et omnium sibi succedentium, concessisse burgensibus nostris de Wellis jure perpetuo libertates et omnes liberas consuetudines burgensium et burgorum plenariis libertatibus gaudentium, Nos eorum vestigiis inhaerentes, considerantes etiam, et cum diligentia attendentes honestam et plurimum laudabilem eorum fuisse intentionem quod circa statum burgi illius meliorandum et in libertatem majorem provehendum habuisse dinoscuntur, libertates omnes et liberas consuetudines burgensium et burgorum qui plenarias habeant libertates burgo de Wellis et burgensibus universis et singulis infra terminos subscriptos mansionem habentibus plene et integre concessimus in perpetuum, statuentes etiam et jure perpetuo concedentes ut totum territorium subscriptum liberum sit burgum et plenariis ut diximus gaudeat libertatibus—a parte quidem australi, aqua decurrente a molendino et ab angulo virgulti nostri per quoddam vetus fossatum usque pratum de Hela—a prato illo per quendam rivulum usque ad pontem de Kiward — a ponte illo sicut aqua de Wellis defluit usque pontem qui in ingressu villae prope capellam beati Thomae martyris —a parte occidentali, cruce olim sita in via qua itur ad Axebrugge—a parte septentrionali, cruce olim sita qua itur Bristoldum — a parte orientali, via quae praetenditur a lapidicina usque ad montem versus Tidesput[1] per pomerium nostrum. Volumus etiam et praesenti decreto sancimus ut quilibet intra easdem

---

1. "Tidesput." Cf. Reg. Prioratus Bathon. f. 67, inspeximus of charter of bishop Roger, 1245, of lands "in manerio nostro de Wellis in Tithesput furlang qui jacet intra terram Roberti le Sedere et terram Thom. fil Sode super cheminam versus gardinum nostrum de Wellis ex parte orientali."

metas messagium aliquid in presentiarum possidens vel in posterum possessurus liberam habeat licentiam commorandi et cum catallis suis recedendi necnon et revertendi. Liceat quoque cuilibet burgensium domos suas impignorare vendere sive etiam donare secundum perpetuam dispositionis suae voluntatem, plenamque habeant facultatem eas in quemcunque eis placuit transferendi praeterquam domibus religiosis, quod facere non poterunt sine licentia nostra vel successorum nostrorum, retento nobis annuo redditu duodecim denariorum de singulis messagiis.

Concedimus itaque ut si lis aliqua forte damnosa infra ambitum messagii alicujus eorum emerserit, liberam habeant potestatem ut advicem concordes fiant in curia sua, justitia nostra in nulla exigente consuetudinem vel emendationem donec burgenses in justitia defecerint, nisi mortale vulnus vel damnum perpetuum corpori inflictum fuerit; salva in omnibus justitia et dignitate domini regis et regni.

Inhibemus autem ne aliquis in eodem burgo pelles crudas aut coria cruda emere presumat nisi fuerit in luna et laga burgensium Wellensium. Statuimus etiam et in perpetuum concedimus ut quicunque illic in quatuor festivitatibus quacunque negotiationis causa convenerint, scilicet in inventione Sanctae Crucis, in festivitate Sancti Kalixti, in festivitate Sancti Andreae, in die anniversario dedicationis capellae beati Thomae Martyris, qui est dies crastina Sancti Joannis Baptistae, in plateis burgi illius negotiationes suas fecerint, et ab omni prava consuetudine et inquietudine et molestia et exactione liberi exerceant, et nullatenus ecclesiam Wellensem et atrium ecclesiae negotiaturi intrare vel violare praesumat. Concedentes et in perpetuum statuentes ut omnes ibi convenientes quieti sint in perpetuo de teloneo in omnibus praedictis festivitatibus et earum vigiliis et crastino earumdem, ut per triduum illa gaudeant libertate in singulis festivitatibus supra nominatis. Et quod haec omnia rata et firma perseverent ea praesenti carta nostra et sigillo nostro et ecclesiae nostrae Wellensis duximus confirmanda.

Hujus testibus: Alexandro decano Wellensi · Gaufrido archidiacono Berkescire · Thoma subdecano Wellensi · Magistro Radulpho de Lichel · Magistro Rogero de Doveliz cancellario Wellensi. Johanne Camel · Roberto de Essio · Hugo de Wellis, clericis nostris · Radulpho de Auio seneschallo nostro · Willelmo filio Ricardi · Alan de S. Georgio · Radulpho Teissun · Gileberto · Helia filio Ricardi · Hugone de fontibus · Willelmo de Banwell · Et multis aliis clericis quam laicis.

Seal: small oval in green wax.

Device: figure of bishop.

Legend: SAVA[RIƆVS ƐPISƆOPVS BATh]ON. [ƐT 6LAS]TON.

Another seal in bag.

The boundaries in Savaric's charter are marked—
I. On the south (a) by the watercourse from the bishop's mill, and from the angle of the bishop's withy-bed, running down an old cut[1] to Helesmead;
  (b) thence up the stream-course to Keward bridge on the Glastonbury road;

---

1. Vetus fossatum, an artificial channel.

(c) up the Wells stream (*i.e.* the water from St. Andrew's well) to the bridge by the chapel of St. Thomas the Martyr, at the entrance of the town.

II. On the west — by the cross on the road to Axbridge, *i.e.* Little Elm, at the point of divergence of the road to Wookey and Axbridge.

III. On the north—by the cross on the road to Bristol.

IV. On the east — by the road from a quarry (under Stobery) to the hill towards Tidesput through the bishop's ground (*i.e.* the Tor hill).

APPENDIX O.

Charter of king John to the town of Wells. 1201.
Town Hall, Wells.

JOHANNES dei gratia &c.—Sciatis nos concessisse et praesenti carta confirmasse quod Welles in Sumerset sit liberum burgum, et quod homines ejusdem villae et heredes eorum liberi sint burgenses et quod ibi liberum sit mercatum singulis dominicis diebus sicut ibi est et esse consuevit, et liberae feriae sicut annuatim ibi esse solent, in festo beati Andreae, beati Calixti, in Inventione Sanctae Crucis, in crastino beati Johannis Baptistae, et praeterea una feria de dono nostro singulis annis in translatione beati Andreae per octo dies duratura, infra vicos ejusdem burgi in locis quibus praedicta feria beati Andreae ibidem teneri consuevit, nisi sit ad nocumentum vicinarum feriarum. Quare volumus et firmiter praecipimus quod praedicta villa de Welles liberum burgum sit et omnes homines ejusdem villae et heredes eorum liberi burgenses sint in perpetuum, et quod habeant praedictum liberum mercatum et praedictas ferias quae ibi esse solent, et de dono nostro praedictam feriam per octo dies duraturam, et quod ipsi et heredes eorum habeant omnes libertates et liberas consuetudines liberi burgi et liberorum burgensium et ad hujusmodi mercatum et ferias pertinentes bene et in pace, libere et quiete, integre et honorifice in perpetuum. Volumus etiam quod ipsi et eorum res et possessiones sint in manu, custodia, et protectione nostra, prohibentes ne quis eos vel heredes eorum contra hanc cartam nostram vexet vel disturbet super forisfacturam[1] nostram.

Testibus: Willelmo Marescallo Comite de Pembroc · Willelmo Comite Sarisburiensi · Willelmo de Rupibus seneschallo Andegavensi · Stephano de Pertico · Gerard de Fornivall · Warino filio Geroldi · Petro de Stok · Fulco de Cantelupo · Roberto de Plesseto.

Datum per manum Simonis Wellensis archidiaconi apud Chinonem septima die Septembris anno regni nostri tertio.

Seal gone. Green tags remaining.

APPENDIX P.

A TRADITION at Wells has assigned to Savaric a pastoral staff and a pontifical ring which were found in a stone coffin dug up in the western burial ground

---

[1]. "The king's right of enforcing demands."

of the cathedral church at the beginning of this century, in the time of dean Lukin, 1799—1812.

"The staff is exactly twelve inches high, and consists of three parts: (a) the crook; (b) the knot; (c) the neck; the whole being of copper-gilt and enamelled. *(See Frontispiece)*. The crook is formed of the body and head of a serpent; the scales are filled with dark-blue enamel, and a serrated crest runs along the outside of the curve. Inside the crook is a winged figure, probably St. Michael, striking a spear into the body of a two-legged lizard or wingless dragon, whose tail runs through the snake forming the crook and terminates in foliage. The dragon's body is set on either side with seven turquoises, and the eyes are, like those of all the figures on the crozier-head, formed of some dark stones, seemingly garnets. Both the serpent and the dragon have the heads so formed as to show a face on each side of the crook. The junction of the crook and knot is masked by a bold indented cresting, once set with turquoises. The knot is a flattened circular boss of gilt copper with a casing of open-work formed of six wingless dragons like that inside the crook, three above and as many below, each biting the tail of the one preceding, an ornate belt dividing the two groups.

The neck of the crozier-head is four inches long, ornamented with beautiful scroll-work of conventional foliage on a field of dark blue enamel. This is divided lengthways and slightly spirally by the bodies of three serpents, heads downwards and their tails curving outwards under the knob. The serpents are gilt, and have each five turquoises on the back and garnets for eyes. The whole of the work is of excellent character, and still in very good preservation. The crozier-head was put together in 1834, under the advice and assistance of Mr. Douce and Mr. Gage, then Director of the Society, before which it was exhibited on February 6th of that year. The wooden staff to which it is now fixed, and the bronze ferrule, made after one in Mr. Douce's possession, were added by Mr. Willement.

There is no historical ground for the tradition that it belonged to Savaric. The workmanship and similarity of pattern to many other croziers of bishops of the twelfth and thirteenth centuries, probably gave occasion for the assumption.

The peculiarities of the pontifical ring, a massive gold ring with a pale uncut ruby, do not help to fix the date."[1]

APPENDIX Q.

Canons of Wells at the time of bishop Jocelin's death.

A.D. 1242. Archer, *Long Book*, p. 35.

CANONICI Wellenses qui defuncto Jocelino controversiæ inter Wellenses et Bathonienses de electione Episcopi se immiscuerunt.

Johannes Saracenus, Decanus. R. i, f. 73.
Willelmus de Button, Archidiaconus Well. f. 73.
Walterus de St. Quintino, Archid. Taunton. f. 73.
Will. de Maydeneston, f. 73.
Phil. de Gildeford, f. 73.

---

1. A coloured plate is given in *Archæologia*, Vol. LI, part 1, p. 106. *Savaric, etc.*, with this description written by Mr. W. H. St. John Hope, Assistant Secretary of the Society of Antiquaries.

Hugo Subdecanus, f. 74.
Lucas de Membury, f. 74.
Walterus de Sarum, dictus de Button, f. 74.
Johannes de Cerde, *ib*.
Will. de Brugwalter, *ib*.
Robertus de Mariscis, f. 74. 1259, f. 105.
Sylvester de Everdon, clericus domini Regis, f. 75.
Johannes de Uffinton, missus ad papam, f. 75.
W. de Eboraco, præpositus Beverlacensis, f. 76.
Walterus de Cussinton, f. 65. 1259, f. 103.
Ricardus de Dinham, *ib*.
Jocelinus Capellanus, *ib*.
Johannes Mansel, f. 78.
Johannes Odelin (f. 80), præb. de Yatton, R. iii, f. 404.
Johannes de Button (f. 80), præpositus, 1259, f. 104.
Will. de Pilton (f. 80), 1259, f. 103.
Will. de Kaynesham (f. 80).
Wall. Bruno, *ib*.
Rad. de Chyw, *ib*.
Ric. de Langport, *ib*.
Milo, *ib*.
Rog. de Wynesham, *ib*.
Will. de Lechlade, *ib*.
Walt. Sarum, *ib*.
John de Kaynesham, *ib*.
Rog. de Westbury.
Luc. de Bristol.
Walt. de Cerda.
Thomas de Kent.
Robert de Welles.

APPENDIX R.

Master Workmen in bishop Jocelin's time.

MASONS, goldsmiths, sculptors :   Masons.

(a.) The family of Lock.—Adam Lock, father, Thomas Lock the son, *cementarii*, are possessed of houses in Wells, which they make over for the use of schools in Wells. R. i, ff. 33, 34 ; anno 1229, 1234.

With them are connected as witnesses attesting their grants the names of two other *cementarii*, Deodatus, and Thomas Noreis, and of different officers of the church, and of the bishop's household; the subdean and two canons of Wells; three vicars; Elyas de Derham, seneschal and steward of bishop Jocelin ; Walter the chamberlain ; Lawrence and Ivo Cade, provosts of Wells.

(b.) The family of Noreis, Norais, Noreys, appears about this time. Master Thomas Norreis, 1235, 1243, in Charter 43, and also in other documents belonging to the old Almshouse in Wells. Richard Noreis attests in Henry III's time a grant to John Glaston, aurifaber (goldsmith) of a messuage in Wells.   Goldsmith. A. H. No. 5. (Cf. Charter 35, Godefrey aurifaber attests grant of houses in Wells.) In Edward I's time John le Noreys, son and heir of Robert le Noreys of Wells, makes a grant of houses in Southover, Wells. A. H. No. 6. Thomas (Norreys) the mason (*cementarius*) attests at Glastonbury (13 December, 1249) a release from Ralph Page, son of Alwyn de Vinea, of messuages and lands in Glastonbury to William son of Roger Bunetone, together with Nicholas de Lostehulle, then seneschal (steward) of Glastonbury, and others.

A. H. No. 3, with seal of Ralph Page fil. Alwyn de Vinea, a fleur de lys elegantly designed.

Sculptor. *(c.)* The Bunetone Family "dictus sculptor."—William de Bunetone, called "sculptor" in Edward II's time grants twelve houses "in vico qui vocatur Boneton in villa Glaston." and lands to his son John de Boneton, charged with payment of two shillings to the abbot, and to heirs of William aurifaber (goldsmith) a pair of gloves (A. H. Nos. 11, 12).

(d.) Elyas de Derham, witness to the grants of the Lock family (R. i, f. 34), is the name of one of the executors of the early draft of the will of Hugh bishop of Lincoln in 1212, co-executor with bishop Jocelin, then in exile in France. He bears the same name as the canon of Salisbury, the "rector ecclesiæ" of Salisbury, 1225-1229 (Osm. Reg., ii, cxxii, Rolls Series), and the traditional builder of the church of Salisbury; the "incomparable architect" of St. Thomas' shrine at Canterbury, 1220 (Matt. Paris, *Hist. Angl.*, ii, 242); the master of the works in the king's hall at Winchester, 1232 (Rot. Lit. Pat. 16 Hen. III, m. 5, 6; Rot. Claus. 20 Hen. III), whose death is mentioned by M. Paris in 1245.[1] (*Chr. Maj.*, iv, 418.) Others of the family of Derham (Dyrham in Gloucestershire) are named in the Wells registers.

Walter de Derham, canon in 1234. R. i, f. 33.
John de Derham, canon 1243-7. R. i, ff. 64, 65, 78.
R. de Derham, canon 1247. R. i, f. 96.

---

1. Vide a paper on Elias de Derham, read at the meeting of the Royal Archæological Institute at Salisbury, 1887, by Rev. J. A. Bennett, F.S.A. *Archæological Journal*, xliv, 365. Also an article in *R.I.B.A. Journal*, 12 April, 1888, by Mr. Wyatt Papworth.
A. H. here stand for Almshouse Charters.

APPENDIX S.

Inspeximus. 1242. *Original Documents, Nos.* 39, 40, 41.
Penes Decanum et Capitulum.

UNIVERSIS Christi fidelibus ad quos presens scriptum pervenerit J[ocelinus] Bathoniensis. W[illelmus Brewer, 1224-44] Exoniensis. et W[illelmus de Ralegh 1239-45] Norwicensis Dei gratia episcopi salutem in Domino. Noveritis quod inspeximus quedam instrumenta autentica, et etiam ipsa originalia que nobis ex parte Decani et capituli Wellensis fuerunt exhibita, quorum transcripta prout inferius continentur de verbo ad verbum absque adjeccione et diminucione ad ipsorum peticionem presenti carte inseri fecimus in hec verba : Recital.

Alexander episcopus servus servorum Dei dilectis filiis Decano Archidiaconis et Capitulo Wellensi salutem, et apostolicam benediccionem. Intelleximus ex litteris vestris, et ex testimonio plurium magnarum personarum ; nichilominus innotuit nobis quod vos recepta libertate celebrandi eleccionem in ecclesia vestra dilectum filium R[eginaldum] Archidiaconum Saresberiensem unanimiter et concorditer in pastorem vobis et episcopum elegistis. Cum autem idem electus pro sciencia et literatura sua, et pro fervore devocionis quam circa nos et Romanam ecclesiam gerere comprobatur, carus nobis sit plurimum et acceptus, et conversacio sua se nobis commendabilem reddat, unanimitatem vestram et concordiam super hoc commendamus ; volentes vos in proposito vestro stabiles et firmos existere, et in omnibus que spectant ad commodum et profectum ecclesie vestre, et prefati electi vestri Ratification of Wells election of Reginald. A.D. 1174.

inveniri unanimes et concordes. Unde quia predictum electum sicut virum providum et discretum, literatum et nobis valde devotum ferventer in Christo diligimus, et libenter quantum secundum Deum possumus ad ejus commodum intendimus et honorem, discrecioni vestre per apostolica scripta precipiendo mandamus, quatinus ei sicut electo vestro omni contradiccione et appellacione remota debitam obedienciam et reverenciam impendatis, et ejus monitis et mandatis humiliter et devote parere curetis. Ita quod ipse in vobis filialem subjeccionem inveniat, et nos obedienciam et devocionem vestram in hac parte debeamus non immerito commendare. Datum Anagnie . xiiij kalend . Maij.

Ratification of Wells right of election.

Alexander episcopus servus servorum dei dilectis filiis, Decano, Precentori, Archidiaconis, et capitulo Wellensis ecclesie salutem . et apostolicam benediccionem. Justis filiorum ecclesie peticionibus nos convenit libenter annuere, et eas effectu prosequente complere, ut cum a sede apostolica quod racionabiliter postulant fuerint assecuti ei debeant omni tempore firmiori devocione adherere, et ejus honori et exaltacioni fervenciori studio invigilare. Eapropter dilecti in domino filii racionabilibus votis et desideriis vestris grato concurrentes assensu vobis et per vos ecclesie vestre canonicas consuetudines, libertates quoque et immunitates, et episcoporum vestrorum elecciones sicut eas a ducentis retro annis usque ad tempora bone memorie Johannis quondam episcopi vestri, qui sibi in bathoniensi ecclesia sedem constituit habuisse noscimini auctoritate apostolica confirmamus, et presentis scripti patrocinio communimus.

Ita tamen ut idem episcopo a vobis eligendo tractari debuerit ne inter vestram et predictam ecclesiam aliqua possit imposterum de eleccione controversia suboriri, vos et monachi ipsius ecclesiæ ad electionem tractandam, et faciendam conveniatis, et cum inde perfectam honestam et ydoneam conveneritis, tu, fili Decane, secundum antiquam ecclesie tue consuetudinem ipsius eleccionis debeas sollempnem pronunciacionem habere, ut persona electa Cantuariensi archiepiscopo examinanda et promovenda sine contradiccione qualibet presentetur. Decernimus ergo ut nulli omnino hominum licet hanc paginam nostre confirmacionis infringere, vel ei aliquatenus contraire. Si quis autem hoc attemptare presumpserit, indignacionem omnipotentis Dei et beatorum Petri et Pauli apostolorum ejus se noverit incursurum. Datum Anagnie . vj idus. Januarij.

Agreement for joint action recommended.

¶ *Item pacem postmodum factam inter ecclesiam Wellensem et ecclesiam Bathoniensem super eleccione Episcopi sui inter eos communiter facienda.*

Agreement.

In nomine Patris et Filii et Spiritus sancti Amen. Facta est hec pax subscripta inter ecclesiam Bathoniensem . et ecclesiam Wellensem . et conventum Bathoniensem . et capitulum Wellense super eleccione pontificis utrique ecclesie prefitiendi vacante episcopatu. Videlicet quod cum secundum deum et consuetudinem regni de eleccione tractari debuerit prior et monachi Bathonienses, et decanus et canonici Wellenses, in loco idoneo proper hoc convenient, et de eleccione futuri Episcopi communiter tractabunt. Et cum communiter in idoneam personam convenerint, prior

Bathoniensis debet denuntiare ex parte utriusque ecclesie, et postulare personam de communi assensu electam. Si vero prior Bathoniensis vel monachi, vel decanus Wellensis, vel canonici, in eleccionem episcopi contra predictam formam in aliquo proruperint, diffinitum est et concessum ex utraque parte quod irritum sit et inane quicquid fuerit ab eis contra hoc super eleccione attemptatum. Si vero partes communiter consenserint in personam prioris decanus Wellensis ejus eleccionem debet denuntiare et postulare. Eodem modo convenit inter partes, quod si ecclesia Bathoniensis caruerit priore tempore eleccionis, quod decanus Wellensis eleccionem illius in quem partes consenserunt denuntiabit et postulabit. Decanus vero et capitulum Wellense non impedient quo minus episcopus illorum prius in ecclesia Bathoniensi intronizetur quam in Wellensi, nec procurabunt quod prius intronizetur in Wellensi quam in Bathoniensi. Convenit etiam inter predictas ecclesias quod nunquam contra hanc formam pacis utentur aliquibus privilegiis impetratis vel impetrandis. Hec autem omnia fideliter observandas tam prior et conventus Bathoniensis quam Alexander decanus et capitulum Wellense juraverunt. et sigillo utriusque confirmaverunt.

Election of Jocelin at Bath.

¶ *Item instrumenta utriusque ecclesie vacante tunc ecclesia Cantuariensi directa summo pontifici super eleccione domini Jocelini episcopi sui communiter inter dictas ecclesias facta, videlicet instrumentum ecclesie Bathoniensis in hæc verba:*

Sanctissimo patri et domino Innocentio Dei gratia summo Pontifici, devotissimi sui Robertus Bathoniensis ecclesie prior et totus ejusdem ecclesie conventus salutem, et tam promptum quam debitum in omnibus famulatum. Cum pie recordacionis episcopus noster Savaricus viam universe carnis fuisset ingressus, convenimus in unum nos et decanus et capitulum Wellensis ecclesie ad quos una nobiscum episcopi nostri noscitur electio pertinere, ut de prefitiendo nobis episcopo communiter tractaremus. Tandem vero post diutinam et diligentem deliberacionem communi omnium hinc inde voto et desiderio in magistrum Jocelinum clericum ecclesie nostre et canonicum Wellensis ecclesie, virum industrium et literatum et honestum vota nostra contulimus ipsum in pastorem, et episcopum animarum nostrarum, invocata sancti Spiritus gratia solempniter eligentes. Pedibus itaque vestre Paternitatis provoluti quanta possumus devocione supplicamus quatinus eleccionem nostram, concurrente tam cleri quam populi voluntate celebratam, et principis assensu subnixam, auctoritate apostolica confirmare dignemini, ne si ecclesie nostre diutius pastoris provisione caruerint irreparabilem quod Deus avertat tam in spiritualibus quam in temporalibus jacturam incurrant. Ego Robertus prior . s[ubscripsi] ✠ Ego Aluredus . s . + Ego Vincentius . s . + Ego Hamo . s . + Ego Hugo . s . + Ego Johannes supprior . s . + Ego Aurelianus . s . + Ego Martinus camerarius . s . + Ego Adam . s . + Ego Reginaldus . s . + Ego Ricardus . s . + Ego Willelmus thesaurarius . s . Ego Ricardus subsacrista . s . + Ego Willelmus . s . + Ego Anselmus succentor . s . + Ego Walterus . s . + Ego Serlo subcellerarius . s . + Ego Robertus granatarius . s . → Ego Walterus . s . + Ego Walterus . s . + Ego Nicholaus . s . + Ego

Arnaldus . s . + Ego Urbanus cellerarius . s . + Ego Radulfus infirmarius . s . + Ego Robertus . s . + Ego Marchus . s . + Ego Willelmus sacrista . s . + Ego Walterus refectorius . s . + Ego Johannes custos operum . s . + Ego Johannes elemosinarius . s . + Ego Robertus . s . + Ego Symon precentor . s . + Ego Johannes tercius prior . s . + Ego Fulco . s . ✠ Ego Willelmus . s . ✠ Ego Hugo . s . + Ego Johannes . s . + Ego Walterus . s . + Ego Robertus . s . + Ego Johannes . s . ✠ In hujus itaque rei testimonium robur, et majorem firmitatem huic scripto sigillum nostrum apposuimus.

Election at Wells.

¶ *Item instrumentum ecclesie Wellensis in hec verba:* Sanctissimo patri et domino karissimo J. dei gratia summo pontifici devotissimi sui Alexander Wellensis ecclesie decanus et totum ejusdem ecclesie capitulum salutem et tam promptum quam debitum in omnibus famulatum. Cum pie recordacionis episcopus noster Savaricus viam universe carni fuisset ingressus convenimus in unum nos et prior et conventus Bathoniensis ecclesie ad quos una nobiscum episcopi nostri noscitur eleccio pertinere ut de prefitiendo nobis episcopo communiter tractaremus. Tandem vero post diutinam et diligentem deliberacionem communi omnium hinc inde voto et desiderio in magistrum Jocelinum canonicum nostrum virum industrium litteratum et honestum vota nostra contulimus ipsum in pastorem et episcopum animarum nostrarum invocata sancti spiritus gratia solempniter eligentes. Pedibus itaque vestre paternitatis provoluti quanta possumus devocione supplicamus quatinus eleccionem nostram concurrente tam cleri quam populi voluntate celebratam et principi assensu subnixam auctoritate apostolica confirmare dignemini ne si ecclesie nostre diutius pastoris provisione caruerint irreparabilem quod Deus avertat tam in spiritualibus quam in temporalibus jacturam incurrant. Ego Alexander Wellensis Decanus . s . + Ego Willelmus [de Sancta Fide] 1185-1208 precentor Wellensis . s . + Ego .[1]H . Wellensis archidiaconus . s . + Ego .[2]R . cancellarius Wellensis . s . + Ego . T . thesaurarius Wellensis . s . + Ego W . cancellarius domini Regis . s . + Ego . [3]P . archidiaconus Bathoniensis . s . + Ego . [4]W . archidiaconus Tantoniensis . s . + Ego .[5]T . subdecanus Wellensis . s . + Ego . [6]A . Succentor Wellensis . s . + Ego Abbas Beccensis canonicus Wellensis . s . + Ego abbas Muchelnensis canonicus Wellensis . s . + Ego . R . archidiaconus Wyntoniensis . s . + Ego Magister . R . de Lechel [ade] . s . + Ego Stephanus Ridel . s . + Ego magister Amandus . s . + Ego . P . Canutus . s . + Ego . J . Chauvel . s . + Ego . T . de Lond[on] . s . + Ego Reginaldus Buzun . s . + Ego magister . W . de Tantonia . s . + Ego . R . de Tresgoz . s . + Ego magister . T . de Heselle . s . + Ego . S . de Elmeham . s . + Ego . T . de Tornaco . s . + Ego . H . de Welles . s . + Ego . J . capellanus . s . + Ego . P . de Inglesh . s . + Ego . A . Scottus . s . + Ego Hugo de Wylī .

1. Hugh de Welles 1204-10.
2. ? Richard de Kenelworth, 1219.
3. ? Peter de Cicester, dean, 1227.
4. William de Wrotham 1216.
5. Thomas de Dinan 1199.
6. Adam ?

s . + Ego Arnisius de Constantiis . s . + Ego Mauricius de Berkele . s . + Ego Johannes de Bohun . s . + Ego Iterus de Wandesti . s . + Ego Philipus de Lucy . s . + Ego . R. de Tymbresƀ . s . + Ego . R . preciosus . s . + Ego . R . de Staweya . s . + Ego . R . de Camera . s . + Ego . W . de Sarum . s . + Ego . H . de Wyflescumba . s . + Ego . A . Lugdunensis . s . + Ego . H . de Berkele . s . + Ego . T . de Cycestria . s . + Ego . J . de Kainesham . s . + Ego magister . R . de Wyltoñ . s . + Ego . T . de Dundeñ . s . + Ego . W . de Dinre . s . + Ego . J . de Calna . s . + Ego . R . de Bathonia . s . + Ego . N . de Welles . s . + Ego . H . de Traco . s . + Ego . R . de Bercħ . s . + Ego . R . de Sanf . s . + Ego . S . de Torn[aco] . s . + Ego Willelmus de Cerda . s . + . In hujus itaque rei testimonium robur et majorem firmitatem huic scripto sigillum nostrum apposuimus.

¶ *Item litteras testimoniales quorundum Episcoporum Anglie super eleccione sic communiter facta summo pontifici directas in hec verba:*

Sanctissimo in Christo patri J . dei gratia summo pontifici humiles et devoti filii sui W . de Londoñ G . Roffensis H . Exoniensis H . Saresberiensis E . Elyensis G . Coventrensis M . Wygorniensis J . Norwicensis W . Lincolniencis S . Cicestrensis et P . Wyntoniensis episcopi salutem et cum omni devocione ac reverentia debitam domino et patri obedientiam. Noverit sancta paternitas vestra quod cum venerabilis frater noster Savaricus bone memorie Bathoniensis episcopus concessisset in fata et tam Bathoniensis quam Wellensis ecclesia sua fuisset viduata pastore, prior et conventus Bathoniensis et decanus et capitulum Wellense ad quos jus eligendi episcopum pertinere dinoscitur in unum pariter convenerunt, . habitaque prout moris est super eleccione episcopi diligenti tractatu, pari tandem voto et unanimi assensu in magistrum Jocelinum canonicum Wellensis ecclesie virum providum, litteratum et honestum, consenserunt ipsumque invocata sancti Spiritus gratia, in pastorem et episcogum suum canonice et solempniter elegerunt. Cui nimirum eleccioni illustrix rex Anglie Johannes suum adhibuit benignus assensum. Quia vero Cantuariensis ecclesia suo noscitur orbata pastore supplicamus sancte paternitati vestre quatinus nuntios dictarum ecclesiarum benignius admittentes prenominato electo munus confirmacionis conferre dignemini.

¶ *Item similiter litteras testimoniales eorundem episcoporum directas super hoc domino . J. Sancte Marie in via lata diacono cardinali tunc venienti legato in Angliam in hec verba:*

Venerabili patri et domino karissimo J. dei gratia Sancte Marie in via lata diacono cardinali, apostolice sedis legato W. Londoniensis G. Roffensis H. Exoniensis H. Saresberiensis E. Eligensis G. Coventrensis M. Wygornensis J. Norwicensis W. Lincolniensis S. Cicestrensis et P. Wyntoniensis episcopi salutem et sincere devocionis affectum. Noverit paternitas vestra quod cum venerabilis frater noster Savaricus bone memorie Bathoniensis episcopus concessisset in fata et tam Bathoniensis quam Wellensis ecclesia suo fuisset viduata pastore, prior et conventus Bathoniensis et decanus et capitulum Wellense ad quos jus eligendi episcopum pertinere dinoscitur in unum pariter convenerunt, habitaque prout moris est super eleccione episcopi diligenti tractatu . pari tandem voto et unanimi assensu in magistrum Jocelinum canonicum Wellensis ecclesie virum providum litteratum et honestum consenserunt ipsumque invocata spiritus sancti gratia in pastorem et episcopum suum canonice ac sollempniter elegerunt, cui nimirum eleccioni illustris rex Anglie Johannes suum adhibuit benignus assensum. Quia vero Cantuariensis ecclesia suo noscitur orbata pastore supplicamus paternitati vestre quatinus nuntios dictarum ecclesiarum benignius admittentes . prenominato electo munus confirmacionis conferre dignemini.

¶ *Item litteras domini regis super assensu suo dicte eleccioni prestito directas domino . J. Sancte Marie in via lata diacono cardinali tunc venienti legato in Angliam, qui omnibus predictis instrumentis receptis et visis, vacante tunc ecclesia Cantuariensis, vice domini pape dictam eleccionem sic communiter factam confirmavit. Tenor vero predictarum litterarum domini regis talis est:*

King's missive.

Venerabili patri in Christo J . dei gratia sancte Marie in via lata diacono cardinali et apostolice sedis legato J . eadem gratia Rex Anglie, dominus Hybernie Normannorum et Aquitanorum, comes Andegavorum salutem et debitam cum devocione reverentiam. Mittimus ad vos dilectum et fidelem nostrum magistrum Jocelinum ecclesie Wellensis canonicum a decano et capitulo Wellensi et priore et conventu Bathoniensi ad regimen episcopatus Bathoniensis de assensu nostro canonice et sollempniter electum paternitati vestre supplicantes quatinus eleccionem suam confirmare velitis. Teste Domino P. Wyntoniensi episcopo apud Dokemerfelde, xx°iii° die Aprilis.

In omnium vero predictorum testimonium presenti scripto sigilla nostra apponi fecimus. Datum mense Julii Anno incarnacionis dominice Millesimo ducentesimo quadragesimo secundo. Commissioners warranty under seal.

On the flap: "W. scripsit."

APPENDIX T.

Pacification, A.D. 1246. CHARTERS 45, 46, 47.

OMNIBUS ad quos presens scriptum pervenerit T. prior et conventus Bathoniensis salutem in domino.

Litteras venerabilis patris domini Rogeri Bathoniensis et Wellensis episcopi nostri super reformacione pacis inter nostram et Wellensem ecclesias inspeximus in hec verba.

> Omnibus Christi fidelibus ad quos presens scriptum pervenerit. Rogerus miseracione divina Bathoniensis et Wellensis episcopus salutem in domino sempiternam.
>
> Mediator Dei et hominum dominus Jhesus Christus a patre procedens sibique coeternus et consubstantialis existens, ut nos primorum prevaricacione parentum dampnatos a potestate seductoris eriperet, et summo patri genus reconciliaret humanum in se inmortalis existens et impassibilis, homo factus se

passibilem exhibuit et mortalem, et demum voluntariam resolutus in mortem professionis diverse fidei christiane rectores instituit, ut sicut ipse semper cum patre unus extitit non divisus, nos in fidei et caritatis unione conservent, hos quidem juditiali gladio reprimentes, illos suavitate moderaminis demulcentes.

<small>Both chapters consent to award.</small> Nos igitur licet inmeriti in partem hujus sollicitudinis evocati que jam premisimus sollicitius attendentes, et pii magistri doctrinam pacificam totis viribus amplectentes, questiones quasdam et controversias pridem subortas earumque materias inter ecclesias Bathoniensem et Wellensem quibus disponente domino presidemus amputare penitus affectantes, de consensu et voluntate dilectorum in Christo filiorum prioris et conventus Bathoniensis et capituli Wellensis qui ordinacionibus apostolicis super eleccionem pontificis prefitiendi ecclesiis memoratis communiter inter ipsas ecclesias perpetuo fatienda ipsamque eleccionem contingentibus per decanum et capitulum Wellensem impetratis ac promulgatis salvis et in suo robore per omnia duraturis a quibus capitulum Wellense sollempniter et publice tam viva voce quam per litteras suas patentes se per tractatum ordinacionem suposicionem dicto vel facto seu etiam quocumque alio modo in nullo velle recedere protestati sunt, consimili a priore et conventu Bathoniensi super ordinacionibus supradictis protestacione premissa. Quibus etiam protestacionibus salvis per omnia

Appendix T.

super inferius annotatis se provisioni et disposicioni nostre subjecerunt. Quibus ordinacionibus apostolicis ab Innocentio papa quarto per Johannem Sarracenum decanum et capitulum Wellensem impetratis una videlicet sub datum Laterani decimo kalendarum Aprilium, pontificatus ejusdem anno primo, alia vero sub datum Lugduni tercio nonarum Januarii pontificatus ejusdem anno secundo, sicut nec possumus obviare nolentes, sic inter dictas ecclesias in nomine domini nostri Jhesu Christi providendum duximus et disponendum, videlicet quod utraque ecclesia denuntiet alteri quando primo sciverit episcopatum vacare, item major illius ecclesie presens in qua occurrit eleccio ea vice fatienda denuntiabit cum qua convenit et fieri poterit celeritate capitulo illius ecclesie in qua non fuerit adtunc eleccio fatienda diem quo debeant convenire apud Ferntoñ per procuratores suos litteratorie constitutos ad ordinandum hinc inde procuratores suas ad curiam domini Regis sine more dispendio destinandos pro petenda communiter licentia eligendi, qui simul eant veniant ad dominum Regem petant et redeant termino competenti tunc ibidem ab eisdem communiter statuendo quo dominum Regem possint adire et utraque pars eat sumptibus ecclesie sue cum litteris procuratoriis ecclesie sue, in quibus contineatur quod procuratores suos propriis nominibus eorum expressis destinant ad dominum Regem una cum procuratoribus alterius ecclesie

Papal bulls on the case.

Award.

similiter propriis nominibus eorum expressis ad petendum communiter ab eodem licentiam eligendi prout ad utramque ecclesiam similis spectat eleccio, et hoc ipsum coram domino Rege pariter protestentur litterasque suas simul domino Regi presentent, hujus tamen peticionis pronuntiacionem et priorem litterarum suarum porrectionem habeat procurator illius ecclesie in qua tunc fuerit eleccio fatienda. Licentia vero eligendi optenta, major presens illius ecclesie in qua ea vice non fiet eleccio per litteras capituli sui denuntiabit capitulo alterius ecclesie sine more dispendio diem certum quo convenient procuratores utriusque ecclesie loco superius assignato ad providendum communiter certum terminum competentem, ad quem et infra quem utraque ecclesia omnes de capitulo suo in regno existentes qui eleccioni interesse debent volunt, et possunt, faciant et valeant commode convocari. Cum autem partes die et loco sic sibi ad eligendum prefixis convenerint, invocata Spiritus sancti gratia secundum formam canonicam quam eis Deus tunc inspiraverit, communiter ad eleccionem procedant. Quod si forte primo die eleccioni faciende prefixo partes non poterunt concordare cum communi accione trium vel quatuor dierum secundum quod fuerit necesse procedant donec per aliquam formam canonicam eleccio vel postulacio ibidem incipiat *Te Deum laudamus*, et dicat collectam que fuerit dicenda super electum. Idemque sollempniter denuntiet clero et populo sicut negocii series se habet fideliter nomine utriusque ecclesie eleccionem factam, assistente sibi tunc ibidem majore alterius ecclesie, leganturque ordinaciones papales tunc ibidem et hec eadem scriptura. Decretum autem eleccionis incontinenti communiter et sollempniter unum fiat loco quo tunc celebrata fuit eleccio, et ibidem mox post publicationem consignetur sigillo ejusdem ecclesie, et cum celeritate qua fieri poterit per nuntios communes utriusque capituli fideles transmittatur ad alteram ecclesiam in qua ea vice non fit eleccio sigillo statim illius ecclesie consignandum, et sub sigillis ipsorum procuratorum inclusum fideliter conservetur, nisi quotiens communiter necesse fuerit illud presentari vel exhiberi iterato sub sigillis procuratorum recludendum et conservandum per procuratores ecclesie in qua tunc non fit eleccio usque ad necessariam ipsius exhibicionen. Presentetur autem eleccio celebrata domino Regi per procuratores et litteras procuratorias utriusque ecclesie . et in utrisque litteris fiat mencio de communi eleccione et presentacione, cujus presentacionis pronuntiacionem et priorem litterarum suarum porreccionem habeat procurator illius ecclesie in qua tunc non fiebat eleccio, simul tamen eant veniant ad dominum Regem et redeant, et cetera fiant ut supra in peticione licentie eligendi scriptum est, et super assensu regio optento super eleccione facta et de persona electa nomine utriusque ecclesie impetrentur littere regie dirigende domino Cantuariensi, vel alii presidenti et confirmandi protestatem habenti. Quod si eleccioni dominus rex suum assensum adhibere distulerit vel denegaverit nomine utriusque ecclesie et sumptibus et per procuratores earundem prosecucio dicti fiat negocii husjumodi sumptibus et aliis quibuscumque circa eleccionem vel ipsius eleccionis negocium, qualitercumque contingentibus factis et fatiendis ab electo confirmato vel consecrato, et possessionem temporalium optinente. utrique ecclesie reddendis. Item fiat presentacio eleccionis electi et decreti domino Cantuariensi vel alii presidenti et confirmandi potestatem habenti . et peticio confirmacionis eiusdem ab eodem simul per procuratores utriusqe ecclesie. Quam peticionem et decreti presentacionem primo fatiat procurator illius ecclesie in qua ea vice eleccio facta fuit. Examinenturque super eleccoione et electi persona et meritis ijdem procuratores et alii qui fuerint presentes de utraque ecclesia. Et si fuerit eleccio conconfirmata major illius ecclesie in qua non fuerit eleccio celebrata qui presens fuerit et potens incipiat *Te Deum laudamus*, et dicat collectam que fuerit dicenda super electum. Optenta itaque confirmacione fiat presentacio eleccionis confirmate et electi domino Regi prout superius scriptum est in presentacione eleccionis facte fatienda eidem, nonineque utriusque ecclesie impetrentur littere domini Regis super possessione temporalium optinenda, et fidelitatem fatiat electus, domino Regi nomine utriusque ecclesie. Item neutra partium procurabit quocumque modo aliquod impedimentum quo minus altera partium admittatur ad eleccionem et ad omnia alia ipsam eleccionem contingentia prout ordinatum est per dominum papam et utrinque concessum. Item omnia que dicta sunt circa electionem observentur in omnibus et per omnia circa postulacionem si per postnlacionem procedatur salvo jure canonico statuto circa naturam postulacionis. Procuret autem utraque dictarum eccleisarum cum apud eam fuerit eleccio fatienda omnem securitatem et tranquillitatem in villa sua personis alterius capituli illuc ad eleccionem venientibus et familie eorundem compescantque suos ab omnibus probris injuriis et contumeliis inserendis eisdem. Item fiat postulacio consecracionis a consecratore per procuratores utriusque ecclesie et nomine utriusque. Pronuntiacionem autem postulacionis predicte habeat major presens illius ecclesie in qua ea vice non fiebat eleccio, assistente sibi majore alterius ecclesie qui presens fnerit leganturque tunc ibidem ordinaciones papales et hec scriptura. Item professionem suam fatiat electus nomine utriusque ecclesie. Item in examinacione, in consecracione sua et in aliis contingentibus ipsam consecracionem stet a dextris electi major illius ecclesie qui presens fuerit in qua illa eleccio facta non fnit, et major alterius ecclesiie presens a sinistris. Item offitia episcopalia vicissim et successive fiant in ipsis ecclesiis, ut synodi, ordinum ordinacio, et crismatis consecratio, quantum in capitulis est ipsis contrarium non procurantibus. Item in synodis et in aliis congregacionibus publicis in dyocesi fatiendis, Prior Bathoniensis sedeat a dextris Episcopi Wellensis et Decanus a sinistris, Bathoniensis e converso, in aliis vero locis cum convenerint pro disposicione Episcopi. Item quod cape abbatum benedicendorum alternatim et successive cum professionibus suis ipsis ecclesiis conferantur, et professiones ipsorum semper fiant nomine utriusque ecclesie. Item quod nec prebende Wellenses antique, nec de novo imprebendate seu ecclesie commune Wellensis, sed nec ecclesie spectantes ad jurisdictionem Decani et capituli vel alicujus canonici sequantur processiones Pentecostes ad loca in quibus monachi Bathonienses recipiunt oblaciones Pentecostes, nisi ille tantum in quarum possessione nunc sunt.

Hanc autem provisionis et disposicionis nostre formam utraque pars sibi recitatam sollempniter approbavit et ad ipsam per omnia et in omnibus fideliter et bona fide inter se perpetuo observandam, seque nullo umquam tempore in aliquo contravenire pro se et successoribus suis juramento in animas omnium et singulorum utriusque ecclesie corporaliter prestito per procuratores suos hinc inde per litteras patentes Capitulorum ad hoc ita jurandum, et ad hanc provisionem et disposicionem nostram admittendum et recipiendum spetialiter constitutos, se obligavit. In cujus rei robur et testimonium Prior et conventus Bathoniensis et capitulum Wellense una cum sigillo nostro presenti scripto sigilla sua apposuerunt. Actum apud Staweye in parochia de Chyv, Idus Augusti anno incarnacionis dominice millesimo ducentesimo quadragesimo sexto.

Nos igitur predicte provisionis et disposicionis formam ratam habentes et gratam ei nostrum per omnia adhibemus assensum . et hoc presenti scripto nostro protestamur. In cujus rei robur et testimonium de communi consensu eidem sigilla nostra apposuimus. Datum Bathonie in capitulo nostro quartodecimo kalendarum Semptembrium anno incarnacionis dominice millesimo ducentesimo quadragesimo sexto.

Endorsed :—Confirmacio provisionis. *(13th cent.)*
    1246. Prior et Conventus Bathonie. *(15th cent.)*
    Formula electionis Episcopi per Rogerum Episcopum. *(Late.)*

APPENDIX U.

Letters of pope Innocent IV.

1.—Add. MSS. British Museum, 15355, f. 116.
Innocentius etc. Priori et Conventui Bathoniensi.
Ann. i. Epist. 567.

Preamble.

1. Prolixa litis dilatio, pacis emula, nutrix discordie, comodi parca, larga dispendii, gladii judicialis ictum non sine litigantium jactura multiplici et gravi justitie lesione suspendit, exactrix quidem sumptuum, et laborum extortrix, sic ei veritatem implicite confusione processus involvit ut vix postmodum adhibita etiam attentionis manu sollicite audeat explicari propter quod sepius litigantes post expensas inutiles et labores inanes dampnum sustinent sui juris.

Unde sedis Apostolice providentia illud circa causarum strepitus quantum est in ipsa moderantie studium adhibet, ut prorogationis detrimento vitato post debite ventilationis examen vel juste mucrone sententie decidantur, aut amicabili sopiantur concordia, seu etiam meta ipsis equa provisione figatur quatinus partium parcatur sumptibus, quieti provideatur eorum et cuique jus suum integre conservetur.

Prayer of Wells chapter for cassation of Roger's election rejected.

2. Sane bone memorie Episcopo viam universe carnis ingresso vos dilectum filium nunc Electum vestrum, tunc precentorem Saresberiensem in Episcopum elegistis vobis tandem electionem nobis hujusmodi per Thomam et Gilibertum monachos vestros nuntios presentantibus eamque petentibus confirmari, dilectus filius J. Sarracenus capellanus noster Decanus Wellensis Ecclesie pro eadem ecclesia ex adverso respondit, quod cum contemptis eo et capitulo Wellensi

qui debebant de jure requiri, et erant in possessione vel quasi una vobiscum Pontificem eligendi, predicta electio celebrata fuisset, confirmanda non erat sed potius irritanda.

3. Nobis itaque ne diu maneret grex dominicus absque cura, et episcopatus ex longa vacatione grave in spiritualibus et temporalibus incurreret detrimentum, prefatum Electum eidem episcopatui sine cujuslibet prejudicio in episcopum preficientibus de plenitudine potestatis utriusque partis nuntii humiliter petierunt ut ne in posterum cum episcopatum eundem vacare contingeret posset ex hoc super electione Pastoris litigium exhoriri previdere in hac parte paterna sollicitudine curaremus. *Confirmation of Roger's election.*

4. Nos igitur futuris volentes obviare periculis omnemque litis materiam amputare, de fratrum nostrorum consilio ex eadem potestatis plenitudine, sic super his duximus providendum ut decetero cum episcopatus ipse vacaverit, vos et iidem Decanus et Capitulum simul electioni celebrande de Presule intersitis pares in hoc penitus existentes, ita quod utraque partium licet forte plures sint ex una quam ex altera parem et equalem in eligendo, postulando, et alias procurando eidem episcopatui provideri habeat potestatem. Et si earum aliqua uni vel duobus ex ipsa super hoc commiserit vices suas illius vel eorum non minus valeant quam omnes relique partis voces, statuentes ut electionis processus aliter habitus sit omnino vacuus et irritus ipso jure, utrique ipsarum in aliis jure salvo videlicet vestri sit electio celebranda, in qua ecclesia Sedes esse debeat Cathedralis, et fieri habeat Pontificis installatio, et etiam cujus ecclesie sit Episcopus nomin- *Provision for future elections.*

andus. Datum Laterani Kalendis Aprilis anno primo (*March* 23, 1244.)

F. 153.
2.—Ann. ii. Epist. f. 185. (*Jan.* 3, 1245.)
Innocentius etc. Decano et Capitulo Wellensi.

After preamble reciting the former judgment of March 23, 1244:

Nos periculis futuris occurrere ac Bathoniensi, et Wellensi ecclesiarum paci et tranquilitati plenius consulere cupientes . . . . . statuimus, ...

Ut cum episcopatus ipse vacaverit, prima vice in Bathoniensi, alia vero in Wellensi ecclesiis, et sic vicissim semper in ipsis Pontificis electio celebretur, et utraque Cathedralis existat. Ubi autem celebrata fuerit electio, ibi primo installetur Pontifex, et utriusque ecclesie Episcopus nominetur, Bathoniensis videlicet et Wellensis, et sic in sigillo contineatur ipsius. . . . . .
Lugduni. iii Nonas Januarii anno secundo.

F. 235.
3.—Ann. ii. Epist. 556. (*May* 14, 1245.)
Innocentius etc. Bathoniensi et Wellensi Episcopo.

Cum juxta ordinationem nostram Bathoniensis et Wellensis Episcopus debeas nominari, idque in tuo sigillo debeat contineri, tu hoc pro tue voluntatis arbitrio facere denegas, prout dilectorum filiorum decano et capitulo Wellensis exhibita nobis patefecit. Volentes igitur ut talia corrigas per teipsum fraternitati tue per apostolica scripta firmiter precipiendo mandamus, quatinus juxta prefate ordinationis tenorem Bathonień et Welleń te nomines, et id apponi facias in sigillo. Mandatum nostrum taliter impleturus, quod super hoc aliter scribere non cogamur. Datum Lugduni, ii. Idus Maii anno secundo.

APPENDIX W.

Notices of Chapels and Altars in the Church of Wells,
A.D. 1136-1333.[1]

High altar dedicated to *St. Andrew*. R. i, f. 46, A.D. 1148; cf. R. iii, f. 5, A.D. 1246; R. i, f. 112, A.D. 1281.

Altar of *St. Cross*. Charter 5, R. iii, f. 245, A.D. 1148-1166: in north part of the church: east aisle of north transept: at the entrance to the chapter house. Cf. R. ii, f. 77, A.D. 1500.

Altar of *St. Calixtus*, in east aisle of south transept. Charter 5, R. iii, f. 245, A.D. 1148-1166.

> Chantry of dean Peter. R. iii, ff. 5, 131; A.D. 1238.
> Chantry of dean Hussey. R. i, f. 52, R. iii, f. 277, A.D. 1307.

Chapel of *St. Martin juxta fontem*, in east aisle of south transept, A.D. 1206-1242; R. i, f. 124; cf. Charter 759; Ledger D, f. 30.

Chapel of *St. Mary*. R. i, f. 31; A.D. 1088-1136.

> Repaired. R. i, f. 41; A.D. 1196.
> Daily mass instituted by Savaric. R. i, f. 46; iii, f. 136.
> Daily mass instituted by Jocelin. R. iii, f. 127; i, f. 43.
> . . . *retro magnum altare*. R. iii, f. 124; A.D. 1277; i, f. 128; A.D. 1298.

---

1. See plan of church.

Chapel of *St. Mary* in burial ground east of cloister.[1]
    R. i, f. 64; A.D. 1243.
        . . . *in australi parte ecclesiæ juxta claustrum.*
        Charter 83; R. iii, f. 291; A.D. 1250.
        Charter 95; A.D. 1268.
        R. iii, ff. 282, 293; A.D. 1269. R. i, ff. 22, 90; A.D. 1269-1271.

Altar of *St. Nicholas* in *Chapel of St Mary.*
    R. i, f. 22; iii, f. 124; A.D. 1276.
    R. i, f. 62; iii, f. 175; A.D. 1277.
    R. i, f. 127; A.D. 1301.
    R. i, f. 179; A.D. 1330.

Altar of *St. Saviour.* R. i, f. 2; iii, f. 180; A.D. 1254.

Altar of *St. Mary Magdalene, in boreali parte.* R. i, ff. 63, 116; iii, f. 127; A.D. 1263.

Altar of *St. Edmund, Confessor, in navi ecclesiæ.* R. i, f. 87; A.D. 1269.

Altar of *St. Cross*, at entrance into the church on the north side under the belfry. R. iii, f. 284; A.D. 1305.

Altar of *St. Catherine, St. Mary Magdalene, St. Margaret.* R. i, ff. 181, 184; A.D. 1329.

Altar of *Corpus Christi.* R. i, ff. 179, 180; A.D. 1330 "adhuc dedicandum."

"Extract from a MS. note book formerly belonging to the Rev. Mr. Bowen, one of the Priest Vicars of the Cathedral" (circa 1800?), found in Mr. Serel's notes to Britton's *Wells Cathedral.* In Serel Collection in Taunton Museum.

"In the south aisle in the back side of the Quire

---

1. See plan of chapel near the cloister.

are three ancient effigies of bishops of this church before the present fabric was built; the first is bishop Burwold, died in 1088; the next above is bishop Ethelwine, he died 1023 ; the next is bishop Brythwyn, died 1074.

In the north aisle bishops Brighthelm, Kineward, Alwyn, Giso, the last bishop before removal of the see to Bath, four effigies put here after the re-edifying present fabric, and the Founder placed those four effigies in memory of those sixteen antient bishops who governed the see from its first foundation before the removal and died here bishops."

Then follows the account of bishop Drokensford's tomb, quoted in note to p. 313: "In a chappell beyond the quire is a curious tomb for bishop John Drokensford. It was neatly arched and painted and gilded, and his effigy lying thereon, which arching was taken down in 1758, when the high altar was being decayed and seemed in danger of falling. So the tomb for bishop William Bitton the second,[1] died 1274, was finely painted and arched over, and pinnacled above upon the top and at the sides and corners, but being decayed, was in 1758 taken down."[2]

"The high altar[3] was full of niches with images of apostles and saints therein finely painted, which, after the Reformation, were all broken and the whole plastered up as a plain wall; and so it stood till about the year 1758, when the whole was taken down and removed entirely away, many of the broken images

1. A mistake for 1st, who died 1264.
2. This monument was restored by dean Goodenough, 1840-1845.
3. Is Reredos here meant?

being found therein, particularly one almost entire of the woman with child and the dragon ready to devour."

APPENDIX X.

Plan of Chapel, " juxta claustrum," *east of cloister*.

Extensive excavations in the ground south of the church and on the east side of the cloister have been carried on by the dean and chapter during the spring of 1894.

It had been generally known, from evidence contained in the chapter documents, that buildings existed on this ground from very early times until their destruction in 1552. But the exact sites and character of these buildings were matters of conjecture.

The foundations of two buildings have now been laid bare, on different levels, and with different lines and dimensions.

One was a small rectangular building of somewhat less than 50 feet from cloister wall to eastern end, consisting of nave, and two aisles. A base of a column with mouldings of the latter part of the 13th century attached to the cloister wall remains to show that there was an arcading between nave and south aisle. Some floor tiling has been found *in sitû*, at the lower level in the nave, and on the inside edge of the southern wall. Numerous fragments of similar tiles and of different designs have been found in most of the trenches dug in this part. Two stone coffins were seen lying below the level of the floor. The lids of these coffins were broken across, but no attempt was made to disturb the graves.

There is a remarkable peculiarity about these foundations, that the lines of building tend in a direction rather north of east, and their orientation does not exactly agree with that of the great church.

There can be no doubt that this rectangular building was "*the chapel of the Blessed Virgin Mary which is set in the south part of the great church near the cloister,*" so described in many documents of the thirteenth century. It was a chapel of great antiquity, and the foundations may be of an earlier date than the church of the thirteenth century. There is a continuous history of a building on this site called "the Lady-chapel by the cloister," from the middle of the thirteenth century until 1552. But within this time there were two chapels, one succeeding the other, on the same ground.

This first chapel was richly endowed for the celebration of funeral services, or obits, of two bishops and other members of the Bytton family in the thirteenth century—of dean Godley and others in the fourteenth. It was the court of the dean's official also in the fourteenth and fifteenth centuries. Ordinations were frequently held here. Entries in the register of bishop Stillington (1466-1491) show that ordinations were held here up to the year 1469. After that year no ordinations in that chapel are recorded, until the first year of bishop Fox's episcopate, 1492.

It is very probable that it was in that interval the old chapel was pulled down and a new and larger chapel was built there by bishop Stillington. Of this later chapel the foundations have now been traced of north and south walls of a nave, starting from the cloister wall and the present door in the east cloister wall, and resting on the older foundations—of north and south transepts ending in circular or octagonal turrets, and of a chancel extending more than 120 feet from the west end of the cloister.

These foundations ran in lines exactly parallel with the orientation of the great church.

Some of the bosses of the vaulting of this later building which were found in the ground, are of great size and elaborate carving, and give evidence of the sumptuous character of the internal architecture of this building of the fiifteenth century, which was contemporary with the chapel of St. George, at Windsor, where Edward IV was buried in 1473, and a little earlier than the chapel of Henry VII at Westminster begun in 1503.

There is no doubt that we have here the foundations of the chapel built by Bishop Stillington, which was destroyed in 1552.

I am indebted to Mr. Edmund Buckle, the diocesan architect, under whose superintendence the late excavations have been made, for the accompanying plan of the earlier Lady-chapel.

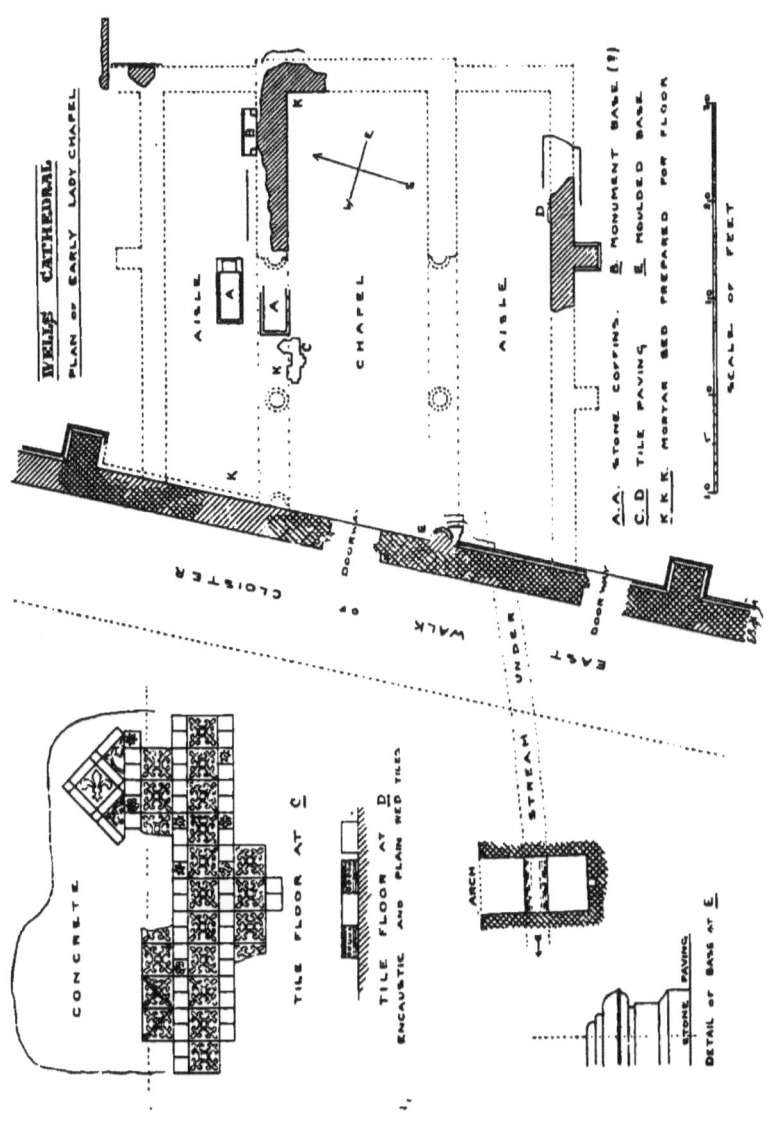

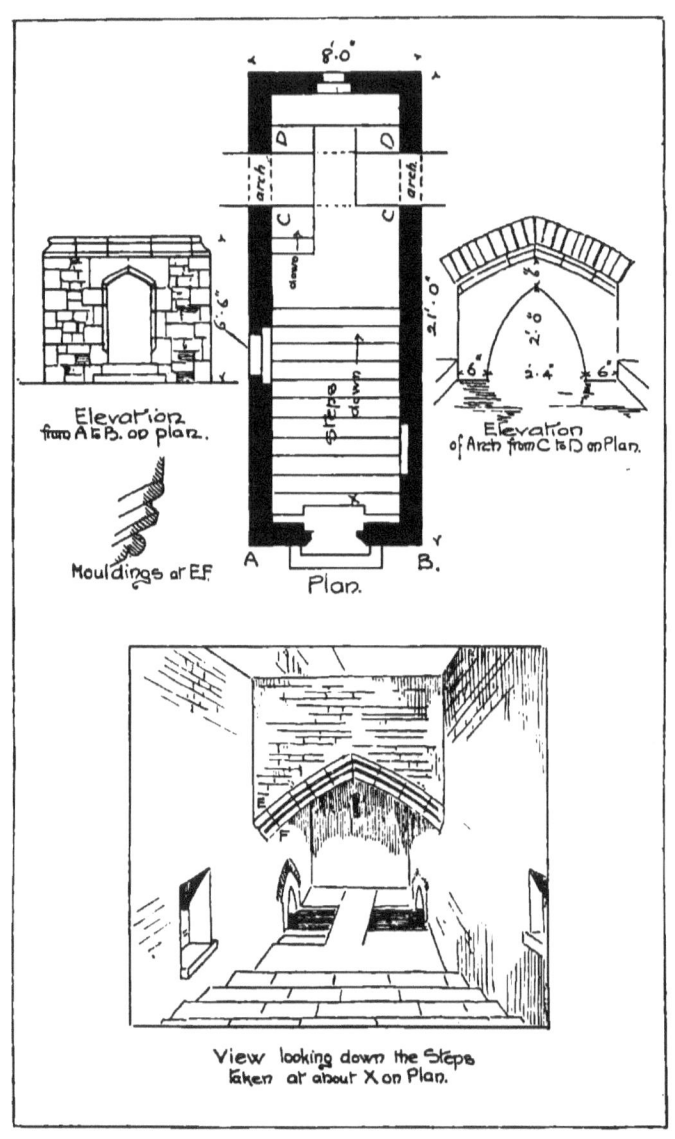

BUILDING OVER OLD WATERCOURSE IN BURIAL GROUND
SOUTH OF CATHEDRAL CHURCH, WELLS.

APPENDIX Y.

Plan of building over watercourse in " Palm Churchyard."

LATE excavations have also brought to light the foundations of a building over an old watercourse in the Palm Churchyard, of which a plan is given, drawn by Mr. F. J. Dollman, from "Carter's Ancient Architecture of England."[1]

A watercourse, conducted in a channel of very strong and carefully worked stone masonry, from the spring head in St. Andrew's well and through the ground south of the church, passes under the wall of the east cloister into the " Palm " churchyard, and thence under the houses on the north side of the market place, and falls ultimately into the bed of the old mill stream.

The building over it, of which the plan is given, was in existence in the memory of some now living at Wells. The position in relation to the present cloister buildings seems to indicate that it belongs to an earlier arrangement of buildings on this ground.

Carter gives this account of the building as drawn by him in 1794:

"*A. B.* Plan, with elevation, in north view of a lavatory in the area of the cloisters of Wells cathedral. The design is walled round, and a plain doorway gives admittance therein.

" View in ditto, looking south.

---

[1]. Carter's *Ancient Architecture of England*, folio, plate xliii, p. 36 (1795).
See also Carter's *Architectural and Monumental Drawings*, Vol. VIII, ed. 1794. Add. MSS. 299-32 : British Museum.

"Having descended the introducing steps, we see on our left an aumbury, or cupboard, for keeping of linen, etc. Before us is an arched headway, directly over the bathing place, and to the right and left are the arches of the aqueduct: through that arch, on the left, the water issues, and from thence runs into the town.

"*C. D.* Foot-stones over and on the sides of the stream, with elevation of the arch through which the water issues. At the side are the aumburies and a niche at head of archway.

"*E. F.* Architrave to the arch in the lavatory."

INDEX.

ABBEYS.—
Athelney, 119, 142, 203, 218. Bath, see "Bath." Bec, 21 (n.), 36, 269. Cluni, 27. Evesham, 101. Eynsham, 98 (n.). Lacock, 209. Lonley, 203. Malmesbury, 27, 101, 192. St. Alban's, 97 (n.).

Abbots of—
Athelney, 19, 334; cited for breach of canonical oath, 269. Bec, 21 (n.), 119 (and n.), 142, 169; stall for, 328, 334. Clairvaux, 51. Evesham, 101, 383. Feversham, 72. Glastonbury, 7, 94, 99, 116, 199. Malmesbury, 101, 383. Muchelney, 19, 114, 142, 169, 186, 187; stall for, 328, 334. Reading, 72, 197. St. Alban's, 173. St. Augustine's, 41. St. Edmund's, 107. St. Exuperius, 40, 41, 73. St. Michael, Martock, 202. "St. Michael de periculo mortis," in Normandy, 210. Sherborne, 100, 383.

Abbotsbury, 100, 114, 217, 383.
à Becket, see "Becket."
Acton Burnell, (Salop), 288.
Acton, Roger de, 317 (n.).
Adam de Ammeville, 261.
Adam de Budeford, 216.
Adam de Domerham, 8 (n.), 56, 57, 58, 95, 96, 99, 103 (n.), 105 (n.), 106 (n.), 107 (n.), 110, 111 (n.), 114 (n.), 117, 176, 191, 192, 196, 197, 219, 221, 230.
Adam de Litton, priest, 177.
Adam de Sutton, 364.
Adrian IV, pope, 22, 50, 97 (n.).

Advowsons.—
Axbridge, 190. Bertun (Barton) St. David's, 179. Chew, 190. Congresbury, 143. Dinder, 207. Dogmersfield, 191. Hinton St. George, 203. Ilton, 203. Lideard, 143. Mudford, 143. Norton, 209. Nunny, a moiety of, 179. Stoke Giffard, 190. Sutton, 203. Wells, St. Cuthbert's, 143. Weston in Gordano, 203. Whitchurch, 208. Winscombe, 143.

Agnellus, Thomas, archdeacon of Wells, 62; preaches funeral sermon on young king Henry, ib.
Ailtredehull, 205 (and n.).
Alan de Fornellis, justiciar, 373.
"Alba Aula," see "Whitehall."
Albigenses, condemned by the Lateran council, 51.
Albiniato, Philip de, seneschal, 224.
Aldford, Michael of, 82.
Aldhelm, 1.
Alexander, canon of Wells, 148.
Alexander, dean of Wells, 62, 82, 89 (n.), 100, 104, 128 (n.), 131, 167, 169, 185.
Alexander III, pope, 22, 42, 51, 64; canonizes Thomas à Becket, 43.
Alexander, subdean, 81, 128 (n.).
Alfonso of Castile, 133.
Alicia, mother of Robert de Vallibus, 186.
Alitheford (Alford), Thomas of, 227.
Alneto, Fulco de, 358.

Altars of—
The Holy Cross, 32. St. Andrew, 286, 324, 329. St. Calixtus, 228. St. Cuthbert, 313 (n.). St. John Baptist, ib. St. Mary, 286, 324, 325, 331; site of in thirteenth century, 331. St. Nicholas, 280 (and n.).

Altars and Chapels, A.D. 1136-1333, 419.
Altariste, 346 (n.), 348.
Altaville, Reginald de, 179.
Altaville, Thomas de, 203.
Alured de Ponson, lord of South Barrow, 81; grandson of, 227.
Amandus, Magister, 169.

428 *Index.*

Ambresbury, 46.
Andrew, St., church of, at Wells, 1, 2, and passim.
Anjou, Henry, duke of, 33, 34.
Annellarii, 346 (and *n*.).
Anselm, 36, 39, 216.
"Antiqua institutio" of Lincoln, 20.
"Antiqua Statuta" of Wells, 15, 20, 340.
Apulia, Simon of, bishop of Exeter, 176.
Arbitration by Jocelin between Elias and the archdeacon of Wells, 217; about patronage of South Barrow, 227; about prebend and advowson of Warminster, 224.
Arbitrators, persons suggested for, at home and abroad, 250.
Archbishops.—
Of Aragon, 104. Baldwin, 52, 62, 69, 71, 72, 91, 97, 104 (*n*.). Becket, Thomas à, 33, 83. Boniface, of Canterbury, 233. Of Bourges, 51. Of Canterbury, 113, etc. Of Dublin, 69, 113. Geoffrey, of York, 103. Hubert Walter, 95, 97, 104, 110. Lanfranc, 5. Langton (Ste.), 134, 174, 209. Of Narbonne, 51. Rich, Edmund, of Canterbury, 219. Of Ragusa, 113. Richard (prior of Dover), 42, 44, 51, 90. Roger de Pont l'Evêque, 33, 42, 83. Of Rouen, 69, 74. Tarentaise, Peter of, 47 (and *n*.). Thurstan de Bayeux (of York), 12, 354. Of Trèves, 69. Walter de Gray (of York), 169 (*n*.), 243, 261. Walter of Rouen, 74, 92, 93. William de Corbeil, 12. York, 33, 42, 83, 103.
Archdeacons.—
Benthelius, 5. Of Canterbury, 104. Hugh, of Wells, 166, 169, 171, 181, 210. John, son of Hildebert, 6. Peter of Blois, 62, 169. Richard, of Bath, 61. Robert de Geldeford, 81. Robert, of Wells, 19, 29, 30, 31, 61. Savaric, of Canterbury, 90. Thomas, of Bath, 19, 29 (*n*.), 30, 31, 61. Thomas, of Glastonbury, 194. Thomas, of Wells (Agnellus), 62, 78, 81, 128 (*n*.). William of Bardeney, of Wells, 193. William de Wrotham, of Taunton, 166, 169, 171. William, of Winchester, *ib*.
Archer, 23 (*n*.), 25, 37, 144, 145 (*n*.), 190 (*n*.), 196, 202, 224, 237, 299 (*n*.), 312 (*n*.); discredits a group of charters, 188 (*n*.)
Arches, court of, bishop William Bytton cited to by the chapter, 266.
Archives of Siguenza, 133.
Area Canonicorum, 140.
Arthur, king, invention of his bones, 57; legend of, *ib.*
Arundel, Matilda, wife of Gerbert de Perci, 373.
Ascelin, bishop of Rochester, 27.
Ashill, advowson of, 186.
Assessment on prebends, 268.
Athelney, 19, 119, 203.
Audit, one per annum, 233, 274.
Audits, four required, 274, 300.
Aulescombe, 373.
Avenant, Thomas de, 203.
Avenel, Oliver, chaplain to the Lady Matilda, 202.
Avranches, Henry II's purgation and penance at, 43.
Axbridge, advowson of, 190; John de, subdean, 274, 279; the vill of, sold, 181; bought up by Jocelin, 210; granted by Hugh, 212.
Aystona (Easton), 358.

BALDOCK, Robert, chancellor, 293 (*n*).
Baldwin, archbishop of Canterbury, *see* "Archbishops."
Banwell, 4, 18, 359; dues to the hundred of, reserved, 230.
Barbarossa, the emperor Frederick, 45
Barewe, Nicolas de, 81.
Barlynch Priory, 67, 183.
Barn, the canons', 78 (*n*.)
Barons unite to compel king John to confirm the liberties of Henry I, 188.
Barrow, religious house at, 183.
"Barton" given to the "communa," 179.
Bath Abbey granted to see of Wells, 6; for 150 years the burial-place of the bishops of the see, 241; chapter of, acquiesce in the election of William of Bytton, 264; attempt to secure the election of their own nominee, 241; their mode of proceeding, 241, 242;

ratify the Wells election of Reginald, 397; church at, begun by John of Tours, 24, 26; city seized in the name of the king, 97; "civitas Bathoniensis," 145; complains against Savaric, 114; hospital of St. John Baptist at, 358; lepers' house at, 183; precedence of prior over dean of Wells, 200; prerogative of, over Wells, 146; prior and convent surrender certain advowsons, 190, 191; protests against Savaric, 96, 97; refuses conference with Wells, 244; Reginald's buildings at, 86; Robert, prior, elected abbot of Glastonbury, 207; the "sedes praesulea," 50; transfer of see from Wells to Bath decreed, and carried out, 5, 6; "Bath and Wells," not the original joint title, 23; earliest assumption of, 144; ordered by Innocent IV to be the bishop's style, 146; Thomas, prior of, 228, 232, 233.
Battle of Evesham, 276; of Hastings, 32; of Lewes, 276; of Lincoln, 33.
Bayeux 13 (and n.)
Bec, 21 (n.), 36; abbot of, defaulter, 269; abbot of, excommunicated, ib.
Bechamstede, William de, canon, 222.
Becket, Thomas à, archbishop of Canterbury, 33; canonized, 43; displeased with Henry III, 83; excommunicates Reginald and Ffolliot, 41; Henry II counselled against him, 38 and (n.); Henry's proceedings, 42; murdered, 42; reaction in favour of his cause, 42, 48; record of his murder, 133, 134; sent on an embassy to Paris, 40; withdraws from England, 41.
Bedford, Henry III's siege of, 208.
Benedict, abbot of Athelney, 203, 207.
Bennett, Rev. J. A., 298 (n).
Benthelius, archdeacon, 5
Berihal (Beryl), land at, 139, 204, and (n).
Bernard, bishop of St. David's, 33.
Bernard, T. D., chancellor of Wells, 73 (n.), 123 (n.)
Bethshemesh, 31.

Beverley, William of York, provost of, 246.
Bidding Prayer, 336.
Biddisham, manor of, 16, 18, 20; prebend of, 20, 343.
Bishops.—
Aldhelm of Sherborne, 1. Ascelin of Rochester, 27. Baldwin of Worcester, 52. Bangor, Robert de Shrewsbury, bishop of, 172. Bernard of St. David's, 33. Burnell of Bath and Wells, 285, 324. Bytton, William I, of Bath and Wells, 80 (n). Bytton, William II, 328. Chester, 11. Coutances, 38, 48. Drokensford, 80 (n.) Dudoc, 26. Durham, Hugh Pudsey, 68, 70. Eustace of Ely, 107. Fighting Bishops, 11. Giso, 3, 4, 5, 16, 17, 26, 31, 32, 84, 85. Godfrey, 6, 7, 17. Godwin (of Llandaff and Hereford), 6 (n.), 23 (n.), 25 (and n.), 37, etc. Gundolf of Rochester, 27. Henry of Sully, bishop of Worcester, 99 (n). Henry of Winchester, see "Henry of Blois." Hugh of Durham, 68, 70. Hugh of Lincoln, 98 (and n.), 129, 209. Hugh Nonant of Coventry, 70, 97. Jocelin of Bath and Wells, 79 (n.), 87, 115, etc. Jocelin of Sarum, 25, 41. John of Tours, 6, 11, 16, 85, 144. Llandaff, Henry of Abergavenny, 172. London, William of Ste. Mère l'Eglise, bishop of, 99 (n), 172. Osmund of Sarum, 7. Peter of Winchester, see "Peter des Roches," 195. Poictiers, 51. Poore, Herbert, and Richard, bishops of Sarum, 136. Rainard, 128 (n.) Ralph of Shrewsbury, 321. Reginald, see under " Reginald of Wells." Reiner of St. Asaph, 172. Remigius of Lincoln, 7. Richard de Bohun, bishop of Coutances, see "Coutances." Richard [Poore] of Salisbury, 208. Robert of Bath, 27, 155. Robert de Bethune, bishop of Hereford, 25. Robert de Bingham, bishop of Salisbury, 217. Robert Burnell, see "Burnell." Robert de Chesney, bishop of Lincoln, 14. Robert Grossetête of Lincoln, 219. Roger of Bath and Wells, 24 (n.), 29, 80 (n.),

144 (*n.*) Roger of Sarum, 12, 27, 28, 147, 354. Savaric of Bath, 38. Seffred of Chichester, 72. Simon of Apulia, bishop of Exeter, 176. Simon of Worcester, 12, 25, 354. St. David's, Geoffrey de Henlaw, bishop of, 172. Stephen, bishop of Waterford, 229. Sutton, Oliver, bishop of Lincoln, 290. Walkelin of Winchester, 27. Walter Haselshaw, 324. William Brewer of Exeter, 209, 210. William Longchamp, bishop of Ely, 69, 93. William de Marchia, 288. William Warelwast of Exeter, 12, 354.

Blackford in Wedmore, 372.

Blois, Henry of, 7, 8, 12, 27, 35, 55, 56. Peter of, 19, 41.

Bohun family, 38, 89, 376. Engelger de, his evil counsel to Henry II, 38 (*n.*) Franco de, 38, 89. Jocelin de, bishop of Sarum, 38, 39. John de, canon of Wells, 89. Reginald Fitz-Jocelin de, 38, 39. Richard de, bishop of Coutances, *ib.* Roger de, 89 (*n.*) St. André and St. George, villages, 38.

Bolonia, Thomas de, 207.

Boniface of Savoy elected archbishop of Canterbury, 233; letter of pope Innocent IV to, 251.

Bonneville, Robert de, 375.

Bonneville, William de, 203.

Books given to library at Bath by bishop Reginald, 53.

Borough of Wells receives its first charter from bishop Robert, 7, 29; freed from tolls, 30.

Bovey Tracy, 67, 179, 374.

Bovey, South, 199.

Boys, *see* " Pueri canonici."

Bozun, Simon, 375.

Bradenstoke, 171, 192, 230.

Bradshaw, Henry, 13 (*n.*), 15 (*n.*), 20 (*n.*), 23, 24, 272, 275 (*n.*).

Braose, Wm. de, 372.

Breaute, Fulk de, 208.

Brent, South, church ceded to archdeacon of Wells, 56.

Bretanche, William, senior, erects a chapel at Trubbewell, 237.

Brewer, William, counsellor of kings John and Henry, 210.

Brewer, William, bishop of Exeter, 210, 239.

Bristol, convent of St. Augustine at, 234.

Brito, Simon, 67.

Britton, John de, adverse to canonization of William de Marchia, 293 (*n.*).

Britton, John, F.S.A., 87, 156, 313 (*n.*).

Bromley (al. Bromfield), 16, 353.

Brotherhood of St. Chad, 300; of St. Gatien, *ib.*

Bruce, Egidius de, bishop of Hereford, 172.

Brugge, church of, 358.

Bruton, John de, canon, 314.

Buche (Buck), Alicia, 214.

Buche (Buck), William, *ib.*

Buckland, nunnery at, 180, 183, 234; vicarage, 206.

Building operations, evidences of, 148.

Buckerel, Andrew, mayor of London, 227.

Bull for the canonization of Thomas à Becket, 43 (*n.*).

Bunton family, 162, 396.

Burgeys, Roger, 11, 213.

Burgo, Hubert de, justiciar, earl of Kent, 132, 206, 216, 224.

Burnham, right of presentation to, recovered, 206.

Bury, Richard de, dean, 317.

Burying grounds, arrangements of, 152.

Burnell, Robert, bishop of Bath and Wells, 285; chantry to him endowed by dean and chapter, 286 (*n.*); grant to the fabric funds, 286; regent, 276.

Burnell, William, canon, 214.

Buticlarius, 357 (*n.*).

Byham, Gilbert de, precentor, 274.

Bytton, Sir Adam de, 281; family, 279, 331.

Bytton, John de, 279.

Bytton, manor of, 261.

Bytton, Richard, vicar, 243.

Bytton, Thomas, dean, afterwards bishop of Exon, 272, 277 (*n.*), 280 (*n*), 281.

Bytton, William, I, archdeacon of Wells, 217, 238, 242, 261; bishop of Bath and Wells, 257, 275; consecrated at Rome, 257; claims fruits of vacant prebends, 265; is resisted by the chapter, *ib.*; makes

over the sequestrations, 269; sub-dean, 225.
Bytton, William, II, elected by both chapters, 276; his seal described, 277, 278 (*n*.); his tomb, 277 (*n*.), 328.
CADBURY, barony of, 83 (*n*.).
Cade, Ivo, 222.
Cade, Laurence, 222.
Cade, Richard, son of Ivo, 213.
Caerleon, the bishop of, 243.
Caerleon, Walter of, 224.
Calixtus, *see* "St. Calixtus."
Campo florido, Henry de, 203.
Campo florido, John de, 216.
Campomoldo, Speronus de, 122.
Camville, Gerard de, 70, 71.
Camville, Joanna de, 371.
Camville, Richard de, *ib*.
Cannington, religious house at, 183.
Canon of Wells, the, 16, 23, 25, 37, 76, 85, 87, 144, 154, 155, 280 (*n*.).
Canonical houses, grants of, 141, 177, 199; to be annually visited and dilapidations valued, 348.
"Canonicorum magna porta," 140, 154, 177.
Canonization of Thomas à Becket, 43; bull for, *ib*. (*n*.).
Canons' barn, 78 (*n*.).
Canons of Hackington, near Canterbury, 71.
Canons of Wells, 2, 4; assessment made on them for the fabric, 148; complain of Savaric's policy, 114; in the time of bishop Jocelin, 393; lose position by transfer of the see to Bath, 6, 22; pay tithes to adjacent parish churches, 19; precariousness of their tenure, 5; required to live in the town, 6; rivalry of Bath and Glastonbury against, 240; specific grant for their daily sustenance, 17; treated as stipendiaries of the provost, 12; at the time of Jocelin's death, 393.
Canons of Salisbury, their pledge in behalf of the fabric, 196.
Canterbury cathedral, 85; the choir destroyed by fire, 49; dispute with the prior and monks of, 71, 72; double election to the see, 174.
Canutus, P., subscribes to Jocelin's election, 169.
Canutus, William, son of P., 222.
Capitular constitution, first draft of, 11, 13, 21; gradual growth of, 18, 20; become a separate corporate body, 21; relations of Wells with Bath readjusted, 22.
Cardinal, honorarium of, 249. John de Colonna, 249. Octavian, 279. Otho, 209, 227, 231, 249. Richard, 267.
Carenton (Carhampton), 22, 90, 119.
Carlyle, Thomas, 350.
Carthusian house, the first in England, 46; cell at Cheddar, 54; house at Hinton, 208.
Cary (al. Kari), Robert de, 80.
Castle Cary blockaded, 10; church of, 80.
Castle of Harpetre, 10.
Castles, numbers of, 11.
Cathari, *see* "Albigenses."
"Cathedralicum," 226, 300.
Ceddre, church of, 374.
Celestine, *see* under "Popes."
Cenis, Mont, passes of, 45 (and *n*.).
Chambers, J. D., 335.
Chana, wife of Ralph, lord of Beaumont, 38.
Chancellor, duty of, 14; T. D. Bernard, 78 (*n*.); John Forte, 274; Peter of Winchester, 61; Ralph Fitz-Stephen, 57; Richard, 169; Thomas of Retford, 307; the lord high, 169 (and *n*.).
Chantries, endowment of, 312.
Chapels and altars, A.D. 1136-1333, 419.
Chapels of the B.V.M., 17, 82, 84, 331, 419, 422.
Chapel of St. Catherine, 312 (and *n*.); St. Martin, 287; St. Thomas the Martyr, 125.
Chaplains.—
Baldwin, 83. Elia, 183, 187, 213. Jocelin, 61, 82. Roger, 183. William, *ib*.
Chapter House, first notice of, 283; ascent to, 287; date of, according to tradition, 289; diagrams of plan still traceable, 295; finished, 300; first summons of chapter to meet there, 301; gradual erection of, 332; stalls in, differently ordered from those in the choir, 333; style of, 283; the "domus capitularis," 327, 333.
Chapter of Wells, first officers of its new constitution, 61; second

generation of ditto, *ib.*; daily recitation of the psalter by, 20; relations with Bath readjusted, 22; ordinances made upon Jocelin's return, 185; ruridecanal, 81, 82; exempted from fines "de murdris," 212; appeal to king and pope, 243; assert right to sequester vacant benefices, 263; expenses of litigation, etc., 266, 267; independent conduct of, 261; jealous of Roman interference, 268; join that of Lincoln against bishop Grossetête, 262; mortgage their receipts to pay off debt, 268; progressive alteration in their governing power, 258, 259; protest against proceedings of Bath chapter, 242; protest against separate action of Bath, 244; relieved from debt, 269; summoned for first time in new chapter house, 301; alarm of, not due to subsidence of building, 307.

Cerde (Chard), church and manor of, 366.

Chandos, Matilda de, 376.

Chard, vicarage, 220; exemption of, 229; patronage of, *ib.*

Charlton Mackerel, institution to, 195.

Charlton, Walter de, 295.

Charmouth, chapel of, 192.

Charters, 138, 240, 290, 303, 312, 316, 317, etc.; of Adrian IV, 22; of Alexander III, 22, 64, 65; of Clement III, 65; confirmatory of rights, etc., 3, 64; of Editha, 5; of king Edward, 3; of free warren, 33; the Great Charter of 1215, 99, 189 (*n.*); of Henry II, 32, 64; of Innocent III, 187, 349, of Jocelin, 149, 204, 212, 230, 235, 241; relative to Jocelin's family, 128 (*n.*); of king John, 125, 138, 175, 390; of queen Matilda, 4; for the "New Work" at Wells, 82; 121; of pope Nicholas II, 3; Nos. 9, 10, and 13, 128 (*n.*); Nos. 20 and 639, 349 (*n.*); preserved at Wells, 3 (and *n.*); of bishop Reginald, 61, 359; of Richard I, 65, 66, 370; of bishop Robert, 29, 84; of Robert's time, 11, 29; of Robert, prior of Bath, 129; of Savaric, 119 (and *n.*), 121, 123, 124, 125 (and *n.*); of king Stephen, 8; supplementary to institution of prebends, 19; undated, 202; of William I, 3, 4.

Chartreuse, the Great, 40.

Chaseporc, Peter, 243, 244.

Cheddar, Carthusian cell at, 54; forest of, 139; the hundred of, 190; the manor of, *ib.*; grant of, confirmed, 212; liberties of, confirmed, 217.

Chesney, Robert de, 14.

Chester, bishop of, 11.

Chew, advowson of, 190; church of, 118, 193; grant of, 3; grant of land confirmed, 216.

Chewton Church appropriated to the abbey of Jumièges, 234.

Chichester, Henry of, 176; Peter of, 181, 183; Thomas of, 205.

Chilcot, manor of, 16, 29; lands at, granted for altar lights, 329; tithes of, 229.

Choir of Cathedral, extension of, 309.

"Choristarum domus," 142, 349.

Chronicon Wellense, 37.

Chudderleigh, Johannes de, 317 (*n.*)

Chudderleigh, Ricardus de, *ib.*

Churches.—

Aldford, 82. Andrew's, St., Wells, 1, 2, 82. Banwell, 359. Brugges, 358. Carenton [Carhampton], 90, 119. Chew, 118, 193, 329. Combe, 220. Compton Dando, 118. Congresbury, 226, 266. Cuthbert's, St., Wells, 2, 17; dedication of, 17; made over to the canons of Wells, 17. Decuman's, St., 67. Doulting, 1. Easton-in-Gordano, 179. Evercreech, 218. Hache, 243. Ham, 207. Haselbury, 34. Holecumbe, Devon, 176. Huish, 56. Lideard, 119. Lovinton, 80. Malmesbury, 28. Margam, 127. Martock, 202, 210. Milverton, 209. Pancras, St., Lewes, 7, 27; Pilton, 55, 119, 124. Placentia, 122. Sarum, Old, 27. South Barrow, 81. South Brent ceded to the archdeacon of Wells, 56. St. Lo, St.*Thomas, 48 (and *n.*); desecrated, *ib.* (*n.*) Sutton, 119. Waltham, 31. Welinton, 193, 329. Weston, 118. Yarlington, 82.

Cirencester, Thomas de, sheriff of Somerset and Dorset, 203.
Clarembald, abbot of St. Augustine, 41
Clarendon, council of, 41.
Clayton, J. R., 330 (*n*.).
Cleeve Abbey, 21 (*n*.), 67, 119.
Clement III, pope, 65.
Clement V, pope, 344.
Clevedon, Matthew de, 179.
Clifford, Roger de, 206.
Cluni, abbey of, 27.
Cluniac house of St. Pancras, 7, 27.
Cnole, Edward de la, dean, 214.
See under " Deans."
College of Priests at Wells, 2 ; of chantry priests established by bishop Erghum, 141.
Colonna, John de, cardinal, 249.
Combe, John de, 363.
Combe St. Nicholas, manor of, 16, 221 ; præpositus of, 219, 220 ; prebend of, 195.
Combe, Simon de (Cumba), 181.
Commemoration of the departed, 347, 348.
Communa, the first draft of, 11 ; Alured de Ponson's gifts to, 81 ; augmentation of, 231 ; Hugh's gifts to, 137, 183 ; Jocelin's, 193, 194 ; contribution from Nunney, 179 ; Reginald's, 78 ; in bishop Robert's time, 14, 17, 21 ; lands of Hatche and Wrentich confirmed to, 166 ; manor of North Curry confirmed to, *ib*.
Communarius, 223.
Commune of Milan, 109 (*n*.).
Composition between dean and chapter and John of Alre, 218.
Compton Episcopi consecrated and endowed, 225.
Compton Martin, 34.
Comyn, Eustace, 105.
Conclave at Reading, 185.
Concordat between Savaric and Glastonbury, 107 ; to be final, 108 ; provisions of, 108, 109 ; for election of bishop between the chapters of Bath and Wells, 166.
" Concordia finalis," about canonical lands, 219.
Congé d' élire to Glastonbury retained by Jocelin, 116, 133.
Consuetudinaries of Exeter, Salisbury and Wells, 335.

Cormailles, Robert, 312 (*n*.).
Côtentin, the, 38, 48, 99 (*n*.).
Councils.—
Canterbury, 50 (*n*.). Clarendon, 41. Lateran, 50 (*n*.), 51, 65, 68. London, 5, 9, 50 (*n*.), 51. National, 50 (*n*.). In Normandy, 50 (*n*.). Oxford, 93, 206. Pipewell Abbey, 50 (*n*.), 69. Toulouse, 50 (*n*.), 51. Westminster, 44, 50 (*n*.), 51. Woodstock, 50 (*n*.).
Courtenay, Robert de, 179.
Coutances, bishop of, 38, 48, 86.
Coutances, Richard, archdeacon of, 128 (*n*.).
Craucumb, Godfrey de, 224.
Cross, invention of the, 31, 32.
" Cruce signati," 137 (and *n*.), 201.
Crypt, 283, 284, 332.
Curia, the Roman, selfish policy of, 98.
Curry, *see* under " North Curry."
Cuthbert, St. *see* " Churches."
Dacus, William, founds " Alba Aula," 211.
Daily mass in honour of B. V. M. instituted, 123, 137, 331.
Daily recitation of the Psalter (*see* also Psalter), 20.
Daily requiem, 124.
" Dalmatius, Seneschallus Lugdunensis," 90.
Deafforestation of Congresbury manor, 215 ; of North Curry, *ib*.
Dean and chapter a corporate body, 21 ; borrow money for building, 300 ; enforce discipline, 270 ; jurisdiction over town and suburbs, 226. petition the bishop to remove his official principal, 304.
Deans.—
Alexander, 62, 82, 89 (*n*.), 90, 100, 104, 128 (*n*.), 167, 169. Burnell, Walter, 288. Bury, Richard de, 317. Bytton, Thomas, 272, 277 (*n*.) Fordham, John, 194. Giles of Bridport, 271. Godelee (Godley), John, 295, 298, 299, 312, 321, 347. Haselshaw, Walter, 272, 288, 295, 345. Husee, Henry, 295. Ivo, 19, 29 (*n*.), 30, 33, 61, 360. John Saracenus, 151, 194, 232, 246, 260, 262, 270, 271. Knoll (Cnoll), Edward de la, 214, 271, 273 (*n*.), 274, 275, 279, 284. Leonius, 79

K K K

(n.), 185, 187, 188. Littleton, Wybert de, 318. Merton, William de 225. Peter of Chichester, 183, 184, 199, 208, 213, 228, 229. Ralph of Lechlade, 96 (n.), 148, 193, 194. Richard de Spakeston (Spaxton), 33, 61, 62, 78. Stephen de Pempell, 194. Walter de London, 318.
Deanship instituted, 13; election to, 14 and (n.), 21; endowment of, 13, 15; duty assigned to, 14; church of Wedmore made over to, 140; process for appointment to, set forth, 260 (n.)
De Burgh, see "de Burgo."
Decuman, St., 67.
Dedication of the cathedral, 24, 25, 29; of St. Cuthbert's church, 17; of the monastery of St. Pancras, Lewes, 27; of the new church at Glastonbury, 57.
Derham family, 162.
Derham, Elias de, 181, 187, 200; one of the executors of St. Hugh's will, 182, 183.
Desecration, painful instance of, 48 (n.), 3.
"Dictum" of Kenilworth, 276.
Dinder, fee of, unjustly taken by William Fitz-John, 10; prebend of, 260; "imprebendation" of, 340;
Diocesan synod summoned to attest a deed, 19.
Dogmersfield, 290, 312; prebend, 237.
Domerham, Adam de, see "Adam de Domerham."
Domesday survey, 4.
Dominicans come to England, 199.
Domus Capitularis, 327, 333.
Domus Choristarum, 142, 349.
Doulting church, 1.
Dover, Richard, prior of, made archbishop of Canterbury, 44.
Downhead, Alfred de, 177.
Downhead, Ernisius of, 214.
Downhead, Walter de, 139, 177 (and n.), 203, 213.
Drokensford, John de, bishop, 188 (n), 293 (n.), 296; arms on seal, 313 (n.); conflict with dean and chapter as to jurisdiction, 303, 304, 305; obtains license of mortmain, 312; his register, 278, 296, 308 (n.), 310 (n.), 311 (n.); takes the queen's side, 310; tomb described, 313 (n).

Drokensford, Philip de, 313 (n.).
Dudeman, "vallet" and clerk to treasurer, 247.
Dudoc, bishop of Wells, 26, 329.
Dultingcote, (Dulcot), 16, 29, 138.
Dunstan, St., 2, 367.
Dunster, 10.
Durandus, prior of Montacute, 180.
Durham, Hugh, bishop of, 68.
Durham, Philip of Poictiers, bishop of, 104.
Dürrenstein on the Danube, 92.
Dynham, Oliver de, 371.
Dynham, Richard of, rector of Mark, 237.
Dyrham, John of, canon, 246.
EARTHQUAKE, 278.
Easton (Aystona), 358.
Editha, queen, 3.
Edmund, Richard, archbishop of Canterbury, 232.
Edmund, king of East Anglia, 2 (n.).
Edward the Confessor, 3, 26, 31, 38.
Edward the elder, 2.
Edward de Welles, father of Jocelin, 127, 128 (n.).
Edward, I, II, and III, see under "Kings."
Edyngton, Wm. of, bishop's official principal, 304 (n.).
Ela, countess of Salisbury, 187, 208, 215.
Eleanor, daughter of Henry II, 133.
Eleventh century, growth of the see in, 3.
Elias, chaplain, etc., 183, 187, 213, 222, 225, 321; founds an obit, 214; prebendary of Compton, 217.
Ely, see of given to William Longchamps, 69.
Emoluments of cathedral staff increased, 235.
Emperors.—
Frederic Barbarossa, 45 (n.). Henry VI, 73, 88, 89, 91, 93, 102, 121; his compunction and death, 102.
Empnett, chapel of, in parish of Compton, 237.
Empress Matilda, 33.
Engelger de Bohun, 38 (n.)
Erghum, bishop, establishes a college of chantry priests, 141.
Ernisius of Downhead, 214, 223, 363.

Ernulf, nephew of Iterius, prebend, 187.
"Eruditi Sancti Thomæ," 36; among à Becket's followers, 40 (*n*.)
Escheator's accounts in the chapter archives, 32.
"Espeltamentis canum, de" charges, 234.
Estrangia, wife of Geldewin Fitz-Savaric, 38.
Ethelwold, 2.
Euphemia, St., her body given to the convent of Bath, 53, 358.
Eustachius, Magister, 361, 363.
Evercreech Rectory, 140.
Everdon, Sylvester de, 243, 261.
Eves and Feasts on which markets were to be held, 30; why chosen, 31; additions made by Reginald, 59.
Excommunication, power of, left by Savaric to the chapter during his absence, 120, 121; pronounced by Thomas à Becket against Reginald and Ffoliott, 41; solemn, by Wells chapter, 262.
Exchange, deed of, between Walter of Downhead, William of Wyke, and Jocelin, 204.
Executors of bishop William de Marchia, 289 (*n*.)
Exuperius, St., Reginald made abbot of, 40, 41.
FABRIC of the cathedral, Wells, 11, 16, 24.
Fabric, architectural features of, 25, 86; benefactions to, from vacant benefices, 78; contemporary grants to, 80, etc.; grant by Alexander, canon of Henstridge, 196; by Henry III, 208; particulars of, from contemporary charters, 80, 81, 82; Reginald's work upon, 76, 85; suspended during the litigation with Glastonbury, 122; for some years no account of work on it, 278; causes of anxiety about it, 319.
Ferdinand, king of Castile, 264.
Ferentinus, John, legate, 172.
Ferenton (Farrington Gurney), 247, 276.
Festivals and fairs fixed by charter, 31, 59, 361.
Fighting bishops, 11.

Fines "de murdris," 212.
Fitz-Arthur, Richard, 179.
Fitz-Arthur, William, 203.
Fitz-Edward, Richard, 227.
Fitz-Godfrey, Hamo, 175.
Fitz-Hamo, Robert, 364.
Fitz-John, William of Harpetre, 10, 216, 372.
Fitz-Richard, Hugh, 216.
Fitz-Stephen, Ralph, chancellor, his munificence, 57.
Fitz-Urse, Robert, 67.
Flandre, William, de Dinre, 207.
Flaxman on the sculptures of the west front of the cathedral, 163.
Ffoliott, bishop of London, excommunicated by à Becket, 41.
Florence, proposed loan by merchants of, 267.
Font, ancient Norman, 124.
Fordham, John, dean of Wells, 194.
Forest laws of Henry I, 66.
Forests, Royal, 139, 148.
Fornellis (Furneaux), Alan de, 373.
Freedom from tolls granted to burgesses of Wells, 7; to tenants of bishop, dean, and chapter, 215.
Freeman, Prof. E. A., 21 (*n*.), 26, 28 (and *n*.), 60, 76, 157, 278, 322.
Fulco de Alneto, 358.
GARSTONE, land at, 219.
Gaufridus de Noiers, St. Hugh's architect, 161 (*n*.)
Geldeford, Philip, canon, 243, 261.
Geldeford, Robert de, 128 (*n*.)
Geoffrey, archbishop of York, 107.
Geoffrey de Henlaw, bishop of St. David's, 172.
Gerard de Camville, 70, 71.
Gerbert, Sir, 220.
"Ghersuma," 178 (and *n*.), 206.
Giffard, Robert, canon, 270.
Gilbert de Sarum, 216.
Gilbert de Schipton, *ib*.
Giles of Bridport, dean, 270
Giso, bishop of Wells, 3, 4, 5, 16, 17, 26, 31, 32, 84, 85, 329, 331, 354; Harold's treatment of, 4 (*n*.); introduces stricter discipline, 5.
Glastonbury, abbot of, holds a prebend in Wells cathedral, 55; a barony of the crown, 108; building work of Henry of Blois, 56; conflict with Wells, 58, 97; controversy with Martin de Summa, 218;

destroyed by fire, 56; exempt jurisdiction conceded to, 56 (*n*.); expenses of litigation with Savaric, 111; foundation of the " major ecclesia," 57; held by the king, 56; Henry II makes himself and his heirs responsible for its fitting restoration, 57; historical notices of, 1, 2, 4, 55; income, nett divisible, 108; mead contributed to church of Wells, 367; monks of, dissent from Jocelin's election, 131, 132; monks, number of, in the abbey, 108; new church dedicated, 57; particulars of Savaric's concordat with, 108 *seq.*; protest against the king's possession of the abbey, 96, 97; put into commission, 56; respective proceedings of Reginald, Savaric, and Jocelin towards, 117; revenues of consumed by litigation, 58; Robert, prior of Bath, elected abbot, 207; Rome appealed to for a dissolution of the union between the see of Wells and the abbey of, 176; Savaric's invasion of the abbey's independence and exemption, 117; his violent possession of the abbey, 104, 105, 240; sequel of the conflict after Savaric's death, 113; three stages in the history of the struggle, 99; transfer of the *patronatus*, 118; union between Glastonbury and the see of Wells dissolved, 134; war again renewed, 116.

Godelee, Hamelin de, canon, 314, 317 (*n*.)

Godelee, John, dean, 295, 312; executors of, 317; monument of, 316 (and *n*.); obits for, 314; work going on under him, 298, 299.

Godfrey, bishop of Wells, 6, 17, 354.
Godfrey de Craucumb, 224.
Godfrey de Dinre, 364.
Godfrey de Hercredeb, 363.
Godfrey de Mandeville, 208, 228.
Godfrey de Sto. Georgio, 364.
Godfrid the Frenchman, 128 (*n*.), 364.
Godwin, bishop of Hereford, 6 (*n*.), 23 (*n*.), 25 (and *n*.), 37, 76, 85, 87, 123, 127, 144, 154, 155, 277 (*n*.), 280 (*n*.), 285, 288, 289, 294, 324 (*n*.).
Golclive convent, 187.

Grammar School, The Cathedral, 78 (*n*.).
Grandison, John de, 293 (*n*.); promoted to the see of Exeter, 311.
Gratian and Vivian, legates, 42.
Gray, Walter de, *see* under " Walter " and " Archbishops."
Great Chartreuse, The, 46.
Gregory IX, pope, 115, 122, 260.
Grenne, Adam, 205.
Gresham college, 206.
Gresteign, convent of, 234.
Grossetête, bishop of Lincoln, 219, 274.
Gualo, papal legate, 134, 195.
Guertrie, Robert, " vallet " of sub-dean, 247.
Gundulf, bishop of Rochester, 27.
Gurnay, Robert de, 215, 216.
Gyan, Simon, lands and tenements given by, 232.
Gyford, Robert, chaplain of St. Cuthbert's, Wells, 229.
Gyffard [Giffard], Walter, sub-deacon and canon, chosen bishop, 276.

HACHE (Hatch), church of, 243; land at, 166.
Hackington, college and church of secular canons at, 71; peremptory order of Celestine III for the destruction of the new buildings, 72.
Ham (Hamme), church of, 207.
Ham, William de, precentor, 179, 184, 187.
Hameldun, patronage given to bishop of Lincoln, 217.
Hamo Fitz-Godfrey, 175.
Harold, earl, 31, 32; his treatment of Giso, 3, 4 (*n*.); prior of Bath, 96.
Harpetre castle, 10; charter of king John dated from, 138; William FitzJohn of, 10; grant of West Harpetre, 211.
Haselbury church, 34, 372.
Haselbury, William, canon of, 61, 364.
Haselshaw, Walter de, dean and bishop, 324; his gravestone, *ib.*; ritual in his time, 335; statutes of, 345.
Hawking, bishop Reginald's love of, 40.

Henry of Anjou, 33, 34.
Henry of Bath, 245.
Henry of Blois, 7, 8, 12, 27, 33, 35, 55, 56, 95, 147, 354; builds at Glastonbury, 56.
Henry de Campo Florido, 203.
Henry of Chichester, 176.
Henry I, king, 34, 38; his forest laws, 66.
Henry II, king, his charters, *see* "Charters"; his coronation, 42; counselled against Thomas à Becket, 38; foreign policy of, 39; founds first Carthusian house in England, 45; grant of a charter to Witham, 54; interdict against him suspended, 43; protests against nomination of English bishops by the pope, 44; purgation and penance, 43, 49; sends embassy to Rome, 42; undertakes to found three religious houses, 46; his death, 68.
Henry III, king, confirms Magna Charta, 208; his grant to the fabric, *ib.*; letters patent acknowledging grant from the prelates, *ib.*; grants congé d'élire to church of Bath, 244.
Henry VI, emperor, 73, 88, 89, 91.
Henry of London, canon of Wells, 225.
Henry of Sully, abbot of Glastonbury, 94; consecrated bishop of Worcester, 96, 99 (*n.*)
Henstridge, 148.
Herbert of Bosham, 39.
Hida, William de, 216.
Hildebert, precentor, 61; provost, 6.
Hinton Monachorum, Carthusian house at, 208; refounded, 187; confirmed by royal charter, 231.
Hithe or wharf, 66, 67.
Hobhouse, bishop, notes by, 79, 137, 204, 296 (*n.*).
Holcombe Rogus, 374.
Homer quoted, 256 (*n.*)
Honorarium of a cardinal, 249.
Honorius, pope, 116, 193, 194; dissolves union between Bath and Glastonbury, 197.
Hope, W. H. St. John, 27 (*n.*), 323, 392, 393 (and *n.*)
Horrington, land at, 139, 204 (*n.*).
Hospital of St. John Baptist, 137; ordinance about, 201; grant of Evercreech church to, 218; of St. Bartholomew, London, release by society, 227; at Whitehall, 211.
Hounds and hunting, rights of, 66.
Houses for canons, 140, 199.
Howden, Roger de, 102 (*n.*).
Hubert, archbishop, 95, 97; supports Savaric, 100.
Hubert de Burgh, 132, 206, 216, 224.
Hugh, archdeacon of Wells, and chancellor of the kingdom, 181; appointed to the see of Lincoln, 182; consecrated at Melun, *ib.*; death of, 219; early draft of his will, 137, 201 (*n.*).; exiled with his brother Jocelin, 182; grants to see of Wells, 189 *seq.*; later will, 184; legacies to Bath, Lincoln, Wells, etc., 183.
Hugh of Avalon, bishop of Lincoln, St. Hugh, 20, 28, 46, 47, 53, 54, 86, 98 (*n.*), 112, 129; bull for his canonization, 199; canonized, 155, 199; his conduct contrasted with that of Savaric, 98 (*n.*); work at Witham, 53, 86; death and burial, 112, 113.
Hugh de Dinan, 372.
Hugh of Grenford, 201.
Hugh Pudsey, bishop of Durham, 68, 70.
Hugh de Romenal, treasurer, 247, 274, 279.
Hugh de Vivone, 244
"Hugh of Wells," 128.
Huish annexed to archdeaconry, 56; grant of, to canons, 18, 19; attached to prebend of Compton, 213; arbitration connected with, 217.
Husee, Henry, dean, 295; his obit, *ib.*
IDEAL conceived and enforced during the thirteenth century, 350.
Ilbert, precentor, 363.
Ilchester, lepers' house at, 183.
Ilditius, vicar of Christian Malford, 200.
Ilminster church, 119.
Incense, 349.
Ine, king, 1; pretended charter of, 56 (*n.*).
Innocent III, pope, 99, 106, 107, 113, 114, 115, 174; cancels the double

election to Canterbury, 174; orders the kingdom to be put under an interdict, 180; his intimate knowledge of English diocesan affairs, 187, 349.
Innocent IV, pope, 54 (*n*.), 146, 169; arbitrates between Bath and Wells, 251; further arbitration, 253; issues a peremptory order for the full title of the see, 263.
Insecurity of the canons' tenure 5; of the rights of property, 64.
Instauramentum, disposal of, 221.
Interdict on Henry II, 43; suspended, *ib.*; ordered by Innocent, 180; relaxed by the papal legate, 189; taken off, 185.
Invention of a relic of the Cross, 31.
Invention, festival of, 30, 31.
Irvine, Mr., 157, 296 (*n*.)
Italians (300), pope desires benefices to be found for, in England, 260, 261.
Iterius, prebendary of Wanstrow, 187.
Ivo, first dean of Wells, 19, 29 (*n*.), 30, 33, 61, 360.
Ivo Cade, 222.
James of Mountsorel, 373.
Jesse window, 311.
Jocelin de Bohun, bishop of Sarum, 25, 38, 41, 89, 128 (*n*.); excommunicated by à Becket, 41.
Jocelin de Treminet, 373.
Jocelin Troteman, accepts the suzerainty of the pope, 133; appointed one of the judges on circuit, 195; again appointed, 199; arbitrates between Goldclive and the dean and chapter of Wells, 187; arbitrates between Elias and the archdeacon of Wells, 217: chaplain, 61, 82, 128 (*n*.); character described by the chapter of Bath, 168; and by the chapter of Wells, *ib.*; charters of 149, 212, 230, 241; chronicon of, 165; consecrated, 131, 173; early life, 127; elected bishop, 167; estimate of Savaric, 124; in exile from 1208-1213, 182; family traced in contemporaneous documents, 128 (*n*.); one of his first acts as bishop, 124; founds hospital of St. John, 137, 201; gives up the abbacy and the title of bishop of Bath and Glastonbury, 134; Glastonbury dissents from his election, 131; goes abroad, 133; grants to the *communa*, 143; king Richard's grant to keep dogs for the chase confirmed by king Henry III, 211; incloses a park and begins the palace, 138; institutes a daily mass to B.V.M., 137; joins Savaric against the monks of Glastonbury, 106; last and greatest of the master builders of Wells, 161; obtains two charters from king John, 138; lead and iron from Mendip, 139; license to stock his park with deer, 139; from papal legate public sanction of his title of "bishop of Bath and Glastonbury," 188; papal legate's letter, 189; proclaims Innocent III's interdict and flies the kingdom, 180; remains in exile, 134; retains his hold on Glastonbury, 116; revises the constitution of the cathedral, 181; his seal of dignity and counterseal, 146 (*n*.); his work on southern doors, 154; state of the fabric in his time, 146; statutes defining residence, 233, 273; style of the bishop in his day, 143; in magna charta, 189 (*n*.); subscribers to the instrument of his election, 169-171; succeeds to the see of Wells, 115; summary of his work on the fabric and the constitution of Wells, 163, 321; tradition that he was the builder of the *whole* church accounted for, 159, 160; unanimously elected by the two chapters of Bath and Wells, 130; withdrawal from Glastonbury, 133; retains four manors ceded by the latter, 240; death of, 238; bequeaths his body to Wells, 240; his tomb, 328.
John of Abbetestun (Abson), 216.
John de Axbridge, subdean, 274.
John, cardinal of St. Praxidius, 200.
John of Cossington, 105.
John de Campo Florido, 216.
John of Chard, vicar, 243.
John of Glastonbury, 117 (*n*.).
John of Ileford, 187.

John, king, 60, 85, 93, 99, 103, 113, 390.
John of Oxford, dean of Sarum, 41; excommunicated by à Becket, *ib.*
John of Palton, 214.
John de Ros, 344.
John of Salisbury, 36.
John of Tours, 6, 11, 16, 24, 26.
John of York, 183.
Jordan la Ware (Warr), 216.
Joy, William, dean Godelee's master mason, 296, 302, 321.
Jus patronatus claimed by St. Hugh, 98 (*n.*).; and by Savaric, 117; obtained by Jocelin, 118, 132.
Justiciar, the king's, 74, 91, 92, 93, 129, 206, 216, 371, 373.
KAERLEON, *see* "Caerleon."
Kardonville family, 178, 213; lands, 214.
Kardonville, John of, 213.
Kardonville, Lucia, *ib.*
Kardonville, Mirabel, *ib.*
Karenton vicarage, 375, 376.
Kari, Robert de, *see* "Cary."
Karole, de la, 325, 326 (*n.*), 327.
Karscumbe [Croscombe], 82.
Karswell, 204 (*n.*), 205.
Kenilworth, the "dictum" of, 276.
Kentiswood, Richard, chancellor, 225.
Kilwardly, Robert of, 277.
Kings.—
Arthur, 57. Cnut, 31 (and *n.*). Edmund of East Anglia, 2 (*n.*). Edward the Confessor, 3, 26, 31, 38. Edward the Elder, 2. Edward I seizes treasury of the Temple for Welsh war, 293 (*n.*). Edward II murdered, 311. Edward III and his Queen keep court at Wells, 315. Ferdinand of Castile, 264. Henry I, 34. Henry II, 32; his penance at à Becket's tomb, 49; death of, 68; Henry, Prince of Wales, joint king with his father, 44; his coronation, 83, 135. Henry III crowned, 195, 200; his grant to the fabric, 208. Ine, 1, 56 (*n.*). John, 60, 85, 93, 99, 103, 112, 113, 125 (*n.*), 131; his anger at Innocent's interference in the election to Canterbury, 175; confirms the union between Bath and Glastonbury, 191; his donations to hospital at Bristol, 180; grants immunity from market tolls to chapter of Bath and Wells, etc., 176; grants Jocelin license to inclose park, 175; grants the patronatus of Glastonbury, 191; his quarrel with pope Innocent, 184; secret communication with the pope against the barons, 193; supports Jocelin against Glastonbury, 132; surrenders the crown, 187, 188; his death, 195. Louis VII of France, 40, 51, 73; his deed of appointment to the abbey of St. Exuperius, 357. Philip II (Auguste) of France, 71, 91 (and *n.*), 92, 93. Richard I, 58, 85, 88, 90, 91, 92, 99, 110; his conflict with Celestine, 99; and with Innocent, 100, 101; forbids the execution of papal mandates, 101; goes to the Holy Land, 91; is made prisoner, 92; delivered up to Emperor Henry VI, 93; ransomed, 94, 118; repudiates his concession of Glastonbury to Savaric, 99; returns to England, and is crowned a second time, 94; Savaric extorts from him the exchange of Bath city for the abbey of Glastonbury, 94; stations and dates of his imprisonment, 94 (*n.*). William I, 3, 32. William II, Rufus, 6. William the Lion of Scotland, 112.
Kingsbury vicarage, 186.
"Kirnellare," licence to, 285, 286 (*n.*).
Knight's fee, 190 (*n.*); half fee, *ib.*
Knights who murdered Thomas à Becket, 42 (*n.*), 67.
Knole, Edward de la, dean, 271; manor of, in Wookey, *ib.*
LADY-CHAPEL, constructed by dean Godelee, 332; earlier building, *juxta claustrum*, endowed by Giso, 331; daily mass endowed by Savaric and Jocelin, *ib.*; scene of obituary services, *ib.*; pulled down by bishop Stillington, 332; eastern, behind the high altar, 331, 332; finished, 310; gifts to, 331 (*n.*); first definite mention of (1279), 331; offerings made at the image of St. Mary (1298), *ib.*
Lambert, sub-dean, 213, 222.
Lamelegh-by-Stoke, land in, 219.

Lancherley, 129.
Lands of dean and canons, 15; divided into prebends, *ib*.
Lanferley, land at, 128 (*n*.)
Lanfranc, 5, 36.
Langport, Richard, vicar, 222.
Langton, Stephen, elected to the primacy, 174; consecrated at Viterbo, 175; death of, 212.
Lateran, council of, 51, 65, 68.
Lechlade, Ralph of, 61, 82.
Legates, papal, 42, 51, 134, 145 (*n*), 172, 184, 185, 188, 195.
Legend, Arthurian, 57.
Lentenay, Gilbert de, 247.
Leodgaresburgh (Montacute), 31, 32.
Leonius, dean, 79 (*n*.), 185, 187, 188, 192, 193.
Lepers' houses, 183.
Levy for seven years on all canons and prebendaries, 234.
Lewes, church of St. Pancras at, 7, 27; Cluniac monastery at, 7.
Lexinton, 171; Robert de, 207.
Liber Albus, 297, 298 (*n*.)
Liber Niger, 298 (*n*.)
Liberty, the, formed, 140, 141 (*n*.); growth of, 141.
Library and *capitulum*, 326, 327.
Lideard (Lydiard), 203, 367; advowson of, 143; confirmation of Savaric's grant of, to the chapter, 186; confirmed to the canons by Jocelin, 229.
Lideford, church at, 375.
Lights for the high altar, 24 (*n*.), 29, 219, 329; lands at Chilcot granted for, 329; before the cross in the nave, 348.
Lincoln, architecture at, 28; battle of, 33; Gerard de Camville, sheriff of, 70; recitation of the Psalter at, 20; William de Romara, earl of, 67.
Litigation between Glastonbury and Wells, 58, 97, 111, etc.
Littleton, Wybert de, 318.
Litton, 4, 16, 353; Adam de, priest, 177, 178.
Loans, 267.
Lock family, 141, 161, 162, 222, 321, 395.
"Locus Dei," 209.
"Locus beatæ Mariæ," *ib*.
Lombards, 39 (*n*.)

London, synod of, 5, 9; Walter de, dean, 318.
Longchamps, Wm., bishop of Ely, obtains the chancellorship by bribery, 69, 70.
Lonley abbey, 203.
Longsword, William, earl of Salisbury, 208.
Loretta, countess of Leicester, 180.
Louis VII, *see* under "Kings."
Lovel family, 10, 80, 372, 376.
Lovesert, Henry de, endows Wynescomb church, 225.
Lovington, church of, 80.
Lovington, Robert de Kari, lord of, *ib*.
Lucia Laundrey, wife of Nicolas le prest, 331.
Luc de Membury, proctor, 243.
"Luna et Lagha," 363.
MAGISTER *Scholarum*, 349.
Magna Charta, 189 (*n*.); granted, 192, 193; confirmed by Henry III, 208.
Magna porta canonicorum, 140, 154, 177.
Malet, Jordan, 192.
Malet, W., 176.
Malford, Christian, 198, 200.
Malger, Walter, priest-vicar, 177, 178, 179, 213, 214.
Malherbe, Robert of, 202.
"Malleus canonicorum," etc. (Hugh of Lincoln), 219.
"Malleus monachorum" (Savaric), 121.
Malmesbury abbey, 27, 28, 101.
"Mammon of unrighteousness," 251.
Mandates, papal, illegal, 101; their execution forbidden by king Richard I, *ib*.
Mandeville, Godfrey de, 208, 228.
Mandeville, Robert de, 181, 192, 217.
Manors.—
Ashbury, 109 (*n*.), 198. Axbridge, 66. Badbury, 109 (*n*.), 198. Banwell, 18. Berges (Berrow), 109 (*n*.), 110. Biddisham, 16, 18, 20. Blackford, 109 (*n*.), 198. Bromley al. Bromfield, 16. Buckland, 109 (*n*.), 198. Calveston (Kelston), 365. Cheddar, 143, 190. Chilcot, 16. Christian Malford, 110, 198. Combe St. Nicholas, 16, 119, 142, 221. Compton Episcopi, 66. Congresbury, 148. Cranmore,

109 (n.), 198. Downhead, 139. Dulcot, 16. East Brent 109 (n.). Hinton, 209. Huish, 18, 19. Keinton, 198. Kingston, 110. Litton, 16. Lyme, 109 (n.), 110. Meare, 198. Mells, 100. North Curry, 70, 119, 143, 215. Norton, 209. Poulet, 215. Pucklechurch, 109 (n.), 198. Wanstrow, 16. Wedmore, 15, 33. Winsham, 16. Wiveliscombe, 119. Wormistor, 16. Wynescombe, 109 (n.), 143, 149, 150, 198, 230, 263.

Mansel, John, canon, 248, 261, 264, 265
Manuscripts unpublished, in the chapter library, 239.
Maperton, 83 (n.)
Marchia, William de, bishop of Bath and Wells, 288, 289, 339, 345; his character, 293; desire to canonize him, 293 (n.), 306; money raised for his canonization, 311 (and n.); release to Godelee's executors for sums so raised, 317; his registers, 289 (n.); accused of sacrilege, 294.
Marci, Peter de, administrator of Glastonbury, 56.
Margam, church of, 127.
Margaret, daughter of Louis VII, 40.
Marisco, Robert de, canon, 243, 261.
Mark, 3, 15, 18, 237.
Market held in the church, 29; removal of, 30, 359; times for, fixed by charter, 30, 31; offerings at, 32; tolls, immunity from, granted, 176.
Marmion, Robert, *armiger* of archdeacon of Wells, 247.
Marshall, earl of Pembroke, 132.
Martin of Karscumbe, 82.
Martin, legate, 252.
Martin IV, pope, 288, 290.
Martin de Summâ, 105 (and n.), 109 (n.), 111.
Martin's, St., chapel, 124 (n.)
Martire, Ralph, 29, 30.
Martock, church at, 202; rectory of, 140; William of, 82.
"Martyn's masse," 124.
Mary, St., chapel of, 84; service in honour of, augmented, 230.
Mass at the altar of St. Calixtus, 228.
Mass of B. V. M., 193, 220.
Mass, daily, instituted by Savaric, 123, 385; by Jocelin, 173.

Mass for the departed, 123.
Masses ordered in the "antiqua statuta," 20; two weekly required by, 340.
"Mater ecclesia," 145.
Matilda, the empress, 33; the lady (widow of Otho of Wanstrow), 202; Queen, 4.
Matthew of Westminster, 294.
Matthias de Winton, 128 (n.)
Mauduit, Thomas, 224.
Maulesbury (Melbury), William of, 228
Maurice of Gaunt, 181, 210; his foundations at Bristol, 215.
Maurienne, St. Jean de, 45.
Maydestone [Maidstone], William de, canon, 225, 238, 242.
Mead, contribution of, from Glastonbury, 367.
Meare, vineyard at, 18.
Meauleberger, Richard de, 205.
Meisy, Robert de, 179, 195.
Melbury (*see* also Maulesbury), 128 (n.)
Membury, Lucas, 214.
Merchants of Florence, 267.
Merchants of Siena, 268.
Merton, William de, elected dean, 225.
Michael of Aldford, 82.
Michael of Easton, 310 (and n.).
Michael, St., "in periculo mortis," the abbot of, 202, 210.
Midhurst, Sussex, 89.
Mill-dues granted to the *Communa*, 78.
Mills, 220, 221, 229, 366.
Mills at Fordyngton, 229; Hornysbowe, 229; Radewik, 215; South Chard, 229; Weare, *ib.*
Milo, 214.
Milverton, 3; made a prebend, 210; annexed to the archdeaconry of Taunton, 232.
Mining rights of the see of Wells, 66.
"Missa pro defunctis," 220.
"Missa in capitulo," 327.
Mission-priests, early settlement of, at Wells, 1.
Mitres, 305 (and n.).
Mohun, William de, of Dunster, 10.
Molinarius, Rufinus, 122.
Monasticon of Somerset, 378.
Montacute, cross found at, 31; convent at, 180.
Morevill, William de, 179.
Mortarium, Reginald's ordinance respecting, 329.

L LL

Mortimer, Roger, regent, 276.
Muchelney, 19, 114, 119, 186, 187.
Muddesley, 202, 353.
Muddesley, Alexander de, *ib.*
Muddesley, Henry of, *ib.*
Mudgeley, 15, 18.
Mudford church resigned to bishop, 231; granted to the *Communa*, *ib.*
Muntoria, "Muntorey," la Mountereye (Mont-Roy), 141, 142, 177, 179, 213, 214, 349.
Muntoria, grant of, by Elias the chaplain, 213.
NEW BUILDINGS, preparations for, 279
Newmarch, Henry, 83 (*n.*).
Nicholas de Barewe (Barrow), 81, 82.
Nicholas II, pope, 3.
Nicolas, the clerk, 247.
Nicolas, bishop of Tusculum, papal legate, 185, 188, 191; his letter, 189; relaxes the interdict, *ib.*
Noiers, Gaufridus de, 161 (*n.*)
Nonant, Hugh, bishop of Coventry, 70, 97.
"Norma eligendi," formally established between the chapters of Bath and Wells, 255.
Norman architecture, 28.
Norreys family, 161, 321, 395.
Norreys, Deodatus and Thomas, 222, 395.
North Curry, 16, 70, 119, 202, 207, 215, 221, 229, 274, 324, 377.
North Curry confirmed to the *Communa*, 166, 211.
North Wootton, chapel of B. V. M. at, 17, 354.
Norwich, church of, 114.
"Nova constitutio," of Salisbury, 273.
"Nundinæ," markets, 29 (*n.*); offerings made at, 32.
Nunniz (Nunney), church at, 179.
OBITS, memorial, 123, 124, 142, 213, 214, 223, 280 (*n.*), 281, 287 (*n.*), 294, 324, 331, 346.
Octavian, cardinal, 279.
Odo, 178.
Offices of dean, precentor, etc., early existence of, 13, 14, 15, 61; second generation of, 61.
Offington, *see* "Uffington."
Okehampton, lands at, 312.
Oratory at Stathe, 202.
Ordinale, importance of, 275 (*n.*); revised, 233.

Ordinance of Innocent III, 107.
Orlton, Adam, bishop of Hereford, 310, 344.
Orlton, John de, canon, 343.
Osmund, bishop of Sarum, 7.
Otho, cardinal legate, 209, 227, 231, 249
Otho of Wandestre (Wanstrow), 202.
Oxford, provincial synod at, 206.
PACIFICATION of Winchester, 70; between the chapters of Bath and Wells, 240; bishop Roger's scheme of, 254, 263.
Palace at Wells begun, 138, 139; chapel of, 285; hall, *ib.*
Pamborough, vineyard at, 18.
Pandulf, papal legate, 145 (*n.*), 184, 185, 197.
Papal interference, growth of, 98; exemplified.
Paris, Matthew, his character of bishop Jocelin, 219, 238; account of cardinal Colonna, 249; account of a violent storm in November, 1242, 242; of an earthquake, 278; testimony respecting bishop Roger, 252.
Park, the bishop's, inclosed, 138, 176.
"Passion of St. Andrew," 218.
Patronatus of Glastonbury, 197, 265.
Paulet vicarage, 234.
Paulton, John de, 203, 223, 225.
Pedigree of bishops Reginald and Savaric, 379.
Pempel, Stephen de, dean, 194.
*Pepper, annual payment of, 227.
Perci, Gerbert (al. Gilbert) de, 373.
Perreton (Petherton), 16 (and *n.*).
Peter, archbishop of Tarentaise, 47 (and *n.*), 358; papal legate, 51.
Peter, archdeacon of Bath, 169.
Peter, prior of Bath, 19.
Peter of Blois, 19, 40, 41, 62, 71 (*n.*); archdeacon of Bath, 62, 63; archdeacon of London, *ib.*; illustrations of his character, 41 (*n.*), 62; his letter to Savaric, 110; his opinion of Savaric's proceedings, *ib.*; his sarcasm on Reginald's death, 75.
Peter of Chichester, dean, 228, 229.
Peter de Marci, administrator of Glastonbury, 56.
Peter des Roches, bishop of Winchester, 61, 128 (*n.*), 132, 195, 206, 209, 364.

* *See* Bailey's *History of Notts*, i, 234.

Philip, king of France, 73.
Pica, William, abbot of Glastonbury, 100, 105, 107, 382; excommunicated by Savaric, *ib.*; dies at Rome, 384.
Pighele, Cristina, 205.
Pighele, Thudricus, *ib.*
Pilton, church of, 119, 124, 217, 370; vineyard at, 18.
Pipewell abbey, council of, 69.
Pitney, grant of land at, 218.
"Placebo" and "dirige," where to be sung, 327 (*n.*).
Placentia, "major ecclesia," of, 122.
Pointed arch, 26, 27, 28.
Polydore Virgil, 294.
Ponson, Alured de, 81, 376.
Pontigny, à Becket withdraws to, 41.
Pontoise, John de, bishop of Winton, 290 (and *n.*).
Poore, Herbert and Richard, bishops of Exeter, 136.
Popes.—
  Adrian IV, 22, 50, 97 (*n.*). Alexander III, 22, 42, 51, 64, 65, 250, 364. Celestine III, 72, 92, 96 (and *n.*), 97, 99, 100, 103, 110, 233. Clement III, 65. Clement V, 344. Gregory IX, 115, 122, 194, 211, 233. Honorius III, 97, 116 (and *n.*), 117, 133, 134, 145 (and *n.*), 193, 194, 197, 198, 211. Innocent III, 97, 99, 100, 103, 106, 107, 110, 111, 113, 114, 115, 116, 134, 169, 174, 180, 184, 193, 233. Innocent IV, 54 (*n.*), 416. Martin IV, 288, 290. Nicholas II, 3, 199. Nicholas, IV, 290. Urban III, 72, 90.
Porta Canonicorum, 140, 154, 277.
Postulatio, 167 (*n.*).
Poulesham, 128 (*n.*).
Prayers for the departed, 336, 337 note 1.
Preaching friars come to England, 174
Prebendaries, daily recitation of the psalter by, 339.
Prebends, lands divided into, 15; made in Robert's time, 17; in Reginald's episcopate, 66; increased by Savaric, 119; increased by Jocelin, 142; ordinance for five new ones, 220; their number and titles in 1298, 339; papal nomination to, 343, 344.
Precentor, duty of, 14, 18.

Precentors.—
  Gilbert de Byham, 274. Ilbert, 363. Ralph, 181. Reginald, 6, 16, 29 (*n.*), 30, 61. Thomas de Tornaco (Tournay), 185, 195. William de Ham, 179. William of St. Faith, 71 (*n.*), 78. William of Wells, 101, 167, 169.
Precinctum, royal licence to inclose, 285.
Preciosus Radulphus, 170, 213.
Presbytery in the cathedral, 328.
Priddy vicarage, 229.
Priests, college of, 2.
Priory, Barlynch, 67.
Priors.—
  Bath, 19, 29 (*n.*), 52, 96, 167, 213, 228, 232, 233. Bradenstoke, 192. Bruton, 19. Canterbury, 71, 107. Glastonbury, 19, 100, 105, 107. Montacute, 19, 180. St. Swithin, 7, 8 (*n.*). Taunton, 19. Winchester, 55. Witham, 53.
Processional stones, 336.
Processions, 335, 336; on Sundays, 336; on Palm Sunday, 337.
Protests of Wells chapter against that of Bath, 242, 244.
Provincial synod at Oxford, 206.
Provost, 5, 6, 12, 195, 196, 219, 220, 279.
Psalter, daily recitation of, 20; at Lincoln and Sarum, *ib.*; distribution of, amongst the prebendaries of Wells, 340-342; early statute that the whole should be said daily, 340.
Pucklechurch, 216.
Pudsey, Hugh, bishop of Durham, 68, 70.
"Pueri canonici," 328, 349.
Pumeraye, Hugo de la, 179.
Purgatory, etc., 280.
Purley, Walter de, canon of Wells, 203, 270

"QUASIMODO," 281.
"Quatuor articuli" referred to the pope's decision, 250.
"Quatuor personæ," 273.
Queens.—
  Editha, 3. Eleanor, 248 (and *n.*). Isabella, 306, 310. Matilda, wife of William I, 4. Matilda, wife of Henry I, 34. Philippa of Hainault, 315.

"Quotidians," 142 ; money substituted for, 143, 235 ; increased by Jocelin, 150, 151, 235 ; scale of, according to Jocelin's statute, 236 ; refused to a papal nominee, 344.

RADCLIVE, power to create a borough at, granted, 66.

Radulf, bishop of Chichester, 224.

Radulf Fitz-William, 376.

Radulfus de Waravill, canon of Lincoln, 212.

Ragusa, archbishop of, 113.

Rainaud, bishop, 128 (*n*.), 364.

Ralegh, William de, canon of Wanstrow, 203.

Ralegh, William de, bishop of Norwich, 239, 253.

Ralph, lord of Beaumont and St. Suzanne, 38.

Ralph, bishop of Chichester, 27.

Ralph of Chichester, chancellor, 215.

Ralph de Diceto, 36, 40 (*n*.), 43, 47, 49, 63 (*n*.), 90, 102 (*n*.).

Ralph Fitz-Stephen, chancellor, 57.

Ralph of Lechlade, canon, archdeacon of Bath, and dean, 61, 128 (*n*.), 364.

Ralph Martire, 29, 30, 361.

Ralph Preciosus, 170, 213.

Ralph of Shrewsbury ("de Salopia,") elected bishop, 305 (*n*.), 313, 314, 347 ; his testimony as to dean Godelee's work, 315.

Ralph de Wilton, 128 (*n*.).

Ralph of Yarlington, 82.

Re-adjustment of relations of chapters of Bath and Wells, 22.

Reginald, ("Master"), of Chester, 183.

Reginald de Wudeforde (Woodford), 205.

Regents during king Edward I's absence, 276.

Reginald Fitz-Jocelin, abbot of St. Exuperius, 40, 41, 73, 357 ; archdeacon of Sarum, 40, 43, 45 ; assists at the coronation of king Richard I, 68 ; attends the council of Lateran, 51 ; of London, *ib.* ; of Westminster, *ib.* ; benefactions to the church, 77, 78 ; character of, 75, 76 ; characterized by Herbert of Bosham, 39, 40 (*n*.) ; by Peter of Blois, 40 ; by Richard of Devizes, 75 ; his charter to the borough, 362 ; commissioner in the affairs of a secular college at Hackington, 72 ; comparatively overlooked, 37 ; confirms and increases the privileges of the town of Wells, 58 ; consecrated bishop of Bath, 45 ; at S. Jean de Maurienne, 47 (and *n*.) ; consecration, why objected to, 39 ; contemporaries of, 355 ; dedicates new church of Glastonbury, 57 ; drawn into political and court intrigues, 68 ; elected to the primacy, 74, 91 ; engaged in contest with Glastonbury, 97, 113 ; enthroned as bishop of Bath, 49 ; epitaph on, 75 ; founds hospital of St. John Baptist, at Bath, 52, 86 ; gifts and endowments to cathedral of Wells in his time, 52, 66 ; gifts to the convent of Bath, 53, 358 ; gives "Barton," and tenth of mill-dues to the *communa*, 78 ; growth of the see during his episcopate, 64 ; "Italian," why so called, 36, 39 ; keeps up his connection with Coutances 128 (*n*.) ; "Lombard," why so named, 39 ; nominated to see of Bath, 44 ; precentor of Wells, 6, 16, 18, 29 (*n*.), 30, 61 ; proceedings at Wells, 58, 86 ; public life, 50, 75 ; purges himself of complicity in à Becket's murder, 47 ; puts an end to the controversy between Wells and Glastonbury, 55 ; related to Savaric, 38 ; his seal and legend, 362 ; supports the king against à Becket, 41 ; surrenders his hereditary tenure of estates received through his uncle, 16, 18 ; surrender contested, 18 ; the claim compromised, *ib.* ; suspected of bidding for the chancellorship and the primacy, 68, 69, 73 (and *n*.) ; visits the Grande Chartreuse, 47 ; visits Rome, 41, 42 ; withdraws from à Becket's party, 41 ; work in his diocese, 52, 86 ; work on the fabric at Wells, 76, 85, 147 ; his death, 74, 91.

Reginald Fitz-Reginald, sheriff of Kent, 206.

Reginald de Sarum, 216.

Register, mutilation of, 224.

Registers of the chapter show the activity of dean and chapter, 265; particulars of, *ib*.
"Reinaud, bishop of Bath," 370, *see* "Reginald."
Relics of the holy cross, 31.
Religious houses, attempt to restrain their excessive powers, 97; the bishop's jurisdiction over, 65, 66.
Remigius, bishop of Lincoln, 7.
Renger, Richard, 227.
Renningmede [Runnymead], 192.
Requiems, 123.
Residence, obligatory, defined, 233; scale of payment regulated by, 235; stricter rule ordered, 274, 275.
Rich, Edmund, archbishop of Canterbury, 219.
Richard, archbishop of Canterbury, 42, 44.
Richard, archdeacon of Coutances, 128 (*n*.).
Richard of Bytton, vicar, 243.
Richard of Devizes, 53 (*n*.), 69, 70, 75, 83 (*n*.), 91, 92.
Richard, bishop of Durham, 224.
Richard I (king), charters of, 65, 66; grants additional privileges to the see of Wells, 66; refuses the abbey of Glastonbury to Savaric, 99; sells rights and privileges, 69.
Richard de Marisco, chancellor of the king, 191.
Richard Richeman of Wells, 300 (*n*.).
Richard of Spakeston, dean, 33, 78.
Richard de Wells, canon, 222, 224.
Richard de Wrotham, 234.
Ridel, Stephen, 169.
Robert de Berkeley, canon of Wells, 216.
Robert de Bethune, bishop of Hereford, 25.
Robert de Bingham, bishop of Sarum, 217.
Robert de Chesney, bishop of Lincoln, 14.
Robert Fitz Pane, sheriff of Somerset, 128 (*n*.).
Robert of Guildford, 82, 128 (*n*.).
Robert de Gurnay, 215, 216.
Robert of Lewes, bishop of Bath, 7, 8, 27; builds church at Bath, and designs that at Wells, 7, 24; his character, 9, 35; charters of his time, 11, 84; confirmed in the temporalities of the see by king Stephen, 8; constitutes chapter, 7, 13; grants new charter of freedom to the burghers of Wells, 7; institutes the deanship, 13; his part in public affairs, 33; visits St. Ulfric in his cell, 34; works out the new constitution, and the new fabric of the church at Wells, 11, 29, 35; his death, 35.
Robert de Mandeville, 181, 192.
Robert de Marisco, 246.
Robert, prior of Bath, 167.
Robert of St. Lo, 128 (*n*.)
Robert, bishop of Sarum, 217.
Robert, subdean, 29 (*n*.), 61.
Robert, prior of St. Swithun's 53 (and *n*.)
Robert de Vallibus, 186.
Roche Andely, castle of, 102.
Roches, Peter des, bishop of Winton, 206.
Rochester, bishop of, with bishop Bytton, secret agents, 264.
Roger, abbot of Athelney, 218.
Roger, bishop of Bath and Wells, 24 (*n*.), 29, 80 (*n*.)
Roger Burgeys, 213.
Roger, chaplain, his obit, 142, 349.
Roger of Chewton, canon and chaplain, 222; grants houses for canons, 223; for schools of Wells, *ib*.
Roger le duc, 227.
Roger de Pont l'Evêque, 33, 42, 83.
Roger, bishop of Sarum, 6, 7, 9, 12, 27, 28, 147, 354.
Roger of Sarum, first bishop of the united dioceses of Bath and Wells, with full title, 239, 256; nominated by monks of Bath, 245; chosen, and consecrated, 252; his charter of pacification accepted, 255.
Roges, lady Alicia de, 67.
Romanesque architecture, 26, 28.
Romanus, St., uncertainty as to day of, 150 (*n*.), 230.
Romara, William de, earl of Lincoln, 67.
Romenal, Hugh de, subdean, treasurer, proctor, 243, 274.
Ros, John de, 344.
Rouen, archbishop of, 74, 92, 93; church of, 13.
Rufinus Molinarius, 122.
Russell, Ralph, 216.

ST. ANDREW, fraternity of, 299.
St. Anselm, 70.
St. Calixtus, altar of, 228; festival of, 30, 31, 32.
St. Cuthbert, church of, at Wells, 2, 17; made over to the *Communa*, 17.
St. Decuman's, 67; the prebend of, a defaulter, 269.
St. Euphemia, V. and M., 53.
St. Exuperius, Reginald, abbot of, 40, 41, 73, 357.
St. Faith, William of, 71 (*n*.), 78, 167, 361.
St. Hugh of Lincoln, 28, 47, 54, 70, 71, 219.
St. Jean de Maurienne, 45, 46.
St. Lo, 48 (and *n*.).
Ste. Mère l'Eglise, 99 (and *n*.).
St. Pancras, Cluniac house of, 7.
St. Praxidius, John, cardinal of, 200.
St. Quintin, Robert de, clerk, 247.
St. Quintin, Walter de, archdeacon of Taunton, 238, 242, 267.
St. Swithun, priors of, 7, 8 (*n*.), 53 (and *n*.).
St. Ulfric, 34, 35 (and *n*.),
Sacristan bound to sleep in the Thesauraria, 333.
Sacristy, 285, 332.
Salisbury, architecture of, 28; church of, 114; "nova constitutio" of, 136; recitation of the psalter at, 20; register of, 135.
Samford Bret, 67.
Sandford, Roger de, 171.
Saracenus, John, dean, 151, 194, 232, 246, 260, 262, 270, 271.
Saracenus, Peter, *civis Romanus*, 232.
Sarum, *see* "Salisbury."
Savaric, bishop of Bath and Glastonbury, 88; absence from his diocese, 121; from England, 101; from his see lamented by the chapter of Wells, 168; adds three prebends, 119; aims at the primacy, 95; annexes the abbacy of Glastonbury to see of Bath, 89; archdeacon of Canterbury, 90; of Northampton, *ib.*; his archdeaconry sequestrated, *ib.*; asserts himself at Glastonbury, 104; at king John's coronation, 104; at St. Hugh's burial, 112, 113; at Worms, 93; attends king Richard to the Holy Land, 91; ditto, to Normandy, 105, 111; attests William the Lion's homage to king John, 112; betakes himself to Rome to work out schemes of ambition, 91; chancellor of Burgundy, 102, 121; character of his career, 88; charters granted by him, 119, 120, 121, 123, 125, 386; commissioner on Geoffrey of York's appeal to Rome, 103; consecration to Bath, 92; *cultus* of the B. V. M., 123; death, 121; debts owing by him, 111, 166; disappointing character of his policy, 114, 122; epigram on his wandering life, 123; exempts prebends from the jurisdiction of the archdeacon, 120; extorts from king Richard exchange of Bath city for the abbey of Glastonbury, 94; favoured by king Richard, 90, 91, 95; fined in earlier life, 89, 90 (*n*.); gifts to convent of Bath, 118, 385; goes to Rome, 103; government, his, condemned, 122; institutes daily mass in honour of B. V. M., 123; ditto, for his predecessors, *ib*; interests himself to advance Reginald to the primacy, 73, 91; invades the rights of Wells chapter, 120; last appearance at Wells, 120; leaves power of excommunication to the chapter during his absence, 120, 121; "malleus monachorum," 121; negociates with the emperor in behalf of king Richard, 93; nominated to the see of Bath, 92; obit, directions for his, 124; one of king John's court at Lincoln, 112; ordered to Rome, a commissioner, 103; pastoral staff and ring assigned to, 391; pedigree of, 89, and *App. I*; his policy characterized, 98; disappointing nature of, 114, 122; public life, his first appearance in, 89; refuses to receive the pope's letters, 111; relations with the diocese, 118; requiem mass for, appointed by bishop Jocelin, 124; still paid for in 1535, *ib.*; satire on his debts, 122 (*n*.); on his life, *ib.*; savage treatment of Glastonbury monks, 106, 383; secures the abbacy of Glastonbury, 96; king John's order for his institution to Glaston-

bury, 104; sequence of events in his life, 380; title of bishop of Bath and Glastonbury, 97; treasurer of Sarum, 90; violent measures at his instalment to Glastonbury, 104, 105; with king Richard at Rouen, 102.
Savaric Fitz-Chana, 38.
Saxon priests, early settlement of at Wells, 1.
Schipton (Sifton), Gilbert de, 216.
"Scholæ grammaticales," 142, 349.
Scholars of Wells schools to sing an antiphon to B.V.M., 224.
School of St. Thomas, 36.
Schools of Italy, 39.
Schools in Jocelin's time, 14, 142, 349.
Seal and counterseal of Jocelin, 146 (n.).
"Sedes præsulea," 50, 145 (and n.), 240; changed, 6.
See of Wells, 2; growth of, 3; local endowments, ib.; royal endowments, ib.
Seffred, bishop of Chichester, 72.
Selwood, forest of, 139; lepers' house at, 183.
Seneschal of the bishop, 203.
Sequestration of benefices, 304.
Shalford, grant of, by Hamo Fitz-Godfrey, 175, *App. K*.
Sherborne, original seat of western bishops, 1.
"Signati cruce," 137 (and n.), 201.
Siguenza, archives of the cathedral of, 133.
Simon of Apulia, bishop of Exeter, 176
Simon the physician, 245.
Simon, bp. of Worcester, 22, 25, 354.
Sinibaldi, cardinal, elected pope, 248.
Skenefrith, 232.
Sonnets, by Rev. G. Thring, on Wells cathedral, v; on west front, 164.
Spakeston (Spaxton), Richard de, dean, 33, 78.
Spaxton on Quantocks, 33.
Speronus de Campomoldo, 122.
Spineall, William de, 364.
Springs at Wells, 1, 2.
Staford, Elga de, 216.
Stalls, new, 308, 309, 328; in the chapter-house, 333, 334.
Stanford, St. Peter's, 217.
Stathe, oratory at, 202.

"Stations," 336, 337, 338.
"Statuta antiqua," 15, 21.
Statutes defining residence, 233.
Statutes of Westminster, 285; of Winchester, ib.
Staweia (Stowey), 187, 254.
Stephen, king, 7, 8, 33; first appointment, 8; grants a short charter, 9; grants the temporalities of Wells to Robert bishop of Bath, 8; lawlessness in his reign, 10, 35; promises to respect the canonical election of bishops, etc., 9.
Stephen de Pempel, dean, 194.
Stephen de Segrave, 216.
Stephen de la Strande, 227.
Stephen of Tor, canon of Wells, 128 (n.).
Stephen de Tornaco, parson of Welinton, 193, 206.
Stephen O'Brogan, bishop of Waterford, 229.
Stobery, land at, 139, 204 (n.), 205; conveyed to Roger of Chewton, canon and chaplain, 222, 223.
Stoke Courcy, 203.
Stoke Giffard, advowson of, 190.
Stubbs, bishop, 71 (n.), 88, 89 (n.).
Stuble, Geo. de la, 179.
Stuble, William de la, ib.
Sub-dean, 15, 29 (n.), 61, 81, 128, 167, 169, 213, 267, 274; his prebend transferred to Wookey, 140.
Submission of Scottish chiefs to king Edward I, copy of in the archives of Wells, 289.
Succentor, 140, 169, 274.
Sully (de Soliaco), Henry, 94, 96, 99 (n.).
Summâ, Martin de, 105, 109, 111.
Sutton, church of, made a prebend, 119.
Sutton, Oliver, bishop of Lincoln, 290.
Sylvester de Everdon, canon, keeper of exchequer, 243, 261.
Synod, diocesan summoned to attest a deed, 19; of diocese of Bath, 135; at London, 5, 9; provincial, at Oxford, 206.
TABELLARIUS, 348.
Talbot, Galfrid, 377.
Tarentaise, Peter, archbishop of, 47 (and n.).
Taxation of one tenth of all income for five years ordered, 348.

Tenth century, revival of discipline and learning in, 2.
Tenths confirmed to the church of St. Cuthbert, 231.
Tenths from the clergy for the crusade, 288.
"Terra Gisonis Episcopi," 4.
Tervic, Clericus, 216.
Tervic de Colonia, 227.
Theobald, archbishop of Canterbury, 18, 27, 35.
Thesauraria, 285 (and *n*.), 332.
Thetford, Robert of, 245.
Thirteenth century, interior arrangement of the church in, 322.
Tholus, 278.
Thomas à Becket, account of his murder in the archives of Siguenza (*see* also under "à Becket,") 133, 134.
Thomas, archdeacon of Bath, 19, 29 (*n*)
Thomas, prior of Bath, *see* "Bath," 30, 31, 61.
Thomas, prior of Glastonbury, 194.
Thomas, prior of Wells, 62, 78, 81, 128 (*n*.).
Thomas Mauduit, 224.
Thomas of Retford, chancellor, 307.
Thomas, St., the school of, 36.
Thomas, St., of Canterbury, festival of, appointed, 43, 200; translation of, 135.
Thomas, sub-dean, 128 (*n*.), 167.
Thomas de Tornaco, precentor, 185.
Thorn, Thomas de, 181.
Thring, Rev. G., poetical tribute to bishop Jocelin, 164; on Wells cathedral, v.
Tithes paid by the canons, 19.
Tithes, greater, divided between Wells and Salisbury, 232.
Title, full, of the see, appears in charters and grants, Jan., 1245-6, 254; ordered by pope Innocent, *ib*.
Tolls, freedom from, granted to citizens of Wells, 59; at the fair resisted, 319.
Toulouse, court of inquiry at, 51.
Tracy, Bovey, 67, 179.
Tracy, Henry de, 179, 199.
Tracy, Oliver de, 179, 374.
Translation of St. Thomas of Canterbury, 135, 153; festival of, 43, 200.
Treasurer's office, Jocelin's special ordinance concerning, 140.

Tregoz, Richard de, serves church of Hache, 221.
Treminet, Jocelin de, 373.
Trèves, archbishop of, 69.
Troteman, surname, 127.
Tusculum, Nicolas, bishop of, papal legate, 185.
Twelfth century, change in the architecture of, 26; growth of liberality towards the church, 63.
UFFINGTON, John de, prebend, 224, 249
Ulfric, St., 34, 35 (and *n*.), 372.
Ulward, Godfrey de, 244.
Umbert, count of Maurienne, 45.
Undated Charters, 202.
Urry, Robert, 292.
VACANT benefices, fruits of, granted to the fabric fund, 78, 79.
"Vallet," 247.
Vallibus, Robert de, 186.
Variety in titles of the bishop, 246.
Veir, Henry de, 216.
"Venator," Thomas, of bishop Jocelin, 247.
Vezelay, à Becket issues excommunication from, 41.
Vicarages, perpetual, enforced, 142; formation and endowment of, 220.
Vicars choral, 16, 20, 139, 142, 275, 346; appointment of, during vacancy of prebend, 186; no one to lodge alone, 346.
Vicars, priest 21 (and *n*.); with cure of souls, 186.
Vicars, leave of absence "for bloodletting," 233.
Vigeroys, "vallet" of the archdeacon of Taunton, 247.
Vincent, vicar, 222.
Vineyards, 17, 18, 229, 366.
Violent acts of Savaric at Glastonbury, 240.
Violent storm of Nov., 1242, 242.
Virgil, Polydore, 294.
Vivian, papal legate, 42.
Vivone, Hugh de, 244.
WAC (Wake), Baldwin, 375. Radulf, *ib*.
Waar, Laurence de la, the king's ambassador, 293 (*n*.)
Walkelin, bishop of Winton, 27, 364.
Walter de Bridport, vicar, 222.
Walter, the chamberlain, 222.
Walter of Colchester, 200.
Walter of Cossington, 234.
Walter de Derham, 224.

Walter de Downhead, 139, 177 (and *n*.), 203.
Walter de Gray, lord chancellor and archbishop of York, 169 (and *n*.), 243, 261.
Walter Herbert, bishop of Sarum, advanced to the primacy, 95.
Walter de London, dean, 318.
Walter de Muntoria, 177.
Walter, precentor of Sarum, 128 (and *n*.)
Walter, prior of Bath, 52, 53, 54.
Walter de Purley, canon of Wells, 203, 270.
Walter Rofend, 203.
Walter, archbishop of Rouen, 92, 93.
Walter of Wyke, 203.
Waltham, cross at, 31 ; Henry of, 223; Katherine, widow of Henry de, 224; Reginald de, 223; religious house at, 46.
Wamberg, R. de, collector, 308.
Wanstrow, 4, 16, 18, 353.
Warelast, William, bishop of Exeter, 12, 354.
Warenne, William de, earl of Surrey, 7
Warminster, Wilts, 376.
Wax, annual tribute of, from Weston-by-Worle, 218.
Wayford, Baldwin de, 203.
Weaver, Rev. F. W., 316 (*n*.).
Wedmore, 3, 4, 16 (*n*.), 352 ; prebend of, reconstituted, 237 ; when vacant by cession, 186.
Wedmoreland, 15, 352.
Weleslia (Wellesley), 128 (*n*.).
Welinton (Wellington), 193, 219.
Welinton, William of, 294.
Wells cathedral and see.—Architectural features of cathedral, 86, 156 ; bishop's jurisdiction over religious houses, 65, 66 ; building, progress of, 84 ; causes which checked it, 147; canons of, *see* under " Canons of Wells ; " central lantern of, 322 ; choir screen, 323, 327 ; complaints made to Innocent IV of the state of the church, 130 ; consecrated, 230 ; constitution of chapter, first draft of, 11 ; "convent" of, 19, 114 ; custodians of the see, 166 ; dilapidation accounted for, 152 ; doors de la Karole, statute for opening and closing, 325 ; early stages in its architectural history obscure, 161 ; employés, a few names of, traceable, *ib*.; end of church apsidal or square, 330 ; enrichment of see by cession of Glastonbury manors, 149; Professor Willis' opinion, *ib*. ; era of computation, a new one in the registers, 135 ; gifts and endowments in Reginald's episcopate, 52, 76, 82 ; gradual growth of the capitular constitution, 11, 18, 35, 258, etc., history of Reginald's acts in unprinted manuscripts at Wells, 58; interior arrangement of the church in the XIIIth century, 322 ; local endowments, 3 ; loses its pre-eminence by transfer of see to Bath, 5, 6, 22; nave, resort and traffic in, 324 ; statute, forbidding games in, *ib*.; not entitled " Bath and Wells " before bishop Roger's episcopate, 23 ; plan of choir and presbytery in 13th century, *App. X*; possessions of the see in Giso's time, 3, 4; privileges granted by crown to the bishop in Reginald's episcopate, 66 ; *pulpitum*, 323 ; reconsecration of the church, 149; why necessary, 152 ; rood-loft, 323; variation in the date of reconsecration, 150 (*n*.) ; war with Glastonbury, 97; west front of cathedral discussed, 157, 158 ; work at, continuous, 311 ; new do., money collected by dean and chapter for, 306, 308, 309, 310.
Wells city, constituted a borough, 7 ; burghers revolt against the privileges and claims of the bishop, 319; city charter annulled, 319 (*n*.); fair-days appointed, 59, 125 ; first royal charter given to the borough, 125, 390; franchises of the borough held as grants from the bishop, 59 ; appeal to the bishop reserved, 60 ; freedom from tolls granted, 29; interesting municipal history of, 59; landowners and townsfolk sign first deed of incorporation, 61; privileges of the citizens confirmed, 125; riot at, 319; Savaric's charter to the town, 386 ; springs at, 1, 2.
Westminster, council of, 44 ; statutes of, 285.

Weston-by-Worle, annual tribute from the parson of, 218.
Wharton, Henry, 11 (*n.*), 23 (*n.*), 25, 37, 76, 144, 145 (*n.*).
Whitchurch, Dorset, advowson of given to Jocelin, 208; Hugh of Greneford admitted to, 201; instituted and endowed, 232; Richard, parson of, 192; William de Wellia admitted to, 192.
Whitehall hospital, ("Alba Aula,") 211.
Whitelackington, prebend of, 373.
White Monks, 229.
White Stanton, 220.
Wilelminus, clerk, 247.
Will, royal licence for making, 217.
William de Bechamstede, canon of Wells, 222.
William de Bratton, 228.
William of Brugge [Bridgwater], vicar, 243.
William, abbot of Glastonbury, 116.
William, canon of Haselbury, 61.
William de Chiue (Chew), 153.
William Coquus, 205.
William of Dinr (Dinder), 128 (*n.*).
William the Englishman, 147.
William, bishop of Exeter, 12.
William Fitz-John, of Harpetre, 10.
William Forestarius, 205.
William I, king, 3.
William II, king, 6.
William Longsword, earl of Salisbury, 228.
William de Marchia, bishop of Bath and Wells, 289.
William Marshall, earl of Pembroke, 206.
William of Martock, 82.
William of Melbury, 128 (*n.*).
William of Mohun, lord of Dunster, 10
William Pica, abbot of Glastonbury, 105, 107.
William, prior of Bruton, 29 (*n.*).
William, provost of Combe, 226.
William de Romara, earl of Lincoln, 67.
William of St. Faith, precentor, 63, 104, 167, 169, 361.
William Ste. Mère l'Eglise, 99 and (*n.*); interdicted by Savaric, 100; appeals to the king and the pope, 101.

William of Sens, 147.
William de Spineall, 364.
William, treasurer of Wells, 29 (*n.*), 61.
William de Trumpington, 173 (*n.*).
William of Weleslia (Wellesley), 128 (*n.*).
William de Wellia, 187, 192.
William de Wilton, parson of Chew, 193.
William de Wrotham, archdeacon of Taunton, 166.
Willis, Professor, 76, 77, 157, 159, 330.
Williton, 67.
Wimarc, wife of Edward de Welles, 218 (*n.*).
Winchester, coronations at, 83, 84; pacification of, 70; statutes of, 285.
Windlesore, 171.
Winscombe [Wynescomb], advowson of, 143; church and manor of, 149, *see* also Wynescumb.
Winsham, 4, 16, 18, 219.
Winterstoke, the hundred of, 190.
Winton, Mathias de, 128 (*n.*).
Winton, Peter de, *ib.*
Witham, Carthusian house at, 46, 113; prior Hugh's work at, 53, 86; obtains a charter from Henry II, 54.
Wiveliscombe, manor of, 119; made a prebend, 186.
Wodeton chapel, tithes of, 208.
Wokiole, 128 (*n.*).
Wookey [Owkey], 16, 155.
Wootton, *see* "North Wootton."
Worcester, church of, 114.
Workmen, master, in bishop Jocelin's time, 395.
Wormestor, Worminster, 16.
Wrentich, land at, 166, 219.
Wrotham, Richard de, 234.
Wudeford, Reginald de, 205.
Wybert de Littleton, 318.
Wyneford church,
Wynescombe church, dedicated, 225; endowed, *ib.*; appropriated to dean and chapter, 233; manor of, 230, 263, *see* also Winscombe.
Wynesham, præpositura of, 221.
Wytenal, 229.
YARLINGTON, Ralph of, 82.
Yatton rectory, leased to abbot and convent of St. Augustine's, Bristol, 226.

Printed by Barnicott & Pearce, at the Athenæum Press, Taunton.

www.ingramcontent.com/pod-product-compliance
Lightning Source LLC
Chambersburg PA
CBHW051237300426
44114CB00011B/780